Supersudaca
Incomplete Works

Supersudaca

Supersudaca
Ana Rascovsky
Cesar Becerra
Esteban Varela
Félix Madrazo
Fernando Puente Arnao
Juan Pablo Corvalán
Martín Delgado
Manuel de Rivero
Max Zolkwer
Sofía Saavedra Bruno
Stephane Damsin

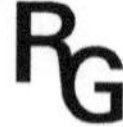 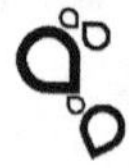

Latin America: Thoughts
BR + USA 10

Romano Guerra Editora
Nhamerica Platform
São Paulo, Austin, 2024
1st edition

For
Teresa,
Ion and
Korina

Incomplete Works

List of
Contents

Supersudaca
A Practice
of Friendship

Fernando Luiz Lara

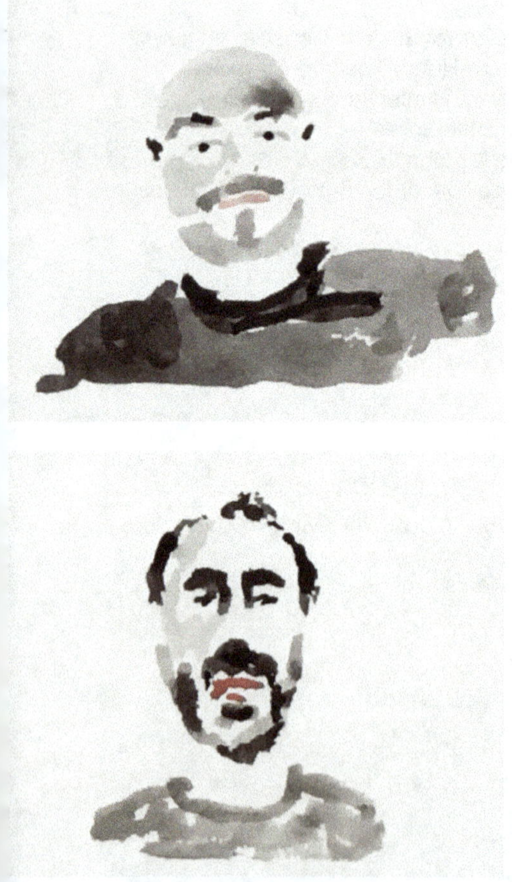
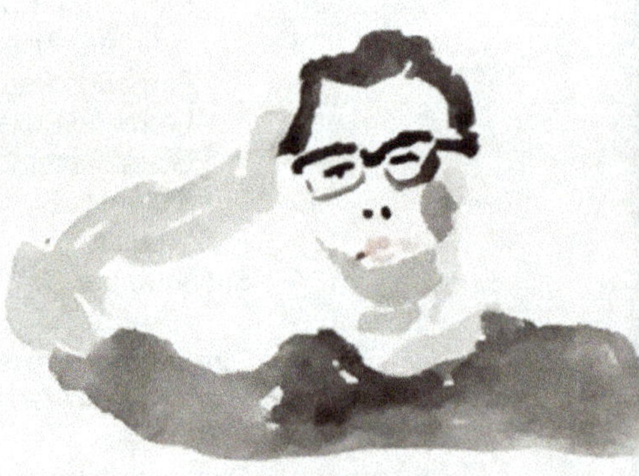
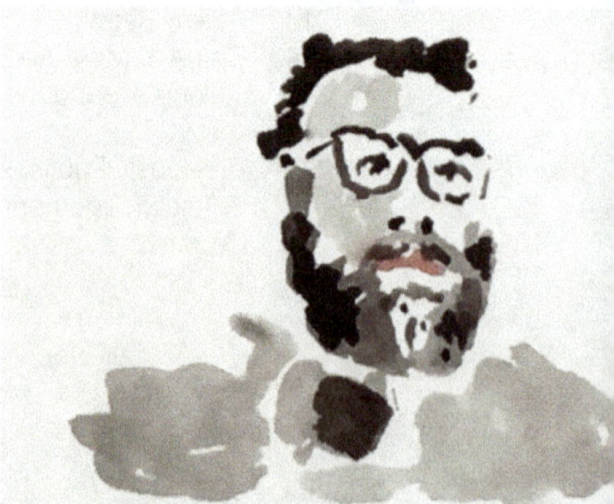

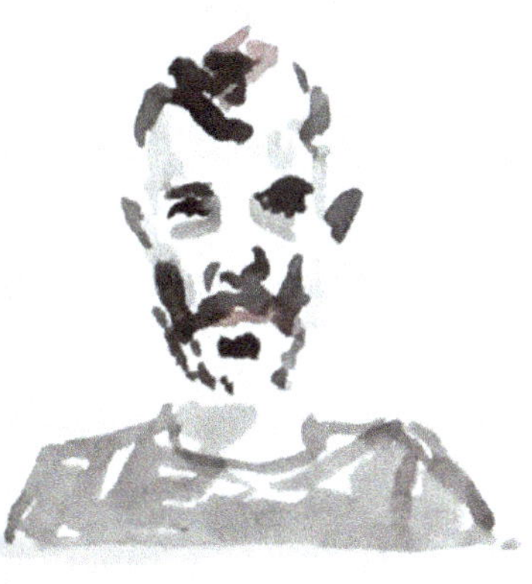
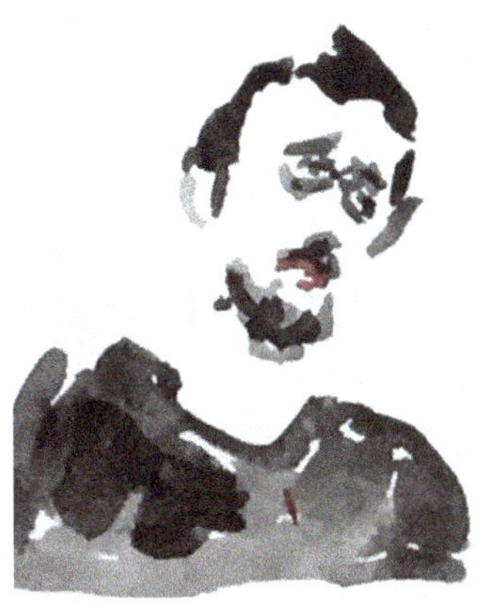
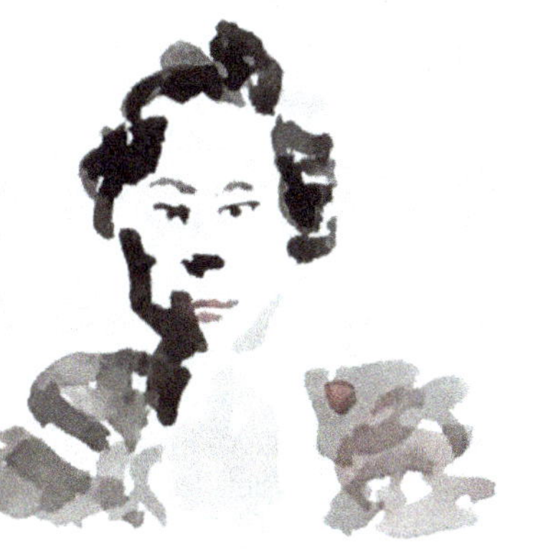
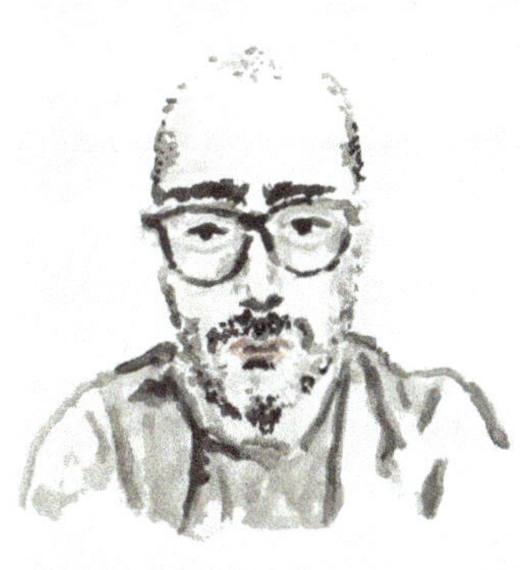
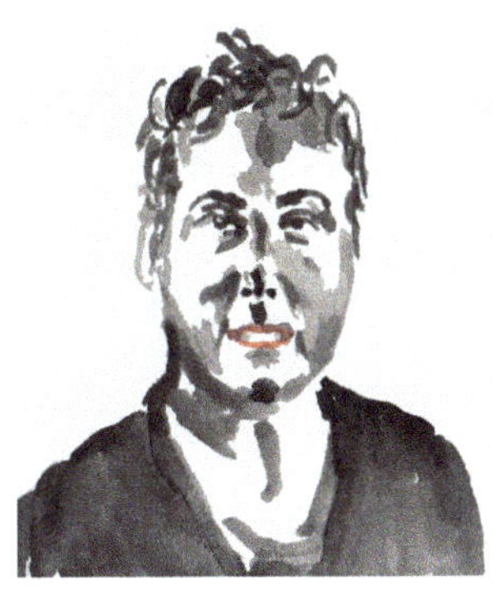
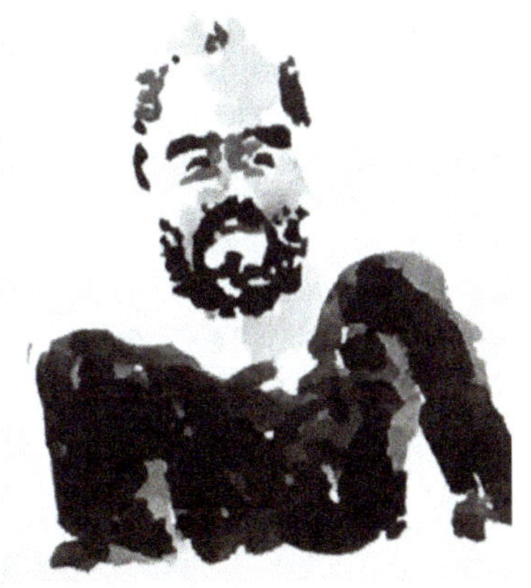
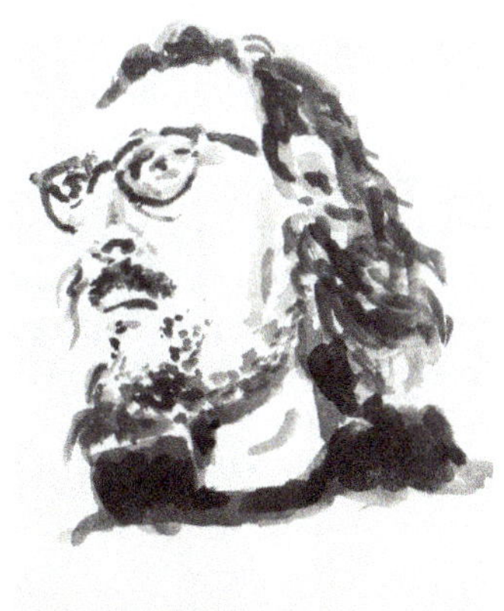

1. Bart Lootsma, *Super-dutch: New Architecture in the Netherlands* (London/New York: Thames & Hudson/ Princeton Architectural Press, 2000).

At the dawn of the new millennium a group of Latin American young architects found themselves in a pilgrimage to one of the centers of design production of the old world. Like pilgrims and migrants have done for thousands of years, they ended up learning more about themselves than about their hosts. Like pilgrims and migrants have done for thousands of years, they thought they were acquiring knowledge in exchange for their cultural currency. Instead, they encountered their own knowledge and learned a lot about the culture of their hosts. From the pilgrimage site they acquired the concept of superlative. It was the time of celebrating the Superdutch,[1] and they decided to ditch the *Dutch* and retain the *super*, a qualifier that spins the demeaning aspects of the label *sudaca* into a whole new orbit. Supersudaca was born at the Berlage Institute, a postgraduate school of architecture based in Rotterdam, Netherlands –, put together by a group that found support and encouragement in each other. As Juan Pablo Corvalan reminded me in one of our conversations, they did not want to choose between the *liberté* of capitalism or the *egalité* of communism, opting instead for the *fraternité*. Supersudaca was born to subvert the orders of center/periphery, North/South, knowledge/culture, and in doing that generate new meanings and new concepts for the discipline and the practice of architecture.

As we know well, *sudaca* is a pejorative term used to label Latin Americans that return to Europe to study or to work. I say *return* because the large majority of those who have the opportunity to cross the Atlantic are descendants of the Europeans who have consistently travelled South since 1492, yet the label is applied with a special degree of cruelty against Amerindians (*los que no vinieron de los barcos*). Interestingly enough, we don't have a pejorative term for the Europeans who came to the Americas. Much to the contrary, we celebrate them as enlightened diasporic entrepreneurs. Our history and theory texts are quite thankful for Richard Neutra, Lina Bo Bardi, Felix Candella, Antoni Bonet Castellana, Clorindo Testa and so many others, but don't really elaborate on the reasons why they were forced to leave their homes and cross the ocean. We know because we know both histories, ours and theirs. When I asked the Supersudacas about what triggered the creation of the collective in 2001 they spoke of indignation, strong emotions in reaction to invisibility. We know their histories but they know nothing of ours.

2.   Fernando Lara, "Five Radical Concepts for Decolonizing the Spatial History of the Americas," in: Decolonizing the Spatial History of the Americas (Austin: Center for American Architecture and Design, 2021), 6-29. The references mentioned in this quotation are the following: Edward W. Said, *Orientalism* (1st ed., New York: Vintage, 1979); Walter Mignolo, "Epistemic Disobedience, Independent Thought and Decolonial Freedom," *Theory, Culture & Society* 26, no. 7-8 (December 2009): 161.

In a recent text I wrote at large about the dichotomy of knowledge and culture, elaborating that:

In his classic *Orientalism*, Edward Said explains how European scholars developed narratives about all other societies on Earth, labeled it culture, and as a result established themselves as the center of human knowledge. Here I need to call your attention to the use of knowledge referring to ideas and concepts from one part of the world and culture as ideas and concepts from another part of the world. Ask people where they think the best knowledge is located and most will inevitably answer Europe, USA and Japan. Ask the same people where they think the best cultures are located and you get a much more diverse answer that spans from Mexico and Brazil to Turkey, India, and beyond. Knowledge became synonymous with science and development, while culture became synonymous with traditions and under-development. What Walter Mignolo calls epistemic disobedience is fundamental to dismantle the idea that "the first world has knowledge, the third world has culture; Native Americans have wisdom, Anglo Americans have science."[2]

In response to this structural inequality, the Supersudaca have always promoted Southern knowledges, and in doing that made Northern cultures visible. When they write about tourism architecture in the Caribbean they turn inside out the guts of architectural practice, showing the ugly side of how hotels and shopping mall sausages are made. When they write about China they dislocate the pendulum away from the centrality of the North Atlantic, revealing global networks that are even more invisible than contemporary Latin American architectures. When they write about *direct architecture* they explode the established boundaries of the discipline, including rickshaw drivers and bicycle delivery workers as subjects of architectural discussions. When asked about why writing about the mundane built environment they remind me that when they arrived at the Berlage all the main characters of the books of yesterday were there, live, speaking to them, and they were all very boring.

The juice of the conversation was not in the accented English of Koolhaas or Tschumi but in the accented Spanish of a fellow student from a different Latin American country. At the café or at each other's apartments they discovered that exactly like their European colleagues they also did not know about Lima, Bogota or Montevideo. With a digital projector borrowed from the school they started doing night sessions to present their own hometowns to each other. The first idea was to create a research office called Space for Urban Research – SUR. But it had no punch, no emotion. Someone proposed the name Supersudaca and a few colleagues got offended, it was not serious enough. However, humor was indeed central to their endeavors and the ones that stayed with Supersudaca developed a strong friendship, or yet a practice of friendship. Felix Madrazo defined Supersudaca as the most longevous WhatsApp group, founded eight years before the successful message software that is completely dominant in the Global South. Like the best social media groups, Supersudaca is fun, spicy, provocative and inclusive. We can only wish our WhatsApp groups would be half as exciting as Supersudaca.

Perhaps they found the secret to social media message groups: A platform in which you can never be a star. At another point in our conversation Manuel de Rivero mentioned that the Berlage educated them to be stars, and Supersudaca does everything possible not to. There is no webpage, no Instagram publicity. When *El Croquis* was publishing the faces of the architects as if they were Hollywood celebrities, Supersudaca decided to draw Leonardo's Vitruvian Man dressed for Lucha-Libre. For years I followed them, finding their publications here and there and wondered who they were, and how could I be in touch with such an interesting concept? In their own words, Supersudaca is an attitude of amateurism, a tree house in which they are allowed not to grow like Peter Pan. Like the best tree houses, Supersudaca is even hidden behind the bushes, much like an illicit love affair. Hidden just enough to keep face, I would add.

So how do they operate? And most intriguing, how did they survived twenty years already? In a text published in 2015 there's an interesting mention of their work as Tarzan jumping from rope to rope. The metaphor could not be more precise and not only because of the Eurocentric idea of Latin America as a jungle. This part we should laugh about and make it SuperTarzan. I am more interested in the idea that ropes are opportunities thrown at you that one can either hang on or not. Ropes can also be swung in the direction that you throw your weight, the opposite of pre-determined roads of arbitrary rails that force you to take one direction or the other. Rope hanging is all about flexibility, ability, dexterity and balance, skills that are fundamental for managing any collective practice and unfortunately never discussed in our architecture schools.

When I asked them that question directly – *how do you operate?* – the answers were all about flexibility and desire. Ana Rascovsky mentioned more than once that Supersudaca is about the desire to be together.

Spend time with any number of them and one learns how much the enjoy talking to each other. Unfortunately all our conversations have been mediated by Zoom platform, the first one in July 2020, the last ones in September 2021. In a way this book is the result of the Covid Pandemic, perhaps another rope that we hand on to in order to keep the conversation alive. Looking at the thousands of pictures that Supersudaca made available for the design of this book I can only imagine how much fun and intellectually stimulating are their travels around the world. In the words of Max Zolkwer, Supersudaca has been the best travel agency they could dream of. Many of the chapters of this book are the result of such travels such as "Chatting Around the World" and "Destination Whatever." From their initial encounter in Rotterdam they have continuously travelled the world, exploring places they did not know well such as Russia and Senegal but perhaps most importantly showing Lima, Santiago, Buenos Aires and Montevideo all over the world.

And travelling all over the world dressed as Supersudaca, hanging from a hope to another, they have managed to challenge the very definition of architecture. In "Europe We Need to Talk" they started to articulate the contribution that Latin America brings to the table of contemporary architecture, something that they discuss further in "Direct Architecture" and the more recent "Papel Latino." Max Zolkwer summarized it when he said that Supersudaca was about the architecture of the world, while traditional practices are about the world of architecture.

For Supersudaca the whole world is the subject of their analysis and their intervention, as long as their practice of friendship is allowed to activate this shield that protects and empower them as kids do in the treehouses around the world. In developing this practice of friendship, they might have created a powerful vaccine to our pandemic of social media isolation: A bubble that allows them to engage the rest of the world, in its glorious contradiction. That's their superpower.

Foreword

At the occasion of Supersudaca's 10th anniversary, came
up the idea to publish a book on Supersudaca's "incomplete
works", a project that was presented and exhibited at the 10th
Architecture Biennial of Sao Paulo, in 2013.

Incomplete Works

Supersudaca does not finish its processes; they move from
one place to another, they come back in circles and follow
unpredictable paths. Compared to the individual approach of
the architect, due to a single position with a predetermined
end, in Supersudaca, it's open, multiple and flexible. "This is it!"
is switched to "Is this how it's going?".

Incomplete works – at least for us. Unconcluded projects are
finished by others or remain available for new, either theoretical, academic, or built versions. It's not possible nor necessary
to close the collective processes in Supersudaca.

The previous method can be inefficient sometimes. Goals are
not set; they change during the course and timing becomes
longer than in conventional formats, but without doubt, it's a
richer and more fruitful experience. If there are different possible endings to a story, why pick one? Or rather, why finish it?

In contrast to a complete work book of solid lifetime accumulation of experience, Incomplete works attempts to expose the
process as the frame. The book exposes Supersudaca content
as temporary stages. Finally, the publication will be finished
when it's incomplete.

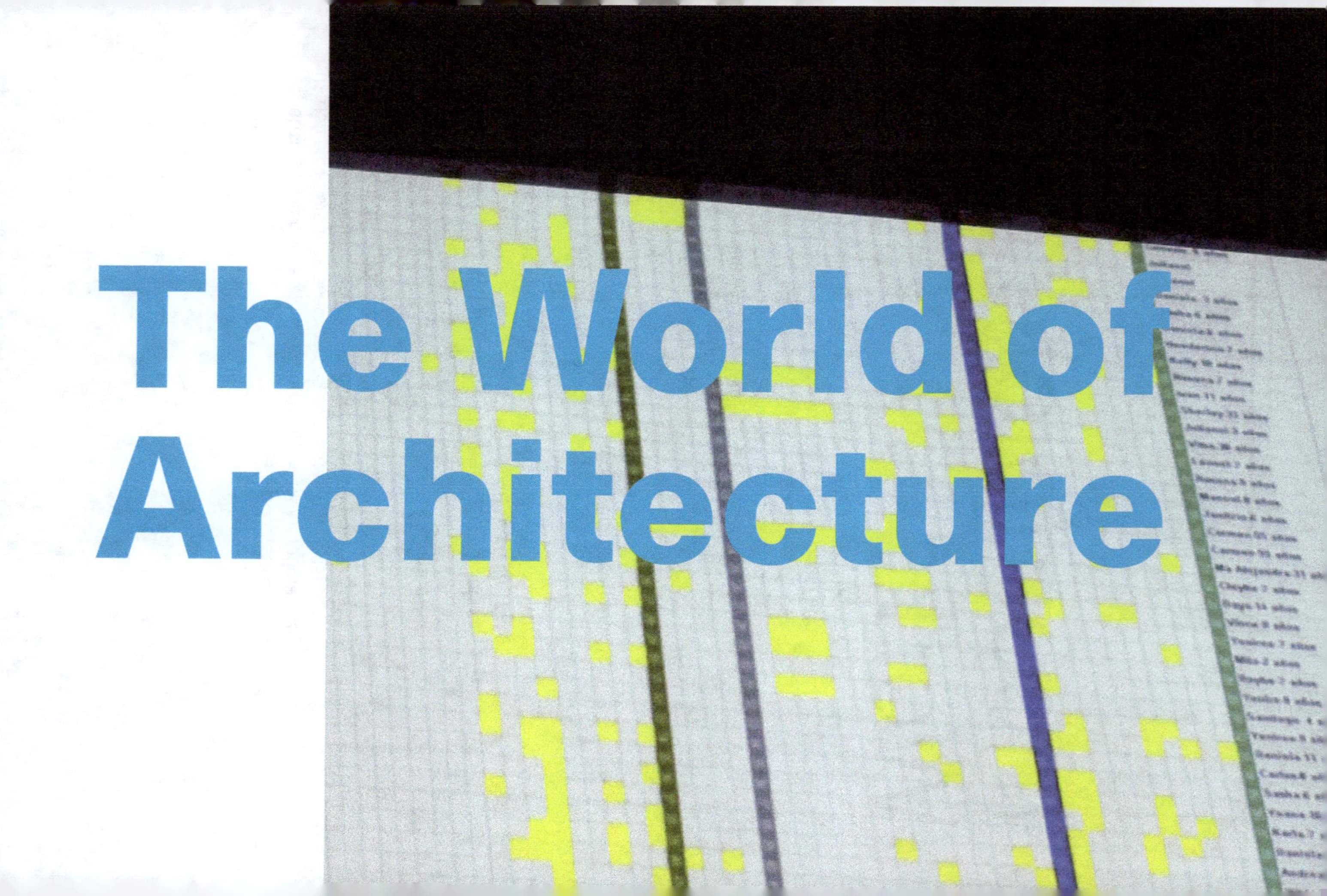
The World of Architecture

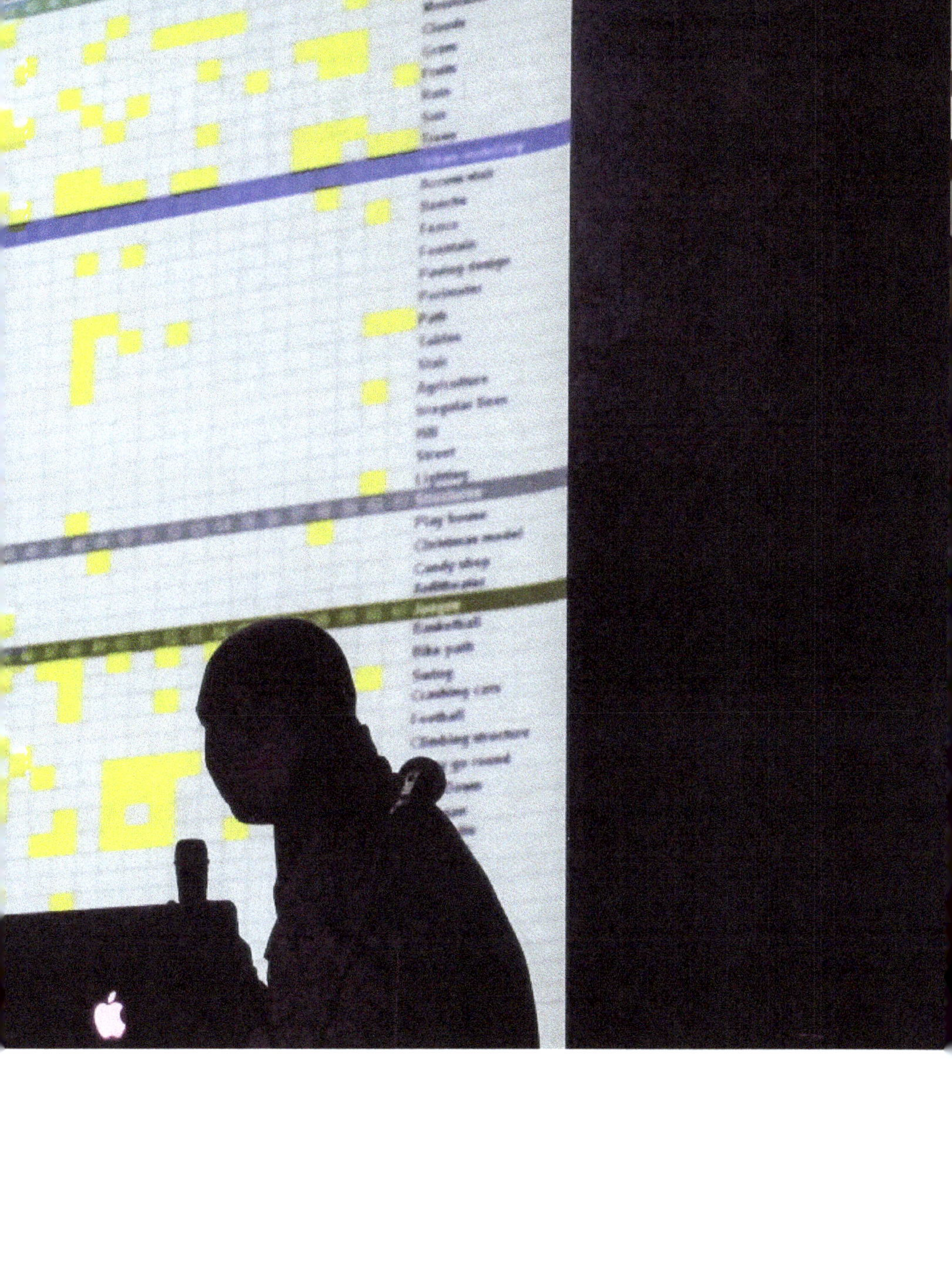

Supersudaca's Turn

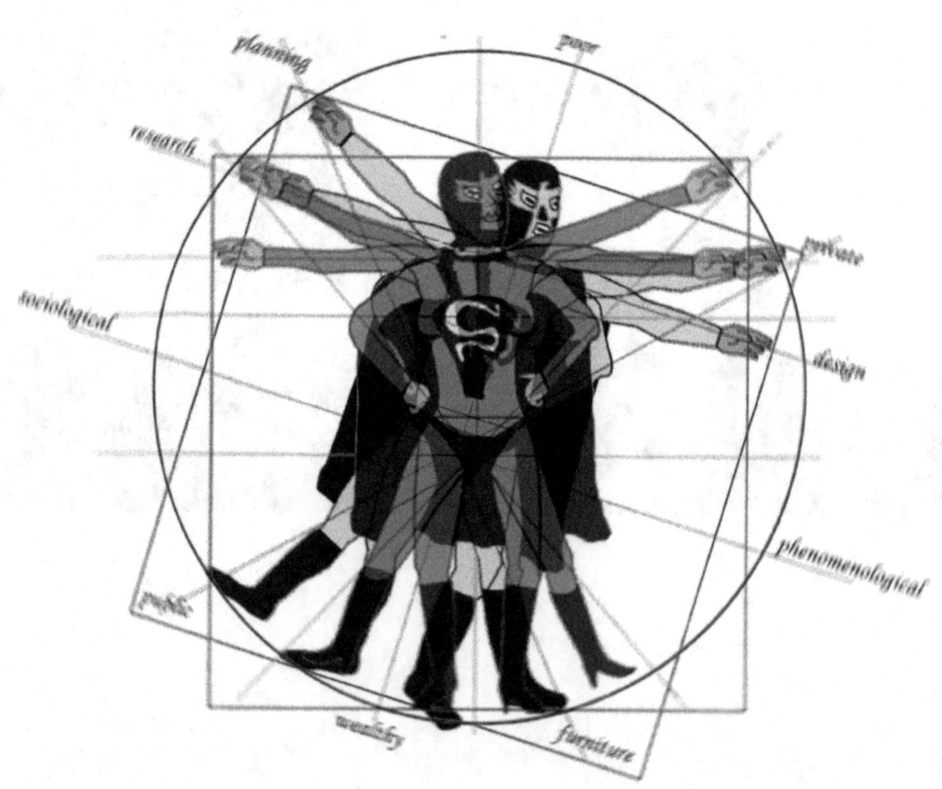

16

During a decade and a half of experience, as a group, wo havo accumulated, developed and debated in Supersudaca disciplinary issues of architecture and its relationship with society. Various theses have been put forward and we have been able to apply, in collaboration, several experimental approaches without an absolute objective, other than the search for content with the aspiration of a global debate from a renewed Latin American perspective. However, from this *cumulus*, recurring reflections and conversations have emerged that herald a possible paradigmatic shift in the discipline of architecture, that rather than a totalitarian, innocent or dangerous twist, it is an alternative, a turning point, which we think it is worth opening up and which we present below. ..

The World of Architecture and the Architecture of the World

Disciplinary autism seems to be a topic of growing debate in architecture, the loss of its link with its space and time, its absence in a broader social project, as well as its mere instrumentality in the installation of a political agenda on the territory with strong multi-scale consequences, where architects' approaches seem to have little or no incidence. We architects aspire to say a lot, but we end up talking within four walls, no matter how solemn or glamorous they may be. We are rarely listened to, as we seem to be romantics detached from all reality, unable to dialogue with the complexities announced in other disciplinary fields, taking refuge in art when it suits us to be silent and in urban theory when we lament. Worse still, in none of these disciplinary areas are we automatically welcomed, as we arrive with approaches that generally appear to be anachronistic and already found in other frameworks of reflection.

Faced with such a drastic diagnosis, at Supersudaca we thought it was key to address the question of the relationship between those who do influence, study and affect space by means of a political agenda, which they systematise and present in ideological terms that seduce and bring to realisation. We call this: the *Architecture of the World* which is in contrast to the current state of the disciplinary art of architecture and its manifestations in works, publications and events that we call the *World of Architecture*. If we reduce it to an overly realistic caricature, we would be talking about the potential relationship between the G7 and the Venice Architecture Biennale. The relationship is clearly none, normal! But is it normal? We already discussed in Supersudaca the need to create a G all minus the 7. These themes when applied to the discipline are difficult to address individually as an architect, particularly from the countries that would make up this theoretical G All minus the 7, where the academic environment perceives them as too broad. We especulate that after years of effort, we would end up discussing these ideas (once again, within four walls).

Why is it so hard to debate and present alternative social utopias and dystopias that would produce an according vocabulary in architecture exercise? Is it possible to speculate on aligning the architecture of the world with the world of architecture? If the above was raised in modernism and lost in post-modernism and its succession of eternal "posts" (post-socialism, post-capitalism, post-criticism...), can we get out of the cyclical redundancy of architecture at the beginning of the 21st century? We believe that the natural answer is yes. Architecture can be part of a change -which of course is not exclusive to its domain- of a planetary reconfiguration, in the same way as it is discussed in other disciplines through the concept of the production of space. How can it continue not to be so? We advocate being more proactive and not only critical, moving from theoretical models to frameworks for action. Certainly, there are today several architects with a similar plan that we have had the good fortune to meet, who express the same concern and claim their right and fundamental role in this disciplinary turn, that of aligning the architecture of the world with the world of architecture, with the consequences that this entails.

But it is not a rebellion without a cause, nor a shout into the void, first we must start with a clear point of discussion. Curiously, we are living in a *momentum* that, from multiple disciplines, coincides in a diagnosis of the current urbanisation process: it generates inequality and is unsustainable, and that manifests itself mainly in the management or lack of it of space. The above has a total reach over the planet, even beyond, if we include satellites and orbiting rubbish. We could cite here, if this were a scientific paper, a thousand authors, from geography, sociology, anthropology, philosophy, economics, history, political science and various urban-related disciplines. Probably reading these lines, several names come to mind. Therefore, can we address from the point of view of architecture the question of how to consider this process of urbanisation? Can we assume that from the process of accumulation of capital over space, broad issues have to be faced? Do you think it is enough, in the face of a problem that is

spread across the entire planet, to respond with a few crumbs
of image-washing or a few emblematic works? If your answer
is yes, we are sorry for wasting your time, we recommend to
stop reading here, thank you. If on the contrary, one takes the
risk of tackling the subject, it opens up to infinite complexity
and enthusiasm, the question is how to do it? For the time
being, the invitation is to a disciplinary turn, we only know that
the way we are practicing architecture has only increased the
inequality of the world and contributing to make it an unsustainable phenomenon, with or without awareness of it. We
think it would be good to take a little more context and breathe
on the matter, as a first step to avoid disciplinary autism.

Polarization, the Critical Vitruvian Turn (or its Return)

One of the conclusions we have reached in our discussions is
the effect of disciplinary polarisation in architecture. Through
curricular renovation, across a broad spectrum of academia
and professional training, a process of specialisation has been
implemented in architecture, as in almost all professions,
promoted as the most appropriate alternative for fostering
innovation and productivity. This is likely to be justified and
necessary in various fields, for specific job opportunities, and
at different levels of participation in society. Thus, in architecture, specialists were trained in urban, theoretical, heritage,
real estate management, even lighting and materials, such as
wood, to name but a few tiny examples. As it turned out, the
development and execution of the architectural works, which
is a different matter, was split up. Moreover, the disciplinary
debate naturally led to binaries of specialisation, the purpose
of which was to claim exclusively each of the areas of specialisation, such as: architecture versus urbanism, social versus art
and craft, theory versus practice, and a long list of etcetera's
that permeate both the training and practice of architecture.
Our thesis at Supersudaca is that this polarised condition of
architecture is fatal; it has atomised the debate and rendered
us ineffective in addressing more complex issues. It's like we
are being worried about washing dirty clothes at home, without ever being able to go out on the street dressed. Even more
important, it is an intrinsic contradiction of the discipline, as it
is a denial of architecture as a general discipline. Indeed, we
know since Vitruvius that in architecture we are concerned
with the reflection and elaboration of what is useful, solid
and beautiful beyond buildings, in his case: from weapons to
clocks, of course with the social review it deserves today. So

1   Ayn Rand, The Foun-
tainhead (1943, repr.
New York, Plume, 2005)

why deny the enabling capacity and this universal character of the discipline of architecture if these aspects are still referential in all architectural education? With the introduction of market capitalism into all spheres of public and private life it has on the one hand engendered an alleged demand for architectural specialists, while at the same time it has discarded the architect as a valid representative figure of a common spatial goal. For Supersudaca the generalist process is exposed in the representations linked to the architecture from Da Vinci's Universal Man, through Le Corbusier's Modulor, where there was an apparent synchrony between society and its aspirations with the contribution of architecture, but perhaps the turning point is represented in the figure of the architect Howard Roark in the novel *The Fountainhead*[1], the one who is capable of dynamiting his own work rather than submitting to the absurd changes imposed on him by society. Here is a symbol of the beginning of the divorce between the desires of the architectural agenda and those represented by society, in particular those of the market. Nor does this process mean that architecture has been completely annihilated, there have been various generational efforts, from resistance to commercial glorifications, to attempts to *operate from within* such as *surfing the wave of the market*, as well as the call for the supposed *autonomy* of architecture, which is basically locking itself in the disciplinary barracks, or the constant anaesthetic escapades in technological odes, - let us admit - architecture has remained afloat on an already very thin (surf) board. The essential question is: What would happen if we avoid polarisation, what disciplinary scopes would be (re)opened up? This is Supersudaca's invitation, and part of the shift we encourage, is to stop worrying about whether we are urbanists or not, whether we can be pigeonholed into one or several subjects at once. Of course, skills develop from opportunities, but the disciplinary starting point of architecture as a generalist, beyond the art of construction, is to have a universal perspective with respect to the art of social space. To assume critically under any circumstances that arise that architecture is to be simultaneously art and part of society.

Direct Architecture: Self-Commission and Self-Management

The question derived from the thesis of polarisation in architecture is: What are the mechanisms at work in this process and how can they be avoided? Without having an exhaustive, let alone total answer, which would be a contradiction as we have described, we propose to examine the *tyranny of commissions*. We question the possibility of basing the architect's training, his intellectual stance, his ability to convey a synthetic message, solely on the basis of the commission and its client. There are already several voices that have warned that in both the public and private domains, the most redundant and uncreative work, the one that least contributes to civil society, is embedded in the content of the commissioning of a work. Incidentally, these are becoming increasingly rarer as the majority of works are now absorbed by a real estate agency, if necessary, in complicity with the architect, who can do something, but often only lends his signature for the permit plans. Then there are very few poets who commission a house, as we have so often seen in undergraduate architecture workshop exercises, let alone a mega-port, intermodal station, or ecological reserve park, as is often done by young architects aspiring to obtain their cardboard diploma, a commission that they will never do alone or probably not even accompanied. So why does this idea of the commission remain the only way of approaching architecture since its academic beginnings? Of course, there is an obvious training to be able to respond to commissions, but surely this must be more linked to the management of uncertainties and restrictions than to the management of a total freedom of architecture. Perhaps it would be better to train architects in how to get commissions without totally abandoning the critical look, the discussion and the contribution in architecture? Better yet: in addition or complementarily, how to transcend the commission and directly put the approaches and concerns of architecture into the space? In a first attempt to address these issues, and inspired precisely by the debate and collaboration with academic institutions, at Supersudaca we have spent more than a decade proposing and carrying out what we define as *Direct Architecture*[2], what in other fields would be understood as interventions, installations and performances, the same but without forgetting the projective angle of architecture. In these instances of direct architecture, an interesting debate has finally opened up, to the extent that within the context of specialisation and polarisation, the question has been asked: Is a temporary 10-day intervention in public/private space really architecture? If studying a context, defining a space for the purpose of reverting, claiming or provoking a value change, managing and optimising resources, building and implementing a work in four and five dimensions, adding a symbolic character, why

2   See chapter Direct
Architecture Genealogy,
pages 26-37.

wouldn't it be architecture? To ensure quality does architecture have to be large in scale, slow in execution and perpetual in presence? If there is one thing that has been certain for a long time, it is that these qualities do not guarantee quality in architecture. So why focus on these aspects alone and ignore other possibilities? Of course, these possibilities must be verified with all the rigour that the architectural debate deserves. Perhaps this statement will come too late for some, there are many experiences of urban interventions, e.g. pallets and street gardens, but it does not mean *per se* that they are successful. There are several warning cries underlining that these urban interventions that aspire to improve a certain degraded context, eventually tend to be only a one-off example for the satisfaction of architects and have little or nothing to do with the inhabitants (here we go again) or end up generating an increase in the value of the square metre and end up displacing the original inhabitants by those with greater purchasing power over the land. Even so, this is a debate that deserves to be had, we must indeed correct certain illusions of corporate image-washing and moral safeguarding innocence's, in which architecture can be co-opted as a victim by undeclared corporate interests. At the same time, architecture does not have the task of solving everything on its own, but it can address a larger field in conjunction with other disciplines, and we return to the previous starting points. Perhaps indeed the turn already has its first inclination, but to avoid going out of the curve, it is necessary to give it constant acceleration and force to avoid the tyranny imposed by the duet commission-client.

CoLab: We Also Build Beach Houses

The above discussion also lends itself to confusions and apparent radicalizations that, once again, end up in polarisations and obvious contradictions in architecture: Never receive commissions! Never work for the rich! Never design, never build, nothing! And a perhaps shorter list of *etcetera's*. These proclamations come from a reflection that may be valid: effectively distancing oneself from processes of segregation and social unsustainability may be perfectly valid on some occasions, but why should it be valid on all? Another of the debates we have carried out in Supersudaca is why should a certain typology, archetype or condition uniformly imply failure or success in architecture? Including, of course, our own conclusions and works of architecture. This is a phenomenal debate that again is impossible to carry out as an individual, let alone in the academy, because it is linked to a process, and it happens mainly when you are collaborating on a project. This is why, in the Supersudaca group, we set up *CoLab*, a collaborative laboratory, a framework for debate that can be about research, but which becomes more intense in a work or indeed in a commission. They influence, from the questioning announced in the previous point, to highlighting the context and specificity of the task to be carried out and in allusion to the classic guidelines of the discipline of architecture. Of course, it is easier when it is a collaboration for a public institution or cultural agent: the debate hardly happens, we assume the above as all aligned, long live the turn in architecture, but what happens when a commission arrives, a rich client, eventually a real estate agency? Do we hide it? Is the -to pay the bills- an opportunistic and misleading quotation to Robin Hood? This is where it gets tasty. There is no definitive answer, but neither is there an experience of paralysis, there are of course experiences of rejection, and here the context influences a lot and each member of Supersudaca takes the freedom to decide without prejudice how to approach it. Clearly it would be pretentious to assume infallibility, but it must be stressed that this is the real trench and the experiences that count. Avoiding polarisation and cynicism, Supersudaca has advocated total openness to the process. No sweeping projects under the carpet, because this is where the learning and debate is. Once the above starting points and positions have been defined, there is the form, but ultimately, we go for the substance of the issues in architecture.

Incomplete Conclusion

In Supersudaca we assume that in Latin America we have been globalised for five hundred years and that we can systematize this heritage and project it into global discussions. It is amazing the level of empathy we have generated, particularly in the so-called "South-South" connections with the East, especially with a name that is half insult, half comic book! But also in the developed countries where we act and discuss. The question of how to deal with uncertainty, the emergence or revelation of informal processes, collusive politics, attacks, governance fragility, etc., has apparently come to the fore in architecture. These are all issues that are becoming increasingly relevant and sound awfully familiar in the previously announced framework of Supersudaca. It seems increasingly evident the condition and process whereby the 1% dominate

3   See chapter LA Col-
ective, Y PREVI?, pages
38, 57.

at the expense of the remaining 99%, something we have experienced historically in Latin America, as the back room of the laboratory, accumulating all the ideological experiments that the West has come up with, and where architecture, the (mega)polis and the territory have not been left out. There are certainly striking stories, such as the Experimental Housing Project (PREVI-Lima, 1969)[3] that we have studied, beyond the fetishism of the alterations to the original architecture proposed by the *starchitects* of the sixties, as a diverse and resilient neighbourhood, to give one of several examples. Since our beginnings we have collaborated with academia, actively and fervently teaching in all the countries where we have set up bases and outside where we have been invited, we have tried to erase boundaries and reverse the rules of the game in architecture. When we teach, we don't simulate, we do spatial practice, when we practice, we discuss and theorize until we use up the last bit of time and patience. When we do research, we draw on both science and art. Most of the results have gone unnoticed or with passing glories, we often go down well, sometimes badly, but the process never seems to stop, although within the group no one cares to justify Supersudaca to anyone, other than *per se*. The group could be dismantled at the end of writing these lines, but it seems that Incomplete Works, it is contagious, when it seems forgotten it resuscitates in the most unthinkable forms, like the concept of the mueblenstein, a multipurpose piece of furniture with architectural properties created collectively. This has a life of its own! All the reflections, discussions and works we have done over the years have led Supersudaca members, if not to seduce bankruptcy - another permanent topic of discussion - to be invited, to have experiences in unlikely places, to interact with admirable people and institutions, all in a seemingly inconsequential effort, which can be said to be inconclusive. While a book of Supersudaca's complete works does not yet exist, and if it does, it would be a book of unfinished operations, a book called *incomplete works*. Supersudaca has been, and perhaps will continue to be, an audacious *travel agency*, in a very broad sense of the concept, to produce, experience and share architectural content, without any pretence and without any heritage other than its questions and discussions. Again, perhaps no one knows, but on this trip, it may be time to invite more people onboard and continue to turn the flight itinerary around.

Direct Architecture Genealogy

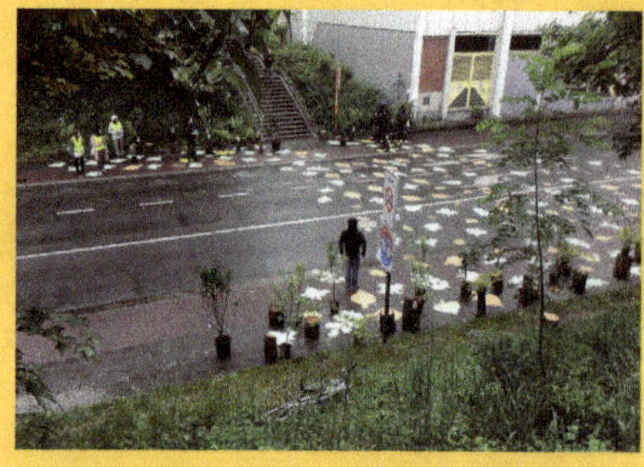

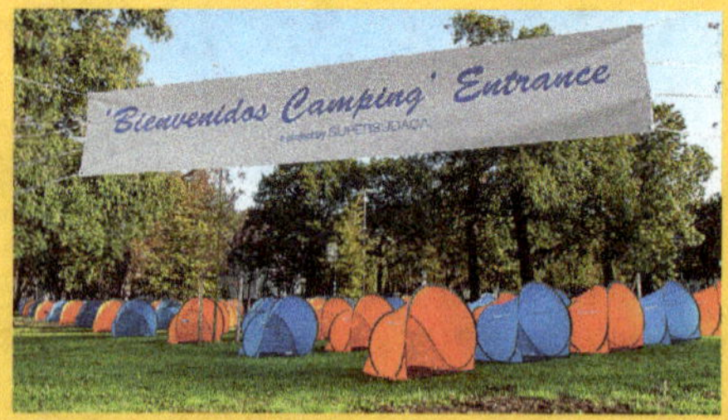

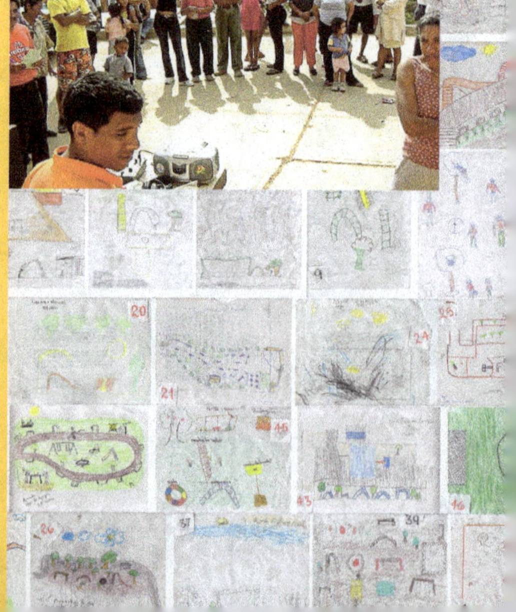

Intro-outro

1. "Paris as a Masterclass jury," Berlage Institute, 2001.

"And why didn't you do it for real?"
Jean-Louis Cohen[1]

It has been an adventure to move from the fiction (or representation) of architecture to reality. First as students, then as teachers, practitioners and researchers, but above all, within the framework and the paths of belonging to Supersudaca.

For its members, Supersudaca is undoubtedly the project that has transcended the most in time, in relation to any other, in the disciplinary, but also in the affective and personal. It has certainly been a great adventure to access a way of looking at *the world of architecture* and *the architecture of the world*, with multiple points of view and multiple realities. This, before the multiverse, before WhatsApp, before YouTube, before Facebook, Instagram and now TikTok and Discord, but at the same time anticipating, in an analogous way, a connection, a collective intelligence, which seems inexhaustible and always enthusiastic, as it is demonstrated every time we meet, even partially or via zoom.

This connection gave rise to the exploration of alternative realities in the performance of architecture, beyond the commission, the client and the competition, at the same time, without discarding them. It also offered the possibility of taking initiatives beyond a disciplinary reading of linear, hegemonic or coherent architecture.

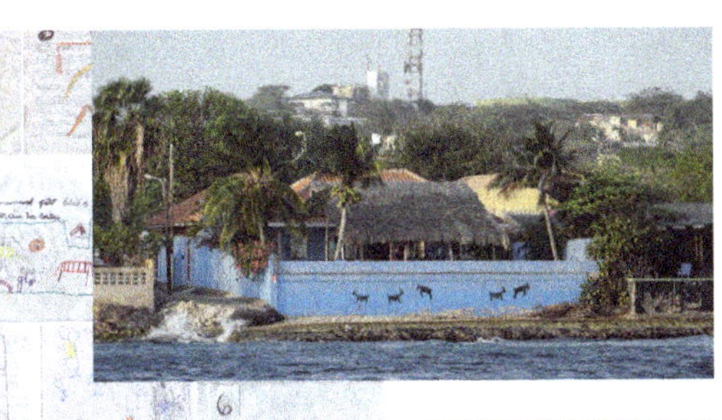

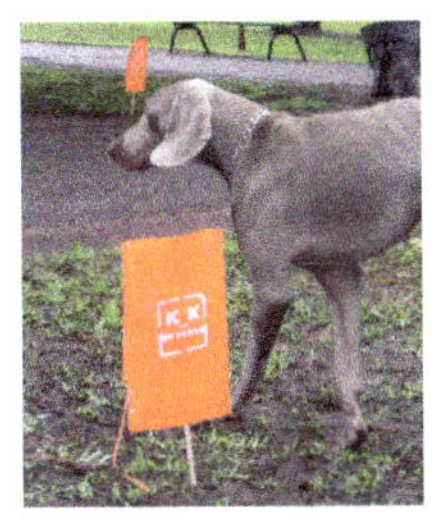

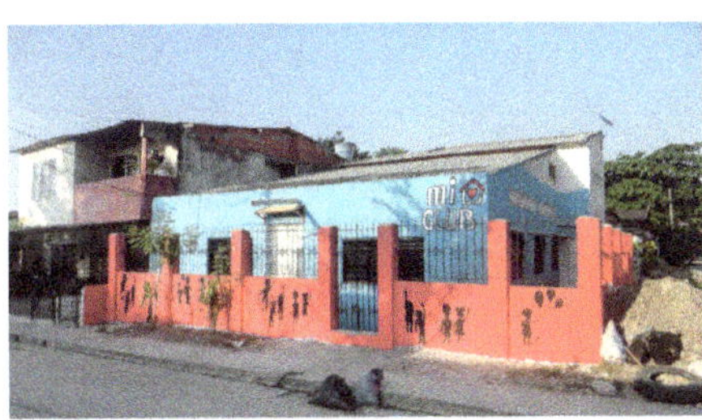

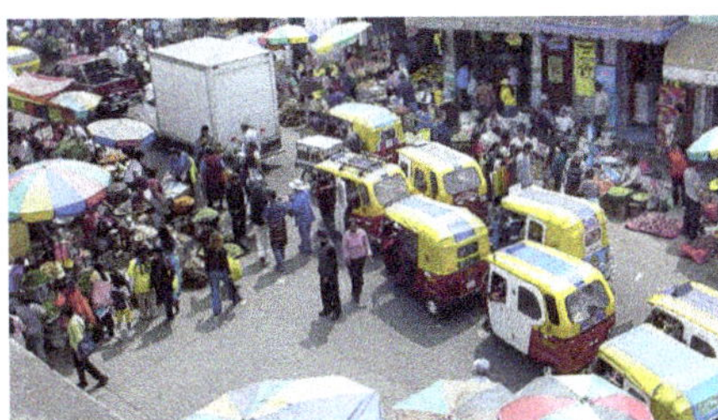

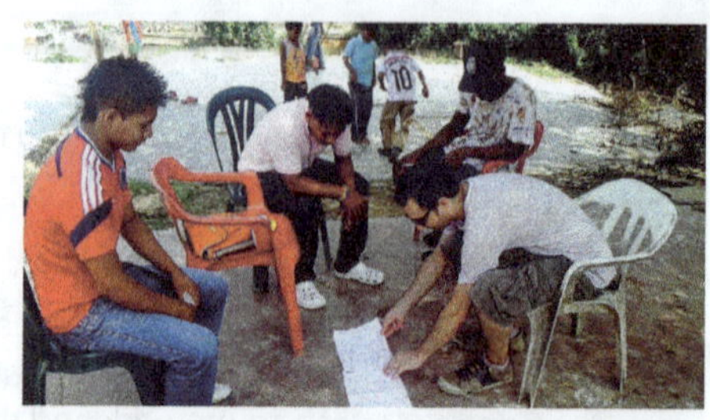

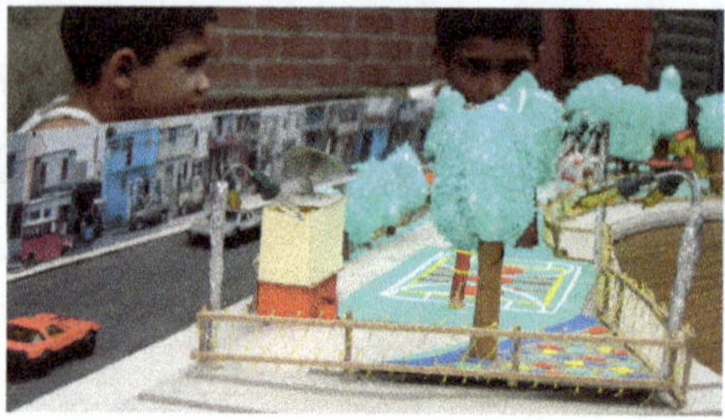

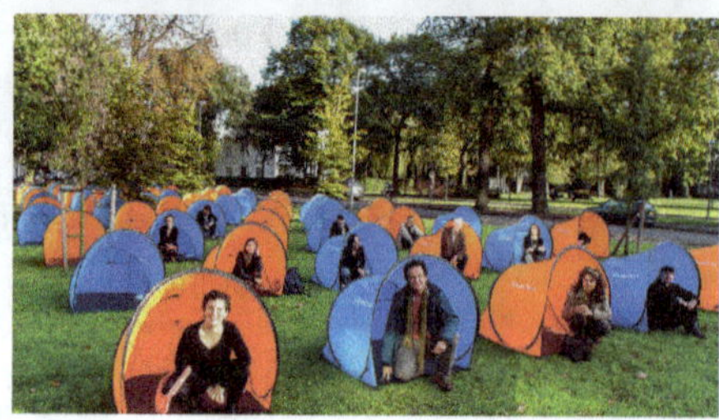

From these incombustible explorations and discussions, *direct architecture* was born, the last component of the Supersudaca trinomial (compiled in *Supersudaca's Turn*). This concept ends up structuring the three-legged stool: the *world of architecture*, which refers to the tradition and state of the disciplinary art. Second, the *architecture of the world*, which frames critical urban research, the link with society and its deployment in space. And finally, *direct architecture*, the approach to which this text is dedicated.

The aim of the essay is to briefly understand the genealogy of the concept of "direct architecture", both its internal epistemology and its ramifications, rhizomes and spin-offs, but also its (self) critique of the current state and to open up its eventual projection. In the following, some cases and references will be mentioned to trace its origin and the lifting of its results and conclusions for its future projections in, ideally, a wider discussion of exit possibilities and disciplinary implication as it relates to the challenges of the current century with marked complexities on the social structure and the impact on its living environment, which differs from any previous condition of architecture.

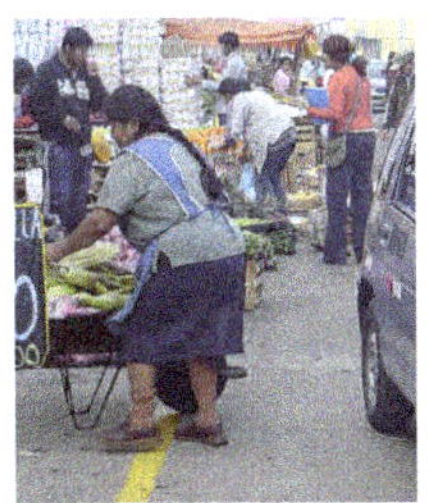
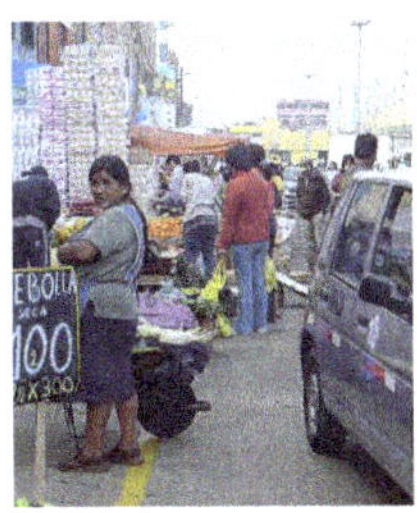
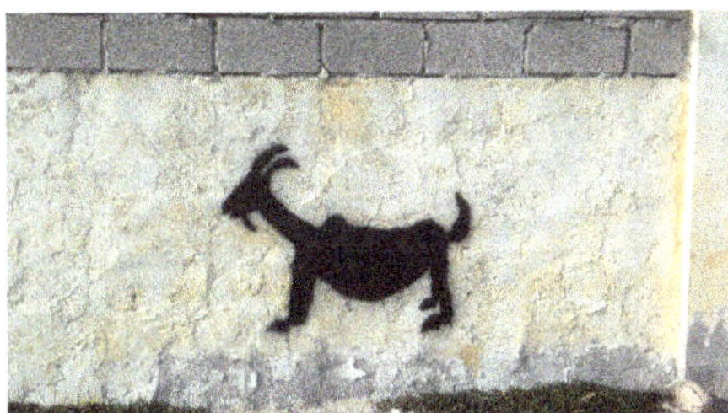
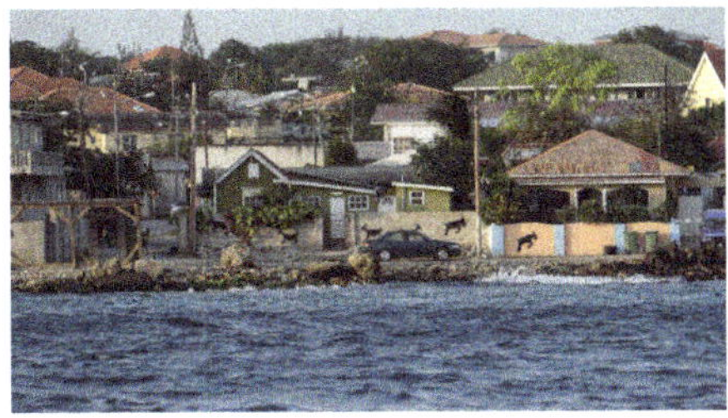

Thesis: Do it Yourself
From Petit Projets to the Berm

There was an experience that was the cornerstone of what was to be the beginning of the idea of *direct architecture*. It was 2001, in an embryonic state of what would become Supersudaca, several of its members, coming from Latin America, were fascinated, as students of the Berlage Institute, to be able to study the city of Paris. The theme of the workshop was "Grands Projets", more than a decade after its implementation.

We traveled from Holland to settle in the office of the prominent architect Dominique Perrault, the author of one of the projects, the Bibliotèque de France, which could be glimpsed on the horizon through the glazed partitions of the studio. We were asked and recommended to collect data, study flows and programmatic analyses of the iconic works of the bicentenary of the French Revolution. All in a state of abstract laboratory, reviewing screens and documents.

However, in a moment of absent-mindedness, it occurred to us to look out of the window and see the city, the question arose, why not put aside our keyboards and notes and go out and experience it. Thus, to establish a link with the assigned case study: the Louvre Museum, and the society in which it operates.

Rather than fieldwork with the aim of collecting a particular piece of information, we were fascinated by what the

Parisian urban space had to offer. We quickly realized that by
simply moving around the city without any other objective than
the city itself (*flânerie*?), it offered a character and a number
of options impossible to represent in a graph or numerically.
What struck us on the way to the Louvre, from our experience,
were the connections between common spaces, mainly parks
and the metro, where one element seemed to be so common-
place as to go unnoticed: the chairs. Public chairs, green, not
anchored to the ground. As they seemed to have a use value
so obvious that all citizens respect them, it seems that nobody
stole, destroyed or threw them into the river. The chairs left
traces, configurations of the city dwellers, as they gathered
and congregated, some looked towards the magnificent
sculptures of Henry Moore, Alberto Giacometti, Jean Dubuffet.
Others, the opposite, but they stayed together. Different day-to-
day situations were recorded in these very obvious devices.

Our conclusion for the workshop was that although the
Louvre was transformed – as a *grand projet*, into a museum
– mall, with commercial premises and rooms for events, by
focusing all the attention on the entrance of the glass pyramid
by I. M. Pei – it left out the *cour carré*, the courtyard of the
medieval origin of the castle, which also connects with the rest
of Paris towards the island by means of the bridge (*des arts*?),
to its fate.

Our proposal then was to populate the *cour carré* with the
same texture of gravel and chairs that the city offers in its illus-
trious common spaces leading to the museum, and automatically (re)establish the connection to the city. The proposal also
reflected on the context of the museum's financial crisis and
pointed a new direction: to move from *grands projets* to *petit
projets*, in allusion to the *little prince*.

It was a daring approach, as most of our colleagues went
in a different direction, but the jury, composed of "starchitects"
and architectural scholars we admired, loved the proposal.
They encouraged us to form a kind of group that would be
concerned with urban issues and would come up with simple
ideas, with minimum resources and maximum public impact.
But Jean-Louis Cohen, a leading architectural researcher, Le
Corbusier biographer, curator and many other award winners,
raised a question: why didn't you do it, why didn't you take
some chairs and try it out?

We were left with no response. It was obvious that we
should have tried, even if it raised alarm bells. We were left
with the last bullet and without realizing it, we committed ourselves, more or less consciously, that on the next occasion, we

should conclude this narration, generate what the situationists had already pre-conceptualized, an urban situation (euh!).

Back in Latin America in 2003, we would propose to do that second click: make the students in the Architecture Studio go out through the city of Talca, to find conflicts or opportunities for improvement and generate a project (classic), but then, manage how to bring it to reality (2xClick!). Some went well and others not so well, but notable cases such as *El museo Callejero* were achieved where a dark, unsafe and smelly level crossing was transformed by painting it white and gathering there the musicians and artisans of the neighborhood who now activated the space indoors. In successive workshops the exercises would be repeated involving different methods to achieve the possibility of actually intervening in the space of the city.

Also in 2003, the German Cultural Foundation together with Caracas Urban Think Tank convened a group of 17 specialists (including photographers, architects, urban planners, semioticians, sociologists, engineers, filmmakers, social communicators and writers) to travel to Caracas to study a place where gasoline is cheaper than water, where heights of city buildings rose from one to some twenty floors in about five years in the economic boom of the '50s.

Supersudaca joined the team. Upon arrival in Caracas, the great energy and hope generated by Hugo Chávez's victory over the failed attempt to overthrow him in 2002 made it more interesting for specialists to investigate the reverse role of specialists and the inhabitants of the barrios. Now the latter were empowered, a new method had to be conceived far away from the office computers. It was a moment to question the authority of the expert versus the knowledge of barrio inhabitants. When we were asked by one community leader to design a park, it was clear that they expected a new approach and recognition of the inverted power roles. So after discussing with the community leaders we decided to test a new method that did not rely on the hierarchical organization of experts and customers.

Inspired by the first experiments on decentralized democracy in America we would test a sort of direct democracy: *direct architecture*. The idea was not only the typical empowerment process of demanding justice, but the initiation of self-reliant organization platforms that could deal with their public needs, including the decision of programs, location, finance, definition of priorities by the affected and the architectural design itself. Rather than showcasing our form giving talents we tested the role of the architect as a midwife guiding and mediating the people themselves to build what they need through the design of a method that included organizing a two stage user competition, where all users could determine what they really want, to then proceed a process of negotiation through smaller collective dreams and finally a commonly agreed design direction supported by the community. It implied a do it yourself attitude: direct architecture was coined.

By 2005, Supersudaca had figured out a trajectory to intervene in the complex metropolis we inhabited. We could adventure beyond the classical theoretical proposal by having a method to work as midwives that articulate the aspirations of a certain community with the available resources and then actually implementing them in space. So, when we got the offer of teaching an Urbanism course in Pontificia Universidad Católica del Perú (PUCP), it was time to formalize Arquitectura Directa into a pedagogy that can "read and write" in our overflowed cities.

The brief of the course Supersudaca taught stated:

> "The social responsibility of architecture is making better cities. But only eventually it has the opportunity to 'make' cities through projects or plans. On those rare occasions, based on the alleged professional competence that the society (s)he 'serves' has held responsible, architects tend to diligently deliver the solutions to change the world. Anointed by omnipotence, they turn studies and reflections into promising interventions and arguments... but... the endless list of intermediaries who assist in the labor of the project, reduce the architect into pathetic levels of impotence. Architecture turns into a discipline with an expertise on Past Perfect Tenses ('if' clause) which – proudly – illustrate full color publications only read by other architects (!). Too much talent and energy turn into too much irrelevance.
>
> How can we transcend this passive condition about intervening in the city? How to solve the uselessness of architecture's task to improve the quality of life of cities? Between cynicism and naivety, do we train – yet another generation – to play the role of the misunderstood intellectual? Do we insist on differentiating architecture from urbanism, so the mud doesn't reach us beyond scale 1/200? How much time will the ostrich hold its head underground?

2.   Ludwig Von Berta-
lanffy. *General System
Theory: Foundations,
Development, Appli-
cations* (USA, George
Braziller Inc., 1969).

Perhaps there are some spaces where our limited power – once assumed – could make a difference. If we cannot control the train that will transform the city, maybe we are capable of driving hundreds of *mototaxis* (motorcycle taxis). If we understand urbanism beyond mere deterministic planning and focus on the induction of situations to happen, we could find ourselves not building a city… but farming its urbanity. By changing to another strategy, we find a great potential in operating at the blind spots of traditional architecture and urbanism. Those interstices where its scale is smaller than a building but whose effects can have urban proportions. There, where nobody claims competence, therefore, no responsibilities or guilt. There, where we can exercise the spatial knowledge of architecture by practicing a budget-less urbanism of minimum resources but maximum impacts. A space where the main tool would be ingenuity, where projects are executed for real, without means or intermediaries: a Direct Architecture."

The mechanics of the 14-week course consisted in applying Bertalanffy *General System Theory* into the study of components and interrelations of a given urban system, once mapped we defined its G-spot: there where with the minimum effort, the maximum levels of change can be achieved, either to solve a problem or to exacerbate a found potential.[2] Finally, a real intervention was made with the minimum of resources. Chairs, plastic bags, yellow lines, banners, paint, balloons, flyers, cardboards, etc. became triggers to unchain virtuous cycles on the urban realm: the awareness of your neighbors, the cleanliness of a street, the animation of a terrain vague, the sense of safety on a dangerous street, the construction of a landmark, etc. In all these interventions the effects have profited on the acknowledgement that relationships between urbanism and citizens, matters the most, on the level of simple ordinary issues that define our quality of life.

A fascinating world was opening up, and so we tested this hypothesis with Supersudaca from Lima to Tokyo mostly in collaboration with architecture students from several universities.

In Lima, students of urban planning reorganized markets using lines of paint, an improvised place of urine was displaced with a stencil. In Buenos Aires the dog "KK" was evident, plagued public parks with orange posters. In Curaçao, interventions over five years put in evidence the lack of public access to the beaches, ultimately led the local government to promote an initiative to open up the illegally privatized access to the sea as well as providing basic infrastructure on the three last public urban beaches in Willemstad. In Cartagena, the area where the Zenu community lives (that doesn´t appear in the city maps) was mapped in order to make it visible and identity was given to a social institution that hosts kids from a risky neighborhood to gather during the day with social and cultural activities, by choosing a name and painting the facades in blue, all decided by vote and work with the children from the institution. In Haarlem, the Netherlands, they camped out in a park. In Antwerp, where a neglected piece of land developed over more than 50 years into an urban natural reserve, interventions helped to discover the blind spots in the governance system leading to a change into a citizens-driven care-for nature protection policy where the policies of "commons" played an important role. And so we explored, prototyped, experimented, for more than two decades in the most diverse contexts, what we define as direct architecture, a way of posing ideas about space in an empirical way.

Antithesis: in Order to be Good... and Other Drifts from India, to the Current Wave

It is to be expected that in experimentation, there will be stumbles or *cul de sacs*, direct architecture is in a preliminary state, though one can trace various experiences, from exercises in Taliesin, to performance and happenings of the 1960s.

While it avoids reliance on commissioning, it depends on supportive institutions, a team willing to give their time and a strong connection to local networks. The academy is therefore an ideal breeding ground, since it incorporates a critical dimension. However, when it is institutionalized at the public level, as a policy, it tends to become uncritical and instrumentalized to promote the authority of the day. Particularly in municipalities, it is used to glorify the mayor of the day. This is what we have seen through so-called tactical urbanism, previously with social urbanism and urban acupuncture.

We have even had experiences where our suspicions were high and we self-critically questioned what we could really contribute in terms of impact in a ten-day workshop. For example, we were invited to work in Daharavi, Mumbai, the largest slum in the world and also one of the most sought-after areas for gentrification, given its central location and lack of available land for development.

The activity incorporated international guests, non-governmental organizations and architects at the highest level such as Charles Correa. However, the complexity of the problem was so great and the first thing we heard in meetings with the community and its representatives was that they were tired of being analyzed and surveyed. They did not see any change in decades. Even at this point, they seemed to believe more in private initiatives than in the government or in nongovernmental organizations (NGOs). A hard start.

Instead of trying to convince the community again of what they seem to distrust, we tried to deliver what they expected. We simulated encounters of private real estate initiatives and projects with our group of students, making seductive images within the vocabulary of representing real estate developers and with a *starchitecture* language that we had learned in the Netherlands.

Of course, this caused discomfort for the organizers, who viewed with suspicion and perplexity how we were ruining the vibe of the activity and selling our souls to the devil. A provocation that might seem unnecessary, but our curiosity was higher, what would happen if we presented these ideas to the community. A performance with brochures and video clips where architects and students were disguised as developers to get a real feeling of the situation. We were perplexed this time, as we realized that most of the people interviewed were fascinated by the real state aggressive approach. We played with fire and (luckily) did not get burned.

This experience, among others, presents a conclusion, a quite blatant look in the mirror, we can make the minimal interventions we want, a party, a painting, a mural, a dance activity, a roof, but the capitalist utopia about the city is rooted to the deepest popular level and it is difficult to regain confidence in the collective and community at the spatial level without having a response of exit and economic welfare. At the same time it gives architecture a useful weapon, double-edged, if it follows the game of private speculation, it can also convince people, sometimes against their own interests, revealing the dark side of direct architecture. When the inhabitants were asked if they were willing to leave their place of origin for generations and move elsewhere for the sake of profit, several community representatives were willing if it allowed them to provide education and a future for their children and grandchildren.

This result generated an internal debate within the group, without resolution, of those who, a priori, believe that it is still possible to contribute something from private real estate logics, versus those who do not. Obviously, there is a big "it depends" on a case by case basis.

There is definitely a need not only for a deeper reflection of expectations, but also for a much greater creative capacity accompanied by a long-term agenda with a change of scale in the politics of space and the city. The key, it seems, must be accompanied by the desire and confidence in another option.

Synthesis: Cantinflas Dialectic, Neither One nor the Other, but the Opposite

Direct architecture, after twenty years, has brought more questions than answers, as they say in academic circles, to make themselves look good. In this case, with a wide range of experiences. This accumulation, without being a summer of San Juan, an act of charity, one of those that are carried out to satisfy oneself morally in the face of an unequal society in environmental crisis, without anything substantially changing.

Arquitectura directa encompasses a catalog of actions, which, although organic, have all had a consequent revision by the participants, systematically, and the rest of the members of Supersudaca, with other actors invited to debate on the experience.

The initiative has been taken as a way to effectively question space, not as an end. Direct architecture is not a way to make oneself feel good, because the sincerity, empathy and trust between the members of Supersudaca leaves little room for complacency and condescension. Everything is questioned, while findings and discoveries are celebrated, validated, kept in conversation.

It is indeed a path, but a path without glories, it is without solution. Yes, with much dedication and affection, it is a genuine affection for those of us who inhabit the planet and its difficult and pathological conditions. We want to continue participating, to continue exploring, to pass the torch, to infect, to pollinate those who will try and are motivated by a greater creation and scale of direct architecture. To promote a questioning from the different professional instances that summon us. From the offices, or what is left of that model in architecture, universities, public institutions.

Our self-criticism is the best element to approach uncertainty with greater certainty. We are not claiming absolute purity in architecture, on the contrary, we are attracted by diversity and crossbreeding. It is, after all, Supersudaca. The above is without any guarantee of success and even less of disciplinary recognition of the world of architecture in its current status quo. Well, at least something is expected in order

3.   This delivery implies suffering from a hypo-critical state which is incongruent in terms of what is demanded in disciplinary terms as a perfect fit between practice, academia and current research. It makes perfect sense when we exchange and try again and again to another version of what dominates and controls urban production.

to continue operating and infinitely grateful to those who have placed their trust in us.

We are still moved to advance towards a knowledge of the cause, to establish a permanent dialectic with reality, even if it means assuming contradictions. Confronting our ideas allows us to unlearn in order to relearn another dimension of discussion and action.[3] To imagine changes, you have to start somewhere and each time we understand that small changes, *petit projets*, can open big lights, and now we did it – we have really done it.

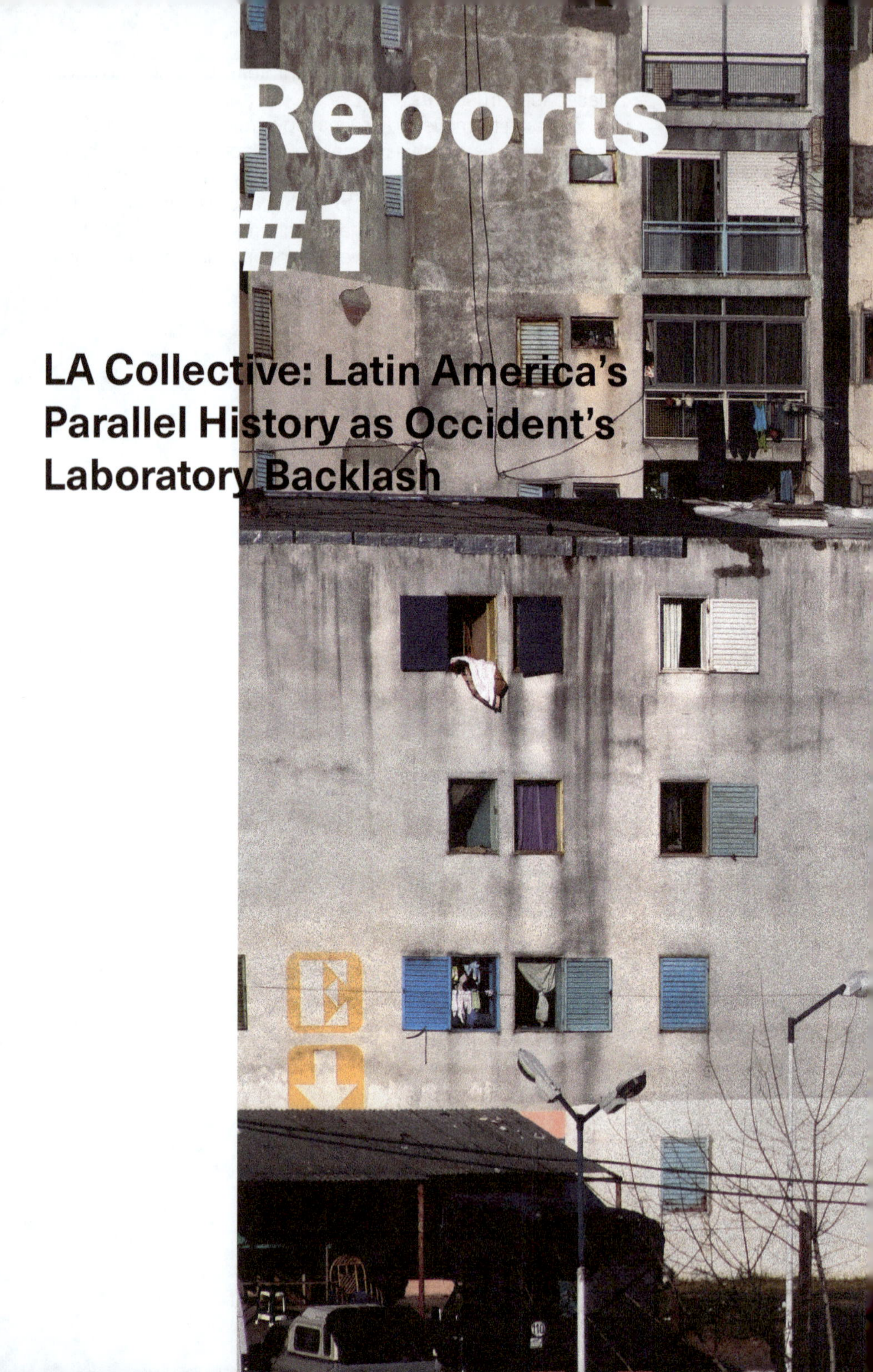

Reports #1

LA Collective: Latin America's Parallel History as Occident's Laboratory Backlash

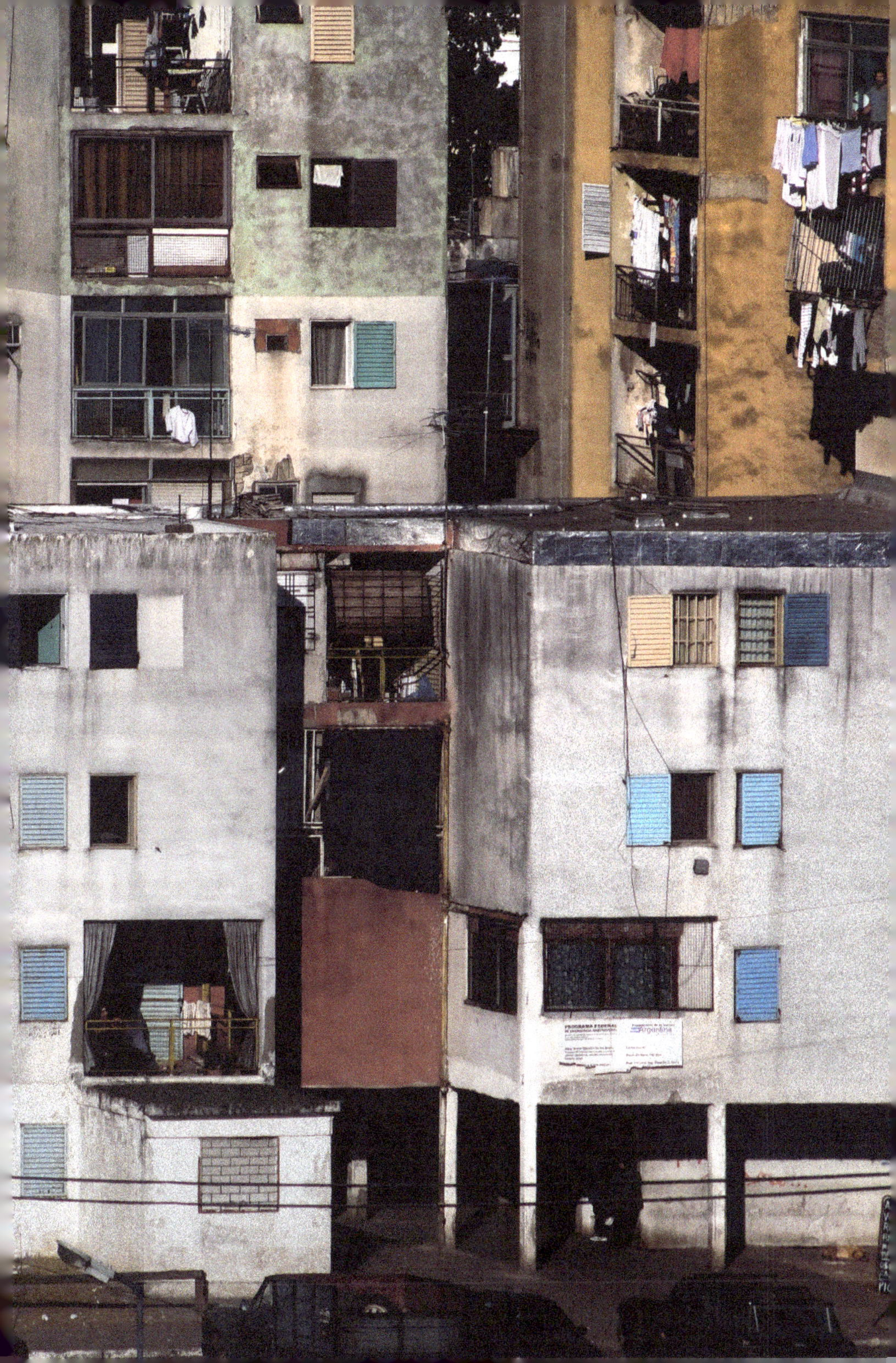

PROGRAMA FEDERAL
Argentina

Mario Pani Avant l'Heure

Guest writer

Miquel Adrià

EN. At Mexico City 1985 earthquake, Nonoalco Tlatelolco became a symbol again. This time with a symbol of destruction and death. The complex was severely damaged: One block collapsed, eleven buildings had to be demolished while four other were shortened.

Mexican architect Mario Pani (1911-1993) inaugurated a scale of projects architects in Europe and America were only thinking about. The emblematic magazine *L'Architecture d'Aujourd'hui* declined to publish his work when they mistook photographs of the buildings for photographs of models. His Tlatelolco project defined the rise and decline of a modern collective ideal: the Linear BLOCK. Coincidentally, it also happened to be the background of the killings of the October '68 demonstration, which constituted nothing less than the assassination of a collective Mexican dream.

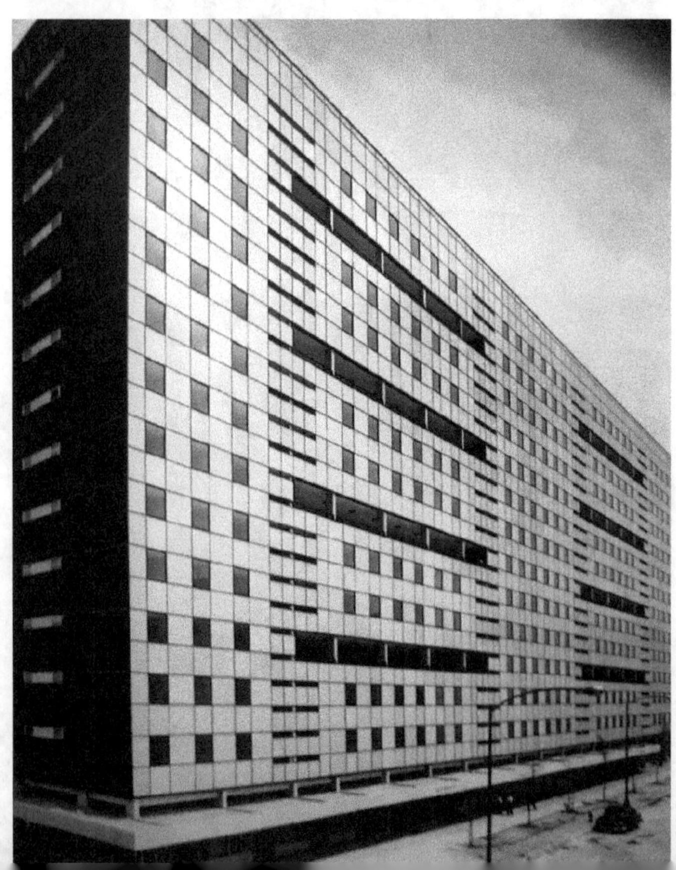

1.   Graciela de Garay Arellano and Mario Pani. *Historia Oral de la Ciudad de México: Testimonios de sus Arquitectos, 1940-1990* (México, Instituto Mora, 2000), 13.
2.   Louise Noelle, *Mario Pani: La Visión Urbana de la Arquitectura* (exhibition catalogue, México, UNAM, 2000), 25.
3.   Mario Pani traveled to France in 1948, intending to visit Le Corbusier and to know on site the works of Unité d'Habitation in Marseille. After several attempts, Le Corbusier never received him since at that time he was under severe criticism for his pilot project and decided not to show anybody the work.
4.   Mario Pani, *Los Multifamiliares de Pensiones* (México, Editorial Arquitectura, 1952), 77.

Pragmatic, and anti-solemn[1] Mexican architect Mario Pani fought on many fronts and bet big on total solutions that included urban, social, economic and political aspects. In Mexico, Pani was the last strategist who sat down at the metropolitan chessboard to move the pieces according to a plan. After him, readings of the city would be fragmented, tending toward autonomous interventions and minor urban episodes.

I had long worried about this idea of residential architecture. The origin of this matter is Le Corbusier's theory on the Radiant City... high-rise buildings that can free up space to make green areas with required service areas on the ground floor. Certainly this idea had never been carried out before, because at the same time it occurred to me to make the first one, the Multifamiliar Miguel Alemán, Le Corbusier was making the Unité d'Habitation in Marseille, a building of only three hundred apartments, but completed it after I finished the housing complex of approximately one thousand apartments.[2]

The Multifamiliar Presidente Miguel Alemán, a collective housing complex built in 1948, was born as an arousing response to an ideal competition held in 1946 by the Civil Pensions for a complex of two hundred houses for public employees. Pani proposed the Corbusian model of high-rise block buildings (arranged zigzag, as is noticeable in photos of the Radiant City's model[3]) occupying only 20% of the site in Coyoacán Avenue, increasing the population density to one thousand per hectare and freeing collective space for green and service areas. The proposal was as tempting as it was unusual for the client. "In a moment of enthusiastic boldness, Pani asked to be granted an extended deadline of fifteen days to submit a detailed project with its corresponding budget."[4] He similarly convinced his collaborators to develop the architectural project in a few weeks, working 24 hours a day in three shifts; and he persuaded a group of enterprising young engineers to assume the risk of providing an estimate and to build at a lower price. These engineers, ICA company (Civil Engineers Associated), would shortly thereafter become the most important engineering firm in Mexico. The architectural result of that intense work session was a complex of nine thirteen-story and six three-story buildings. The first blocks are linked zigzag along one of the lot's diagonals and the lower ones are isolated over the façade of shorter streets. The complex is North-South oriented, allowing most of the rooms to enjoy East-West views. The linked buildings are oriented to the South. The entire *macro-block* becomes a pedestrian area and cars are parked around the perimeter. Ground floors are

5. Arellano and Pani, *Historia Oral de la Ciudad de México*, 76; Graciela de Garay Arellano, *Mario Pani, Vida y Obra* (Mexico, UNAM, 2004), 47.
7. Enrique X. de Anda Alanís, Historia de la Arquitectura Mexicana (Barcelona, Gustavo Gili, 2006), 228.
8. Ibid.

dedicated to commercial and circulation functions. The apartments are duplex; the access level contains the kitchen and dining room and the second level – either up or down – the bedrooms and bathroom. Circulation corridors are reduced to one every three floors. Comparing this project with Unité d'Habitation in Marseille that Le Corbusier was building at the time, Pani remembered: "Our project had the big advantage that corridors were outdoors, like bridges, while Le Corbusiers' were internal corridors."[5] The architect also designed administrative offices, a school for six hundred students, a kindergarten, a laundry room with individual, automatic machines and drying rooms, a medical facility, a dining hall, a theater and sport facilities including a semi-Olympic pool.[6]

In 1964 Mario Pani and his Taller de Urbanismo conducted an exhaustive study to eradicate the so-called *slum horseshoe* – the belt of slums surrounding the city on three sides – that they believed prevented the healthy expansion of the capital city. The neighborhoods analyzed had a density of five hundred inhabitants per hectare on a single level (without services) and was terribly overcrowded. For Nonoalco-Tlatelolco, Pani's proposed one thousand inhabitants per hectare, with 75% green areas and all services integrated within the buildings, thus reversing the proportion of built and empty space. The housing complex was divided into three macro-blocks separated by existing North-South axes, which provided continuity to the urban layout. One could, however, walk through the entire complex from the Tres Culturas plaza passing through La Reforma and continue across 2 kilometers of trees and gardens to Insurgentes without coming across any vehicles. Fifteen hundred apartments were to be distributed in multifamily buildings of various heights. Nonoalco-Tlatelolco represented an exemplary, high-density, application of the modern principles that Pani made his own. His recipes for fighting against urban ailments, often due to accelerated growth, consisted in the creation of new cities *within* and *outside* the city. The latter was carried out in Satellite City and Tlatelolco was the opportunity to implement large-scale, radical surgery within the existing city, taking advantage of precedents such as the Multifamiliar Presidente Alemán and Presidente Juárez complexes.

The Nonoalco-Tlatelolco Unit represents for several generations of architects and Mexican critics a *crime of modernity*, with no territorial entrenchment or social cohesion,[7] one which shows "the decay of the good principles adopted for urban and housing design, praised by Pani himself in his earlier housing

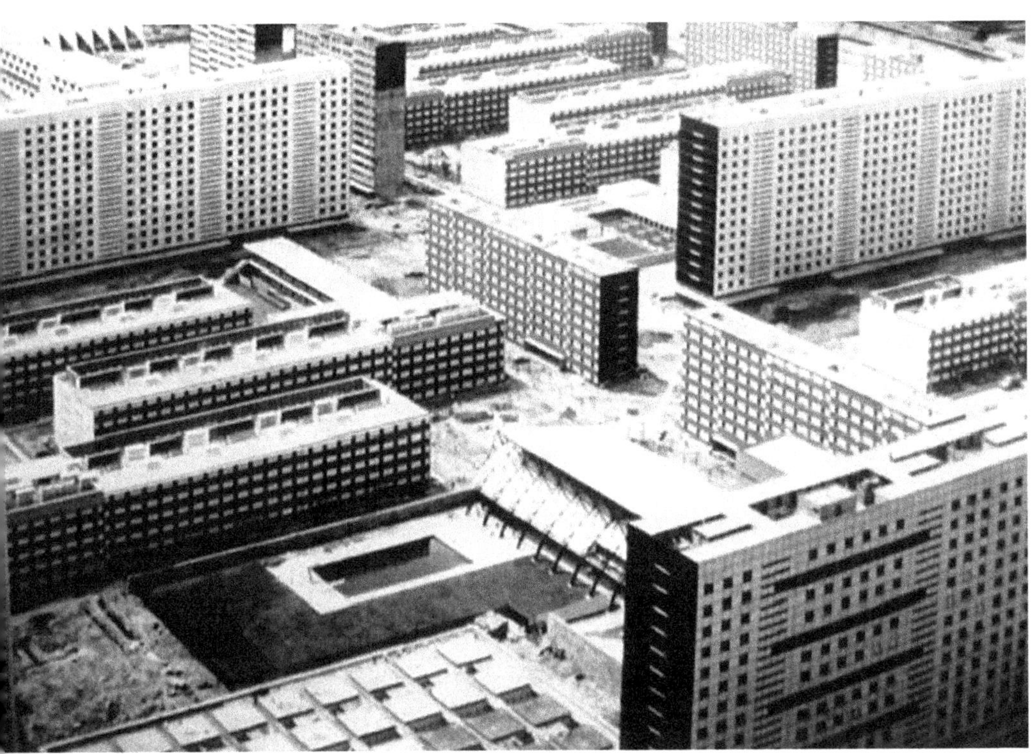

complexes."[8] Nevertheless, these macro-housing units are the
product of the modern movement's utopia, the built dream Le
Corbusier was aiming at with his Plan Voisin (1925) in which
he argued that a radical tabula rasa over the right bank of Paris
was the only solution to urban overcrowding.

The outline of the complex is drawn by the orthogonal
composition of the three building types that correspond to
the three housing typologies. Four-story buildings without
elevators make the stairs into dynamic connectors allowing
access to two apartments every half-floor. This skillful inven-
tion is exposed in the dynamic side-façades. The apartments
offer two bedrooms and a bathroom. Eight-story buildings are
perpendicular to the previous ones and repeat the scheme
used in Multifamiliar Juárez: Circulation on the North side and
façade on the South. The section also shows how to make
stairs efficient by providing access to half-floors. These apartments have three bedrooms and one and a half bathrooms.
The tallest blocks are fourteen-story high with the lower
floors dedicated to commercial use. These are strategically

9. Arellano, *Mario Pani, Vida y Obra*, 51.

equidistant so as to shorten the distance from any of the complex's buildings to the commercial space.

There is an anecdote regarding the impact of this project: It is said that Pani sent some black and white aerial photographs to *L'Architecture d'Aujourd'hui*, the most venerated magazine for this francophone-trained architect. In response he received a very formal letter indicating that journal policy forbade them to publish photographs of models. The French could not believe the images sent – so familiar within the project – were real.

The project was severely criticized for its dimensions, lack of aesthetics and the destruction of historical remains.[9] Nevertheless the syncretism of the macro-plaza preserves some remnants of the pre-Hispanic and colonial past, incorporating them into the representative spaces of modernism abstract blocks and into the cacophonic toughness of black and white façades.

One day in October 1968 the articulating thread of Mexican history was broken in the Tres Culturas plaza. Indiscriminate slaughter ended demonstrations of popular discontent. Paradoxically, and perhaps it is no coincidence, this happened in the new colony of Tlatelolco designed by Mario Pani. If this housing complex for one hundred thousand inhabitants was the paradigm of acritical, modern, high-rise linear blocks – as in so many other metropolitan peripheries across the planet – it would also be the turning point of Mexican architecture and the beginning of the decay of Mario Pani's brilliant and spectacular career. The metaphysical beauty of this artificial landscape would become a taboo, burdened with double meaning that celebrates the loss of freedom and the decease of modernity.

Supersudaca Collective Cases Timeline

Collective housing state policies starts in Latin America with Franklin Delano Roosevelt's New Deal (El Falansterio in San Juan, Puerto Rico, 1937) and in the 1940s mocking welfare states such as Ciudad Evita (Argentina), El Silencio (Caracas) with four story maximum and the paternalistic approach of the time. Afterwards, the modern megablock invented in Europe was imported to Latin America and built massively very early: as, for instance, Carlos Villanueva's 23 de Enero – with 8,206 housing units dated from 1955-1957 – and the emblematic example of Toulouse Le Mirail, designed by the architectural office Candilis-Josic-Woods – with 5,656 housing units dated from 1961-1965. Le Courbusier 's Unité d'Habitation was indeed finished in 1952 but counted only 337 units. Mega efforts proved to be vain in response to the rising housing demand and the fast and flexible self-build house exponentially generated in Latin America. The Assisted Barriada became an alternative to make cheaper cities. PREVI Lima attempts to reconcile low-rise with high density, prefabrication with self-building, modern planning with organic growth; a mid point between the megablock and the Barriada. But it was forgotten. Through the 1970s the megablock and the Assisted Barriada were maintained as in Argentina infamous Fuerte Apache and better the considered Lima's Villa el Salvador and Uruguayans bring the effective housing cooperative model in Montevideo. Lately, in Chile's 1990s new democracy economical boom quantitative subsided housing is promoted to finish with slums, Elemental quests for quality within this model.

Latin-America's Collective Housing Timeline by **Supersudaca**

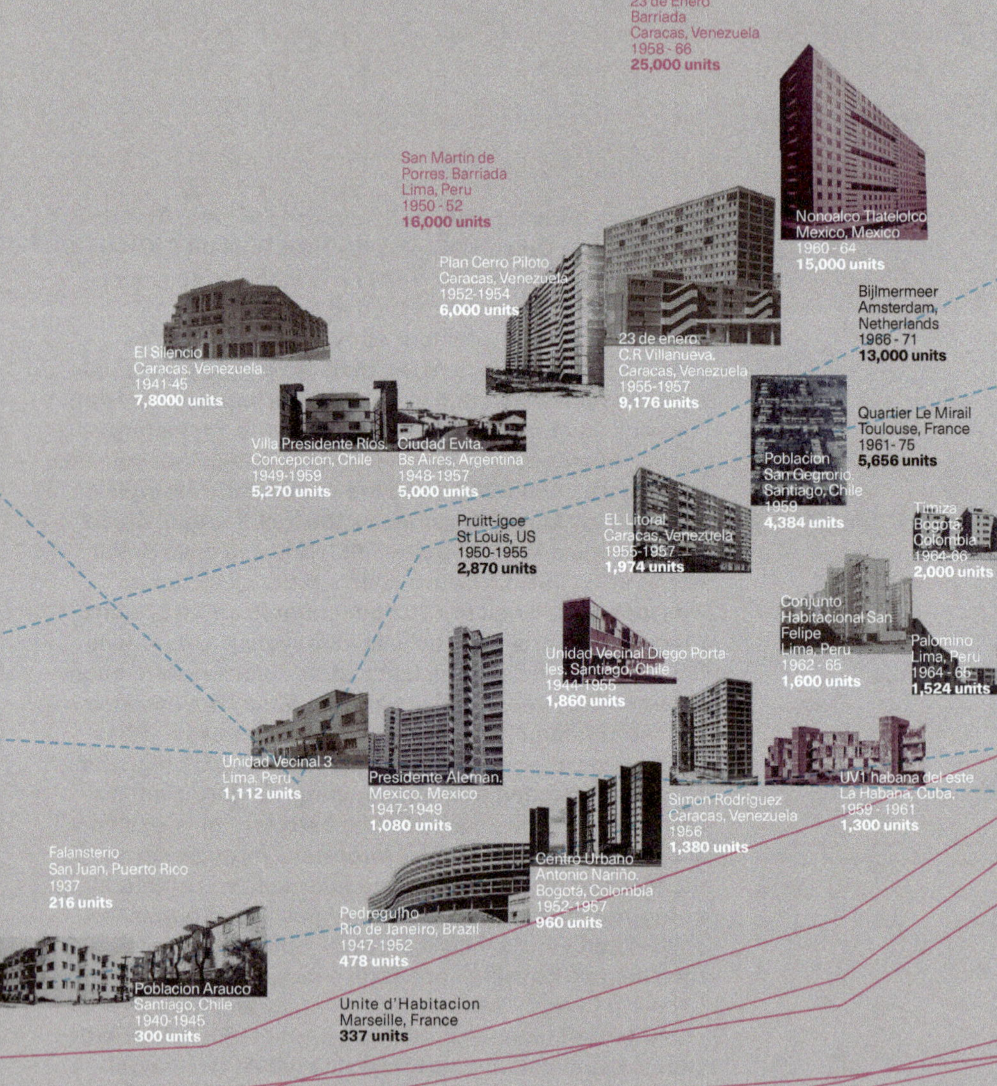

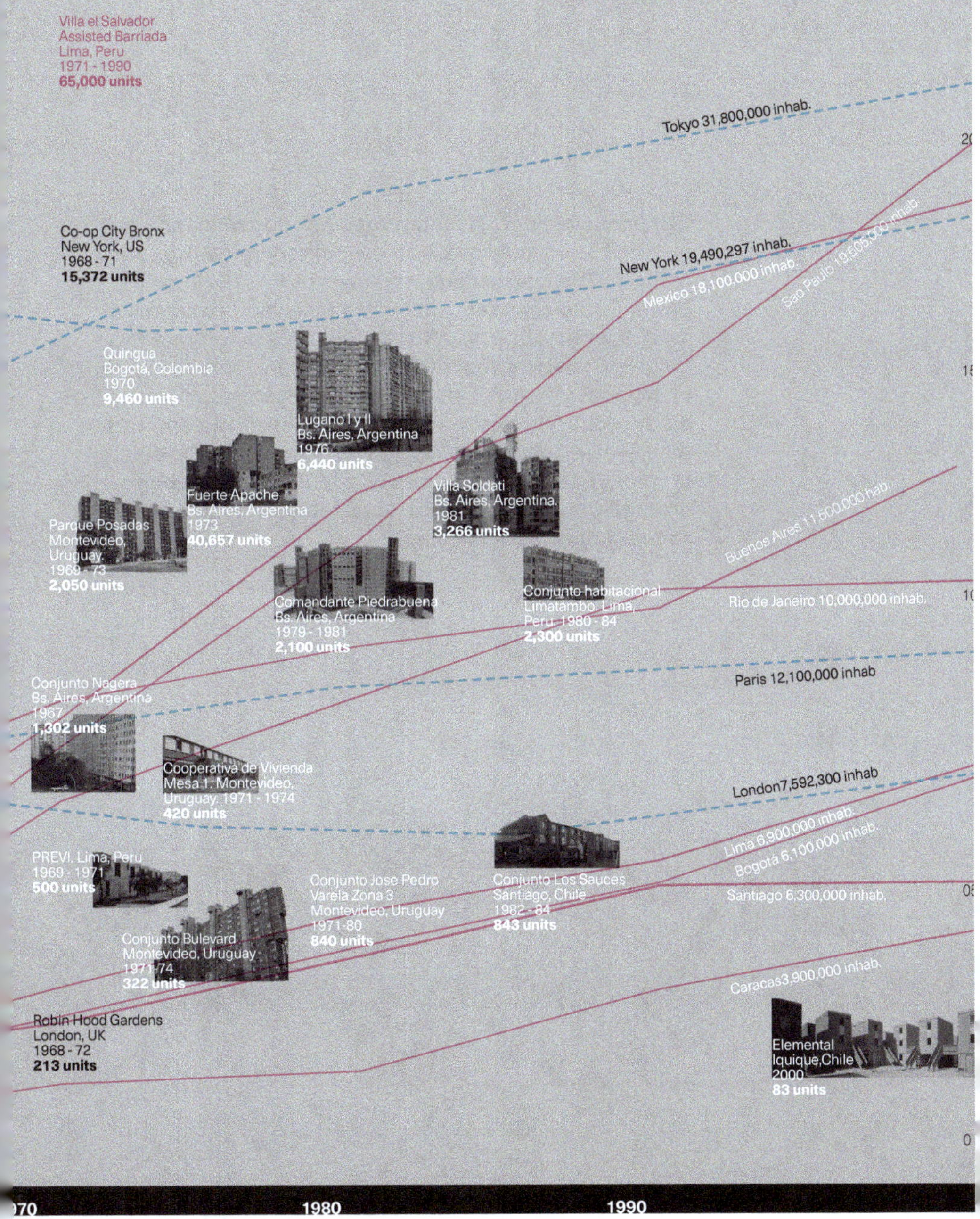

Villa el Salvador
Assisted Barriada
Lima, Peru
1971 - 1990
65,000 units

Tokyo 31,800,000 inhab.

Co-op City Bronx
New York, US
1968 - 71
15,372 units

New York 19,490,297 inhab.

Mexico 18,100,000 inhab.

Sao Paulo 19,505,000 inhab.

Quingua
Bogotá, Colombia
1970
9,460 units

Lugano I y II
Bs. Aires, Argentina
1976
6,440 units

Fuerte Apache
Bs. Aires, Argentina
1973
40,657 units

Villa Soldati
Bs. Aires, Argentina.
1981
3,266 units

Parque Posadas
Montevideo,
Uruguay.
1969-73
2,050 units

Comandante Piedrabuena
Bs. Aires, Argentina
1979 - 1981
2,100 units

Conjunto habitacional
Limatambo. Lima,
Peru. 1980 - 84
2,300 units

Buenos Aires 11,500,000 hab.

Rio de Janeiro 10,000,000 inhab.

Conjunto Nagera
Bs. Aires, Argentina
1967
1,302 units

Cooperativa de Vivienda
Mesa 1. Montevideo,
Uruguay. 1971 - 1974
420 units

Paris 12,100,000 inhab

London 7,592,300 inhab

PREVI. Lima, Peru
1969 - 1971
500 units

Conjunto Jose Pedro
Varela Zona 3
Montevideo, Uruguay
1971-80
840 units

Conjunto Los Sauces
Santiago, Chile
1982 - 84
843 units

Lima 6,900,000 inhab.

Bogotá 6,100,000 inhab.

Santiago 6,300,000 inhab.

Conjunto Bulevard
Montevideo, Uruguay
1971-74
322 units

Robin Hood Gardens
London, UK
1968 - 72
213 units

Caracas 3,900,000 inhab.

Elemental
Iquique, Chile
2000
83 units

1970
1980
1990

Argentina Megablocks Lasts

Enormous residential complexes developed in the outskirts of Buenos Aires when the military ruled Argentina in the 1970s, particularly triggered by the 1978 soccer World Cup. Argentina still blindly believed megablocks would get rid of slums. With no complementary welfare state policies in effect they eventually became three-dimensional ghettos. Their isolation prevents authorities to enter procuring a crime and violence environment. Today, they evolve between stigma to local pride. One example of this is Fuerte Apache's ex-resident and Maradona's protégé Carlitos Tevez who unashamedly declares his soccer origin from the block.

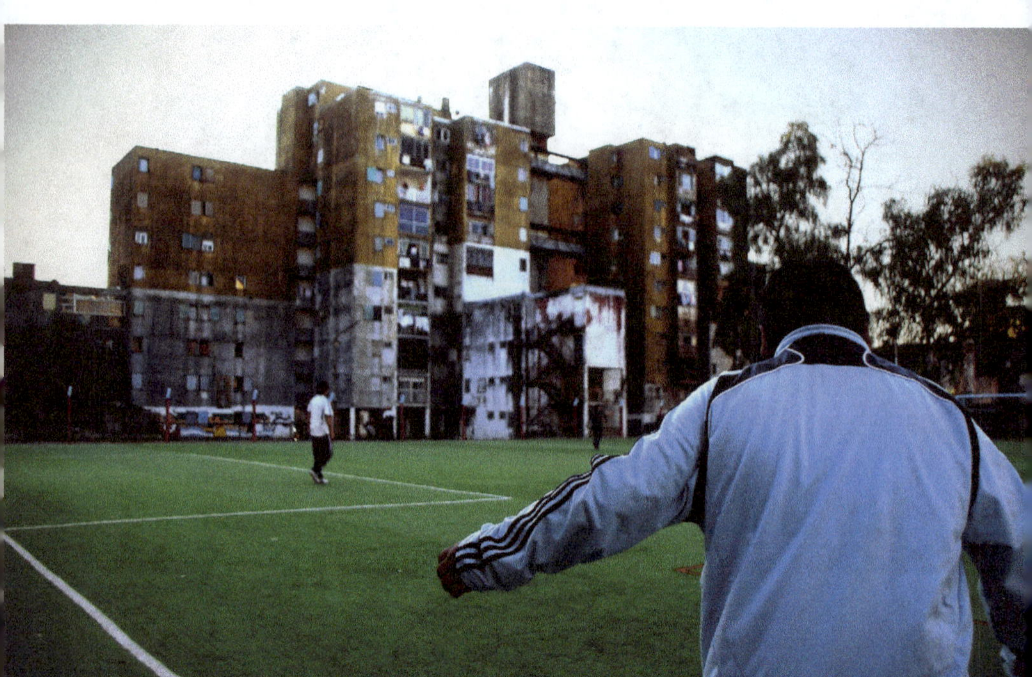

Due to a major urban housing deficit in the 1970s caused by
rural immigration to the cities, the Argentinean state promoted
a new financial system for tenants called National Housing
Fond – FONAVI. The system sought to help low-income population, first time home owners, and displaced families affected
by slum clearances and the recent construction of the A1 highway that crossed Buenos Aires.

Most of the housing financed by FONAVI was built far
from urban centers and was designed to create mass quanti-
ties of units with extremely high densities. It worked as a laboratory, permitting experimentation with a cocktail of modernist
architectural ideas reproduced with great optimism and little
criticism: CIAM dreams of high rise and open spaces, plus
Alison and Peter Smithson's "streets in the air" with prefabrication and standardization methods.

Although these complexes have been absorbed by the
growing city, they have failed to integrate physically or socially
due to a lack of maintenance, overcrowding and the forced
mixture of urban populations.

Megablocks remain ghettos dominated by drugs, crime
and weapons dealers. Still, those who are strong enough, such
as internationally renowned soccer players or local *cumbia
villera* (Argentinean tropical rap) bands, continue to emerge
from these fortresses.

An example is Lugano I and II, which were developed
over eleven years, from 1973 to 1984. Its 92 thousand square
meters (almost 1 million square feet) and forty thousand inhabitants were supposed to function as a satellite city. Services
in its master plan included supermarkets, cinemas, churches,
social clubs, kindergartens, community centers, schools,
sports clubs, medical centers, restaurants, and banks.

The ground floor *flows* underneath the slabs providing
room for parks, parking lots and streets. The second floor
connects its ten bars with elevated bridges over the streets
and provides a commercial and services area. Nowadays the
area underneath the slabs is closed and the entire ground
floor remains a no-go zone. During the day the area is empty of
working family members and rush hours are congested.

Villa Soldati, designed by Estudio Staff – Teresa Bielus,
Olga Wainstein Krasuk and Jorge Goldemberg –, consists
of 3,200 units with a social center, two shopping malls and
17,800 residents, a complex and casual physiognomy with
neighborhoods and *streets* within the megastructure. These
structures are so intricate and diverse that sometimes even
tenants cannot identify their own building and the police

1. Fuerte Apache is an obvious reference to the Bronx's infamous neighborhood Fort Apache.

needs assistance to enter the premises. It was meant to be a programmatic continuity with the rest of the city. Instead it became an isolated ghetto. Some owners privatize common areas next to their apartments, as in jungle law, establishing *macho* ranks in each building.

Internationally renowned architects Flora Manteola, Javier Sánchez Gómez, Josefa Santos, Justo Solsona, Rafael Viñoly, Carlos Sallaberry, and Felipe Tarsitano designed Barrio Piedrabuena in 1974. It has an elevated *plaza* over principal street crossings. Underneath this dark non-place is a center for drug dealers. Lack of identity is so strong that each door of the complex has been customized: Colors, wood, little pergolas, friezes, Greek columns or brick finishing decorate every entrance of each apartment. The complex was so poorly constructed and maintained that in 2005 it was declared a state of emergency by law and the state undertook essential repairs.

Another iconic case is the Barrio Ejercito de los Andes neighborhood. Better known today as Fuerte Apache[1], it was built in several steps between 1970 and 1978 starting during General Juan Carlos Onganía's and ending during General Jorge Rafael Videla's military dictatorships. The aim was more to get rid of slums (especially before the World Cup) than to solve the housing problem. Designed by the same architects who shaped Villa Soldati, it occupies 23 hectares in the Ciudadela district of Gran Buenos Aires. Groups of three towers and strips form rectangular open spaces, aligned to the cardinal points. Each group of towers hosts two hundred units that share only three elevators. The four-story strip buildings connect vertically by external stairs.

The structure of the buildings does not allow for expansion, so when families grow they keep subdividing the interior of the houses in order to accommodate new children and couples. The result is that density soars. With the addition of four new towers the neighborhood expanded forming an extra dense area; the space left by the expanded complex was always considered dangerous. However, after the 2001 economic crisis conditions worsened. Most of its inhabitants lost their jobs, maintenance of the buildings ended, the elevators stopped working and the police was banned to enter by the gangs, converting the complex into a ghetto where police profit from the earnings of the *zona liberada* (free zone). The new scenario led the sensationalist TV journalist José de Zer to label the neighborhood Fuerte Apache,[1] the name by which it is still known today. At that time the area's economic activities were drug dealing and stripping stolen cars. Once inside the complex, the cityscape is out of sight reinforcing its fortress qualities, a perfect hideout. Apparently the only way out of the Fuerte is to become a football star as international player Carlitos Tevez did.[2] It is said that a (supposedly more talented) friend of his found easier to join a gang and was eventually killed.[3]

In 2003 the Gendarmeria Nacional (a branch of the Army[4]) entered the complex, setting up bases along its peripheries and 120 Gendarmes now patrol the zone. Taking into account that the Buenos Aires Province Police (Policía Bonaerense) is considered the most violent and corrupt in Argentina, the residents have welcomed the *Gendarmes*.[5] The control zone works to keep weapons off the street and prevent stolen cars from being brought into the Fuerte. At the same time, a slow government-funded refurbishing of the buildings has started. A facility to make everybody proud is the newly installed syn-thetic grass soccer field where the new Tevez(es) may one day play.

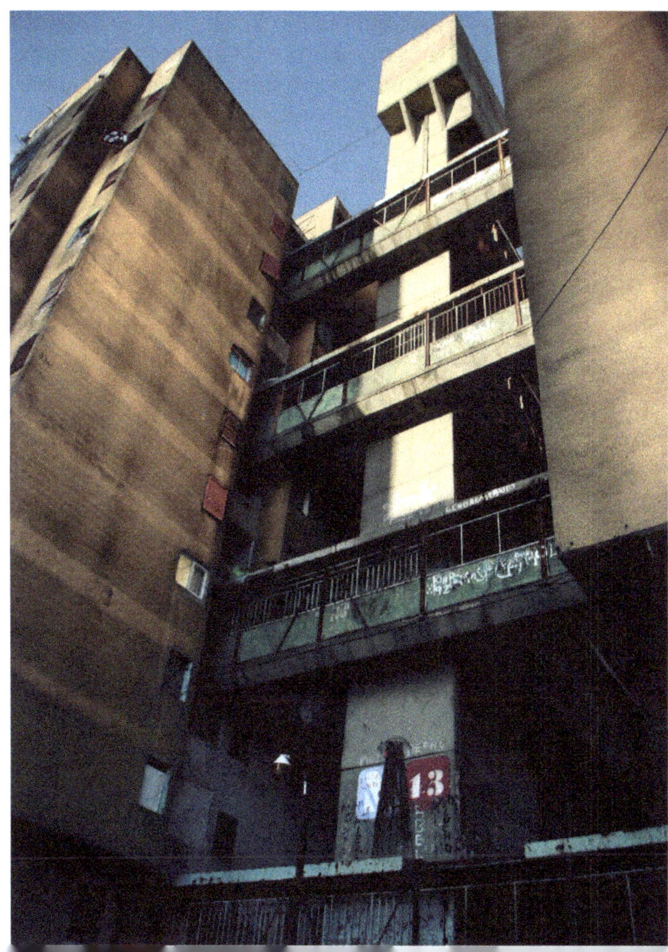

Barriada Experience:
John F. C. Turner Interview
World Bank, Washington D.C., September 11, 2000

Guest writers

Roberto Chávez
Julie Viloria
Melanie Zipperer

EN.
This is an edited version by Supersudaca of the original interview.
1. John F. C. Turner, "The Re-education of a Professional," in: John F. C. Turner and Robert Fichter, eds., *Freedom to Build. Dweller Control of the Housing Process* (New York, MacMillan, 1972), 123. Eduard Neira was a Peruvian architect who studied urban and regional planning at the University of Liverpool. Neira gave Turner his first job in Peru.

After his studies at the Architectural Association, John Turner traveled to Latin America in the 1950s to work on informal settlements in Peru known as barriadas. He exposed the idea that there was more to learn from these self-built enterprises than to teach as Architects. The *assisted barriada* approach he defended replaced the notion of megablocks – only plausible for few – as a feasible way to confront the *big numbers* in housing demand. This interview presents how informal dynamics became his lifetime vocation.

John F. C. Turner I had been working for the director of the Office of Technical Assistance to Popular Urbanizations of Arequipa – OATA for some months, sent by the then Peruvian Ministry of Public Works. Eduardo Neira had set up this office in 1955.[1] Now, that is remarkable, right? I don't know of any national government that had taken official action to assist the development of squatter settlements before the 1960s, or even later.

Roberto Chávez The chart you made in 1959 showed that the areas being built up as Urbanizaciones Populares, that is by the people themselves, actually covered a larger area than that of the city itself?

John F. C. Turner Yes, they did. They covered over a thousand hectares while the legally incorporated city area was less than a thousand.

Roberto Chávez Were Neira and his team aware of this as well? Did they really know what was going on?

John F. C. Turner Yes, they were very well informed. Eduardo's cousin, José Matos Mar, an anthropologist, and John P. Cole, a British geographer who had left Peru before I arrived, had carried out excellent surveys of the *barriadas* – the urban squatter settlements – in Peru for a government report published in 1956. So many leading professionals were quite aware as to the magnitude of the phenomena.

Roberto Chávez What did they have in common? Were they from a school? Were they associated with the Acción Popular party?

John F. C. Turner I don't know about their schools, but Acción Popular was a liberal, left leaning party similar to what we nowadays call a "third sector" bias. Very remarkable, really! This was really thirty years ahead of the rest of the world. As a result of the earthquakes, money was available for post-earthquake reconstruction. The mayor of Arequipa was a bright young man and he listened very carefully. We knew he wanted to spend some of the money on building housing for the earthquake victims which was not really a good idea as so few would had been helped. So we suggested a self-build scheme for those who had lost their inner-city homes and who had vacant plots in the Urbanizaciones Populares. This permitted us to double the number of people assisted. The mayor gave us the go ahead. That was my first really useful experience of working at the grass roots level. Once we got the project going we soon realized that our professional assumptions of design, construction and managerial superiority were exaggerated, to say the least. We soon learned that we needed our supposed clients' own knowledge and the skills of local builders. We also learned how badly our own bright ideas ignored their realities. [Laughter]

Julie Viloria Just to expand a little on that, how do you define your relationship with the people of the Urbanizaciones Populares? Is it contractual or are informal relationships bound by a common goal?

John F. C. Turner Oh, they're pretty formal. After all, there were requirements attached to the money. So it had to be fairly rigidly allocated to people who really were able to use it and were genuine victims of the earthquake. The participants also took their responsibilities seriously as progress

2   "Puerto Rico was the next site for organized mutual-help housing, and since 1949 has been responsible for housing thirty thousand rural families, making it by far the largest organized mutual or self-help housing effort in this country." OSTI Report, 28-29, quoted in Richard B. Spohn, "The Owner-Builder: Legislative Analysis and Recommendation," in: Turner and Fichter, eds., *Freedom to Build*, 22-23. In this project participants were paid only with one quarter of their labor.

depended on the fairly well disciplined contributions of their labor and their work was assessed at regular evening meetings with each group.

Roberto Chávez This is the usual sort of thing today, but this was the first time this was done.

John F. C. Turner Well, I wouldn't say so. *Faena* days (voluntary community work) were traditional and common at that time. The great majority of these people were first and second generation migrants from rural areas where mutual help with house building, roofing especially, was the norm. Relationships were honest. There was no corruption of which I was aware. Agreements were open and verbal, and although there was probably more resistance to the over-organization my associates and I proposed, they voiced no strong objection. We did talk them into the "aided and mutual self-help" model from a Puerto Rican manual Eduardo had given me.[2] All of the 140 participants accepted the idea that it would be quicker if they worked in groups. When it came to our designs for the houses, however, they said little. As the project progressed we learned that these were not the best approaches. Changes came rapidly. Our first approach was really inappropriate which we learned as we began working and talking together. So gradually the relationship changed from a passive one, in which the participants said little and followed our instructions, to working things out together including critically important help from the local builder we had contracted as an overseer, buyer and distributor of building materials. In hindsight we could have done a great deal more with far less effort by allocating tranches of cash by stage: Once you have your foundations, you can get the next tranche for the walls and so on until the work is complete. How you get your materials and how you organize the work is your business. A few years later that's just what Luis Marcial and I did in Lima very successfully.

Roberto Chávez Let me interrupt you here for a minute, John. Do you know of any other countries where they were already experimenting with these types of things besides Peru in the 1950s?

John F. C. Turner Well, some projects along sites-and-services and assisted self-build lines were carried out in colonial Africa in the 1930s, but I don't have more than secondhand references. Apart from the few somewhat

3. A government-sponsored social mobilization agency, the National System for Support of Social Mobilization (Sistema Nacional de Apoyo a la Movilización Social – SINAMOS) was established in 1971 by the military government of General Juan Velasco.
4. Director of the United Nations Centre for Housing, Building and Planning at the UN's HQ in New York.

paternalistic, self-help housing projects in the USA during the New Deal era and a larger program under Governor Rexford Tugwell in Puerto Rico in the 1940s I know of no other comparable innovations until the 1960s and 1970s.

Roberto Chávez The Peruvian model that then evolved into SINAMOS[3] for the Pueblos Jóvenes during the Velasco Alvarado regime seems to have come, well, in part from you through Eduardo Neira, but where were its roots as far as you know?

John F. C. Turner I believe the Velasco regime's constructive policies toward the *barriadas* – under which they were renamed Pueblos Jóvenes – were due in large part to the courses on development at the Escuela Militar given by people like Neira and Matos Mar at the invitation of the young colonels, known as the "young Turks" of the 1950s. It would have been during General Odría's administration that the dictator, impatient with the housing professionals' insistence on building to high modern standards the vast majority could not afford, actually supported the takeover of San Martín de Porres – that huge Barriada or Pueblo Jóven in Lima. *barriadas* became suddenly the architectural limelight.

I should have mentioned the national press coverage of the self-build project in Arequipa. *La Prensa* gave it a center-page spread in its Sunday Supplement. Naïvely, I did not realize that publicity coming from *La Prensa* instead of *El Comercio* (the conservative banker's paper) would anger the administration bosses and since they felt threatened by the publicity given to the self-built project, I was out on my ass in no time! [Laughter]. All I got out of it, at first, was a commission from Ernest Weissman[4] to write up the project.

Roberto Chávez On your experience in Arequipa?

John F. C. Turner Yes. The next significant development, it must have been in 1962, was an article in the *British Sunday Times* supplement magazine by Jan Morris; a very fine writer who, nevertheless, wrote an appallingly misleading, bleeding heart view of the *barriadas*. This not only angered me, but also the British ambassador. They called me and said: "Look, you've got to do something about this." Coincidentally, Monica Pidgeon, the editor of *Architectural Design*, was about to visit Peru. After touring the Lima *barriadas* with her, an immensely impressed

Monica said she must do a piece and asked me to be the guest editor. So the special issue on Dwelling Resources in Latin America was published in August 1963. It was the first illustrated publication that presented what the majority of city builders in urbanizing countries were doing in a positive light. The magazine was picked up by Ernest Weissmann, Wilson Garcès and company at the United Nations. They interested George Movshon, the UNTV commissioner and, in 1964, *A Home of Their Own* was filmed, mainly in Lima: The Peruvian *barriada* formula.

Melanie Zipperer What made this Peruvian experience special? Were there special conditions? Or do you think it would have been possible to repeat it in another region?

John F. C. Turner It is important to put some geographic and historic fact on record. In the first place, there was plenty of accessible, vacant land of no commercial value surrounding all Peruvian cities on the desert coast in the 1950s and 1960s. Second, in Peruvian law, desert land can only be owned privately if it's cultivated. It otherwise belongs to the state, which can lease it only for mining. In effect empty desert land is the people's commons. Opposition to the settlements – technically illegal unauthorized development of the land – was politically counter-productive. It upset the planners and middle classes but politicians could make good use of the opportunities to build constituencies based on the great majority. Quite often there was a show of police force opposing initial settlement but after a usually nominal battle with a few stones thrown and, perhaps, a little tear gas, the settlers would be left to get on with it, especially after some bad press and the interventions of few politicians. Yet there were a few martyrs. A third factor is widely shared with other newly urbanizing societies: The majority can only dream of buying a house or of getting one from the state on affordable terms. The choice is to put up with appalling conditions in overcrowded slums or build your own.

Y PREVI?

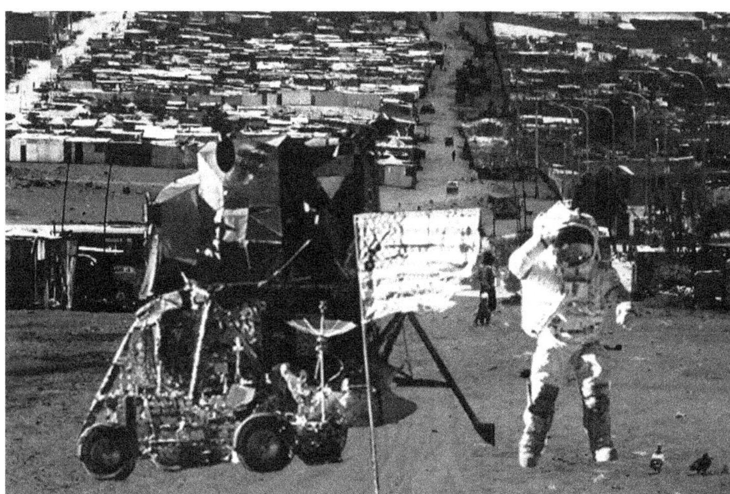

The occasions in architecture when the discipline's intelligentsia gathers to address pressing social issues seem to be few and far away. A last time when this happened it was in response to the demanding living conditions created by Lima's explosive population growth.

The 1960s all-star architects where led by Peruvian President Fernando Belaúnde Terry – an architect himself – into the Proyecto Experimental de Vivienda – PREVI competition. Belaúnde – once labeled "a Latin American architect of hope" on the cover of *Time* magazine – was able to garner the unprecedented support of the United Nations development program for an experiment to cope with the urgent demand of new living areas.

The result confronted an opposing jury minority report, plus an unusual for the time leftist coup jeopardized the whole operation. Finally none of the schemes were fully realized, but all of them would be built jointly. This generated an unexpected mix of a new urban and residential layout missed by almost every book on architectural history. PREVI remains an undiscovered *black box* of collective knowledge to be found.

1. Population growth rate in Lima during 1961-1972 was 5.5% per year.
2. See: "Dwelling Resources in South America," *Architectural Design* 33, no. 8, August 1963. A *barriada* from Lima is featured in the cover, while the whole issue is devoted to portrait the shantytown's architecture.
3. Famous is the case when Charles Jencks places the *barriadas* in his Evolutionary Tree of the 20th century architecture between Archigram and the Metabolists.

Not so long ago, in a far away country...

Despite titanic efforts – like 1950s Carlos Raul Villanueva's 23 de Enero in Caracas or 1960s Mario Pani's Nonoalco Tlatelolco in Mexico City –, squatter settlements in Latin America outgrew every housing program, public or private. The rational and austere high-rise-collective-housing-super-block proved useless next to the faster and more flexible build-it-yourself-forever shack of the *barriadas* (shantytowns). An attempt to reconcile rationality with flexibility was undertaken in Peru. The apparent cul-de-sac for Latin American collective housing might still hide a promising untraveled path.

In 1969, mankind reached the moon... and in Lima, tried to solve the housing problems of the Third World: The Lima Project, PREVI

The most ambitious architectural enterprise of our times lays inexplicably forgotten from the profession's history. In the late 1960s, under the sponsorship of the United Nations, the most lucid architects of the era were congregated in Lima, Peru, in a remarkable effort to use innovative housing to help the low-income sectors of the Third World: The Experimental Housing Project – PREVI. The concepts and techniques they developed constitute a hidden treasure for a discipline that has ceased to deploy its most talented minds where they are most needed.

Barriadas of Lima

In the early 1960s, Latin American cities were growing tremendously fast. Peru's capital Lima was experiencing steady immigration from the countryside as people lured to the city by the chance to improve their living conditions.[1] At that time people solved their housing needs on their own. Squatting empty land near the outskirts of the city, they settled in sophisticated patterns, building their own houses, urbanizing vast territories, and catching the eye of the international architecture community. Jose Matos Mar, John F. C. Turner, William Mangin and other scholars who studied this phenomenon in the field, reported and theorized on these episodes in the main architecture journals.[2] To the iconoclastic intellectuals of the 1960s, the *barriadas* (shantytowns) of Lima turned into an avant-garde form of urbanism.[3] To the Peruvian dwellers, such enterprise meant a hardworking form of survival. Despite the pioneering efforts of the Peruvian government to recognize such heterodox way of settlement and formalize them into better living

4. In 1961, the Peruvian government passed the pioneer law 13,157: The first which recognized a formal status to the *barriadas* and sought for their upgrading into properly urbanized settlements.

5. Peter Land is a British architect graduated from the Architectural Association and Yale. He first went to Peru in 1960, sponsored by the Organization of American States – OAS, to teach until 1963 at the Lima Planning Institute founded by President Belaúnde. Land went back to Lima in 1965 to work for United Nations and then stayed as the main advisor of PREVI until 1973.

conditions,[4] every attempt to stop them proved unsuccessful, due to the scale and speed of the issue. By the mid 1960s, informal housing in Lima outnumbered the formal.

Architect President

In 1963, Fernando Belaúnde Terry was elected President of Peru. In 1965 he was called "a Latin American architect of hope" on the cover of *Time* magazine. He had made himself a prominent figure by organizing the first school of architecture, the planning institute, as well as promoting modern social housing ensembles from the architectural magazine he directed. When he became president, he compulsively built high and mid-rise housing complexes all over Peru. Confronted by the impracticality of his housing policy to cope with the speed of the *barriadas*, he tried a different strategy:

Why not hold an international competition to find innovative housing concepts and techniques, taking into consideration the same parameters the dwellers of the *barriadas* did (a house that grows in a lot in a low rise-high density mode) and using state-of-the-art technology to build homes economically and on a massive scale.

United Nations Class

During 1965, President Belaúnde – with officials from his circle and led by British architect Peter Land[5] – elaborated further on how to organize such project. In 1966, this idea was officially presented to the United Nations Development Program. After examining the Peruvian situation for several months, and recognizing its prototypical condition for application of the findings of the project in the rest of the Third World, the United Nations decided to sponsor the enterprise as a pilot project.

The project aimed for a holistic approach towards the housing problem, which was divided in three priority groups. This way three complementary pilot projects were devised: Design and Construction of a new neighborhood (PP1), Urban Regeneration of an existing Slum (PP2) and a Site and Services self-aid program (PP3).

False Start

The Pilot Project 1 – PP1 (the subject of this essay) was a competition open to Peruvian and a selection of prominent international architects. While the selection process was going on,

6. PREVI was the last project designed by Candilis-Josic-Woods partnership since they split right after it in 1969.
7. Oskar Hansen presented his Open Form concept in the CIAM'59 in Otterlo as well as in the first official Team 10 meeting at Bagnols sur Ceze in 1960.
8. It was demolished in 1990 after the residents voted for it. Residents' chairwoman Margaret Davies said about the estate design: "The architect either had a brainstorm or was suffering from acute depression." *Building Design* (March 3, 1989): 5.

a military coup in October 1968 ousted President Belaúnde. The new military government (which was uncharacteristically left-oriented given the Latin American context) disregarded the PREVI project by identifying it with Belaúnde policies – and intended to cancel it. The United Nations agreement impeded that, and the project went ahead; this was, however, a major setback regarding future support from the Peruvian government. The competition started in March 1969 and thirteen international teams (as dictated by funding) were finally selected.

The Dream Team

The selection of the international teams supported by the United Nations included an all-star cast – most of them in their forties – from the architectural scene sympathetic to housing innovation.

Representing France was the office of George Candilis (1913-1995), Alexis Josic (1921-2011) and Shadrach Woods (1923-1973)[6] key components of Team 10 and Le Corbusier's former collaborators, especially on housing projects such as Unité d'Habitation of Marseille and Arbat in Morocco. Aldo van Eyck (1918-1999) another founder and prominent figure of Team 10, represented the Netherlands. At the time he was famous for his structuralist approach, his Orphanage in Amsterdam (1955-1960) and his quasi-anthropological studies on Dogon culture's use of space. Representing Poland were Oskar Hansen (1922-2005) and Svein Hatløy (Norway, 1940-2015) who had realized the housing estate at Przyczulek Grochowski in Warsaw (1963). Hansen too was a member of Team 10 and the author of the Open Form concept,[7] which allowed the user active participation in the creation process. James Stirling (1926-1992) represented the United Kingdom. Famous worldwide at that time on account of his Runcorn New Town Housing (1967-1976),[8] where he managed to build 1,500 dwellings cheaply via mass production with large precast panels in a low-rise high density neighborhood whose units were clustered around squares, which was precisely what PREVI was looking for. Japan was represented by Kiyonori Kikutake (1928-2011), Fumihiko Maki (b. 1928) and Kisho Kurokawa (1934-2007) who were famous for their Metabolist Manifesto and who had been engaged as consultants for the Japanese Construction Industry at the Nippon Prefabrication Co. developing cheap prototype capsule houses since 1961.

9. "That low-rise, high-density housing is both practical and eminently livable has been more than adequately demonstrated in a number of situations since the end of the 1950s, most notably perhaps in Atelier 5's Siedlung Halen built outside Berne, Switzerland, in 1960 and in the later Thalmatt Siedlung (1985) designed by the same architects." Kenneth Frampton, *Modern Architecture: A Critical History*, 3rd ed. (London, Thames and Hudson, 1992), 342.
10. Albertlund Syd neighborhood experience could be seen as a direct reference for PREVI. See: Thomas Hall, ed., *Planning and Urban Growth in the Nordic Countries* (London, Taylor & Francis, 1991), 110.

From Switzerland came Atelier 5, a young collaborative group of architects who had built the absolute icon of low-rise high-density housing, the Halen Residential Complex near Bern (1955-1961) and later Thalmatt 1 Residential Complex (1967-1972)[9] on their own initiative. Denmark was represented by Knud Svenssons (b. 1925) who had developed with Peter Bredsdorff and Ole Nörgaard the innovative low-rise prefabricated Albertslund Syd neighborhood[10] near Copenhagen (1962).

Finland was represented by Toivo Korhonen (1926-2014), a disciple of Alvar Aalto, who had built the Tonttukallio, a terraced house project in Espoo (1959). Spain's representatives were Jose Luis Iñiguez de Onzoño (b. 1927) and Antonio Vasquez de Castro (b. 1929) authors of the successful managed settlement Caño Roto in Madrid (1957-1969).

From Germany, came Herbert Ohl (1926-2012) who worked at the Department of Industrialized Construction at the Ulm School founded by Max Bill in 1951. Representing India, Charles Correa (1930-2015) had won first prize in an all-India competition for low-cost housing with his climatically designed *tube* house.

Representing a team from United States was the Center for Environmental Design led by the young star of the day Christopher Alexander (b. 1936). The only Latin American team was from Colombia, led by former Le Corbusier collaborator German Samper Gnecco (1924-2019) with his partners Esquerra, Sáenz & Urdaneta who had successfully built a neighborhood with the aid of the dwellers called La Fragua, in Bogota.

Brief

The international competition asked for the design and construction of a neighborhood for 1,500 low-cost flexible dwellings as low-rise, high-density housing. Thus they were not looking for multistory buildings or megastructures. The primary aim of the competition was to come up with pioneering concepts in four levels: The house typology, the construction technique, how it was clustered and a schematic design of the neighborhood.

The only mandatory component of the program was that lots had to have a total floor area between 80 square meters (860 square feet) and 150 square meters (1,600 square feet), and dwellings between 60 square meters (645 square feet) and 120 square meters (1,300 square feet). Initially in one or

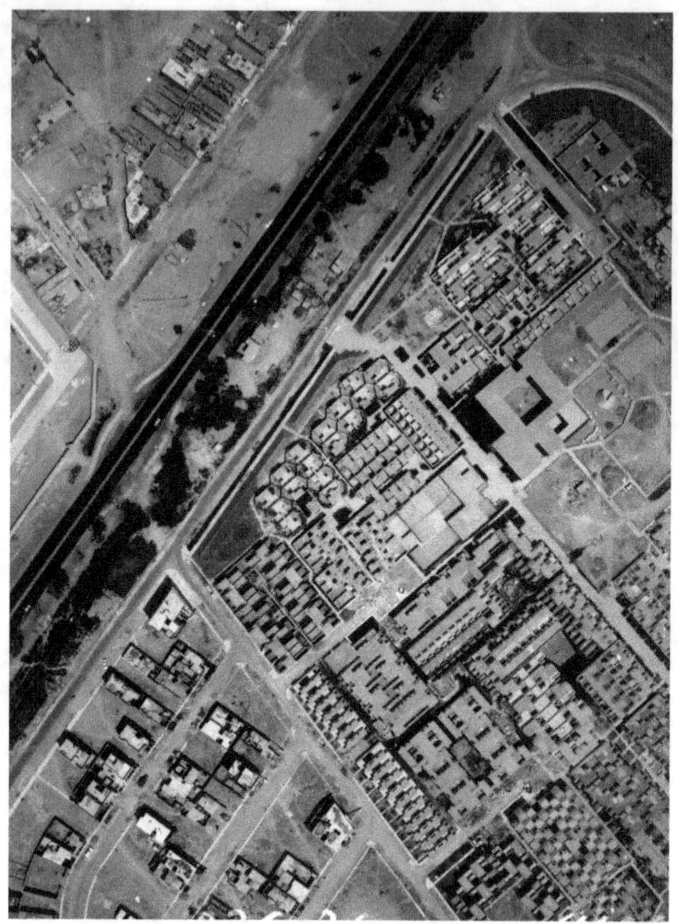

two-story structures built by contractors, but the buildings must be constructed such that the addition of a third floor by the families themselves was possible. Seeking standardization, everything was based on a 100 millimeters module.

In the urban design level, schools, a sports center, a community center and gardens were considered. Automobiles were not to be parked on individual lots; roads were to be kept to minimum due to high costs and separating traffic from pedestrian areas was recommended (prioritizing the design of the latter).

The clustering of dwellings should be studied to stimulate community life around open multipurpose spaces.

Lots were to be entirely enclosed by a 2.20 meters (7.2 feet) high wall and a small private garden needed to be an integral part of the house. Dwelling types were divided thusly: 40% for couples with one or two children, 40% for couples with three or four children and the remaining 20% for couples with 6 or more children. 25% of the units were to be left incomplete, to be finished later by the owners themselves. In the future, houses should be able to grow to accommodate up to ten people including the elderly.

Experiment Proposals

Proposals, especially from the international teams, were highly experimental and groundbreaking.

Urbanistically they ranged from environmentally based solutions (Hansen, Correa, Van Eyck) to user-determined (Alexander) to public square-based (Stirling, Samper) to mat layout (Candilis, Ohl).

Unit Houses ranged from squared patio houses (Stirling, Samper) to narrow and long (Alexander, Japanese, Hansen) to modular (Svenssons, Ohl, Korhonen) to puzzle-like (Correa, Candilis) to H-shaped (Van Eyck).

Construction technologies varied from modular concrete brick (Van Eyck, Correa, Japanese, Samper) to bamboo beams (Alexander) to prefab concrete panels (Atelier 5, Svenssons) to prefab concrete parts (Hansen, Stirling, Ohl) to concrete porticoes (Korhonen).

Jury Frictions

In August 1969 the teams submitted their proposals and the international jury met in Lima. The high profile jury included Spanish architect Jose Antonio Coderch, American prefab guru and designer of Techbuilt kit home Carl Koch, Danish MIT professor Halldor Gunnlogsson, Croatian Ernest Weissmann, former Le Corbusier collaborator, and director of the United Nations Housing Section together with PREVI's director Peter Land and other Peruvian representatives. The high quality and broad spectrum of the proposals generated intense discussion since part of the jury inclined toward the most inventive proposals as concerns construction while others liked those best adapted technologically and sociologically to Peruvian reality. The international winners were Kikutake-Kurokawa-Maki, Atelier 5 and Herbert Ohl. Still, a minority of the jury issued an alternative report due to unconformity with the competition's outcome – especially with the selection of Ohl's proposal – and strongly recommending Alexander's scheme for publication.

PREVI Strikes Back: Why Choose if You Can Build Them All?

Given the experimental tone of the project, in 1970 upon the jury's recommendation it was decided to develop and build all(!) 26 proposals (thirteen international and thirteen Peruvian) instead of just the six winners, in order to test the broadest possible set of concepts. Peter Land and the multidisciplinary Development Group assembled an urban layout based on the best ideas from the competition, which resulted in a patchwork of clusters by the different teams.

Thereafter a new story started: The process of making the proposals reality, known as PREVI episode two. A research and development laboratory was set up in Lima bringing into the project various experts, who tested and evaluated construction processes and materials, in order to bring down costs and speed up construction with relatively unskilled labor. In 1974 the first phase of five hundred dwellings were finally built. Just at that moment the Peruvian military government closed and dismantled the PREVI's Development Group office. The international experts and UN officials went home, the records were archived and the case closed.

The Return of PREVI: How-to-Enlarge-Yourself This Famous Architect's Weird Prefab House

It took two years before the first housing was inhabited. In 1976 families moving in wandered around this strange neighborhood of white, unadorned houses looking for their own. Finnish houses were very popular since they were not built with bearing walls but of columns and were thus easier to modify. No one ever gave these new experimental home residents plans as to how their homes could be enlarged or modified.

With the inhabitation of PREVI a new experiment had started and Peruvian dwellers were on their own... Again.

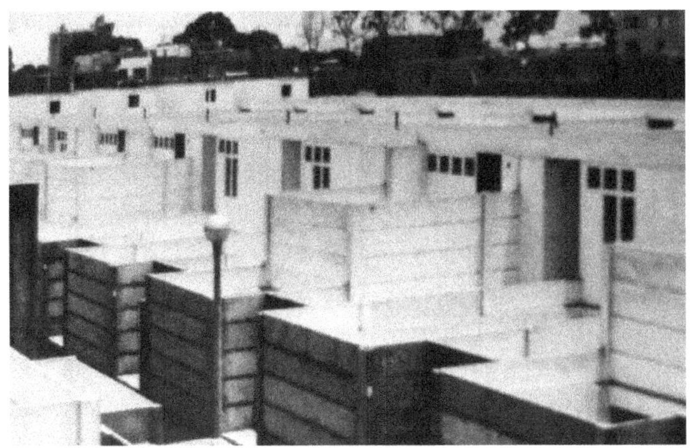

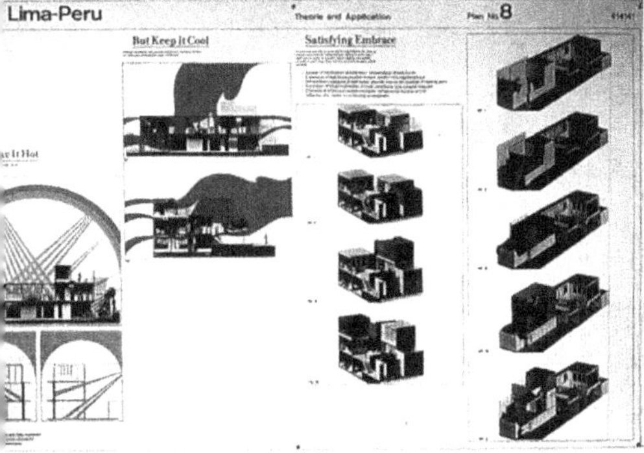

Lima-Peru
But Keep It Cool
Satisfying Embrace
Plan No. 8

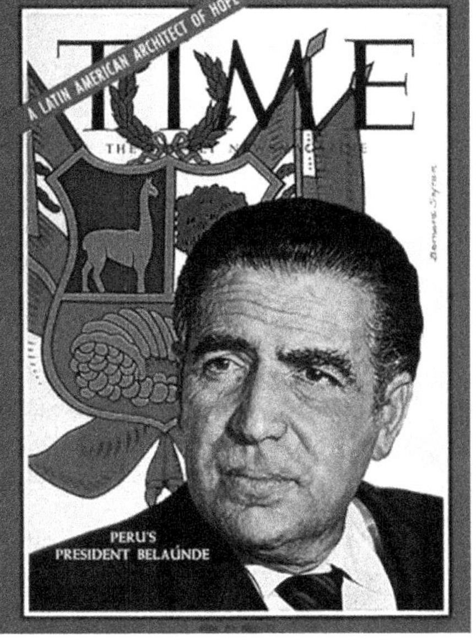

A LATIN AMERICAN ARCHITECT OF HOPE
TIME
THE WEEKLY NEWSMAGAZINE
PERU'S
PRESIDENT BELAÚNDE

"PREVI was one of the last occasions when Western architects were committed to a structural approach to urban problems in the Third World."
Adri Duivesteijn

> Dutch politician, in: Adri Duivesteijn and Harmen van de Wal, *The Hidden Assignment: At Home in the City (Rotterdam, NAI Publishers, 1996)*, 23.

"I hope this project will be called the Lima Project and that it will have as much a beneficial influence on urban and rural planning globally as the Athens Charter did."
Fernando Belaúnde Terry

> Peruvian President and architect, quoted in: *El Peruano,* Lima, June 28, 1968.

"President Belaúnde called me one day and said: 'I am thinking, it is about time for new housing ideas to come up and I think the United Nations will support an international competition.'"
Fernando Correa

> Architect and Peruvian Director of PREVI (1968), interviewed by Supersudaca. Lima, Peru, January 2006.

"Between the suburban low-rise, low density development type and high-rise apartment structures there is a need for another model of urban form for town growth. An objective of the PREVI neighborhood was to develop such a model of low-rise, high density urban form."
Peter Land

> Architect and director of PREVI for the United Nations (1968-1972), interviewed by Stephen White, in: Stephen White, "PREVI Twenty Years After," *Architecture and Design: A Journal for the Indian Architect* 11, no. 2 (March-April 1994): 53-59.

"There is one important lesson experienoc has taught me and no matter what type of cast you use, on site, prefab, conventional etc., the people in this situation are very dynamic and will modify the house in short order."
Ernesto Winkowski

> Architect and director of PREVI for the United Nations (1972-1976), interviewed by Supersudaca. Montevideo, Uruguay, February 2006.

"All the architects and their teams were brought to Peru to have the competition brief explained them, to get acquainted with Peru, to obtain all the information possible. Absolutely everyone was here. Not only did they get lectures on Peruvian life but also they got a chance to visit the slums. I remember that Christopher Alexander lived there for fifteen days with his team of three architects. German Samper went to La Quinta Heeren in Barrios Altos. The architect from Finland went to live in a village nearby. Reading the brief and designing the house was not their goal. They wanted to know people's idiosyncrasies and the design was aimed at a group of humans, not designing housing for the sake of it. There was a need to respond to the characteristics of the community. Nowadays the social aspect is much neglected."
Raquel Barrionuevo

> Engineer and member of PREVI Development Team, interviewed by Supersudaca. Lima, Peru, January 2006.

"We were invited to Lima for fifteen days. They received us, gave us lectures and courses because the concept of social housing for a German, British or French is quite different than ours. It's much poorer."
German Samper

> Architect and Colombian participant in PREVI, interviewed by Elizabeth Añaños for Supersudaca. Bogota, Colombia, April 2008.

"We became members of families. And so, you know, we really immersed ourselves in it."
Christopher Alexande
> Architect and US participant in PREVI, in: Michael Mehaffy, "A Conversation with Christopher Alexander," International Society of Biourbanism, https://bit.ly/3uE4QJm.

"The thing which is different about Peru is the tremendous free-for-all among house owners and builders... We have to allow for this, and organize it into something less uncontrolled. In a way, it is restrictive not to build for some change and adaptation."
James Stirling
> Architect and UK participant in PREVI, quoted in: The Times, London, 1969.

"Whose problems are you trying to solve if not your own? Who calls upon a few in the name of all? The Lord? All? Or just you?"
Aldo van Eyck
> Architect and Dutch participant in PREVI, in: Lecture on Barriadas, Delft, October 1970.

"John Turner and his fascination with Lima influenced and convinced everyone of the capacity of people to provide themselves with decent housing. This has been terribly misinterpreted as a laissez faire attitude of architects in the Third World in which what you should do – at most – is comply with the infrastructure and leave the rest to the people themselves. Turner has been the excuse for architects to remain absent from the topic. Instead, now architects only want to do museums and become famous, starchitects! Why are there so few international competitions on social housing? PREVI was exemplary in this regard."
Charles Correa
> Architect and Indian participant in PREVI, interviewed by Supersudaca, Mumbai, March 2008.

"If Weissenhof Siedlung is the natural childbirth of social housing in the First World, PREVI is the coitus interruptus of Third World housing."
Supersudaca
in: *And PREVI?* First prize winning entry at the IV Iberoamerican Bienal, Lima, October 2004.

"The real competition jury should take place decades after occupation, after all it was a progressive housing challenge!"
Kiyonori Kikutake
Architect and Japanese participant in PREVI, interviewed by Supersudaca, Tokyo, July 2006.

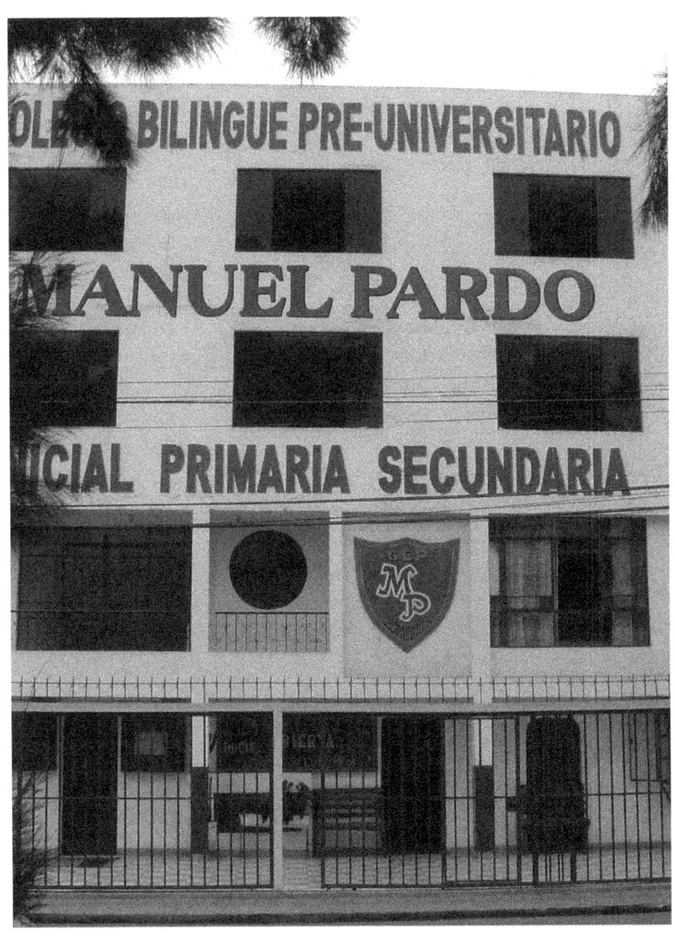

11. See: Turner, "The Re-education of a Professional," 122-147; John F. C. Turner, "Housing as a Verb," in: Turner and Fichter, eds., *Freedom to Build*, 148-175. This book was also published in Spanish and Italian: John F. C. Turner and Robert Fichter, eds., *Libertad para Construír: El Proceso Habitacional Controlado por el Usuario* (Mexico, Siglo XXI, 1976); John F. C. Turner and Robert Fichter, eds., *Libertà di Costruire* (Milan, Il Saggiatore, 1979).

12. John F. C. Turner, "Reflections on scale and subsidiarity in urban development and poverty alleviation: a personal view of development by people." *Urban Forum 2002: Tools, Nuts & Bolts At the World Bank* (Washington, April 2-3, 2002).

Rewind: PREVI Aftermath

The result of the Experimental Housing Project in Lima could be seen not only as an exemplary case to review, but also the inspiration to rephrase architects' will. For example, by replacing *social* with *diverse*, and *housing* with *neighborhood* – more in an anthropological sense rather than an untouchable architectural fetish – PREVI may unexpectedly be offering an understanding of a successful urban environment open to adaptation, integration and opportunities for mid and low-income citizens of the Third World.

As John Turner has pointed out, architects have much to learn about how people live outside developed countries.[11] Overcoming the tendency toward paternalistic utopia and practical indifference, Turner offers a kind of tripod approach,[12] mobilizing the local private and public sectors to create quality sustainable living settings in presently unsteady conditions.

Quite accidentally, today PREVI is exactly what Turner described. It was indeed designed by the most committed generation of architects of the past century, but later massively adapted by their users. This proves that sometimes misunderstandings can have happy endings for PREVI is a successfully modified, personalized, parodied, customized and mutated project. It is a mix that exudes a vital sign of our time; more than informality PREVI is transformality: Not only brilliant pieces by talented professionals but a blend of collective practical intelligence with architects' output as sub-structure.

Forward: Old School = New School

Four lessons can be learned from PREVI's approach for future collective ventures.

Lesson 1: Typological Diversity

As in nature, variety is good. PREVI's typological diversity encourages distinction and identity in an urban environment. Within a rich offering a wide range of people can coexist and complement each other, adding their character to the living milieu and taking care of it as their feeling of belonging increases over time.

PREVI is the execution of the unplanned as all of the competition entries were partially built. This perhaps cancelled the potential experiment in the urban contributions, but this deficit was compensated for with a new output of pluralistic strength,

13 Private interview
with Koyinuri Kikutake,
August 2007. This was a
risky operation as nowa-
days their proposal hides
undistinguishably behind
a multiple program strip.

leaving space for achievements and errors to evolve. As in living processes, biologically diverse crossovers generate *hybrid
vigor* instead of a degenerated endogamy. Mixing Aldo Van
Eyck's honeycomb layout with Atelier 5 constructive scheme
plus Oskar Hansen's pioneering fractal display, to name a few
of the most underestimated urban inventions to date, was both
a sacrilege and a master stroke.

Lesson 2: Blow up Folklore

In dynamic social environments, everything that can grow
will grow and often does so far beyond that which had been
imagined.

One of PREVI's competition requirements was the ability
of the design to develop over time in order to accommodate an
increasing number of inhabitants. An orientation as to how the
residents could expand their dwellings themselves was also
strongly advised. All the proposals offered seamless growth
possibilities in several ways. Some were more *paternalistic* like
Aldo van Eyck's self-imposed angled perimeter wall to avoid
filling setbacks and ensure natural ventilation and light. Other,
more *autochthonous* proposals, like James Stirling's, offered
spiral growth around a central patio. The Metabolist team
explained to have left the front garden for expansion.[13] Yet
none of the precautions and measures were enough to pre-
dict the future: The transformation of the units almost totally
blurred the original intentions. Today, the original designs are
barely recognizable and show an unexpected richness of possibilities, indeed so rich that valuable empirical evidence for
further experiences still to be figured out lies beneath it and is
probably changing even as you read this.

Lesson 3: Programmatic Pandemonium

One of the clearest conclusions is that multi-programmatic
options imply an opportunity to beat poverty. Yet program
shifts and combinations were not an important concern in
PREVI's original proposed schemes. Nevertheless, more than
60% of the area has suffered programmatic alterations. This
self-entrepreneurship has led to the most curious deforma-
tions and unconventional astuteness. Extremely appealing,
almost charming, are James Stirling's four-story high school,
Atelier 5's kindergarten and Maki, Kurokawa and Kikutake's
food strip, a shortlist not just of hybridization, but of the fully
spontaneous generation of a new species.

Lesson 4: La Vecindad
The 1970s Mexican television show *El Chavo del 8* was a children's humor program built around a quite particular – almost dramatic – condition: An orphan (El Chavo) lived in a barrel among characters in the patio of a semi-enclosed community, La Vecindad – a shared space of contiguous dwellings inhabited by a single mother with his son (Doña Florinda and Quico), plus a single father with his daughter (Don Ramon and La Chilindrina), and an elderly woman (La Bruja del 71). In short: No archetypical family configurations here. Misunderstandings and conflicts developed among the characters and others that nourished absurd situations in which El Chavo was always the clumsy protagonist. These initially innocent looking stories ended up not only portraying Mexican social reality, but also are valid for most of Latin American. La Vecindad is more an arrangement than a typology. Somehow without wanting it people took care of each other. This intermediate scaled pattern within the city, between the neighborhood and the particular unit, probably constitutes PREVI's achievement.

Fast Forward: Successful Failure

The tempting judgment is to regard PREVI as another failure in architecture initiatives with a social agenda. It was never really executed as planned for the process was full of exceptions and problems, none of the designs operated as imagined, genius ideas were misused and architectural form disfigured. Some, more generously, argue that it is nothing more than the remnant of a welfare state, an impossible wet dream. This is correct if we think of architecture as a purely static – and aesthetic – event, unable to cope with indetermination. Paradoxically, this makes it impossible for architecture to act for the most demanding of intelligent conceptions.

Of course it's absurd to hold architecture responsible for all the world's evils. Quality architecture may be achieved without any further social concerns. Nevertheless, looking back at PREVI offers a glimpse of another stance: Architecture not only as an end in itself, but also as a medium for a higher objective.

Where unpredictable is at the same time the result of drastic alterations for the benefit of the whole, diversity and incompleteness is an achievement. Implying the disappearance of authorship in an anonymous collection of infinite individual expressions: A true collective architecture.

14. In 1976, Charles Jencks pinpointed the death of modern architecture to a precise moment in time: July 15, 1972, at 9 :32 P.M. (or thereabouts) with the demolition of Minoru Yamasaki's Pruitt-Igoe housing project in St. Louis. Charles Jencks, *The Language of Post-Modern Architecture* (New York, Rizzoli, 1977), 9.
15. 51% of the world population live in slums according to United Nations data on slum populations in urban areas.

No More Social Housing (Anti-Manifesto)

It seems that as soon as the notion of social housing is discarded more possibilities for a new awareness of appealing living proposals for those who need it the most open up. It's no surprise that nowadays nobody wishes to live in a stigmatized area of a city and social housing has become a socialist caviar fixation with segregation as a counter-effect. Social housing has lost its original meaning or, even worse, has turned into a burden and its *failure* set off declarations for changing architectural priorities.[14]

Nevertheless, taking a step back could help further architecture's contribution. This would be a revised and blameless approach for the benefit of the world's population.[15] Speaking freely about collective implications and above all recovering and developing truly innovative architectural thinking could become a continuous challenge for architects.

Nevertheless, taking one step back could help to jump further to broaden architecture's contribution bandwidth. This could tend to a renovated and blameless approach for the benefit of a large number of the world's population's. Speaking about collective implications could become a continuous challenge; above all, an instance to recover and breed truly innovative architectural thinking.

Montevideo Cooperativo: Gustavo González Interview
July 7, 2009

1.   Gustavo González is part of a Mutual Aid Cooperative and former leader of the Uruguayan Federation of Mutual-Aid Housing Cooperatives. At present, he is coordinator for the Housing and Habitat program of the Swedish Cooperative Centre – SCC in Latin America.

2.   Besides the mortgage loan, users pay a monthly fee for day-to-day maintenance as well as building structure conservation.

3.   There are two types of housing cooperatives in Uruguay. The Prior Savings ones, where members contribute with their savings – complementing state credit – and the Mutual Aid ones, that resort to the work of their members as manual labor during the construction. Both may be owners or users type. In owner cooperatives, after the construction phase is completed, each member is given a unit in individual property.

Gustavo González[1] is an initiator of the Mutual Aid Cooperatives in Montevideo, a paradoxical initiative begun in the 1970s and maintained through the 1980s. While the world was looking elsewhere, Uruguayans developed shared property management and self-construction for collective housing. This interview documents an unheard success story and offers clues as to how their success might be packaged for wider implementation now.

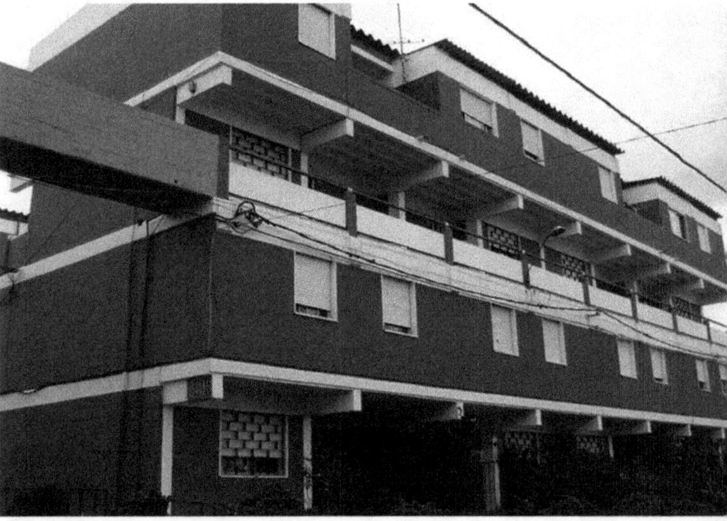

Supersudaca What does the notion of Mutual Aid and User Cooperative imply?

Gustavo González Mutual Aid is a housing solution for those sectors of society that don't have ways to save money but do have the capacity to work to build their dwelling and to pay off a low interest mortgage loan.[2] This self-construction system is generally associated with a *user's regime* in which the family acquires the right to use the dwelling and the cooperative, as a whole, administers a collective property.[3]

4. The National Housing Law No. 13,728 was introduced in 1968 by the government of Jorge Pacheco Areco, who would support, in 1973, the military coup d'état.

Supersudaca What are the fundamentals of collective property?

Gustavo González Time has shown that no solution to the housing deficit in Latin America is possible without state subsidies. That means everyone pays taxes so every family without proper housing can get it. State support of Mutual Aid Cooperatives consists of several tax exemptions, the provision of the land and the aforementioned bank loan financing.

It is very important to understand that collective property is still property. If a group of families come together to build their dwellings, these belong to everyone and no one can go out in the market to sell their own unit because it is the product of everyone's work. There must be an educational aspect, which teaches: "If society satisfies a basic need no individual may profit therefrom." This is the basic idea that divides the two concepts: Housing as a good and housing as a right.

Supersudaca Cooperativism has been strongly linked with trade unions and left-wing groups. Does the Mutual Aid model only take place within these ambiences?

Gustavo González Education and political organization, in the broadest sense, have been very important for the model because they have influenced the capacity of self-management in cooperatives. Without organization and efficiency – in managing and construction – nothing can be achieved. Members in cooperatives need to build, and build well. They must also operate as a company, buying materials and managing finances. For this, people undergo training and broaden their horizons.

Supersudaca Can you explain why *collective property* and the notion of *user* were legally introduced under a right-wing governmen?[4]

Gustavo González The *users's* system is pragmatic: If poor people are given a house and they cannot pay to maintain it, it's wasted money. Through common property, public investment is protected by preventing the beneficiary from selling the dwelling on the real estate market. The state avoids the trap of people making money only to turn around and demand housing again. It protects the investment, even from a capitalist or a liberal-economic point of view.

5.   A solution adopted
by some cooperatives
is paying the departing
user his social capital
monthly during ten
years, enabling the
new user to finance his
entree along this time.

Supersudaca How is the concept of *collective property* made compatible with the dynamics of the real estate market?

Gustavo González When a first generation user leaves the cooperative, the collective returns his social capital to him, namely the hours of mutual help he provided and the capital he contributed, but the dwelling remains in hands of the cooperative and the community chooses the new member who can contribute the same social capital. Nowadays a frequent problem for cooperatives created many years ago is that after many years the social capital is too high for someone with a normal job to afford. A solution might be for the state to subsidize the new member and for the cooperative to transfer this money to the departing *user*. This would ensure that people who enter the system belong to a social sector that deserves the dwelling.[5]

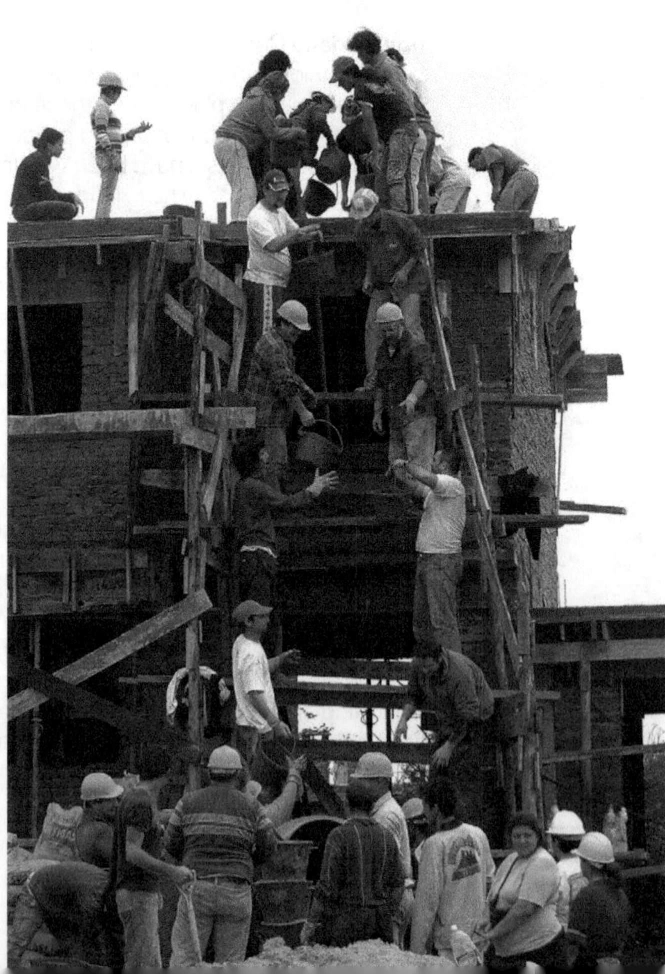

Supersudaca How is the architectural project of cooperatives managed? How has the design evolved?

Gustavo González Architects at the Institutes of Technical Assistance execute the design; multi-disciplinary teams are created expressly to assist cooperatives through a collectively negotiated design process.

As concerns design, there were two prominent periods. The 1970s were the years of housing developments, large mid-rise concrete buildings and very austere architecture on very big lots with little green or recreational spaces and minimum outdoor furnishing. Since the 1980s smaller developments have been built, enhancing social and spatial aspects. The focus was on new smaller-scale volumes, providing outdoor areas with green spaces creating more enjoyable environments. Progress was also made on a typological level, with proposals that could support units of one, two or three bedrooms.

Supersudaca To what extent have standardization and systematization in construction been explored?

Gustavo González In the second period there was access to new technologies, for instance: Water insulated concrete roofs, expanded polystyrene panels with electro-welded meshes and projected mortar. Standardization has largely centered on a few construction elements (e.g., brick tiles, concrete joists) associated with building systems based on brick. A key condition in the systematization of building components is that they can be produced and transported by members of the cooperative who are often women.

Supersudaca Do you consider it possible to extrapolate the model to other social contexts?

Gustavo González Housing as a right is the best investment for any democratic society, by which I do not mean a socialist one. In Cuba, for instance, housing is individual. Collective property with state subsidy has nothing to do with socialism or the Third World. In welfare societies such as Sweden, very good collective ownership projects exist.

The global economic crisis caused by the real estate bubble in the United States demands rethinking the game we are playing. Nowadays states are saving companies from going bankrupt, effectively socializing the losses. Cooperatives are a way of investing collectively in a responsible manner.

Latin American Know-How: Alejandro Aravena & Fernando Pérez Oyarzún Interview
June 12, 2009

During the 1990s Chile's miracle economical growth was obsessed with rankings, new democratic policies promoted massive housing constructions to eliminate slums. Architecture firm Elemental seeks for quality within this model.

Spokesman Alejandro Aravena not only explains how to achieve change by playing with the rules, but in an intense conversation with Fernando Pérez critically analyzes that it's been forty years since urbanization surpassed 50% in Latin America without public funding. Also that a hidden *know-how* should come into the open and public or collective space could still be the new bottom-up entrepreneurship frontier.

How to Urbanize with Hardly Any Money or Urbanizing with Chalk

Supersudaca Within the enigma of what is to come in the near future and in a post-crisis, post-capitalist city situation, it seems that in Latin America, particularly as regards collective issues, we are somehow used to this crisis condition. Is there anything worth saving?

Alejandro Aravena What Urban Age does in London, Rockefeller in New York, or reports like "The Economist 2007" do when they refer to the planet's urban population rates rising over the 50% threshold is in reference to Asia and Africa. Latin America dealt with that question and did so in a very specific way, with a rate of urban population as high as 85% and this achieved through a process that started forty years ago. Not only did this take place as early as the United States and Europe but it was done specifically in Chile with hardly any money. In contrast, Europe achieved these urbanization figures with more resources per family. Thus the specific question we dealt with forty years ago was how to provide housing for roughly US$ 10,000 per family for those moving from rural areas to cities. Having wrestled with this question earlier this now allows us to say we have knowledge the rest of the world does not. This premise should allow us to export know-how.

Fernando Pérez Oyarzún There's a case that in Chile we've forgotten, which is Operación Sitio (or site operation, in free translation) that happened in the late 1960s. This arose during a very fast urbanization process, with strong rural immigration, and was carried out with way less resources than what we have today. That is, the two conditions Alejandro stated pushed to their peak. By the time, people were invading big areas in the periphery and so, the Ministry reacted saying: "Look, we cannot give you a house. What we can do is buy or expropriate this land, make the urbanization outlines and give you a plot. That's all we can do at the time." Political opposition was ironically calling it Chalk Operation: Have you seen this? Instead of housing people, they're giving them chalk, they're tracing lots over soil! As foolish as it may seem, this operation is responsible for the comparatively successful urbanization of very extensive areas of the Santiago de Chile periphery. This was no minor accomplishment for it gave people something very high-valued today: An

1. Cf. Hernando De Soto, *The Mystery of Capital: Why Capitalism Triumphs in the West and Fails Everywhere Else* (New York, Basic Books, 2000).

important piece of land, with its title deed. At the same time areas were planned and lots were traced, streets were being defined, that is to say, what remained was the whole urban base-structure needed to connect to the city's networks. You could then carry on with sewerage or electricity because there was a sense of order. Each person knew – and this was also a collective agreement – what was his own; first they built a shack or two on their land, then came self-construction or they obtained subsidies etc. This demonstrates what Alejandro was saying; all I'm giving you are tracings on the ground, but what these tracings do is situate people's position in the city, connect them and provide coordinates.

Alejandro Aravena Let me elaborate this point because I find it very relevant. Tracing with chalk on the ground, which costs nearly nothing – actually costs what the land is worth – is relevant because it approaches doing those things a family alone cannot do well. If there is not enough money to do everything, families must establish priorities, doing first what cannot be done well individually. The layout of an urban development falls under the category of things that, if done spontaneously, do not turn out well. This is important because the value of the house you build on that plot largely depends on the value of the neighborhood: If the neighborhood is worth nothing, that house will be worth nothing. If one proposes that the core of a housing project is to increase its value over time, the fact that it is an investment and not an expense should be seen as a major at tribute which is what we propose in Elemental.

In Latin America is that we have dealt with this problem before. Informality rates in Latin American cities are over 50% wherever you go: Caracas, Mexico City, Lima. What differs in Santiago is not only a lack of money, but, because of this type of *chalk* operation, the informality rate in Chile is very low. It is the only way to fight illegal land seizures in a democratic system. What happens has been described by the Peruvian economist Hernando De Soto in his book *The Mystery of Capital*: if there's going to be capitalism, it should reach everyone.[1] What allows us to benefit from the current rules of the game is that property may have a parallel life as capital: I buy a property, ask for credit to start a business at home, for a taxi, or a sewing machine. What De Soto studies is how much money is traded in the informal world. The difference between the formal and informal world is that in capitalism the value of

assets also has a parallel value as a capital. This is what
has permitted first world economies to take off. This is
why he titled the book *The Mystery of Capital*; he seeks to
explain why capitalism triumphed in the occident and has
failed everywhere else.

The relevant aspect of the planet's urbanization process is that there is not enough money to do it by building
houses. There are a lot of people asking what happened
to the chalk side? We are going to have to urbanize with
very lit le money in Africa and China and strategies like
Operación Sitio will see 2.0 design versions. This is what
we are going to be facing from now on, and we have the
knowledge. In Latin America we have dealt with this problem before so we must have a comparative advantage.
Finally, we have some knowledge to export to the rest of
the planet.

Public Space and Inclusive Cities

Fernando Pérez Oyarzún From the beginning, Elemental
proposed an issue related to the space outside the house
as another immediate pending issue. The discussions
you had during the development of the social housing
project in Iquique, Chile, related to the existence of pas-
sages or questioning the size of yards and these have
continued to be issues of interest. As important as it is
to use criterion to solve housing units, it is to answer the
articulation between these and the city, which in this
case, can become tremendously relevant. So relevant
that Luis Eduardo Bresciani, head of the Chilean Urban
Development Division of the Ministry of Housing and
Urban Development, called for architects and others to
organize themselves concerning the issue of public space.
He believed the next challenge for Chile, one which would
require significant resources, was public space as concerns small and medium companies. He thought it was
a challenge, that the demand for design was no longer in
the minimum operation of housing, but in questioning how
to incorporate more resources without squandering them
or spending them inappropriately. I think it's a big question
right now in Chile.

Supersudaca Following this line of thought, the issue of
where to put the money when it is scarce in Latin America
has been determined for some time now through public
spaces. Examples include Bogotá, in Colombia; Curitiba,

2. See: Rakesh Mohan and Shubhagato Dasgupta, "The 21st Century: Asia Becomes Urban." *Economic and Political Weekly* 40, no. 3 (January 15-21, 2005): 213-223.

in Brazil, with Jaime Lerner and "urban acupuncture;" or works regarding the favelas in Rio de Janeiro, just to name a few. That is, by thinking about where to put the money, given that it is scarce, and to whom and how many people are going to get hold of it, the issue has reached the topic of public space.

Alejandro Aravena Yes, let me get to it by articulating three points. This space between *public* and *private* is a wedge, a collective space. In Iquique one of our *inventions* was to build a condominium consisting of eighteen to twenty houses. That is to say, the housing project is not on a street but in a place that has controlled access and entries. Security was a big issue given the conditions from which people came; therefore control over their own public space was relevant.

Second, when this occurs, when you make an Operación Sitio with rather small lots, the distance between streets is very small. If anything is visible in the peripheries we have produced it is that there are way too many streets for the number of existent cars; because – if one thinks in terms of private and public – the road is the only way you have to ensure access to each apartment. Therefore there is an excess of streets, when actually they're not necessary. Third, in socially fragile environments this collective space is very important for the economic and social development of that group of families.

Let's examine the cases you named, like Colombia or Brazil, and understand what they have achieved with these infrastructures and public space operations. Cities also concentrate a certain elite that creates knowledge, which is what makes the difference in national economies. The author of this idea is Rakesh Mohan, a Hindu economist from the Central Bank of India,[2] and he proposes that in the future global economics will no longer compete over the value of goods and services or even over the efficiency to move them associated with the infrastructure certain countries build, but rather what will make the difference in international competition will be the professionals capable of creating knowledge. First World cities are investing in being able to attract these professional creators of knowledge. The most emblematic case is probably Chicago, which has improved the rate at which it attracts such people, surpassing even New York City.

When viewed from a global scale, more or less the same occurs with security issues, educational, cultural activities, infrastructure efficiency, connectivity and access to sophisticated services. A particularity of knowledge, Mohan maintains, is that it is generated in face-to-face encounters, not through the internet. The more elites in a certain place, the more chances there are of creating knowledge. For poor people, on the other hand, the city is a shortcut to equality. This means not having to wait for income redistribution, which is almost the only thing one hears, intended to amend inequality or improve people's quality of life.

As a result you have a city for rich and poor, who, more than ever, need one another. That's why what emerges from the recommendations of the United Nations or global forums about urbanization is the inclusive city. More than ever, rich and poor people will need each other. The poor need the opportunities cities provide for; they have no other options. The rich need the city because the critical mass that generates these developmental leaps forward is there. It is what will make the difference in the world's economies.

Supersudaca So, an inclusive city is good business...

Fernando Pérez Oyarzún Business that is also sustainable.

Alejandro Aravena Especially, but sustainable from an environmental, economic and social point of view.

Supersudaca Business that is also capable of opening frontiers, because there will be a need for poor people to be where only rich people are today.

Alejandro Aravena Furthermore, in Latin America all this must be achieved without resources. Bogotá, and especially Medellin, are places where this has been done well. The Colombian case is absolutely extraordinary in its capacity to transform social environments through interventions in the city. You could hardly find a more complex, radical or violent situation than in a Colombian city. Despite this, with specific, well directed and efficient interventions these cities have experienced a turnaround the quality of life. We have seen this in Bogotá with public space and transport and in Medellin with the construction of the Parque España Library, which is actually a public space. Beyond the impressive rock-looking building, what is remarkable about this library is that you can access the interstices between *rocks* at any time; it's raining and there are children who can be within the building instead of on the streets. It has created spaces in which people gather to do nothing. Furthermore, the Metrocable – the most radical operation of all – was built to provide access through the gaps on the hillside which was previously impenetrable. You could not get into this place! The responsible was the Empresa de Desarrollo Urbano – EDU, a public agency directed by Alejandro Echeverri that provided potable water, sewage systems, gas, electricity, telephone etc., such that there was a coordinated upgrade in all services. There is political governance that decides how to do it and coordinates all the systems. The scarcest resource to plan cities well is coordination, not money. The city and its networks are rarely done well spontaneously and in Medellin they made a choice I believe was the right one; what they should keep on doing is to insist on public infrastructure and make it even better.

Supersudaca Elemental played by the existing rules on social housing projects, but at the same time redefined them by making collectiveness, economic and social profitability the important issues. As architects do you think you are compelled to play by the rules or you should at tempt to change them?

Alejandro Aravena Or both.

Fernando Pérez Oyarzún I think the big challenge for today's architecture education is finding a way in which disciplinary practices are faced as honestly as possible; this means facing this problem crudely, with their rules on top. This would only renew practices that are becoming tiresome, acquired, gestural and formal.

Alejandro Aravena Training yourself to respond to a problem within its real restrictions is what allows you to simultaneously maintain distance while having a mechanism that, when you go work in the outside world, will make what you studied and trained worthwhile. I mean restrictions that in general lead you toward new questions, which consequently lead to new answers.

Nevertheless, it seems we are far more concerned about style or the answer itself, rather than the question.

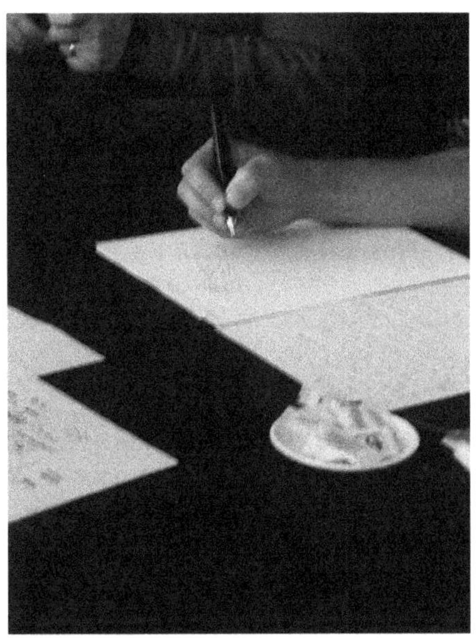

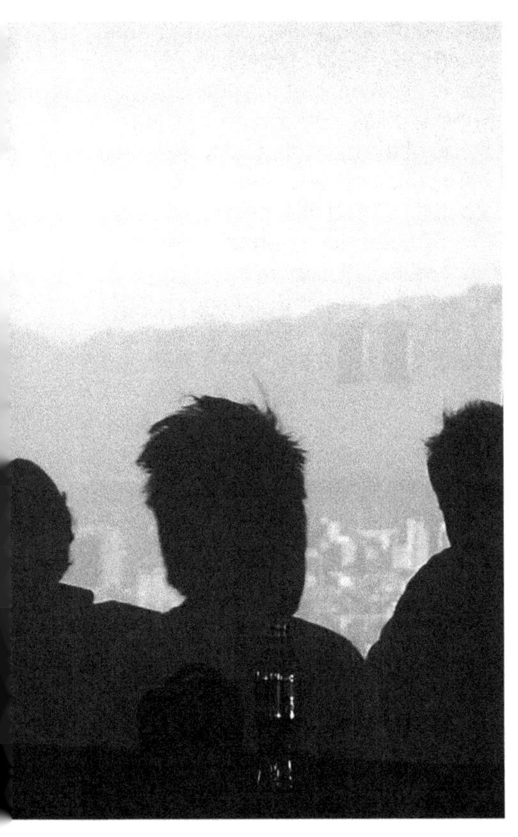

From Big Boxes to Little Boxes

Guest writers   Mario Marchant

Massive changes have been taking place in Latin America since the 1990s when the re-democratization process began to replace most of the continent's military dictatorships. Regardless of the ideological orientation of the new democratic governments neo-liberal politics were implemented. That decade marked the end of the development strategies employed by many Latin American governments since the second half of the 20th century within leftist and/or Socialist ideological and political frameworks. It was an era during which it seemed that architecture's ideals went hand by hand with the collective cultural aspirations of many political leaders: housing projects and urban plans proposed by several prominent Latin American architects (which founded in modernist principles the *perfect* recipe to be applied) seemed to easily convince governments of the urgent social need for housing, envisioning what promised to be a bright future. Consequently, during the 1950s and especially during the 1960s those ideals were crystallized in several – collective? – rational projects locally known as Unidades Vecinales (abbreviated as U.V.), such as U.V. de Matute in Lima, Peru, and U.V. Portales in Santiago, Chile. These developments were essentially modernist *big boxes* (blocks and megablocks à la Ginzburg's Narkomfin, Corbusier's Unité d'Habitation or Soviet microrayons) including never-ending corridors and elevated pedestrian bridges that connected standard housing units. Architecture seemed for a moment to perfectly embody collective life.

During the last fifteen years we have witnessed a major modernization of the continent's urban milieu (tolled highways, private industrial parks, international hotel facilities, shopping malls and so on). Along with that typically Western notion of progress, several Latin American countries also modified their housing strategies leading them to institute subsidy policies, which, in association with the private sector, were supposed to

1. *Little Boxes* is a song written and composed by Malvina Reynolds in 1962, which became a hit for her friend Pete Seeger in 1963, when he released his cover version. Reynolds' version was first released on her 1967 Columbia Records album *Malvina Reynolds Sings the Truth*.

satisfy the social demands for that commodity. That scenario drastically transformed Latin America's collective housing dream into Latin America's individual housing dream. Housing production rapidly changed from *big boxes* to *little boxes*. Little boxes have proliferated in Latin America's cities like forest mushrooms after a downpour, defining enormous urban areas (and not just suburban sprawl as many might imagine) with endless rows of *pequeñas cajitas*. The initial urban tissue woven by these small individual houses is initially a dreary landscape of dull conformity, as the North American folksinger Malvina Reynolds described in her 1962 song *Little Boxes* which lampoons the development of United States suburbia:

> *Little boxes all the same.*
> *There's a green one and a pink one*
> *And a blue one and a yellow one,*
> *And they're all made out of ticky tacky*
> *And they all look just the same.*[1]

Yet there is a significant difference between the United States sprawl Reynolds describes and Latin America's Little Boxes phenomenon. If we carefully focus on that initial postcard of urban homogeneity, we can clearly see how people in Latin American cities have produced interesting, formal and programmatic transformations in their *pequeñas cajitas:* From room additions to the original unit to a variety of non-residential (educational, religious and commercial) uses. For example, in La Florida, a typical low-middle class neighborhood in South Santiago de Chile, a mother could start her day by dropping her child at a *little-box-nursery* and from there walk down a few steps to stop at the next door *little-box-church* for a religious service. Once the service had ended she could go with a friend (recently met at the *little-box-church*) to visit her new *little-box-house* addition (a second floor for the new baby) and then quickly stop by the *little-box-shop* next door to pick up bread, vegetables and a roasted chicken for the family lunch. Thus the new urban landscape that Latin America's little boxes are constructing do not *all look just the same*. There is a significant variety and singularity within a repetitive basic pattern (initially conceived just for housing). Diversity has been mainly produced by the lack of urban services and infrastructure (generated by unsuccessful or non-existing urban planning) that goes along with the rapid construction of those developments, the product of market forces. As a consequence some people have seen those missing urban necessities as something to criticize and demand from local governments. Others have seen it as an opportunity for personal gain. The capacity of little boxes for individualization, flexibility and controlled expansion may explain their demand and popularity. It may also explain why big boxes of the past with limited spatial capacity, little flexibility and badly scaled, unsupervised, open public spaces that surround megablocks have been a failure. In addition, the desire for a *casita con patio* has been strongly embedded in Latin America's social imaginary since colonial times when new cities were constructed based upon the *mini me* urban version of the countryside's Spanish haciendas (creating the typical urban block, a.k.a. *manzana*, of several side-by-side row houses with inner patios).

The architectural ideas behind Latin America's big boxes of the 1950s and 1960s may have confused the notion of *collective* (a group of individuals with similarities but with particular aspirations) with the notion of *massive* (a large structure without individual recognition). Massive clearly does not imply collective. Collective architecture must consider space flexibility, the ability to change and grow as well as smaller sized, supervised social space as essential to individual satisfaction and the creation of a sense of community among urban residents that truly represents the social notion of collective. If the architecture of little boxes results in the United States (and even in parts of Europe) in an ever-expanding monotonous urban sprawl, in Latin America it seems to construct an emerging contemporary collective way of life (with the absence of an architectural vision, plan or discourse), showing that collective aspirations have increasingly become the product of individuals, again, a collective phenomenon.

From Slum to Slim

Neza York or the Perfect Rascasuelos

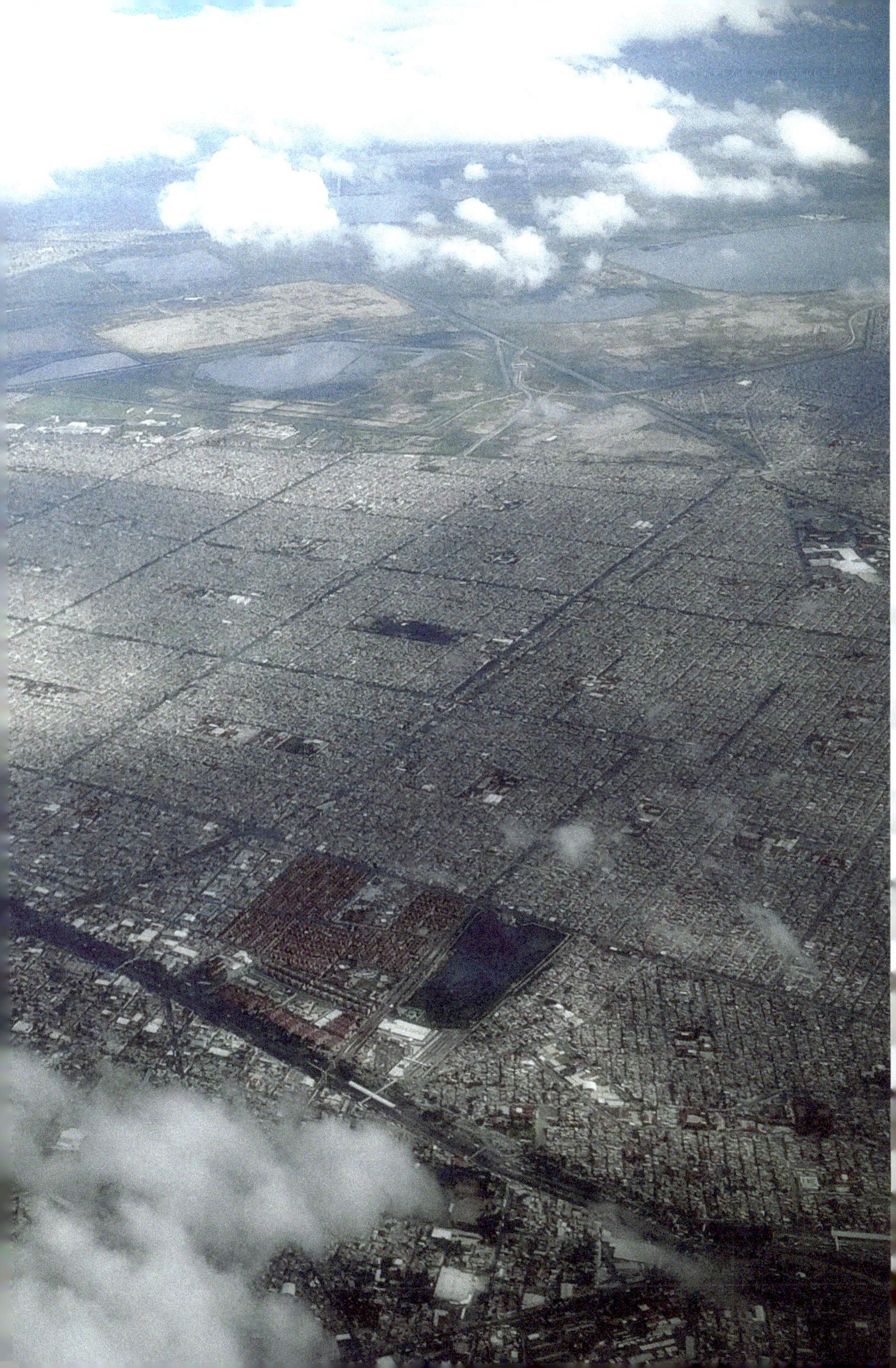

The remake of peripheral slums into attractive neighborhoods is particularly important when addressing the emerging challenges of areas previously on the edge of cities. Not many informal or irregular settlements get out of their dead-end cycle, let alone become successful, but that is all the more reason why it is imperative to look more closely at the sequence of events that turned the peripheral slum and no-go area of Ciudad Nezahualcóyotl (in short, Neza) in the periphery of Mexico City into a highly urban territory that nowadays attracts investors and inhabitants of all types.

The hypothesis leading to the emergence of an attractive city out of a precarious place is not based on any belief of inevitable progress or on blind optimism. Poor slums in similar peripheral conditions in Mexico City might become worse if neither attention nor investment is enabled. Neza's success is a combination of the stubborn struggle of its inhabitants to gain the attention of successive governments – power that emanated from their sheer numbers, solidarity and focus of goals –, which led to the eventual introduction of key infrastructure improvements. Finally, its specific street layout, in the form of a grid, has helped to spread the benefits to all corners of Neza. These are perhaps the secret ingredients of this Mexican urban miracle that continues to improve on a daily basis.

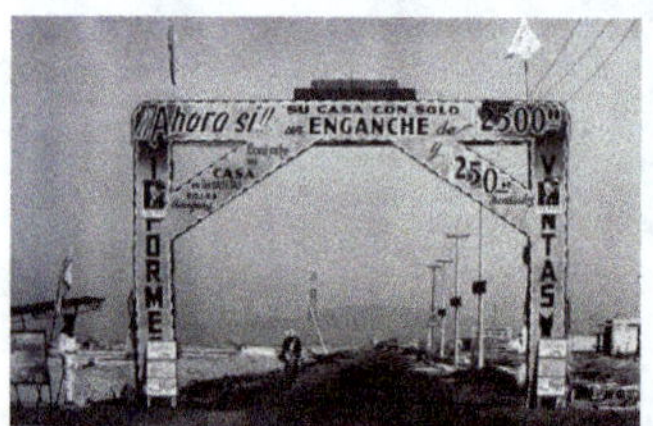

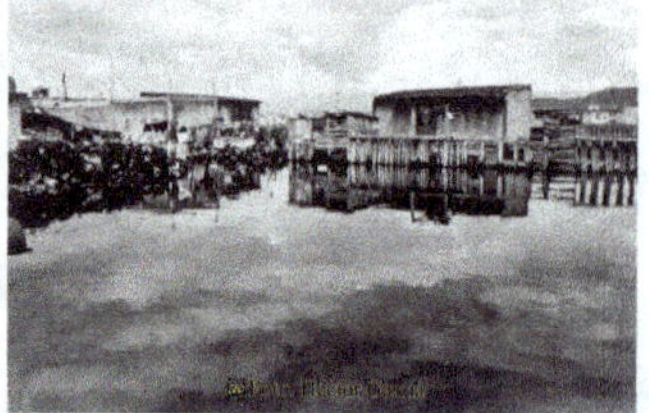

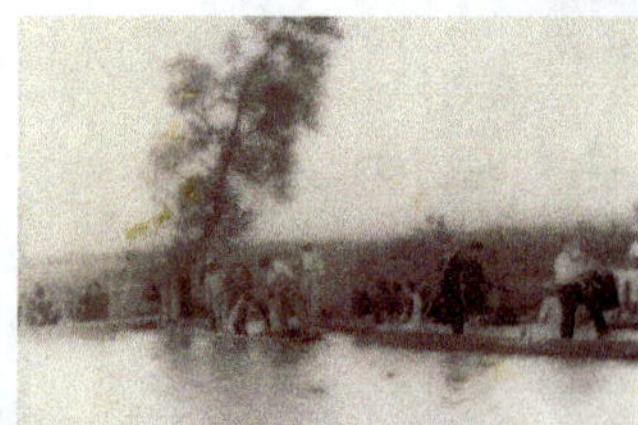

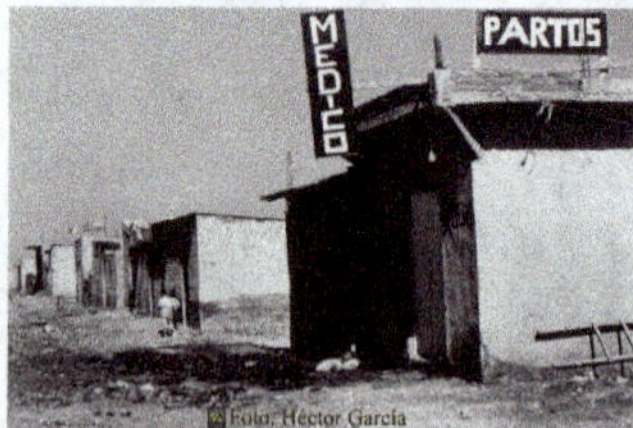

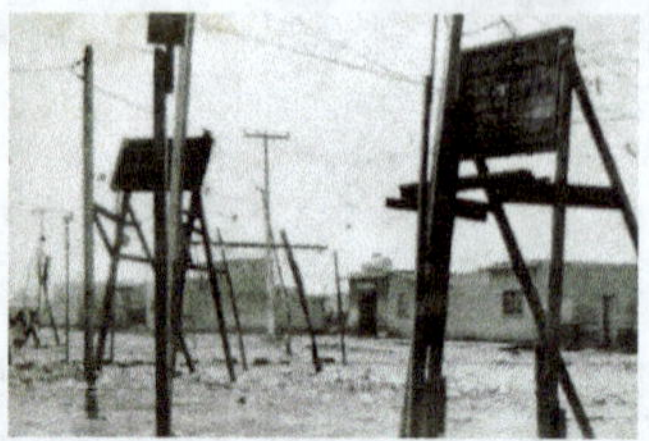

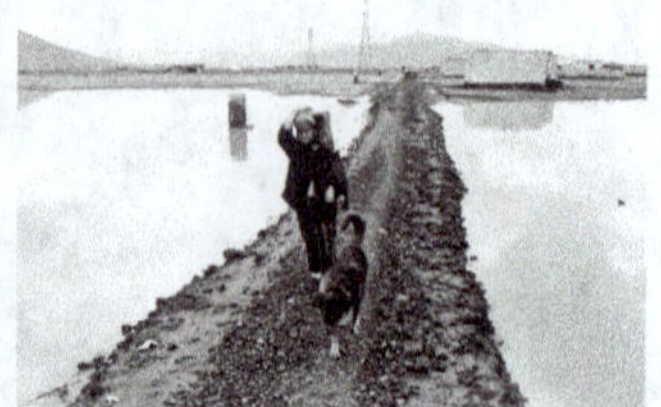

1.   OMA, Rem Koolhaas and Bruce Mau, *S,M,L,XL* (New York, Monacelli Press, 1995). See metaphor used by OMA in the park competition of La Villete in Paris.

2.   Jose Castillo and Sarah Raines, "Urbanisms of the Informal: Transformations in the Urban Fringe of Mexico City." *Praxis: Journal of Writing + Building* 1, no. 2 (2001): 100-111, https://bit.ly/3IN5crD.

3.   Seth Kugel, "Urban Tactics: Destination, Neza York," *The New York Times*, February 15, 2004, https://nyti.ms/331W4sG.

4.   *Censo de Población y Vivienda* (Tultepec/Nextlalpan/Tultitlán, Inegi, 2010), https://bit.ly/3dAKFIP.

5.   Mario Bassols Ricárdez and Maribel Espinosa Castillo, "Construcción Social del Espacio Urbano: Ecatepec y Nezahualcóyotl. Dos Gigantes del Oriente." *Polis* 7, no. 2 (2011): 181-212, https://bit.ly/3dz80US.

6.   Nezahualcoyotl is one of 58 municipalities from the state of Mexico that are included in the Metropolitan Region of the Valley of Mexico. Cf. Fernando Romero, *ZMVM: Zona Metropolitana del Valle de Mexico* (Mexico, Laboratorio de la Ciudad de Mexico, 2000).

7.   The municipality of Nezahualcoyotl was officially created in April 23, 1963. By then it is estimated it had a population of 100 thousand inhabitants. Cf. Gobierno Municipal Nezahualcoyotl, "Breve Historia del Municipio," https://bit.ly/33650NK.

Nezahualcoyotl, a.k.a. Neza York

Nezahualcoyotl, also known as Neza York, is in no way close to the Manhattan city profile; and opposite to Manhattan, you cannot devise Neza until you are inside of it. Yet, in terms of population density, the city of Neza indeed could be read as a horizontal skyscraper.[1] Its urban layout spreads in a surface of around 10km x 4km – in a regular grid that comprises one of the largest and densest low-rise cities in the world with a population of 1,11 million in an area of just 4,190 hectares; a density of 264 people per hectare spread almost perfectly even in its net-like territory.

Densely populated Randstad in the Netherlands with a density of 83 persons/ha, or urban Paris 70 persons/ha are well below Neza's density. Manhattan borough, one of the densest urban areas on earth, has a density of 273 persons/ha, almost the same as Neza. What makes this remarkable is that most building heights in Neza average only two stories.[2] The block size is also remarkably similar to New York dimensions; most of Neza's blocks are 220m x 35m while in Manhattan they are of similar length, but 20 meters wider. No wonder that inhabitants of Neza that have emigrated to New York recently are able to melt easily in its urban culture, showing the compatibilities of both cities and their love for street culture.[3]

Besides this, Neza also shares something else with New York: The exuberance of its architecture. In Neza this is represented by 285,027 self-built houses[4] and the abilities, potential and mental stamina (ego) of each plot owner to improve and expand them over time. Officially founded in what was the periphery of Mexico City fifty years ago, Neza is currently the second biggest municipality in terms of population of the State of Mexico;[5] a self governing state surrounding the Federal District where the Mexican capital is located. Despite being a municipality not belonging to the Mexican capital, Nezahualcoyotl has become a *de facto* part of the Mexican metropolitan region due to its proximity and relevance.[6] Its rise from a barely legal settlement built by thousands of families into one of the most populated and active places of Mexico City in a period of fifty years[7] is worth revisiting.

8.   This ad appeared in the newspaper *El Universal* in October 9, 2013.
9.   The minimum wage in Mexico is 64.76 pesos per day (close to $4.9 dollars per day or $61 cents per hour). If you would earn one minimum wage you will need to work around 100 years to pay the property exclusively or 300 years if you spend 1/3 of your salary for housing costs. See: Comisión Nacional de los Salarios Mínimos, "Nuevos Salarios Mínimos 2013, por Área Geográfica Generales y Profesionales".
10. Another ad at the newspaper *El Universal* featured n apartment for sale in the central neighborhood of Colonia del Valle in Mexico City for $1,800,000 pesos (around $140,000 dollars).
11. For a recent overview of the Nezahualcoyotl reputation, see: Miriam Moreno, "Neza, El Callejón sin Salida," *Letras Libres*, June 1, 2011, https://bit.ly/3IUkomR.
12. *Nacos* is a pejorative word to describe Mexicans of lower classes living in the city with *dubious* taste of style. See the tragicomic portrait of the relationship between the *nacos* in their role as peripheral inhabitants (*paracaidistas*) and the *picudos* (ruling class known also as *fresas*) in their role as landlords with the TV comedian El Pirruris, https://bit.ly/341Lh2Q.
13. Universidad La Salle open its campus in 1996, besides offering high school and university

The Newspaper Ad

Beautiful house in two levels very spacious includes a flat with independent exit. Plot 153 square meters. Construction 247 square meters. Exceptional house in two levels, ready to inhabit, includes living room, dining room, kitchen, five bedrooms all with closet, studio, backyard, two parking places, very spacious in all its surfaces, excellent location, very close to shopping malls, schools, colleges, universities, primary roads, parks, museums, includes all services. Flat includes living room, dining room, kitchen, bathroom, one room, excellent distribution well illuminated, visit it.[8]

Normally if you would read today such an ad in the newspaper of Mexico City you would conclude that the house might just be an attractive property worth considering buying. The price tag at $1,672,000 Mexican pesos (around $125,000 dollars) might be tight for your budget,[9] yet still tempting to find out more.[10] Can such an attractive property be located in the infamous suburb of Nezahualcoyotl,[11] widely known as one of the harshest neighborhoods of the city, a no-go area for many? In the mass media it is still considered a place where only the *nacos*[12] live. Yet, as you read again the ad, you realize that the property remains attractive; schools, parks and many trees are indeed nearby when searching Google Maps. More surprising, there is even a private university around the corner.[13] The airport is actually quite close and not only the Metro, but very soon Metrobus will connect the location with the capital and nearby areas. Shopping – and we are not talking about only informal markets, we are talking shopping malls with top of the line products – and museums are nearby. It is hard to properly assess the depiction of the media, but it is less difficult to believe that price regulation at this level begins to show a city attractive enough for such property prices.

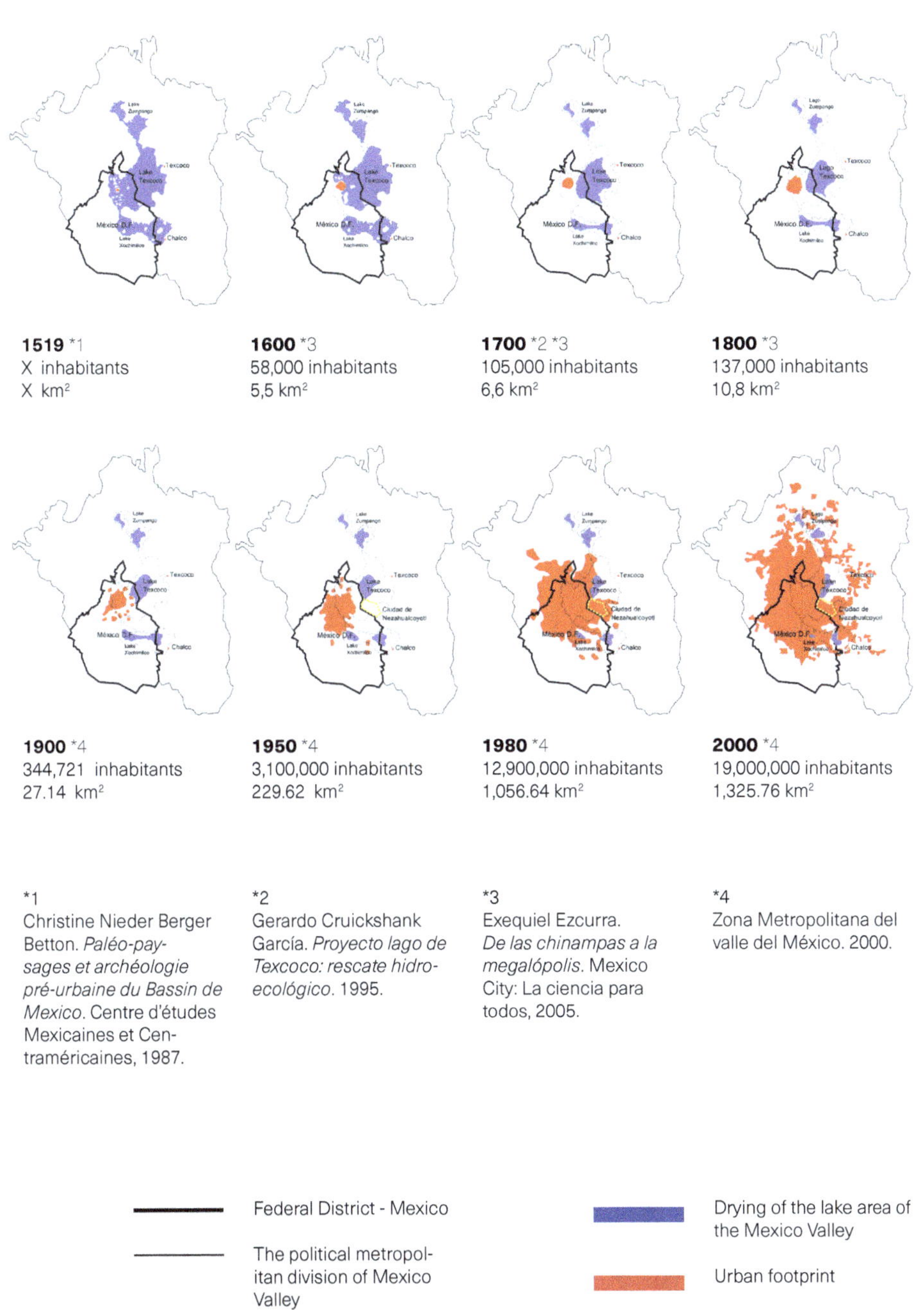

*1
Christine Nieder Berger Betton. *Paléo-paysages et archéologie pré-urbaine du Bassin de Mexico*. Centre d'études Mexicaines et Centraméricaines, 1987.

*2
Gerardo Cruickshank García. *Proyecto lago de Texcoco: rescate hidro-ecológico*. 1995.

*3
Exequiel Ezcurra. *De las chinampas a la megalópolis*. Mexico City: La ciencia para todos, 2005.

*4
Zona Metropolitana del valle del México. 2000.

degrees it also offers postgraduate courses.

14. Maribel Espinosa-Castillo, "Procesos y Actores en la Conformación del Suelo Urbano en el ex Lago de Texcoco," *Economía, Sociedad y Territorio* 8, no. 27 (May/August 2008): 769-798, https://bit.ly/3scGOxr.

15. Ibid. See also: Gloria Valek-Valdés, *Agua. Reflejo de un Valle en el Tiempo* (Mexico, Universidad Nacional Autónoma de México, 2000).

16. Nestor Garcia Canclini, Alejandro Castellanos and Ana Rosas Mantecón, *La Ciudad de los Viajeros: Travesías e Imaginarios Urbanos. Mexico, 1940-2000* (Mexico, Universidad Autónoma Metropolitana/Grijalbo, 1996).

17. Peter M. Ward, "Intra-City Migration to Squatter Settlements in Mexico City," *Geoforum* 7 (1976): 369-382, https://bit.ly/3AN4G3r.

18. Pedro Ocotitla Saucedo, "Movimientos de Colonos en Ciudad Nezahualcóyotl: Acción colectiva y Politica Popular 1945-1975" (master's thesis), Universidad Autónoma Metropolitana, 2000, https://bit.ly/3rjk04l.

Reclaiming Neza

Since its foundation in 1325, the City of Mexico suffered from severe flooding due to its geographical condition of an *endorheic basin*,[14] i.e. a topographical condition that retains rainwater without offering an exit for it by rivers or oceans. To protect against flooding a proper system of water evacuation was required. The infrastructural works to drain the water out of the basin are numerous and go a long way back in history, even to the arrival of the Spaniards.[15] As the lakes had finally been drained out at the beginning of the 20th century, the question of what to do and who should exploit the gradually reclaimed new land are crucial to understand the emergence of the city of Nezahualcoyotl in what used to be the Lake Texcoco, the lowest but biggest of all Mexican lakes.

The drying of the lakes coincided neatly with Mexico City's demographic explosion that started to put pressure on the city housing stock after the 1940s. In just thirty years the metropolitan area went from 1,6 million people in 1940 to 9,2 millions in 1970.[16] As housing rents started to escalate in the city center, the PRI government tried to tackle the unpopular price rise using a decree of *pegged* or *frozen* rents in 1942.[17] The landlords fired back by stopping all housing maintenance. To add more pressure to the mix the *regente* (appointed major) of the city, by 1950 Mr. Uruchurtu had forbidden the creation of new neighborhoods within the Federal District limits.[18] In a few years the combination of decaying rental buildings in the center, demographic growth and increasing densification, forced thousands of recent immigrant families to search for land where they could build their own houses cheaply. The municipalities of the neighboring state of Mexico were an obvious answer and Nezahualcoyotl was one of the first that became available to them.

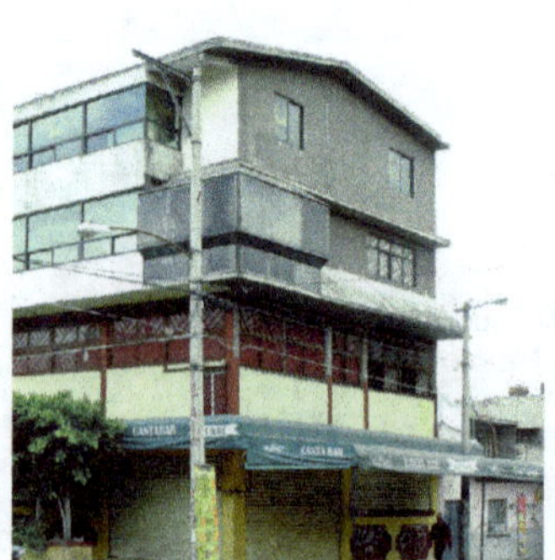

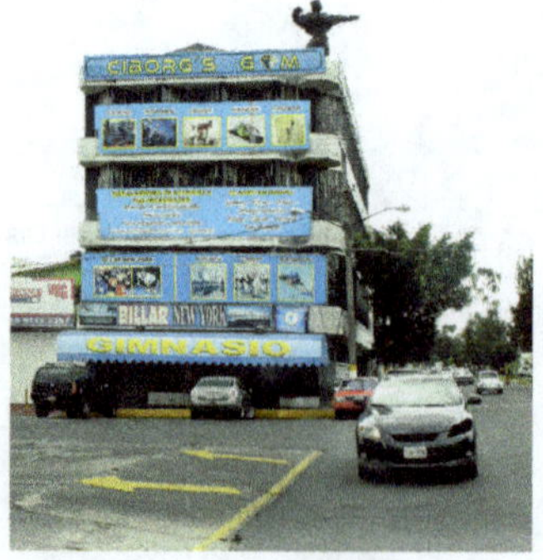

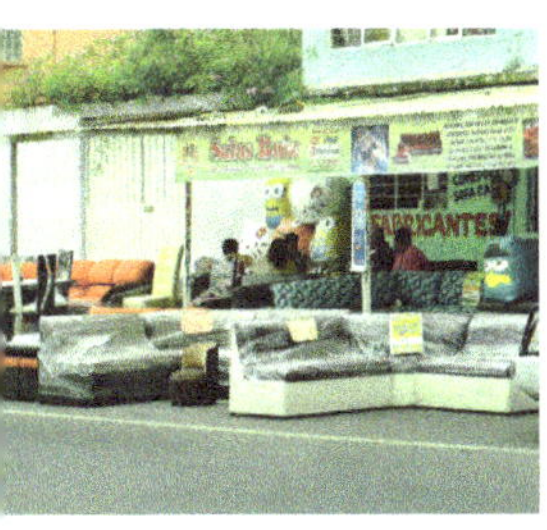
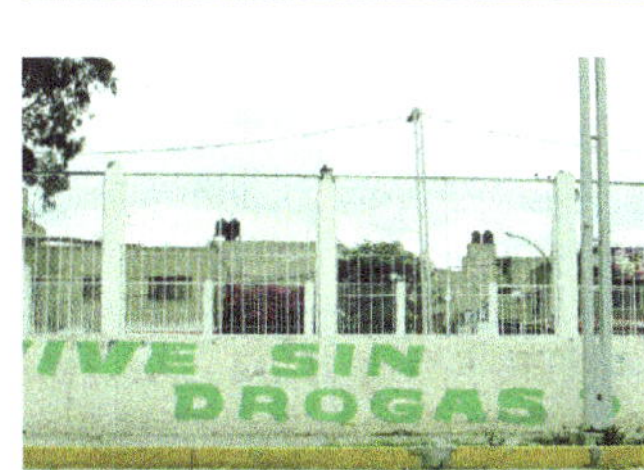
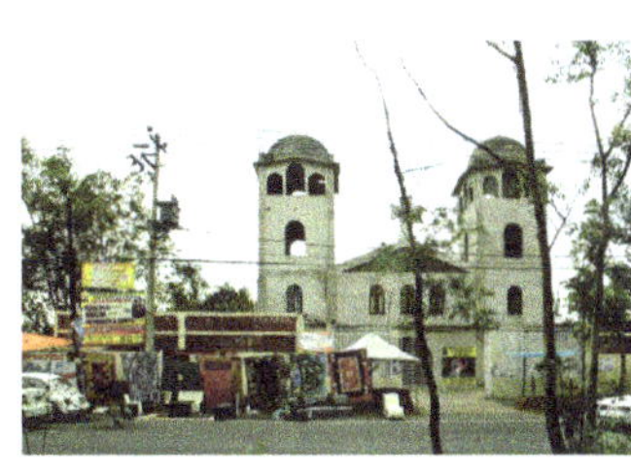
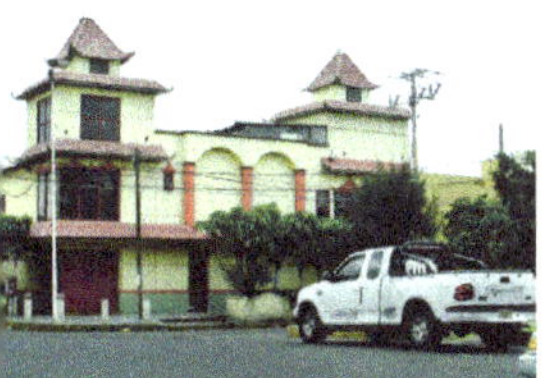
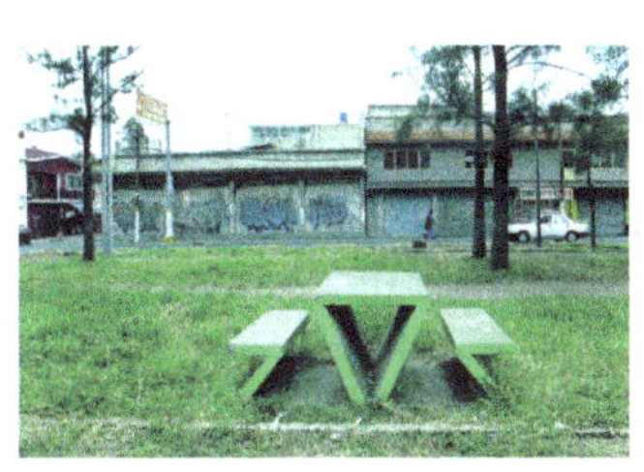
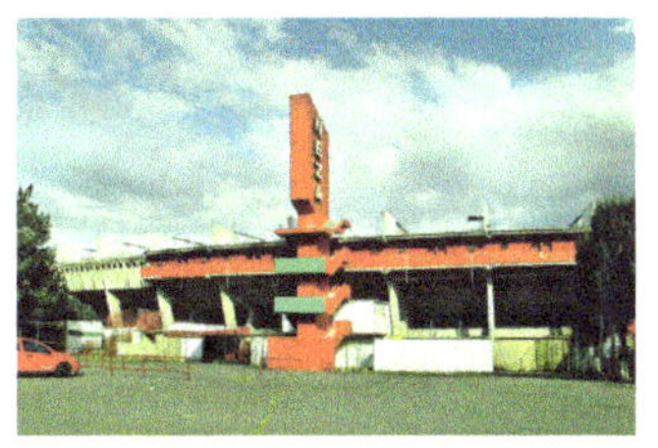
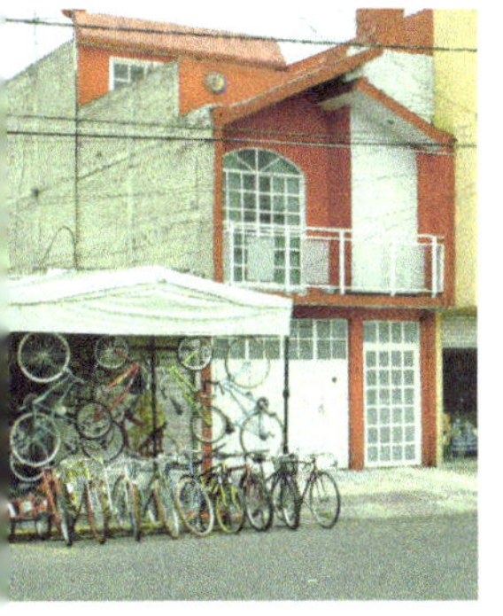
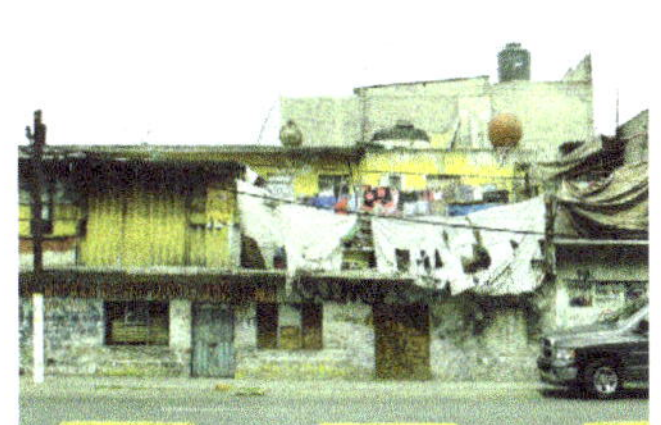
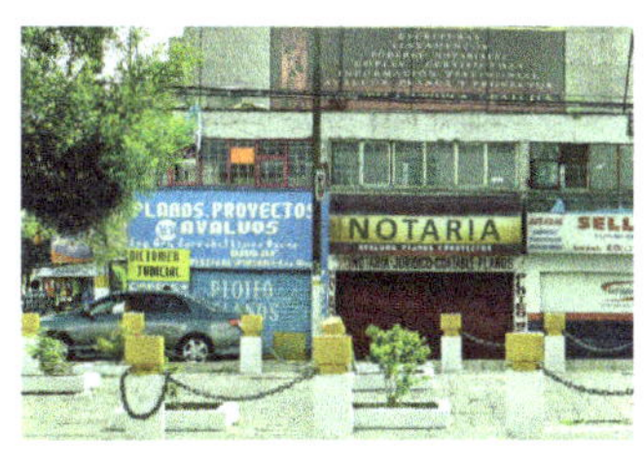
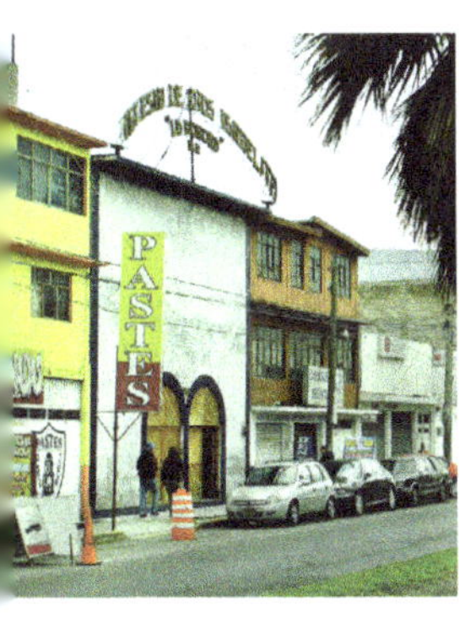
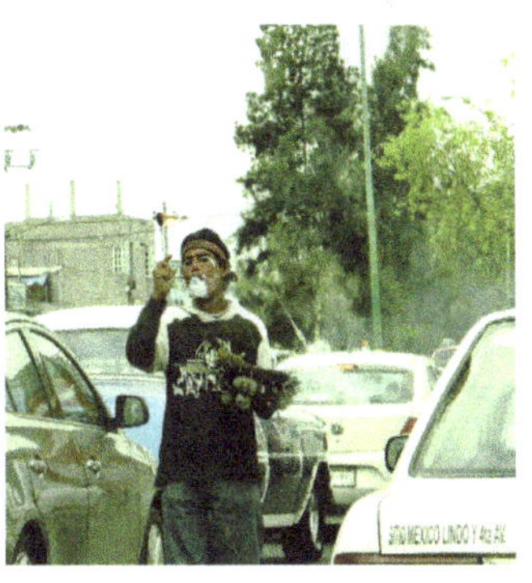
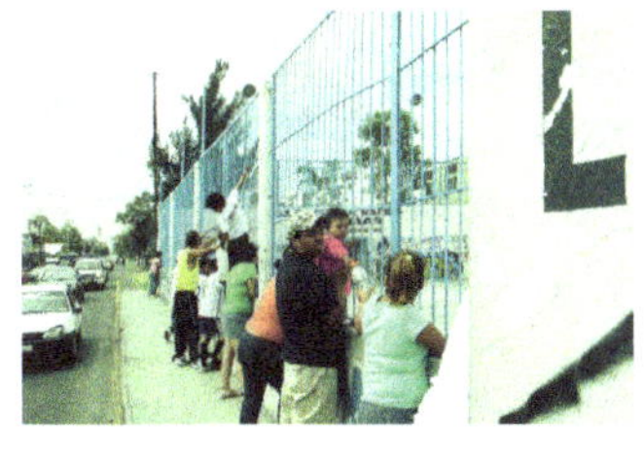
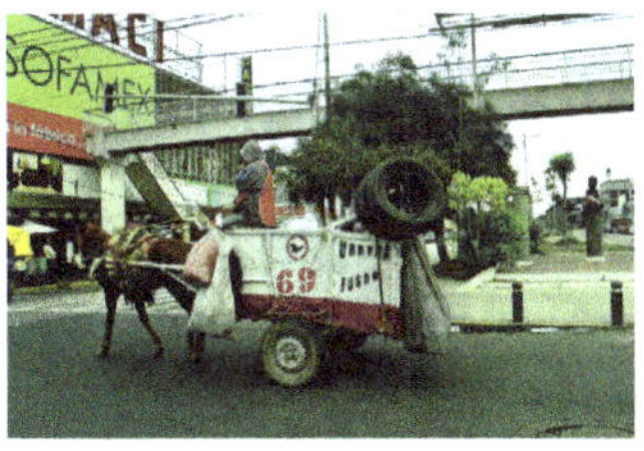

19. Ibid
20. Ibid.

Visions for a New Land

The first attempts to give the dried land a new purpose were carried out in 1919 and 1921 when the situation was considered an emergency, due to the sudden appearance of dust storms coming from the dried lake surface that began polluting the city. The federal government aimed to turn the area into agricultural land and later into a fish farming area, yet both projects failed to take off. This failure led the government to consider the benefit of allowing private capital to offer their vision for the land. In 1930 the engineer Angel Peimbert, and the architect Luis MacGregor, drafted a scenario that combined intensive agriculture, industry and eventual urbanization through the subdivision of plots.[19] The idea of integrating the recently dried area into the expanding city became obvious. By 1932 the governor of the State of Mexico, Filiberto Gomez, released the state-owned land of 7 thousand hectares to a few private hands; land sold by the government at the preposterous price of $1 peso per hectare on the condition that the buyers would treat the land, and clean it from any toxic remains. This unusual sale ended up in the hands of top military generals (including future high rank politicians such as Lázaro Cárdenas, Francisco Mujica and Leopoldo Treviño), federal government officials and even the visionaries of the area: MacGregor and Peimbert. The plot size started at 40 hectares and each personal investor could acquire two plots.[20]

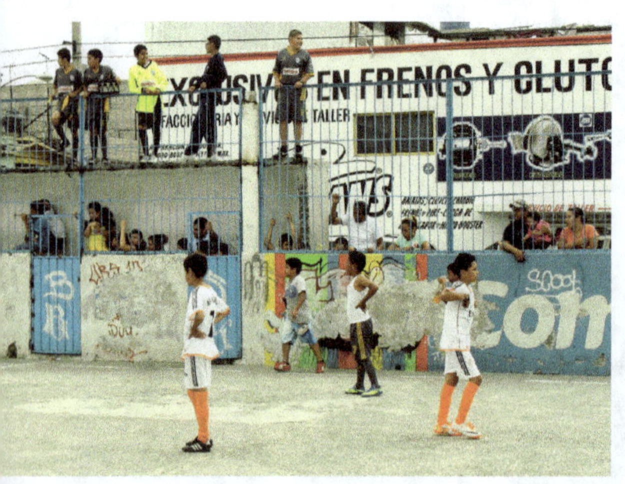

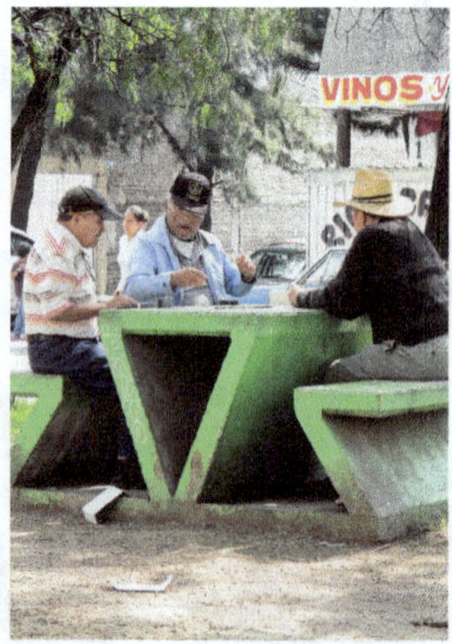

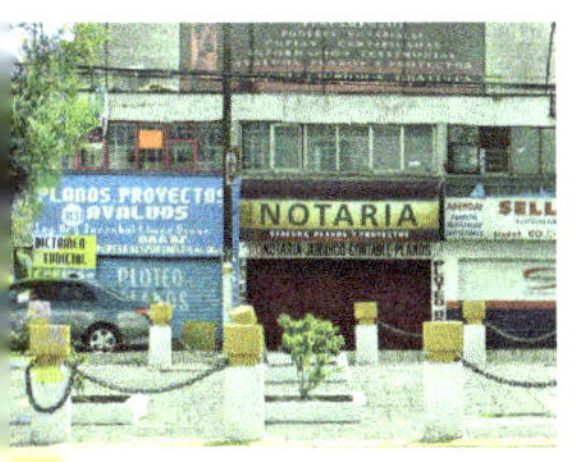

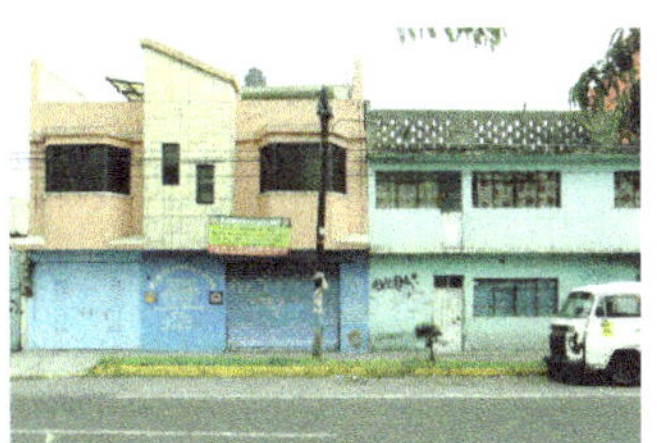

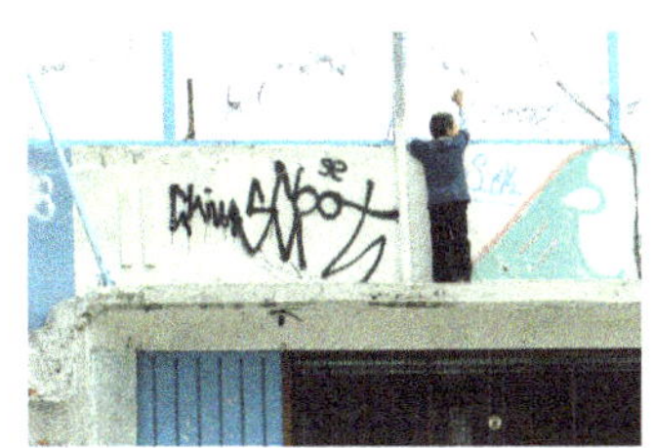

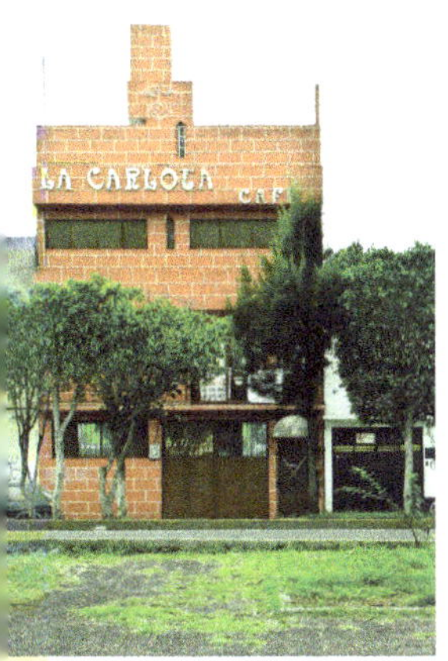
LA CARLOTA
CAFÉ

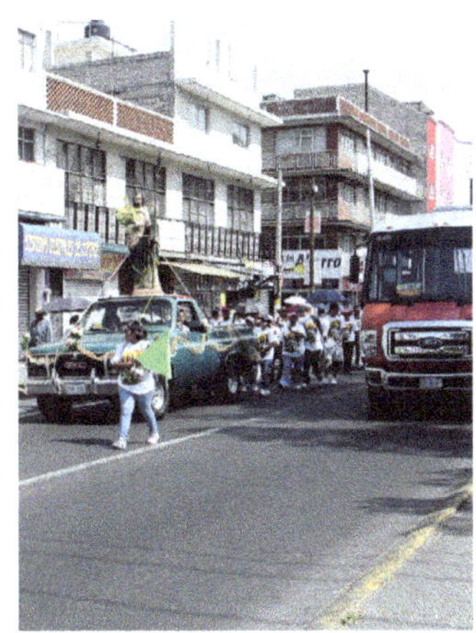

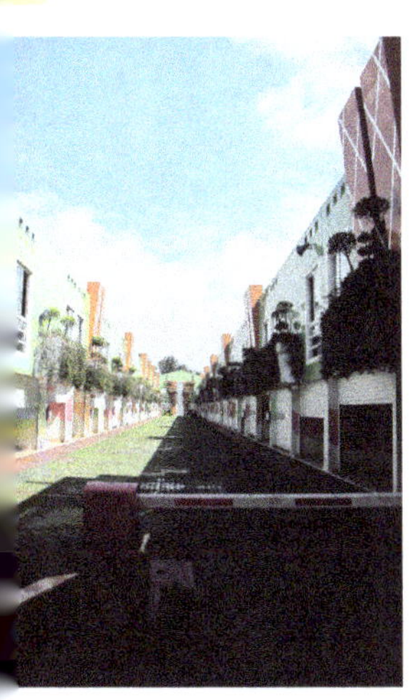

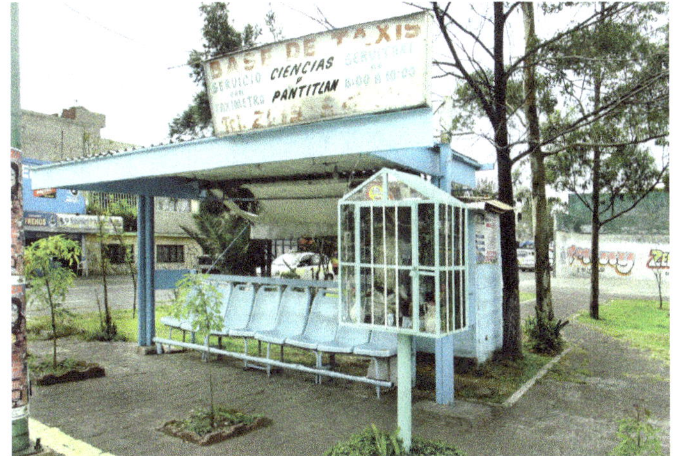
BASE DE TAXIS
SERVICIO
TAXIMETRO
CIENCIAS
Y
PANTITLAN
SERVICIO
8:00 A 10:00

21. These were people mainly from the communal land of Chimalhuacan. See: Saucedo, "Movimientos de Colonos en Ciudad Nezahualcóyotl."
22. Ibid. For example the developer Alejandro Romero previously built the *proletariat* neighborhoods such as Colonia Obrera and Colonia Emilio Carranza. The block dimensions of Colonia Obrera and Neza are almost identical, its only difference being the block *pancoupe* of 45 degrees cut in its corners.
23. Saucedo, "Movimientos de Colonos en Ciudad Nezahualcóyotl."
24. Espinosa-Castillo, "Procesos y Actores en la Conformación del Suelo."
25. Colonia El Sol was supposed to be a flood reserve owned by the federal government. See: Saucedo, "Movimientos de Colonos en Ciudad Nezahualcóyotl."

Let the Fight Begin

Yet once the lake had been dried by the federal government, the transfer of property into private hands was soon contested by communal land farmers (*ejidatarios*) that claimed parts of the dried lake territory as their own, initiating what would become a decades' long fight regarding who was the legitimate owner of the land.[21] Regardless of these troubles, the State of Mexico government proceeded with the plan, and the land became available to investors for development. Several developers, some of them with recent experience in developing *proletariat* neighborhoods in the city[22] noted the opportunity and started to advertise the sale of plots with several modes of payments, usually spreading the installments over a few years. Most developments offered compact plots of 10m x 20m. The massive sale went on without much government supervision or respect to the law. Within a few years thousands of plots were sold without paved streets, sewage, sidewalks, public lighting, water or electricity and for decades many of the neighborhoods remained like that. The basic infrastructure was to be installed once enough buyers had paid their loans to the developers, so that – according to them – there would be enough capital for their investments. Some developers forwarded this responsibility to the buyers of the plots from the very start.[23] However, for several decades many developers never completed (nor even started) to honor their promises.

The Mexican Government was partly to blame for this blatant abuse of power since one of its laws from 1948 did actually allow the developers to shield themselves legally against claims of landowners for not completing the basic infrastructure.[24] As frustration became the norm, political groups slowly started to become more active in fighting for their rights against developers and government. Yet it took years for them to realize how effective they could be if they were properly organized. Repression and threats to leaders kept collective initiatives to a minimum during the first decades. What triggered the first organized (and successful) battle was their anxiety when rumors spread that one developer did not actually own the land they were paying for.[25] The neighborhood organizations managed to arrange a meeting

that included the police, Mexico City government, the devel
oper and the inhabitant's representatives. Their answer to their
demand for property rights was a unanimous *strike* on monthly
payments, until the developer handed over the official property
deeds as promised.

After this first success several grass-roots movements
sprouted, demanding the developers complete infrastructure
works and actions against government efforts to tax them in
order to supply the missing infrastructure. Collectives became
actively operational also against land evictions, since their contracts with developers included a severe measure of eviction
if installments were delayed for more than two months. From
terra indomita, Neza slowly started to gravitate to the voice and
power of organized collectives.

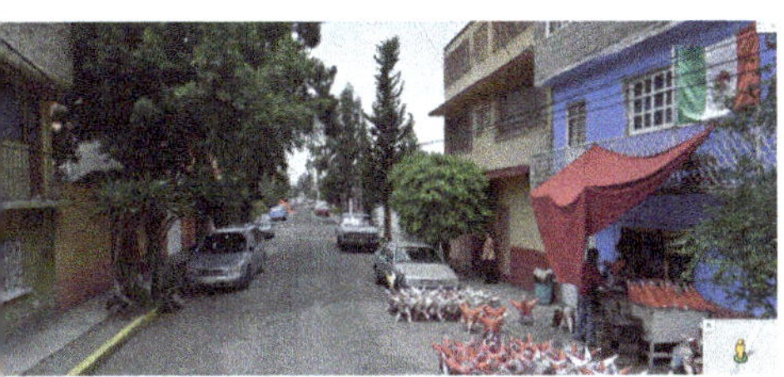
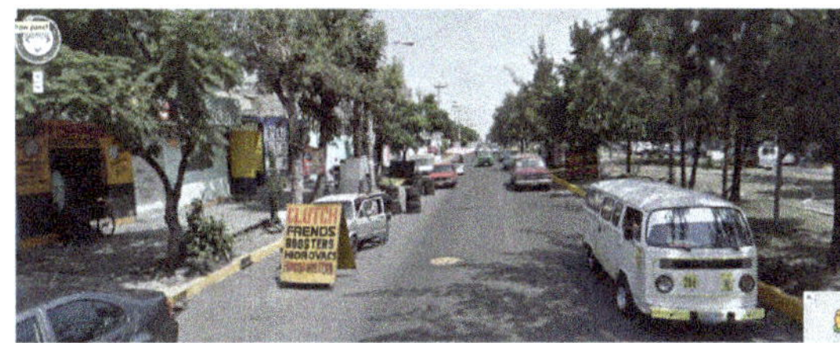

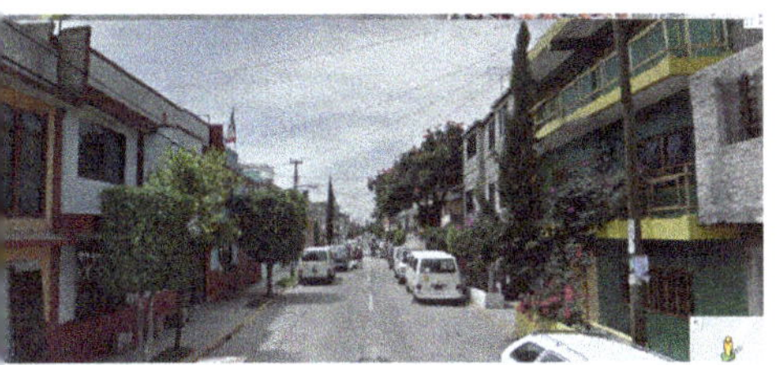
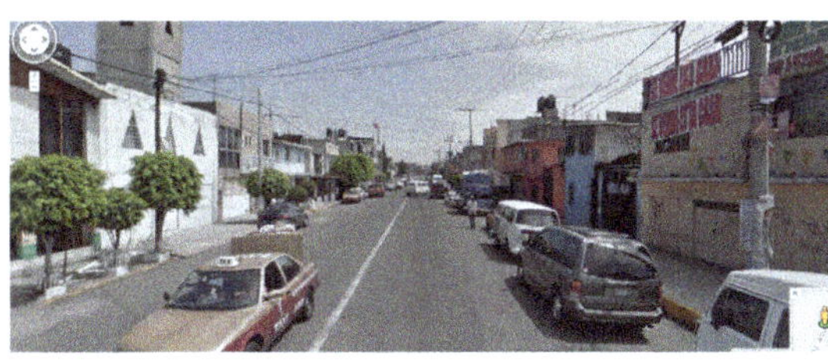

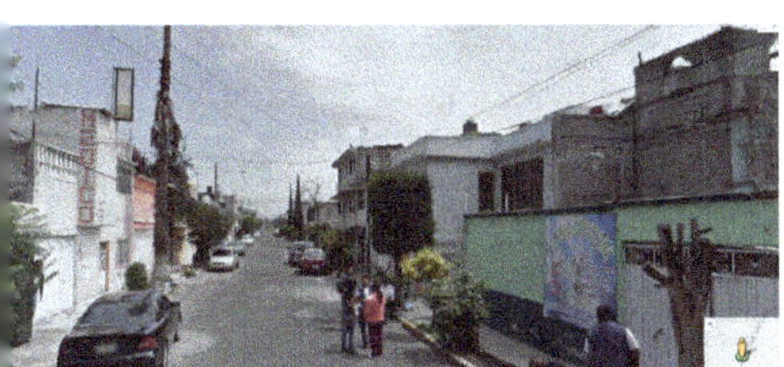
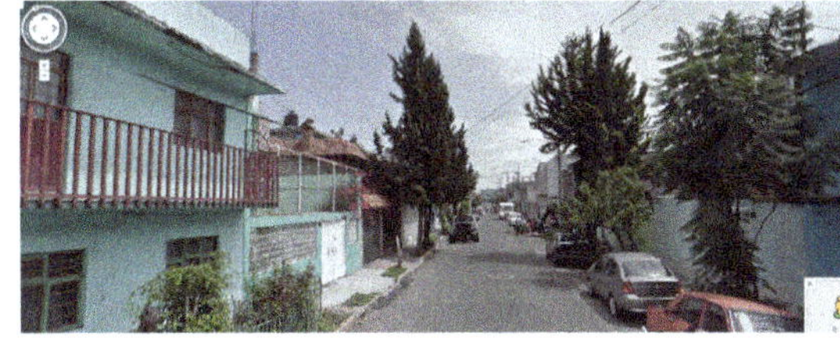

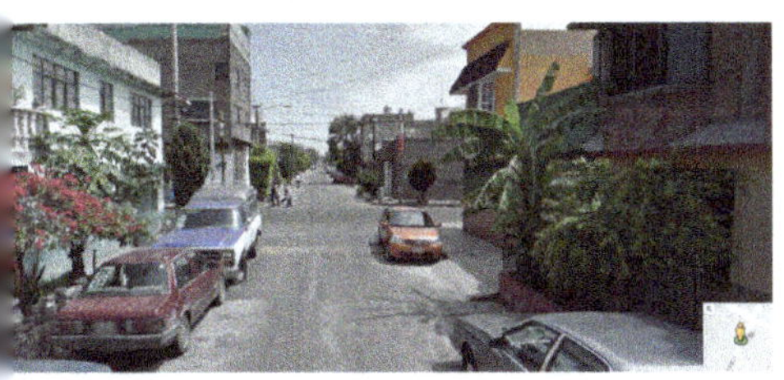
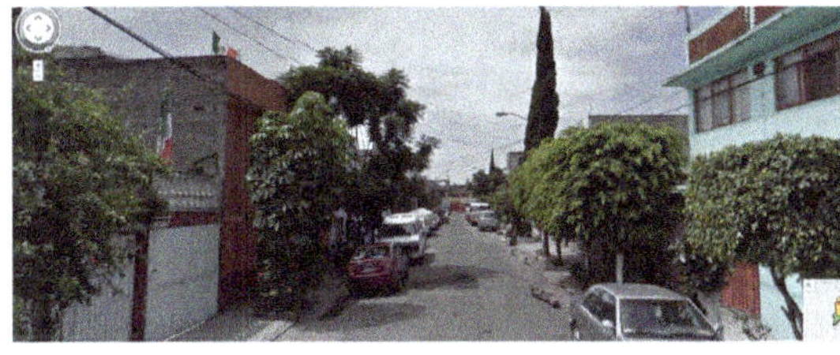

26. Carlos Slim is the world's richest person according to Forbes 2013 list, https://bit.ly/3L1zke8.
27. Oscar Lewis, *Five Families: Mexican Case Studies in the Culture of Poverty* (New York, Basic Books, 1959).
28. Ward, "Intra-City Migration," 380.
29. 98% of all services are covered. See: Ricárdez and Castillo, "Construcción Social del Espacio Urbano."
30. Jan Bredenoord and Otto Verkoren, "Between Self-Help and Institutional Housing: A Bird's Eye View of Mexico's Housing Production for Low and (Lower) Middle-Income Groups," *Habitat International* 34 (2010): 359-365, https://bit.ly/3ISUEjY.
31. Ricárdez and Castillo, "Construcción Social del Espacio Urbano."
32. Ibid.

From Slum to Slim[26]

It was in this period of struggle and desperation that the appearance of Neza at the fringes of the city became a prototypical case study for researchers and journalists in Mexico and abroad. American anthropologist Oscar Lewis described in his research work *The Culture of Poverty. The Life of Five Families of Mexico*. One of them, the Sanchez family, had just started to settle in the barely inhabited settlement of Nezahualcoyotl. The picture the anthropologist depicts is an intimate life of a complex family structure; a family struggling for water, facing badly connected public transport, partly supported by raising animals at home but with an overwhelming feeling of insecurity.[27] Another British-American expert on Mexico City, the geographer Peter M. Ward, despite being more optimistic on the power of self-built environments, considered the area in 1976 a future problem due to its isolation: "For the vast area of *colonias proletarias* in the East of the metropolitan area (Ciudad Nezahualcoyotl), isolated from any convenient commercial or industrial zone, this problem is clearly a real one."[28]

Nevertheless the battles to obtain water, sewage, electricity, paving and property titles were eventually won achieving stability for its inhabitants and to future investors.[29] Slowly the city of Neza gave off a more complex and vivid picture that defied the prevailing concepts of poverty, exclusion, or even the idea of any peripheral slum. The problem of "isolation" addressed by Peter M. Ward eventually ceased to be the main issue, as the main city ring (*periferico*) eventually connected Neza with the city; the city Metro opened parallel to Neza's border the *linea A* in 1991. Though affordable housing production by the state or housing corporations represented a mere 35% of housing demand in Mexico by 1970,[30] Neza inhabitants' self-initiative contributed greatly to *solving* the housing shortage of Mexico City. So much so that by 2011 Neza said goodbye to its characterization of slum in all senses,[31] according to UN Habitat definition:[32]

The final chapter of the Neza York story occurred recently when Mexican heavy weight entrepreneur Carlos Slim proposed to the then governor of the state and now (at the time of the writing of this article) president Enrique Peña Nieto, to turn the Xociaca open waste dump of Mexico City, located in Neza (one of the biggest in the world) into an ambitious theme park: *Parque Bicentenario.* The area of investment covers 138 hectares: Parks, universities, shopping facilities and garbage

33. "Carlos Slim, la ciudad que construyó en Neza," *El Universal*, April 4, 2011.

recycling plants are to become an example to other regions of the World, according to Carlos Slim.[33]

The City in Reverse

During the first decades of its creation, the reasons for the long and constant improvement relied heavily on the citizen's collective modes of mobilization, and eventually the sheer density of its population seems to have played a big role in making Neza a place that no politician can easily overlook – and for that matter no entrepreneur either. Contrary to the problems of European or American cities where the debate is now often centered around how to involve the community in the development of peripheral or poor neighborhoods, Neza puts the question in reverse: How can the community devise strategies to secure the government is involved in solving the challenges of the city?

The skills and perseverance used by the inhabitants of Neza proved that the struggle to be successful are not mere temporal poses, but they are the result of addressing with determination a set of specific and fair demands. This was achieved even though the struggles entailed confrontation with the authorities. Neza demonstrates that citizens are the key component of the improvement of any place in the city; their massive self investment in the improvement of their houses and their constant demands for a better infrastructure and connectivity to the city have eventually become the magnet of more investment from all sectors of society.

When I go back now to Google Maps and to Street View to check again the properties advertisements mentioned before, I notice that the street profile does not show an spectacular city life, there are many bars, markets and places where to play pool, but none seem to be of my taste. Yet I continue strolling in Google Street View and suddenly realize that I am no longer able to distinguish Neza from many other neighborhoods or streets of Mexico City I know. Neza has finally blended into the city: There is no way now to call this anything but a *city*.

Papel
Latino

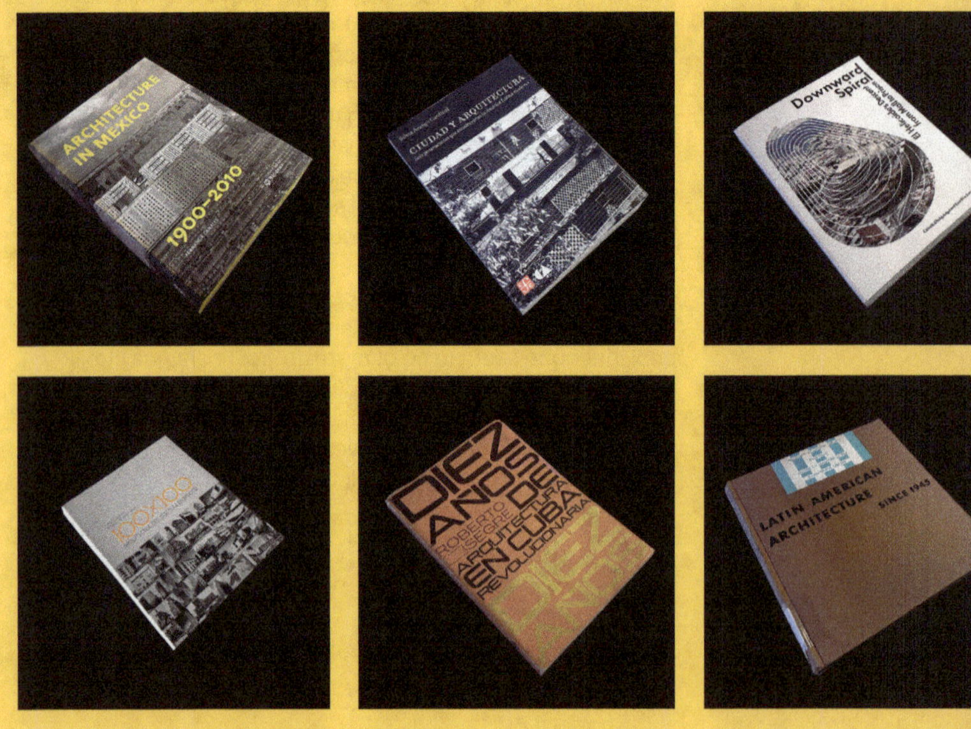

1.   The countries were Argentina, Brazil, Chile, Cuba, Colombia, Mexico, Peru, Uruguay, Venezuela.

2.   According to Encyclopedia Britannica "the people of Latin America shared the experience of conquest and colonization by the Spaniards and Portuguese from the late 15th through the 18th century. They also shared the struggle for independence from colonial rule in the early 19th century" <https://www.britannica.com/place/Latin-America>.

3.   The essay is directly influenced by interviews with architecture historians. For the reflection on the use and the context of architecture the conversation we had with Felipe Hernandez is quite important. On the popular use and interpretation of modern architecture see: Fernando Lara. *The Rise of Popular Modernist Architecture in Brazil*. Florida: University Press of Florida, 2008.

Supersudaca entered the project at the invitation of Prof. Zhao Pei. The original task was to compile a list of essential books to understand the evolution of modern architecture in some selected countries of Latin America. Although the initial request was to focus on those nine countries[1] we argued that we could discover a fresher reading if we could extend this list to all countries of the so-called Latin America.[2] At the same time, we believed it would be useful to have a multi directional reading across countries and not have the list per countries isolated from each other in order to show the relations and differences between the nation's timelines. The bibliography aimed to show how modern architecture was established, evolved and especially how it was reported or ignored in the different countries from the 20th century until now. The research also included a comment on new readings of it, specifically how modern architecture was used in Latin America and in which context.[3] The following reflections come as a point of departure for further inquiry that has crossed our minds while making this bibliographical work.

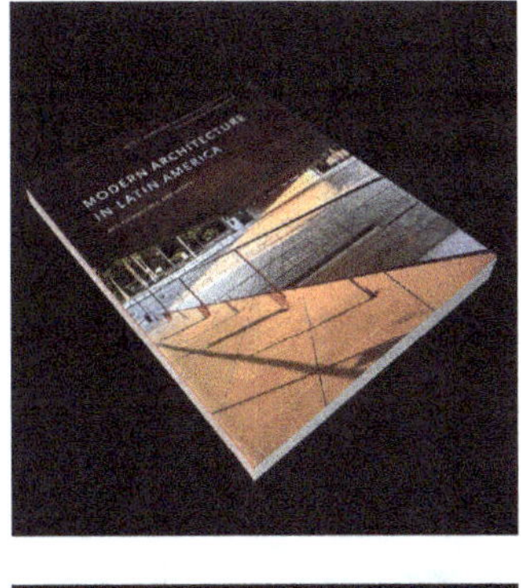
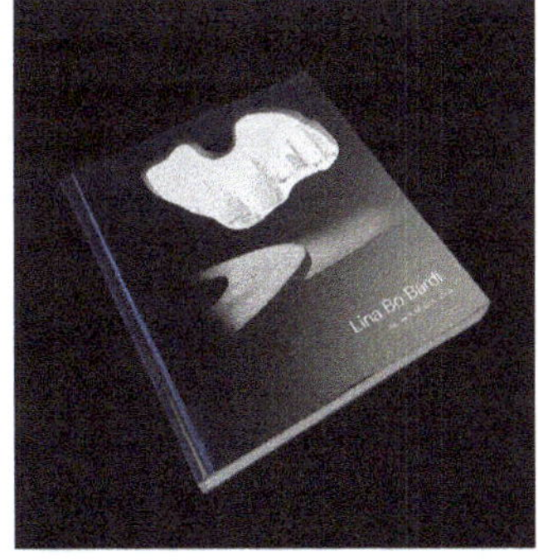
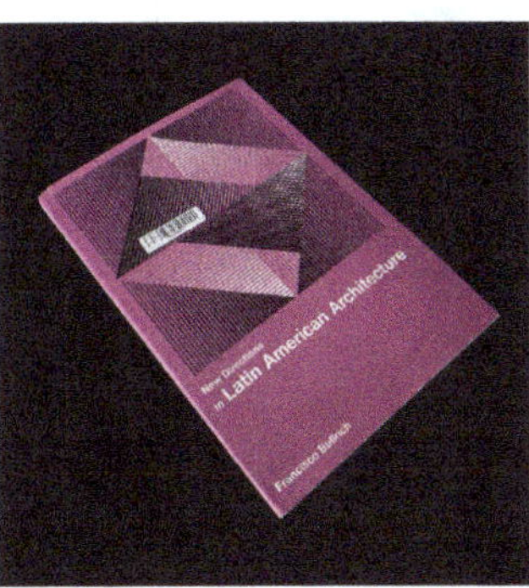
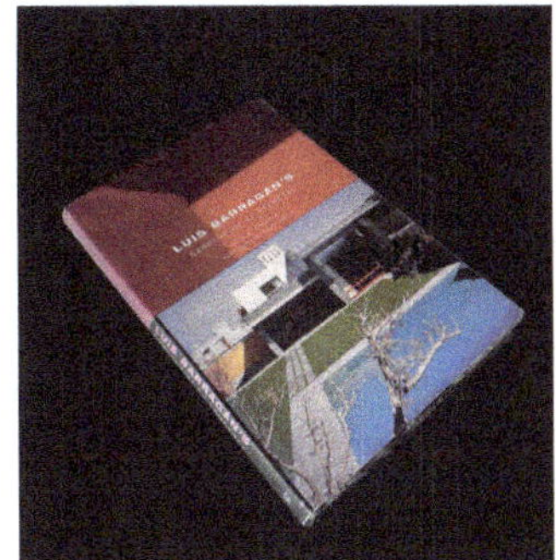

On Ambition

The assignment was exciting (and still is): compiling a library
of modern and contemporary architecture of Latin America. A
question quickly arose: how to approach this titanic challenge?
To begin with, none of our members are architecture or art
historians and although in the group there are architects from
Argentina, Peru, Bolivia, Mexico, Uruguay, and Chile (and even
Belgium) we were missing several other countries where we
did not have a foothold on the understanding of their architecture history. Another aspect also surfaced, should we make a
list of the 'must have' books per country or should we aim to
find common interests between countries? Should we group
these common interests as themes such as exiled architects,
shell structures, informal settlements, building typologies,
architecture education or chronologically, by trends of building
technologies? We began the project with the enthusiasm that
this list would be the first that would be fair regarding gender
balance and the first that would include countries normally
minimized or ignored in standard surveys of Latin America.
In an ideal world it would also be the first to simultaneously
include in it criticism, landscape and urbanism in its catalogue.
Finally, the list should include lesser-known architects to balance the prevalence of the untouchable masters.

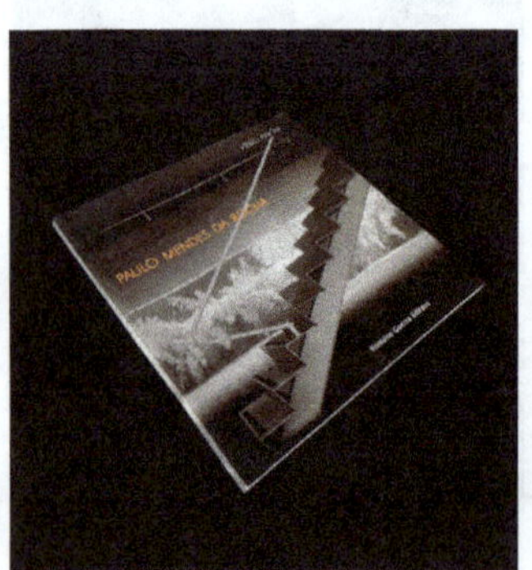
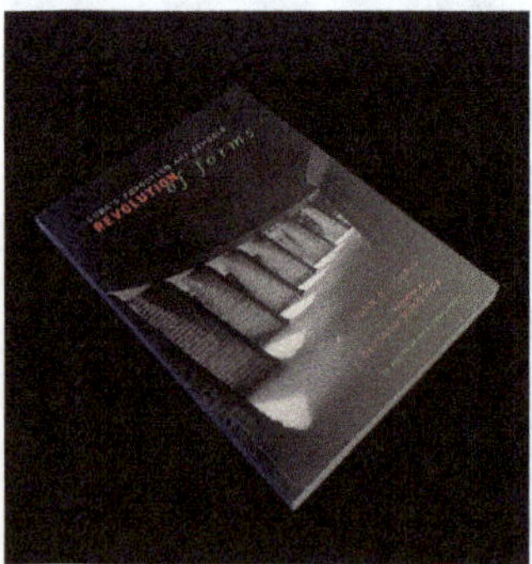
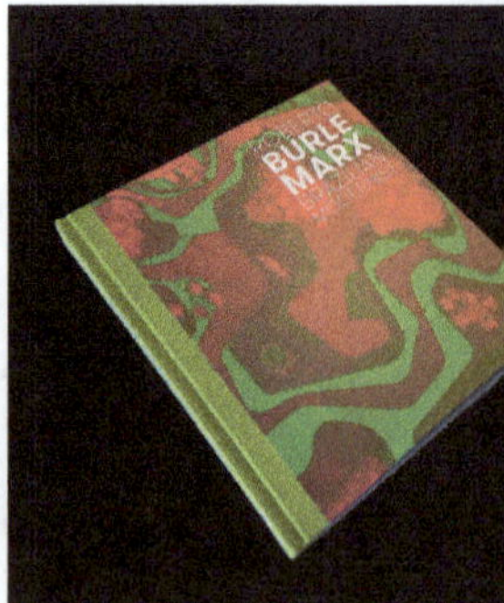

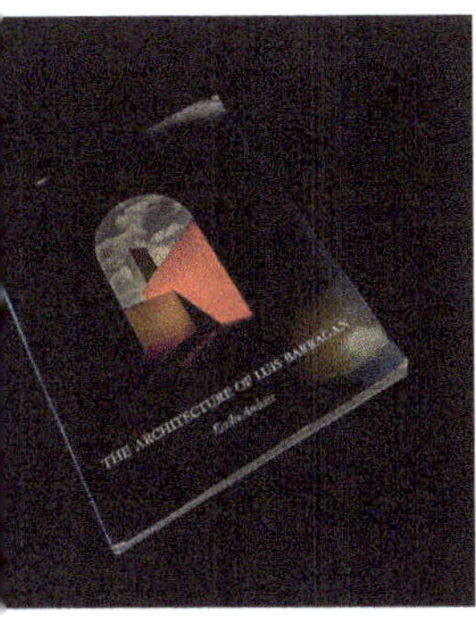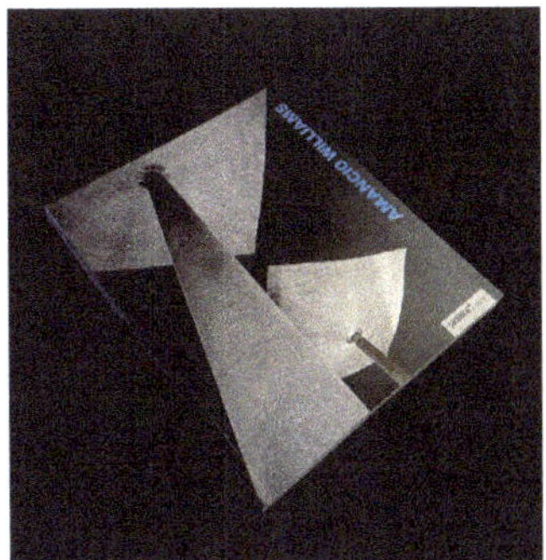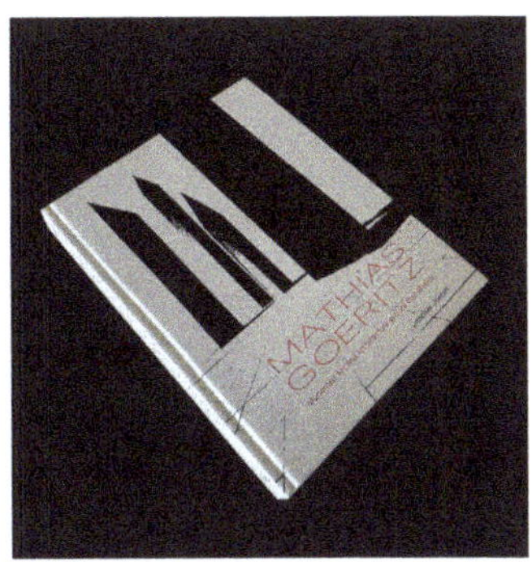

4.   The platform *Arqui-tectura*, sister company of *Archdaily,* shared it in its platform that reaches thousands of people. It also appeared in the national newspaper Clarín, in Argentina and the Instagram platform *Arqpedia*.

On Approaching the Task

It soon became clear that the task at hand was beyond our means. No matter how many hours dedicated to this project, we would never be able to give a fair overview of the bibliography of this great region of the world. We therefore decided to tackle this knowledge gap by two supporting methods: interviews with experts and a public survey. The public survey asked the user ten key questions in order to get a grasp of the list of books that were deemed essential on the point of view of the user. The questions included which architecture or urbanism book were the most influential in their career, which theory or history book of Latin America were considered essential? What is the best emergent Latin American architecture book? And so on. The survey in principle should gather information from several Latin American countries. Yet, despite the effort of distribution and promotion,[4] the survey did not return massive amounts of information, nor amazing discoveries that we were unfamiliar with. The survey did reveal a big issue: many people left several questions unanswered. Were architecture books so unfamiliar in Latin America? Or was it more that Latin American architects were not as widely read as foreign architects? We can't give a full answer to this, but it is clear that from a popular point of view, architecture books of Latin American architecture were not in the priority list of many architects and students. As a possible reason, we´d like to mention that the way architecture schools started in Latin America also led to a bibliography that privileged Europe, western history and also partly the USA culture, especially in the countries that face the Pacific Ocean or the Caribbean. So, many of us are acquainted with the same readings you could find in any international university, but there is a massive lack of knowledge about the local publications between Latin American countries. We can say now that the online publication trend may be a changing factor on this critical issue.

In parallel and ultimately crucial we began to conduct interviews to experts we considered could be helpful in compiling the bibliography. The list includes the following historians and critics: Ana María Durán Calisto, from Ecuador, who kindly suggested to donate books for the catalogue, Claudia Schmidt, from Argentina, who also took the time to revise and compile our list with the addition of several essential books from her point of view. We had a long talk with Costa Rican architect Álvaro Rojas. We spoke simultaneously to Francisco Díaz and Mario Marchant from Chile. In Mexico we interviewed Alejandro Hernández and Miquel Adrià, from Arquine and the architect and historian Fernanda Canales. Also in connection to Mexican architecture we interviewed the historian Keith L. Eggener, from the USA, who also shared a valuable list of journals and other books sources beyond architecture. From Caracas and Miami we interviewed prof. Henry Rueda, who pinpointed the importance of the petroleum industry in Venezuela, as an entry gate for the USA urbanism and architecture ideas (instead of the most common European influence in Latin America). From Peru we had a long session with 94 years-old Adolfo Córdova, one of the key figures of modern architecture from Peru. Pablo Vallejo Urresta, from Quito, Ecuador, talked to us of the publications as a vestige, that shows a map that eventually lets you see a broader context. From Brazil we interviewed the photographer Leonardo Finotti and the former editor of A+U Brazil, Bianca Antunes. Also in Brazil, through Leonardo we got in touch with the young historians Fernando Lara and Luis Carranza who spent a long time explaining us their own trajectory to compile the most complete recent survey on modern architecture in the region. Through them, we arrived to the Colombian historian Felipe Hernández. We also interviewed 2013 Sao Paulo's Biennale curator Ligia Nobre, from Brazil, Guillermo Kliczkowsky (CP67 editorial) and Fernando Diez (Summa+ magazine) from Argentina, and Felipe Mesa from Colombia. As mentioned earlier, we consider this a living project, so we still aim to enrich the list with several more voices.

Finally, besides our own findings we found a few key bibliographical lists which were highly useful to determine the essential library. These included the one published at the

5.   Fernando González Gortázar. *La arquitectura mexicana del siglo 20*. Mexico City: Consejo Nacional para la Cultura y las Artes, 1996.
6.   Historian Luis Carranza mentions the key role of the magazine *Tolteca* as a way to promote modern architecture in Mexico. See: Luis Carranza. *Architecture as Revolution: Episodes in the History of Modern Mexico. Roger Fullington Series in Architecture*. Austin: University of Texas Press, 2010.
7.   Luis Carranza and Fernando Luiz Lara. *Modern Architecture in Latin America*. Austin: University of Texas Press, 2014.

Museum of Modern Art of New York – MoMA, *Latin America in Construction: Architecture 1955-1980* and the Oxford bibliographies on modern architecture in Latin America and per country, in various cases. For the specific case of Mexico, the bibliographical essay by historian Louise Noelle, published at the book *La Arquitectura Mexicana del Siglo 20* was also very useful.[5]

On Readability

Although the budget was limited, this did not stop us for aiming at compiling the most useful or interesting books. We have given priority to English written books since the books are to be read in China but in many cases, key books remain only written in Spanish or Portuguese. Although it´s of great importance, we have not included architecture books that cover worldwide history of modern architecture since we assume Beijing University already has them on their bookshelves. Another aspect that the list does not contain for the moment is the extensive catalogue of magazines. For some countries this is not only a massive source of information, but many times, the only one. This is the case, for example, of the magazine *El Arquitecto Peruano* in Peru, *Trama* in Ecuador, or the magazine *Archivos de Arquitectura Antillana,* from Dominican Republic. In other countries, it remains essential to accompany the scarce presence of books by the vital presence of academic or independent magazines, for example, *Notas CPAU, Anales de Arquitectura UC, Summa+* and recently, *Revista PLOT*, in Argentina, *Boletín del Centro de Investigaciones Históricas y Estéticas*, from the Universidad Central de Venezuela, *Habitat,* from Brazil. From Mexico remains key to include *Arquitectura Mexico* and also the more established magazine *Arquine*.[6]

On Defining What is Latin America

When we were interviewing historians, the first recurring question was: what is the definition of Latin America? In many of their surveys clearly demarked this as a way to establish a clear methodology. For example, in the above-mentioned book of Fernando Lara and Luis Carranza[7] they include Teddy Cruz sharp observation that Latin America begins at the line of the so-called Political Equator, approximately at the 30°N parallel, separating the USA from Mexico. This is helpful about the Caribbean, where countries like Surinam or Belize, although belonging to the continent, because of their different language,

8. Supersudaca. *Proyecto Papel Latino.* Interview with Fernando Lara and Luis Carranza, 2020.
9. The list could be extensive but includes the work of Oscar Niemeyer, Ricardo Legorreta, Jorge Silvetti, Mario Gandelsonas, Diana Agrest and, more recently, Juan Lucas Young to mention some.
10. Juan Pedro Posani. "Por una historia latinoamericana de la arquitectura moderna latinoamericana." *Boletin 9 del Centro de Investigaciones Históricas y Estéticas,* Facultad de Arquitectura y Urbanismo de la Universidad Central de Venezuela (April, 1968): 187.
11. Claudia Schmidt. *Las "Américas Latinas": invenciones desde la historiografía de la arquitectura .*
12. Supersudaca. *Proyecto Papel Latino.* Interview with Claudia Schmidt, 2020.
13. Ibid.
14. Supersudaca. *Proyecto Papel Latino.* Interview with Pablo Vallejo Urresta, 2020.
15. Henry-Russell Hitchcock. *Latin American architecture since 1945.* New York: Museum of Modern Art, 1955, 27.

have remained mostly disconnected from the culture of Latin Americans. What about Los Angeles, which has the second biggest Mexican population? They finally arrive to a practical proposal, their boundary is geographical: architecture built in Latin America, which also includes buildings done in the region by Le Corbusier, Richard Neutra, Mies van der Rohe and John Lautner, among others[8] and not covering the architecture production of Latin American architects building or writing abroad.[9] Carranza and Lara's approach is based on the hypothesis that for the first time we are able to build up a Latin American narrative as the previously disconnected countries started to build up in recent decades several cultural and institutional links. This is a drastic change as the first attempt to build up a proper methodology of a historiography developed by Juan Pedro Posani concluded that "the history of modern architecture in Latin America is and has to be integrated by the particular histories of each of its countries that define it."[10] Yet Claudia Schmidt reminds us that placing an overall thematic covering national histories in a way returns us to the European vision of the new world. She also sees a clear dividing line between the Spanish speaking countries and Brazil.[11] Above all she insists on revising who wrote the documents, where the historian is positioned geographically and culturally speaking, who are his/her contacts.[12] Yet another more subtly but important factor occurs with the assumption that Latin America belongs to the periphery. In this logic, it is expected that the centre (Europe-USA) produces and the periphery rebounds it.[13] Furthermore with the beginning, especially of critical regionalism in the 80's, it became almost compulsory to expect "peripheric" architecture from the "periphery". According to Pablo Vallejo Urresta from Ecuador "from the beginning they (centre) place us on the periphery and demand a peripheral response from us."[14]

On How the Western Historians Registered Architecture from Latin America

It is well known that western based architecture historians have minimized, neglected or mocked the role of Latin American contribution to the modern movement. It is usually an Anglocentric view of the world that occurs also in other parts of culture worldwide and it is expected that the world merely echoes what has been thought in the so called west. Recalling the Argentinean architect Amancio Williams, the historian Henri-Russell Hitchcock famously mentioned in the first survey of Latin American architecture catalogue of MoMA[15] that "for

16. Supersudaca. *Proyecto Papel Latino*. Interview with Claudia Schmidt, 2020.
17. Siegfried Giedion. *Space, time and architecture. The growth of a new tradition*. 3rd edition. Cambridge: Harvard University Press, 1959.
18. Leonardo Benevolo. *History of Modern Architecture*. 2 volumes. Cambridge: The MIT Press, 1977.
19. Ibid.
20. Apparently, Le Corbusier sketched the building over a photograph that Lucio Costa had sent him and included it in his *Complete Works* to claim authorship. See: Carranza and Lara. *Modern Architecture in Latin America*. Le Corbusier again faced Oscar Niemeyer for the design of United Nations headquarters and repeated the trick to claim sole authorship by evidently altering and backdating his sketches. See also: Martin Filler. *Makers of Modern Architecture*. Vol. II. New York: New York Review Books, 2013.
21. In the last edition of Benevolo from 1999 there is a complete chapter on Latin America covering many countries, although this is not written by him but by the Catalan architecture critic Joseph Maria Montaner.
22. Udo Kultermann. *Architekten der Dritten Welt. Bauen zwischen Tradition und Neubeginn*, 1988.
23. Eric Hobsbawm. *The Age of Extremes*. London: Vintage Books, 1996.
24. Kenneth Frampton. *Modern Architecture, a Critical History*. 3rd edition. London: Thames and Hudson, 1992.

the visitor from the north cannot help being stuck by the fact that leading architect is named Williams", despite the fact that the 'Williams' have been in Argentina for few generations.[16] Siegfried Giedion, the author of the first comprehensive book of the emerging movement *Space, Time and Architecture*[17] up to the third revised edition of 1959 gave no mention to the region, although not only Latin America was absent, Asia, Oceania and Africa were also missing. Leonardo Benevolo's *History of Modern Architecture*[18] first published in 1960 in Italian and translated to English in 1966, includes in the last chapter called *New International Field*, three projects done by Brazilian architects. He opens the chapter by stating that "at the beginning of the Second World War the modern movement had affected countries throughout the world, but what happened outside Europe and America was only a consequence of the European and American experiments already described".[19] The projects he includes for this chapter in more detail are Brazil's Ministry of Education (1935), the housing complex of Pedregulho, by Eduardo Affonso Reidy (1950), and the new capital Brasilia (1958). For the Ministry of Education, Benevolo credits Le Corbusier leading authorship although lately this has been disputed.[20] Nevertheless, Benevolo acknowledges that this was the first realization of a building type of which Le Corbusier had been thinking for some time. Before describing the recently built project of Brasilia, Benevolo sensibly introduces the critical voice of Max Bill who, in a lecture in Sao Paulo in 1953, warned architecture in Brazil stands in danger of falling into a parlous state of anti-social academism. Benevolo nevertheless concludes the part of Brasilia with an optimistic remark mentioning that the experiment involves present day planning thought and in various ways anticipates its possible developments.[21]

Right at the beginning of the 80's, the tone of condescendence started to shift.[22] This anticipated the view of the famous British historian Eric Hobsbawm that claimed that the shift from Europe after World War II became most evident in architecture, where the best examples appeared in Brazil and Mexico.[23] The British architecture historian Kenneth Frampton took a leading role in 1980 change of direction with his famous essay *Critical Regionalism: modern architecture and cultural identity*[24] that appeared in his *Modern Architecture, a critical history*. In this essay he has included a series of architects who were able to reinterpret the modern vocabulary through the use of specific solutions that are not simply vernacular and necessarily local and, in this way, they were able to resist

25. For a more critical reception of the essay see: Keith Eggener. "Placing Resistance: A Critique of Critical Regionalism." *Journal of Architectural Education*, 2002.
26. Frampton. *Modern Architecture*.
27. William Curtis (1982). *Modern Architecture since 1900*. New York: Phaidon Press, 1987.

global culture.[25] He begins his essay with the Danish architect Jørn Utzon, moving then to the Spanish architect Josep Antoni Coderch, the Portuguese Álvaro Siza and then to the Mexican architect Luis Barragán. Regarding the latter, he has included two excepts of his Pritzker award speech. More lighthearted, he mentions Brazilians Oscar Niemeyer and Affonso Reidy, Argentinians Amancio Williams and Clorindo Testa and finally, Carlos Raúl Villanueva, from Venezuela. The list continues back to European sources, including the Italian Carlo Scarpa, the Swedish Sverre Fehn, and the Greek Dimitris Pikionis, to finally conclude with the Japanese Tadao Ando. In a field that has been exclusively dominated by European and American architects, it was a welcoming move that finally placed at the same level the emerging relevance of alternative ways of addressing the modern project. The book has seen several editions, but the fifth edition (which by the way, got rid of the subtitle "a critical history") adds a remarkable number of pages to the original book. Out of 351 of the original, the new one has 642, not including notes. The addition aims to give a wider account of the history of modern architecture across the world, with a chapter on the Americas, where the USA and Canada share space with Colombia, Mexico, Peru, Venezuela, Argentina, Uruguay and Chile. The extension seems titanic but paradoxically, instead of bringing a new reading or multiple readings of the unfolding of the history, it merely becomes more inclusive geographically. His story remains on the same paradigm, modern forms originating in Europe and the USA, being absorbed by the periphery.[26]

William Curtis *Modern Architecture since 1900*, from 1982, also devotes a few essays to the issue of regional identity.[27] Yet, as Benevolo before him also stated, he confirms that in certain countries in Western Europe, in the USA and some parts of the Soviet Union, the modern movement in its formative years was an intellectual property. We have to wait until the post-war years, according to Curtis, to witness some experiments that were undertaken in Mexico and South America. Bypassing the renown modern architects of Mexico such as Mario Pani or Juan O'Gorman, he concentrates on Luis Barragán, as Frampton did before him, but he warns of the dangers of oversimplifying the formula of critical regionalism set up by Frampton. Curtis states that to speak of the fusion of regionalism and the international style, of the vernacular and Le Corbusier, is to trivialize Barragán. In touch with the tragic vein in Mexican cultural history, his style expressed an archetypical mood. About lesser-known architects, at the end

28. Udo Kultermann. *Architekten der Dritten Welt*. Bauen zwischen: Tradition und Neubeginn, 1988.
29. Charles Jencks. *Modern Movements in architecture*. Milwaukee: Anchor Press, 1973.
30 Alan Colquhoun. *Modern Architecture*. Oxford: Oxford University Press, 2002.
31. Jean-Louis Cohen. *The Future of Architecture since 1889*. New York: Phaidon Press, 2012.
32. Martin Filler. *Makers of Modern Architecture*. 2 volumes. New York: New York Review of Books, 2013.
33. Oscar Niemeyer. *My architecture*. Rio de Janeiro: Editora Revan, 2000, 29.

of the 80's appeared the book *Architecture of the third world*, by the German historian Udo Kultermann, including architects from regions previously ignored, such as Ricardo Porro, from Cuba, Fernando González Gortázar, from Mexico, Joaquim Guedes, from Brazil or Mario Pérez de Arce Lavín.[28] Yet, much before Frampton or Curtis recognition of Latin America contribution to the modern movement is the role Charles Jencks gave to squatter movements of Peru in the activist and intuitive trend, right in between metabolism and archigram, emphasizing barriadas non-hierarchical self-organization methods.[29] Alan Harold Colquhoun sober *Modern Architecture*,[30] of 2002, mentions the team of Brazil's Ministry of Education that included Affonso Reidy, Oscar Niemeyer, Lucio Costa and Jorge Moreira as an outstanding building done in collaboration with Le Corbusier. Colquhoun mentions that this building better addressed Le Corbusier ideas due to its location that did not have to reference old historical towns. Furthermore, he considers it the first glass skyscraper office building to be built using Mies van der Rohe and Le Corbusier principles. Despite of this exceptional entry, Latin America is completely absent from the rest of the book. More recently, younger historians like Jean-Louis Cohen have aimed to be more inclusive and less biased than the above-mentioned historians and yet again Latin America is barely present in Cohen's timeline: out of 474 subchapters, there is only three subchapters on Brazil and only two on Latin America. In both subchapters of Latin America, he reminds us that in most cases either the architects were trained in Europe and/or have worked for Le Corbusier.[31] There are exceptions that contest the singular vision of Europe and the US as epicentres of creation. For example, the *New York Review of Books* architecture critic Martin Filler in *Makers of Modern Architecture* has included a convincing argument that the leading designer of United Nations headquarters was the young Niemeyer and not Le Corbusier, despite the later claims.[32] To complicate things even more, Niemeyer has also left a sour statement regarding the building in question. According to him, after his own design was chosen unanimously, Le Corbusier launched a last attempt at mixing up his own design with that of Niemeyer´s, compromising the Brazilian's design intentions. "I have nothing else to say about what have happened while we studied the United Nations project. But it does not impede me to feel a bit sad, when I see the photo of the built complex. Oh... the United Nations Square that I designed is missing so much!"[33]

34. See his own motivations in <https://helio-pinon.org/memoria_personal>.
35. Toyo Ito, Xavier Guzman and Victor Jimenez. *Casa O'Gorman 1929*. London: RM Publishers, 2015.
36. Francisco Bullrich. *New Directions in Latin American Architecture*. New York: George Braziller Incorporated, 1969.
37. Supersudaca. *Proyecto Papel Latino*. Interview with Claudia Shmidt, 2020.

A peculiar case or readdressing the Eurocentric perspective is the Catalan architect and lecturer Helio Piñón, who had the hunch that Latin America had very good architecture but acknowledged that he ignored its true dimensions. He went on to write several monographs on the Brazilians Paulo Mendes da Rocha (2003) and Eduardo de Almeida (2005), the Uruguayan Raúl Sichero (2002) and the Argentinian Mario Roberto Álvarez (2002).[34] Also, Toyo Ito, in co-authorship with Xavier Guzmán Urbiola and Victor Jiménez, wrote a book on the house of O'Gorman, from 1929.[35] Perhaps this list will grow in time.

On How the Latin American Historians Registered Latin American Architecture

If the view of Latin America from European or Anglo-American historians has been marginal, the view that Latin Americans have of themselves is even more self-deprecating. Ignorance, humbleness or self-pity in the post-war period was followed in the 80's by a harsh division between who is Latin American and who follows global trends. Also, within Latin America countries outside the editorial powerhouses of Brazil, Argentina and Mexico have also complained of their peripheral role within the Latin American periphery. Fortunately, the recent tone is more nuanced, not precisely celebratory, but fully aware that the region did achieve several critical works that do deserve more attention. In this sense, we expect a whole new generation of historians from Latin America and abroad that will be able to compensate for the neglect and disdain the region has encountered in most of the 20 and the current century.

To prove the lack of self-interest by Latin Americans, we actually have to wait until 1969 for the first survey of Latin American architecture by a local author: *New directions in Latin American architecture*, written by Argentinian Francisco Bullrich.[36] This is almost fifteen years after Hitchcock exhibition catalogue of MoMA's *Latin American architecture since 1945*. Although the title is about Latin America, Bullrich disregards the concept of Latin American right at the beginning. This was not surprising as he had disregarded the concept of Argentinian architecture before by asking what has Peru to do with Argentina.[37] The book is a provocative, concise and intriguing assemblage of affinities that concentrates on a few aspects Bullrich considered essential at the time. What is also special and different from Hitchcock´s catalogue is that Latin America

38 Roberto Segre (editor). *America Latina en su arquitectura*. Madrid: Siglo Veintiuno, 1975.
39. Roberto Segre, born in Italy and Argentinian by nationality, moved to Cuba after the revolution and resided there for nearly 30 years before moving to Brazil. Segre became one of the key historians of revolutionary architecture in Cuba.
40. Ramón Gutiérrez. *Arquitectura y urbanismo en Iberoamérica*. Madrid: Ediciones Cátedra, 1983.

is not presented by countries or chronologically but through autonomous themes. In retrospect, the book seems rather incomplete and missing a few key figures such as Lina Bo Bardi or Barragán (that would be recognized much later), while promoting other architects that have ended up being less essential in retrospect. In 1975, with the support of UNESCO, Roberto Segre edits the book *America Latina en su arquitectura*.[38] Following the Marxist school,[39] the book places architecture history in the context of social, political, economic and technological developments in the region. It focuses on urgent themes such as fast urbanization, poverty, rural under-development and social awareness. The tone is serious and it does not aim to showcase the region as an example to follow, on the contrary, it alerts to the multiple challenges the region faces and calls for architects and urban planners to take a much committed role to the future of the region. Especially the chapter *Current crisis of Latin American architecture*, by Ramón Vargas Salguero and Rafael López Rangel gives an outlook that calls for a much radical position of architects in the face of environmental and social challenges posed by the effects of capitalism. The book once again overlooks the production of several architects and countries in the region. It took until 1983 to see the appearance of *Arquitectura y urbanismo en Iberoamérica*,[40] the most complete Latin Amer-ican architecture survey written by the Argentinian architect and historian Ramón Gutiérrez. The book covers architecture and urbanism since the Europeans arrived to Latin America and until the 1980's, reserving more than 200 pages to the development of architecture and urbanism in the 20th cen-tury. Besides its impressive scope is the sharp eye to detect emergent architects from several countries and link them to an overall narrative of an architecture that responds to social, technological and cultural themes. At times, the book is highly critical and dismissive of several architecture projects that don't follow this thread. The book gives a positive outlook to the most promising examples of Latin America at the time, many of which were hardly known beyond their country's bor-ders. The list is extensive: Jaime Larraín, Osvaldo Larraín and Diego Balmaceda, from Chile, who won the design of Villa Frei neighborhood, that was finished in 1966, the Bolivian Gustavo Medeiros Anaya, the Uruguayan (residing in Ecuador) Gilberto Gatto Sobral and the Guatemalan architect Roberto Aycinena Echeverría, who designed the Centro Cívico in the capital. The historian also reveals the rather anonymous yet crucial engi-neers such as the Brazilian Joaquim Maria Moreira Cardozo,

41. Ibid., 603.
42. Ibid., 611.
43. Ibid., 646.
44. Ibid., 644.
45. Ibid., 643.
46. Felipe Hernández. *Beyond modernists masters: contemporary architecture in Latin America.* Basel: Birkhäuser Verlag, 2010.

who worked closely with Niemeyer in both shells design and the palaces landing elegance of the columns in Brasilia. While this is highly appreciated it is also tempting to dismiss some of its severe judgements, especially when its tone becomes that of a preacher, namely all good architecture examples are always accompanied by a highly Christian oriented scale value, where humbleness and modesty appeared as the ultimate quality while wrong projects come along with intentions of vanity or imported technologies. His position is deliberate as he tries to distance from the dominant position where Latin America becomes "the fertile ground for experimenting foreign novelties while we scorn internal creativity."[41] Perhaps as a provocation, most well-known architects are also diminished. Barragán's is not that relevant as his architecture is, limited to merely three actors: client, artist-architect and the client.[42] Other architects that later became quite relevant are merely or negatively mentioned: Lina Bo Bardi's Sao Paulo´s Museum of Art (MASP), according to the historian, is merely a copy of Affonso Reidy's Museum of Modern Art in Rio de Janeiro,[43] while João Filgueras Lima (also known as Lelé)'s hospital in Brasilia is a mockery of Niemeyer's expressive force.[44] Mendes da Rocha´s name is not even mentioned when referring to Brazil's Pavilion in Osaka in 1970 as if his approach was merely an opportunistic move to merely be trendy.[45] Yet the book is essential as the first that aims to understand the relationships and emergence of figures such as Rogelio Salmona, in Colombia, who builds up on the previous steps of his colleagues dealing with brick, climate and landscape in Bogota.

In a similar but more inclusive line is the attempt to shift the focus from lesser known architects and places as in the book *Beyond Modernist masters: contemporary architecture in Latin America*, by Colombian historian Felipe Hernández.[46] But is not only new names he is after, but new agendas, so the book is organized around interventions on city's edge, public spaces, poverty, and the way architecture relates to the landscape. The book gives attention to the specific spatial and cultural challenges of the region. Specifically, it is the inhabitants or users of architecture that will bring new readings of the performance of architecture. Felipe Hernández begins with this quest in his PhD *Architecture and Transculturation* following on the findings of Cuban anthropologist Fernando Ortiz. The term *transculturation* is opposed to the then dominant *acculturation* to define the areas of the periphery that had lost their culture due to colonization. Transculturation argues that there are several layers latent and that there is not just

47. Supersudaca. *Proyecto Papel Latino*. Interview with Felipe Hernández, 2021.

48. Barry Bergdoll, Carlos Eduardo Comas, Jorge Francisco Liernur, and Patricio del Real. *Latin America in Construction. Architecture 1955-1980*. New York: The Museum of Modern Art, 2015.

49. Supersudaca. *Proyecto Papel Latino*. Interview with Miquel Adria, 2020.

50. Supersudaca. *Proyecto Papel Latino*. Interview with Claudia Shmidt, 2020.

51. Carranza and Lara. *Modern Architecture in Latin America*.

52. Supersudaca. *Proyecto Papel Latino*. Interview with Fernando Lara and Luis Carranza, 2020.

53. Supersudaca. *Proyecto Papel Latino*. Interview with Ana María Duran, 2020. See also: Clara Irina Rivero. "Triple Alliance in Reverse." PhD diss., University of Texas, 2016 <http://hdl.handle.net/2152/61483>. The argument is that architects from Argentina, Uruguay and Brazil support building modernity in Paraguay.

54. Ibid.

55. Esther Baum Born. "The New Architecture in Mexico." *The Architectural Record*. New York: William Morrow & Co., 1937.

56. Roberto Segre. *Diez años de arquitectura en Cuba revolucionária*. Havana: Ediciones Unión, 1970.

the European colonizer and one deleted culture, but multiple vibrant local cultures, including the influence of the African slave's descendants.[47]

In the last years there has been multiple books on the region modern architecture. The exhibition *Latin America in Construction*, held at MoMA in 2015, and its respective catalogue[48] caused a stirred in different parts of Latin America. Miquel Adrià, the director of the Mexican magazine *Arquine* pointed out that the history shown in the catalogue has been astutely manipulated by Jorge Francisco Liernur to benefit Argentina[49], while Claudia Schmidt remarks that the history of Brazil written by Carlos Eduardo Comas does not mention any connection to Latin America at all.[50] As the show was being prepared, a parallel project was about to occur, the book of Fernando Lara and Luis Carranza[51]. While the MoMA catalogue and the book of Ramón Gutiérrez are organized by countries, the authors of *Modern Architecture in Latin America* embed in several chapters' stories that connect the region diagonally. The effort makes sense, according to the authors, as the region slowly transforms from an archipelago of countries with no connection in the 19th century to an increasingly linked region in the 20th century.[52] These bridges occurred through several milestone efforts of curators, critics and architecture schools, but also through inner migration, like the Uruguayan and Argentinian architects migrating to Ecuador or Venezuela.[53] Echoing Bullrich, Lara and Carranza disregard the concept of Latin American architecture, especially in reaction to the historians of the older generation such as Marina Waisman and Ramón Gutiérrez, who deliberately exclude or harshly criticize those that are not contributing to the so called Latin American identity. They disagree with Francisco Liernur view that modern architecture can be neither regional nor national. Instead, they claim "modern architecture has universal ambitions but local challenges, therefore its architecture responses are both regional and universal."[54]

On the Canon

There are several types of books which we believe should be present. Above all, there are the seminal books, those that were ahead of time to report on the subjects they were contemporary with. This, for example, includes "The New Architecture in Mexico," by Esther Baum Born, written in 1937[55] or the first survey of modern architecture in revolutionary Cuba, by Roberto Segre.[56] There were books which everyone wanted

57. Hitchcock. *Latin America Architecture since 1945.*
58. Bergdoll, Comas, Liernur and del Real. *Latin America in construction.*
59. Philip Goodwin. *Brazil Builds: Architecture New and Old, 1652–1942.* New York: The Museum of Modern Art. 1943.
60. Emilio Ambasz. *The Architecture of Luis Barragán.* New York: The Museum of Modern Art, 1976.
61. Fernanda Canales and Alejandro Hernández. *100×100+ Arquitectos del siglo 20 en Mexico.* Mexico City: Arquine, 2011.
62. Ibid.
63. Ibid.
64. Gortázar. *La arquitectura mexicana del siglo 20.*
65. Supersudaca. *Proyecto Papel Latino.* Interview with Fernanda Canales, 2020.
66. Supersudaca. *Proyecto Papel Latino.* Interview with Francisco Diaz and Mario Marchant, 2020.

to be part of such as the two catalogues of MoMA, first *Latin American architecture since 1945*[57] and the latest *Latin America in Construction 1955-1980.*[58] Also published by MoMA is the first survey of Brazilian architecture *Brazil Builds: Architecture New and Old, 1652–1942*[59] and the first monograph of MoMA dedicated to an architect, that of Luis Barragán.[60]

As the canon becomes more solidified, the chances of revising who are the key figures become more challenging. Nevertheless, historians play a critical role in this regard. To counter the usual glorification of the already famous architects, a less hierarchical approach was attempted by Fernanda Canales and Alejandro Hernández in *100x100+ Arquitectos del siglo 20 en México*[61] where names of architects are ordered alphabetically. In this way, architects from different levels of recognition and location were placed next to each other, creating interesting juxtapositions. Fernando Lara and Luis Carranza have also deliberately placed at equal level renown architects such as Luis Barragán or Oscar Niemeyer with less known yet equally important figures according to them such as Sérgio Bernardes, João Filgueiras Lima (Lelé) or Pedro Ramírez Vázquez.[62] It is not only the drastic difference of representation between the so called masters and the lesser known architects, it is also the usually overwhelming coverage of the capital cities, while little is known from arangprovincial cities such as Cordoba, Recife, Curitiba, Guadalajara etc.[63] This last city for example is passionately defended as the capital of regionalism in Mexico by Fernando González Gortázar[64] in a book that has been considered essential to understand Mexican architecture history.[65] Another factor that is quite absent from the canon is the role of certain architects that were politically supportive of the left-wing president Salvador Allende, in Chile. For example, according to Mario Marchant and Francisco Díaz, two almost invisible architects until now are Miguel Lawner and Fernando Castillo Velasco, mainly due to their political affiliations but also to the lack of research of the work of public institutions as opposed to the heroic lonely architect.[66] Finally, countries like Bolivia, Honduras, Guatemala, El Salvador, Paraguay remain almost unknown to historians of modern architecture. This remains an urgent task to be addressed by future historians.

On Achieving Depth

After several books have concentrated mostly on architecture monographs full of blown-up colour photos, there is a current need for a different type of approach that goes beyond this reading and explores in depth themes that were considered exhausted. An interesting approach was tried with the catalogue of the exhibition *Cruelty and Utopia*, edited by Jean-François Lejeune,[67] where key historians and writers deal with one potentially fatal issue of Latin America architecture history, that of achieving the modern utopia despite its shacky foundations of society, political freedom, equality and technological resources.[68] In this regard, the books that deserve attention are those where historians have carefully revisited specific projects and have discovered a completely refreshing look. Such an example is the case of John Loomis approach to the mostly unknown and abandoned art schools in Cuba, where through a series of interviews with the main actors constructs a very nuanced view of a politically charged subject.[69] In the same vein, *Gardens of El Pedregal,* by Keith Eggener, reveals a much more complex perspective on the connection of architecture and politics, finance, culture and marketing in the volcanic neighbourhood designed by Luis Barragán in the outskirts of Mexico City. Eggener also reminds us on how Mexican architecture cannot be understood without the influence of American architects and vice versa and not necessarily only Europeans.[70] [71] The recently published book *Downward spiral: el helicoide's descent from mall to prison* edited by Celeste Olalquiaga and Lisa Blackmore also puts into perspective how architecture is not only a witness to political and social changes of Caracas but how it actually could be at the center of the discussions on the future of modernity as seen by politicians, investors and architects. There are critical books on Brasilia such as *Lucio Costa: Brasilia's Superquadra*[72] or Luis Carranza's *Architecture as Revolution,*[73] in which he carefully follows Mexican architect Juan O'Gorman disappointment with the way modern architecture was quickly adopted by private investors to speculate and brand a movement he considered was meant to serve the underprivileged classes. Another discovery is the way modern architecture is promoted through the magazine *Tolteca*, therefore leading to conclusions of vested interests on what to promote and what to exclude. Modern architecture per se is not necessarily out of the picture, but it is seen with a different lens. Much as Reyner Banham *Los Angeles: The Architecture of Four Ecologies*[74] we can see in Felipe Hernandez's *Beyond Modernist Masters*[75] a specific lens for the type of architecture that responds precisely Latin American "ecologies": how to build in the edge of the city, how to design for poverty, what is the role of landscape in architecture. On emerging lines of research and quite ahead of Rem

67. Jean-François Lejeune. *Cruelty and Utopia. Cities and Landscapes of Latin America.* New Jersey: Princeton Architectural Press, 2003.
68. Hitchcock points out that with the small exempt from Mexico Latin America does not produce structural steel but neither imports it, timber technology is lacking, while plaster and concrete, and recently mosaic tiles, rein everywhere. See Hitchcock. *Latin American architecture since 1945*, 21.
69. John Loomis. *Revolution of Forms: Cuba's Forgotten Art Schools.* New Jersey: Princeton Architectural Press, 2011.
70. Keith Eggener. *Luis Barrágan's Gardens of El Pedregal*. New Jersey: Princeton Architectural Press, 2001.
71. Alfonso Perez-Mendez. *Las Casas del Pedregal: 1947-1968.* Barcelona: Gustavo Gili, 2007.
72. Farès el-Dahdah. *Lucio Costa: Brasilia's Superquadra.* New York: Prestel Verlag, 2005.
73. Carranza. *Architecture as Revolution.*
74. Reyner Banham. *Los Angeles: The Architecture of Four Ecologies.* Los Angeles: University of California Press, 2009.
75 Felipe Hernandez. *Beyond Modernist Masters. Contemporary Architecture in Latin America.* Basel: Birkhäuser Verlag GmbH, 2010.

76. Felipe Correa. *Beyond the City: Resource Extraction Urbanism in South America*. Austin: University of Texas Press, 2016.
77. Supersudaca. *Proyecto Papel Latino*. Interview with Fernando Luiz Lara and Luis Carranza, 2020.
78. Ibid.
79. Ibid.
80. Carranza and Lara. *Modern Architecture in Latin America*.
81. Clara Porset. *La vida en el arte*. Mexico City: Alias Editorial, 2020.
82. Lina Bo Bardi. *Stones against diamonds*. London: Architectural Association Publications, 2013.
83. Zeuler Rocha Mello de Almeida Lima. *Lina Bo Bardi*. London: Yale University Press, 2019.
84. Fernanda Canales. *Arquitectura en Mexico. 1920-2010*. Fondo Cultural Banamex. 2013.
85. Tatiana Bilbao. *Two Sides of the Border. Reimagining the Region*. Zurich: Lars Müller, 2020.

Koolhaas interest on the countryside, there is the research work of Felipe Correa in *Beyond the City*.[76] Resource extraction urbanism in South America, where modernism is part of the exploitation project of Latin America by mostly North American interests, but also a place where modern architecture experiments, even social utopias could be imagined.

On Female Architects

Since we began the project, we had the naïve illusion that history could be unearthed regarding the scant female presence in architecture books. It will take a bit longer to make that story right, as several female figures are hidden from publications "due to the existing patriarchal system", that fortunately has changed for the good in the last ten years, according to Luis Carranza.[77] The process has just begun and relatively unknown female figures from the past start to emerge. The famous bridge house in Mar de Plata is now credited equally to Delfina Gálvez Bunge and Amancio Williams.[78] The landscape architect from Brazil Mina Klabin Warchavchik is now recognized as a precursor of Burle Marx´s landscape design,[79] but also as the first to introduce cactus plants in modern buildings way ahead of both Burle Marx and Juan O'Gorman.[80] The Cuban designer Clara Porset not only is being recognized for her lasting imprint on Luis Barragán furniture design, but also for her critical writings.[81] This recovery of female architects to Latin American architecture is mostly visible in the work of the Italian-Brazilian Lina Bo Bardi, that in just a few years saw the publication of several books and magazine monographs. Her writings have also been recovered in the book *Stones against diamonds*[82] and a carefully research biography accompanied by projects has been published by Zeuler Rocha Mello de Almeida Lima.[83] The book breaks away with taboos but also carefully constructs the life of a person without idealizing her complex biography. It is clear that her talent is unique but also is revealing that it did not come by a miraculous display of skills. Instead, it shows how small decisions in life and the social network one cultivates could deliver amazing opportunities. In recent years, the presence of female architects in Latin America has become almost a normality. In Mexico, a country famous for its machismo, you have now multiple examples of leading practicing architects such as Frida Escobedo, Gabriela Carrillo, Tatiana Bilbao, Rozana Montiel and Fernanda Canales. The last two are also leading contributors to architecture and urbanism research.[84] [85] The female historians also played a

86. Marina Waisman. *El Interior de la Historia. Historiografía arquitectónica para uso de latinoamericanos.* Bogota: Editorial Escala, 1990.
87. Silvia Arango Cardinal. *Ciudad y arquitectura. Seis generaciones que construyeron la América Latina moderna.* Bogota: Fondo de Cultura Económica, 2012.
88. Fabiola López-Durán. *Eugenics in the garden: transatlantic architecture and the crafting of modernity.* Austin: University of Texas Press, 2018.
89. Supersudaca. *Proyecto Papel Latino.* Interview with Fernanda Canales, 2020.
90. Teodoro González de León. *Lecciones. Escritos reunidos 1966-2016.* Mexico City: El Colegio Nacional, 2016.
91. Juan Borchers. *Institución arquitectónica.* Santiago: Editorial Andrés Bello, 1968.
92. Juan Borchers. *Meta arquitectura.* Santiago: Editora Mathesis, 1975.
93. Supersudaca. *Proyecto Papel Latino.* Interview with Mario Marchant and Francisco Diaz, 2020.
94. Antonio Riggen. *Luis Barragán: escritos y conversaciones.* Madrid: El Croquis Editorial, 2000.
95. Ibid. See interview with Elena Poniatowska.
96. Damián Bayón and Paolo Gasparini. *Panorámica de la arquitectura latino-americana.* Barcelona: Blume/UNESCO, 1977.

leading turning point in defining what is Latin American architecture, especially the Argentinian Marina Waisman's incisive historiographic remarks[86] and the Colombian Silvia Arango's crucial recounting of history of Latin American architecture.[87] Not to mention the emerging talented writers and researchers such as the Venezuelan Fabiola López-Durán,[88] recommended by Ana Maria Duran Calisto.

On Architect's Own Voice

Due to their excessive amount of workload or the lack of training in writing reflections, very few architects have adventured in the task of publishing their thoughts beyond the glossy (and many times self-sponsored) portfolios and books. According to Fernanda Canales[89], an exception in this regard is the written texts of Teodoro González de León.[90] But to write and communicate are not per se an easy task. The theoretical books that Chilean architect Juan Borchers wrote in the late 60's[91] and early 70's[92] are cryptic and therefore difficult to become influential, according to Chilean architect Mario Marchant.[93] Little is known on Barragán writings but some are carefully curated in Antonio Riggen's *Luis Barragán, escritos y conversaciones*.[94] It is important to revisit those texts because, despite the propaganda machine of so called Mexican architecture, Barragán states in conversation with the writer Elena Poniatowska that Mexican architecture does not exist, that the vernacular is a connection to the Mediterranean and the colonial, to Spain, while Mexicans have deleted their connections to the prehispanic cultures.[95] In fact, there is little known of what architects really thought themselves. In that sense, the 1977 pioneering book *Panorámica de la arquitectura latino-americana,* by Damián Bayón, is a jewel, since he is able to give us first hand and without much editing the thoughts of then leading architects such as the Cuban Fernando Salinas, the Uruguayan Eladio Dieste, the Argentinian Clorindo Testa, the Mexican Pedro Ramírez Vázquez, and so on.[96]

On the Impossibility of Balance

The initial aims of maintaining balance between gender and countries as mentioned earlier slowly fell apart as we encountered the amazing disparity of amount of book production from countries such as Mexico, Brazil, Argentina or Colombia compared to the rather scarce books presence on books about Peru or Venezuela. Other countries such as Bolivia, Ecuador,

Costa Rica and Panama are just recently starting to produce architecture books, while others such as Honduras, Guatemala, Nicaragua and El Salvador lag until today clearly behind regarding the available written documents beyond journals or internet articles. The list of books from a country such as Cuba remains very limited, although much more could be said about the production of architecture from the island. There are several more parts of the puzzle that need to be carefully explored. But we hope this list of books helps the reader to initiate or continue in its exploration of modern architecture culture in Latin America.

Susucumbre

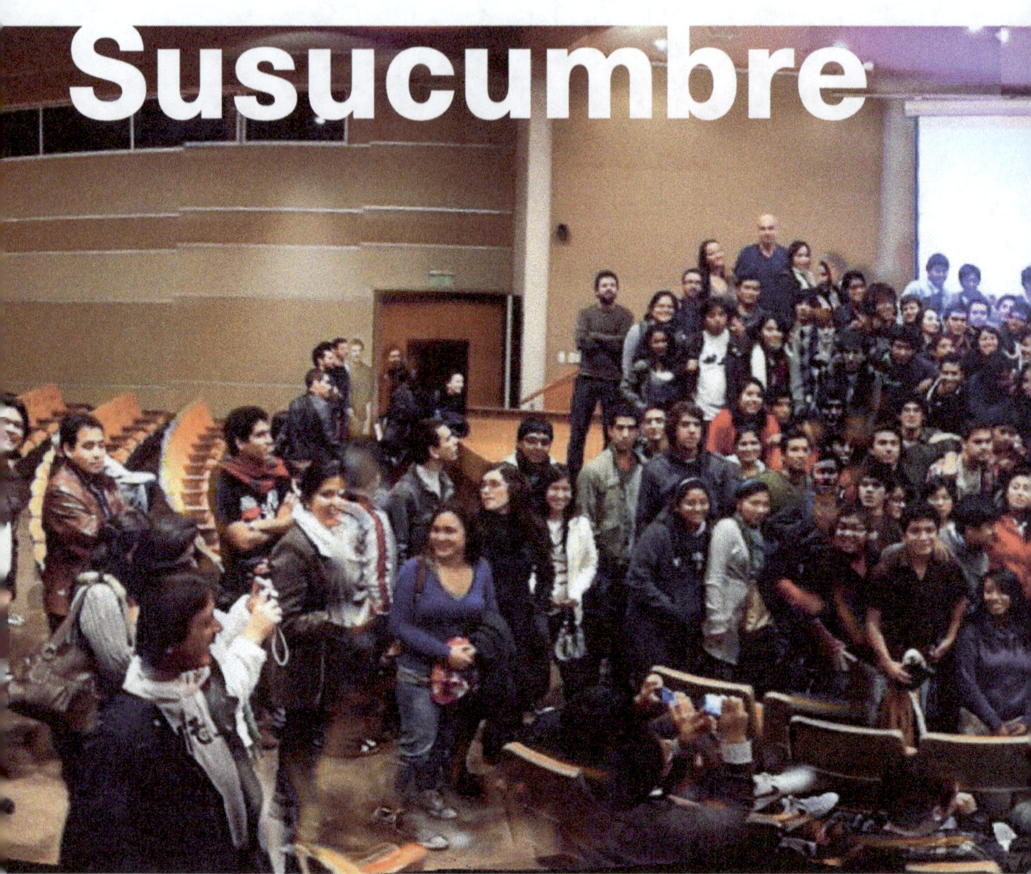

First Day
September 15, 2011

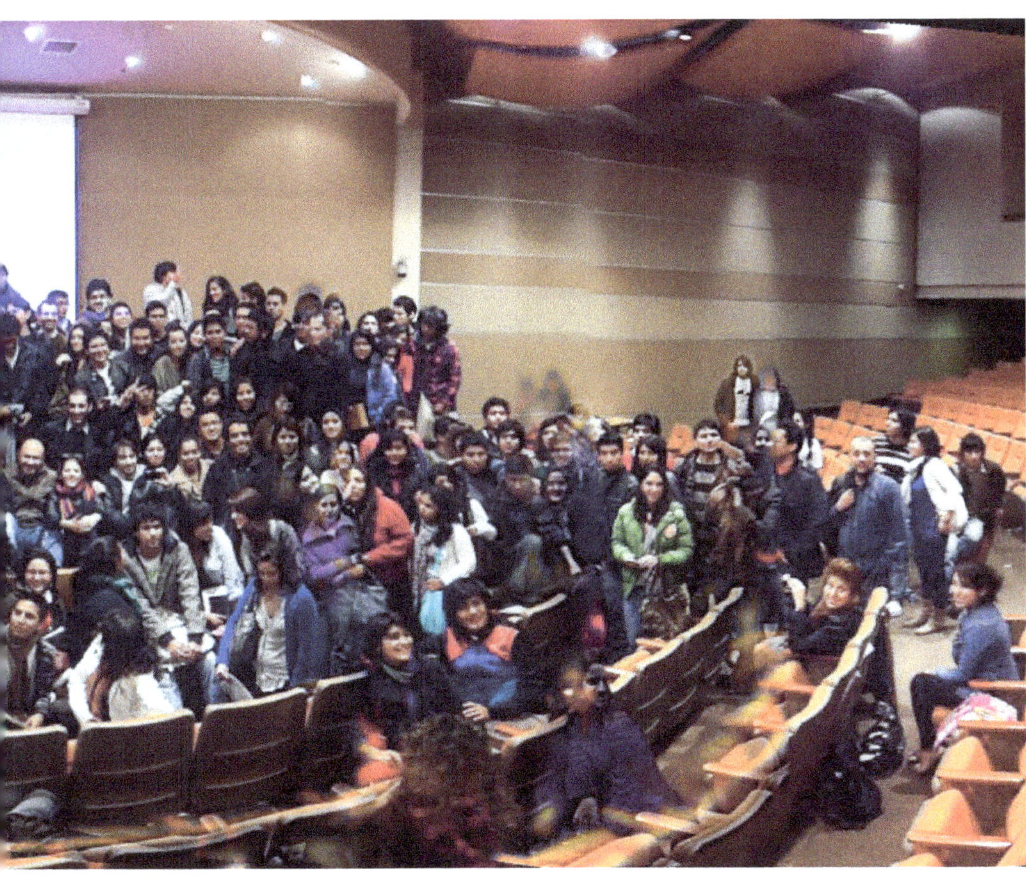

**During the lecture series "Susucumbre" (Supersu-
daca 10 Years Summit) in Lima, two public conversations were held at the end of each session.**

1. "Latin America at the Crossroads," *Architectural Design* 81, no. 3 (May/June 2011), https://bit.ly/3lKqk1o.

2. Supersudaca, "Supersudaca's Asia Stories (aka at Home in the First, Second, Third, Fourth and Fifth Worlds)," *Architectural Design* 81, no. 3 (May/June 2011), 118-123, https://bit.ly/3GCm3qF.

Supersudaca We want to talk openly about the role of the architect, about what is the field in which we should operate. What are the boundaries that define that what we do is no longer architecture? Must we remain focused in making buildings? Or is it that there are more ways of doing architecture and that society needs us as experts in *spatializing* ideas and giving scale to things? We have invited three friends to this conversation: Enrique Bonilla, architect and director of the University of Lima; Jorge Villacorta, art critic, curator, geneticist biologist, and one of the most interesting minds we have around here; and Mariana Leguía, young architect working with a broad spectrum of what is architecture and who has recently edited for the British magazine *Architectural Digest*, one of the most interesting publications on the architectural production of the region, the issue "Latin America at Crossroads."[1] In fact, Mariana invited us to collaborate in that publication and our first reaction was to check who else was invited, and the other invitees were the ones that we are used to listen talk about Latin America: If we want to talk about housing then we would call Alejandro Aravena, and if we want to talk about urbanism we would call Alejandro Echeverri, and so on, a list of personalities and institutions that are very lucid and represent us. Then we, at Supersudaca, in a sort of Houdini act that sometimes characterizes us, asked ourselves: Why don't we just write about Asia?[2] Why is it that every time the British call us to talk, it is always about Latin America? Suddenly, it could be interesting to see what view Latin Americans may have about other parts of the world that they not usually talk about. Because we would go without certain prejudices or perhaps with other subjectivities.

Jorge Villacorta One of the things that most impresses me about Supersudaca is how they present their projects; it becomes a situation of constant creativity. What is fascinating is that their presentations reflect an open attitude towards the real, in other words taking the world as their laboratory. A laboratory where to observe different types of phenomena, provoke some, and edit it in such a way that certain things create systems within a peculiar gaze over the surroundings that does not exclude at all a deep research of things that normally do not belong into the architectural realm. There has always been that idea that a great artist was also an architect, the example that we find again and again throughout the history of art is Michelangelo and how at ninety years old he

was building Saint Peter's Dome which was the masterpiece
of someone who had already proved himself through a series
of steps, masterpiece after masterpiece, then architecture
suddenly is just the cherry on top. But I think that the current
situation of the world has completely turned this the other
way around, many times it is the architect, and here is where
studio experience is very important in a way, and as an art
critic I cannot understand it in its whole complexity. But what
I find interesting is that the architect nowadays has a freedom
that those who have been trained as visual artists do not have.
Even in these times when the visual artist can work in different
medias, and when going from one medium to another does
not necessarily imply opening the mind. It is as if suddenly
the Supersudaca experience would agree to blow their brains
individually and then somehow put the pieces back together,
or exchange the pieces perhaps and bring forward something
with such a perspective that one can connect with the world in
unintended ways. It is as if in each point of the experience they
could build a milestone that could continue being a reference
– or not – as you continue advancing.

That is what I find interesting about these dynamics: That
there is a sense of humor and a constant self-irony that also
makes it possible not to take themselves too seriously, even
when Supersudaca starts every project with a very defined
seriousness. It is also true that sometimes it looks like a jump
into the void, but what I believe is interesting is precisely
that they take that risk, something that is frequently absent
in all cultural projects, and suddenly it becomes a starting
point and Supersudaca does not perceive it as such. Simply,
Supersudaca assumes a risk as a freedom to be conquered
to learn or provoke knowledge and this is the part that I find
particularly interesting: The way in which, through their projects, Supersudaca stimulates the acquisition of knowledge as
something elemental and fundamental.

At moments it is tempting to say that they have absorbed
conceptual art in a fresh and lively way, and, on the other hand,
I think they are onto something else. But at the same time, I
am surprised and excited to see how Supersudaca presents a
possibility of openness towards what we confront in contemporary situations, as if somehow the world had turned familiar
without losing its surprise factor. It is something rather strange
and, if I may say it, in some situations perhaps they won't produce a building but they will definitely produce art.

Supersudaca About the division between art and architecture. When we study cities or when we research, we learn about what has happened, we interpret the information and in the best-case scenario we utilize this knowledge as tools for our own work. But beyond the field in which we use that information it is totally different than what is applicable in art. Or what do you think will be the difference?

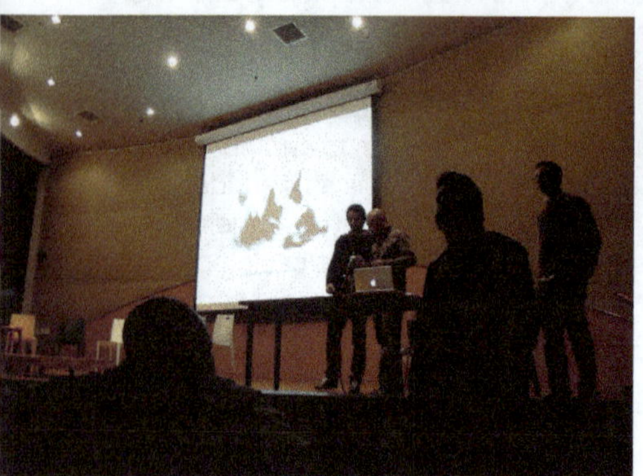 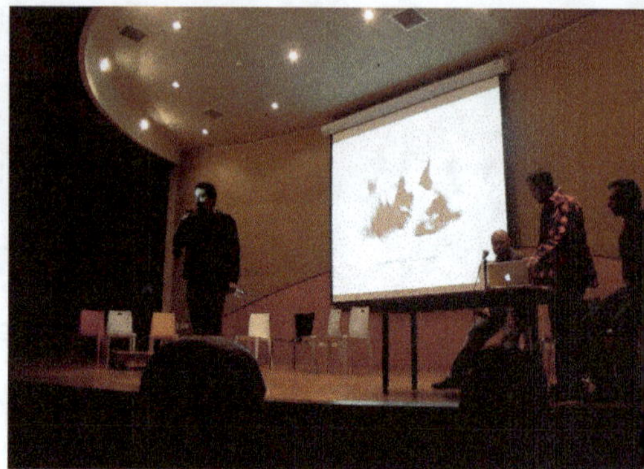

Jorge Villacorta I believe that currently there are artists all over the world who are trying to approach these topics in the way you mentioned. But I believe that it is definitely not something taught in schools. Because even when you look at United States or European schools, they are ever more focused on getting their graduates into the art market. There are a number of subliminal guides in some cases, in other cases they are not so subliminal and it is where the thought is oriented, in one direction only and that is the situation for most visual artists. It is there where it closes. One of the things that have impressed me the most about Supersudaca, from previous presentations, is the way they present photography and graphics – let's say almost scientific in nature – and observe how it becomes a multipurpose tool. You can always go back to the images and graphics and see new things in them and communicate them in a different way each time you make a presentation, so that's where I see that there is constant creation, as a sort of real laboratory. Everything is constantly being tested and because projects are never finished they remain open and we can even imagine more directions. I have seen how you manage to talk about a project that you started seven years ago and suddenly you revisit it and shed new light on it in a powerful way. I think that nowadays the question of whether it is art or not is very often defined by the art market even more so than by the museum as an institution. What I find very stimulating is the power of the idea, even when I have not seen it materialized; Supersudaca's work communicates better through the means of books because of the kind of circulation and diffusion they have to offer, and seems to me it is the way to do real justice to all this work, which is made up of photographic archives and graphic charts that are truly enriching. The experience as an attendee at this conference is a curious one, because the graphic, for example, does not assault you, as in other situations. That is to say, that when you present your graphics they come out as clear evidence. One simply follows the rhythm that you set. The question I have for you is if, in practice –especially in this alliance of minds that you have –, does the notion of the architect as an artist come to your minds? Who wants to answer?

Supersudaca It depends on who you ask, because I would say yes in my case. However, I don't know if this could be for this type of work, so I was interested in your opinion because in reality we often are very critical and we say that what we do is not art, and that it has much more to do with urban planning, with a social situation, which is a way of wanting to change reality by understanding and exposing it. Then there are also layers that the aesthetic systems take into consideration, but what we do, in my opinion, is not art. Although I would like it to be art!

Supersudaca What happens to us is that now they call us from many cultural centers or galleries to do projects that have to do with what the cultural center is proposing, their particular interests, and we go and do our work and we do not think of it as artists. Whether we make art or not, I don't think we think we are artists, we are still researching, observing, and trying to understand the world, and trying to use that understanding of the world to keep doing the things we do.

Enrique Bonilla The topic that concerns this round table is "Is This Architecture?" and I am probably not the one to say that because I think that today, as Manuel said this morning a little between the lines, we are witnessing an absolutely different moment and it seems to me that it must have been the same anguish that the Renaissance guys had when they finally accepted to be called *architects* – because it is not that they always had that title – and that they got into so many issues that this probably will happen to us all the time.

3. See chapter "Al
Caribe!" pages 162-183.
4. See chapter "China
tu Madre," pages
224-243.

I value the ability of this group to do research in an absolutely calm, kind, friendly way and to go into very deep topics
and tells us about those topics in a simple way. I find the
research of "Al Caribe"[3] really fantastic, especially because
they are drawing conclusions and showing things seen
from another perspective and I was looking at "With Infinite
Slowness Arises the Great China"[4] some time ago, which I see
is a process. One of the nice things is that these studies don't
end. Everything continues, you consider other points of view
and make the research topic – that could be so uninteresting
– interesting for architects, apparently so out of place, if our
thing is to create, our thing is to make things, our thing is to
design. The ones in charge of the project have never trusted
the researcher, the theorist etc., and suddenly we see now an
integration process which I find really healthy.

I was also thinking, for example, about the distance that
there is between what was happening in the 1980s, when
groups of Latin Americans would get together. Latin Americans
had Magical Realism as their common theme. Magical Realism
had seduced the literary world and then the architects also got
into it and then they got into critical regionalism.

Suddenly there is this whole idea to generate some sort of
region and at that moment, with postmodernity, they started
saying that there is no one main paradigm – and therefore, one
has to choose between all paradigms, so this whole idea of
regionalism starts slowly dying and when we're about to get to
the end of the century it disappears and no one knows about it
anymore. So, one now asks, what is the destiny of this continent
in the midst of this globalization? Do we have any possibilities
within this whole context? This is when I congratulate this
group that has achieved great boldness, which is to say, we
will not be navel-gazing anymore – that was a bit of what was
going on with the regionalist generation –, now we will take
the initiative and we are going to look at others, and we are
going to look at them from our own perspective. This has been
an international group since its foundation, I have evidence of
this. I recall that I discovered the group in Madrid. I was at a
meeting of architects and a friend of mine asked me "don't you
know Supersudaca?" "No, I really have never heard of them,"
I told her. "Well there is a guy from Peru, his name is Manuel
de Rivero." "Of course, I know him," I said; then she told me:
"He belongs to a group of architects who are doing a bunch of
things," and from then on I started to know the group. I have the
sense that you guys work like Tarzan; that you hold onto a vine
and then jump on to another one that just appeared and on to

another one, so you can go around getting into different things about which you hadn't yet theorized at all and I think that this is the idea of what an architect must do. As I heard Robert Venturi say: "One has to find the other side of tradition."

Supersudaca Well, I'd like to go back to what you said about the vines because of the jungle. You said that in the 1980s there was something similar; in which moment did the vine break? Who fell, what happened?

Enrique Bonilla In the 1980s, commitment was a central topic: There was talk about typology, locus, place, of many things that had to do with tradition, with identity. What they did not see coming was what could happen after. In Latin America there was not a glimpse of an option until these types of experiences appeared, which evidently ended up develop-ing abroad, as it happens when Alfred Bryce said that in the time he lived in Europe, he discovered how Peruvian he was and I believe that this experience of exile helps to understand so many things. Obviously, you have been extremely fortunate to live in a collective exile and to realize how similar you are to each other when out of your own contexts, because surely this experience could not have happened in any of your home countries. There had to be an ocean in between for you to find each other and we pick up again the topic of identity, but in a different way. Without that commitment idea, but from a con-ceptual point of view.

I believe that the idea of identity mutates, it is a kind of virus that keeps changing, then the vines, in good account, end up finding another identity. I think that's what they have and that's what has brought them together and keeps them up to date. That idea without that chauvinistic eagerness of "I am Latin American" – which I think did happen in the 1980s – so I don't have to enclose myself in that, but rather in a calmer way, they are picking up a series of concepts. The reading of the facts is different, what happens is not that important but the reading of what it means, what I perceive. That is what this group is handling, and that is stimulating.

The whole thing of the vines is a metaphor that stuck, but it is true, things are happening too fast resulting in dramatic changes in short periods of time, it is dazing, when you are finally understanding a theory another one appears. Even though you have made references to Vitruvius I believe that there is a post-Vitruvian idea, and that is a different thing, it offers other horizons. I tell my students that if they want to

5. Exhibition "To the Caribe" was shown at the II International Architecture Bienal of Rotterdam 2005.

become architects, nothing related to the human component should be left out. And that is a right that I think we should strive for, because architecture is one of the few professions in which we have the right to stick our nose everywhere. The rest of the professions are scared. Specialization, compartmentalized knowledge, and suddenly there are no *todistas* (experts in the whole), those who come and do an absolute sweep. Today's world is posed in such an open-ended manner. For example, in recent times I have been absolutely seduced by the subject of communication, I have taken drawing courses to increase my communications skills, because I think it is very important that we know how to communicate well, it is something that Supersudaca does successfully, their level of communication is stupendous. We did not have this variable before. And this day is stimulating because it allows us to reflect on a real future and I come back to the question: Is this architecture as well?

Mariana Leguía In relation to what Manuel mentioned about the publication "Latin American Crossroads," I thought that the way you operate was important, that is something that Enrique and Jorge also had mentioned, and to place them right next to Saskia Sassen, who is an expert on the subject of globalization, I thought that was very pertinent, because it was the moment that Latin America was introduced, through this magazine, to the world. I think that you, as a work methodology and as a group have understood a way of approaching this global economic phenomenon, because you are an international image that operates in different countries and the way we know a local office. Enrique went to Madrid and everyone already knew who Supersudaca was and that is something that only happens when one works internationally. On the other hand, after having seen the exhibit,[5] they showed these large-scale experiments in "Al Caribe" and what was behind it. It reminded me of the Latin American housing experiments in the 1950s, when they would show an image of the world that was not real, that tries to hide all of the informal growth that is happening out of sight; I don't know how you interpret this. I think it is a lot of fun to face a problem with a cynical attitude, but obviously I know you see it as a problem nevertheless. On the other hand, it also makes me curious to know what would it be like the day you'll have to face these big global economies, when you have to come up with a masterplan for one million people, how would this methodology or the *know-how*, that you have as Latin Americans, would be applied at that moment. Have you thought about it? Because all this research is an investment, that will have to be tested when a project like that comes to you. Well, I hope so.

Supersudaca In this commitment with what is real and about these successive questions "from vine to vine," that no one knows where they are heading to, the double condition of putting on and taking off the Supersudaca mask whenever is convenient, gives us license to kill and to deal with what is real in a more efficient way. This is why we feel liberated. Part of the power of this group is that this has allowed us to advance on multiple fronts without the need of coordination and especially without the pressure of having to find *the solution*. Rather, as challenges arise, we'll try to face them.

Supersudaca What Mariana just said stuck with me: The word *cynical*, and I find it interesting that it is connected to what Anita says "we never end our researches, we don't close the books, we keep adding topics and pages to them and they are never finished." Perhaps it has to do with the fact that as architects, we are trained – and that is why we don't trust artists – to get a ready possible solution for real issues and precisely for this reason we don't feel that what we do is cynical. It is like Sisyphus' stone, we've been close to make it to the top of the hill but it always falls off our hands, but we still have this idea that we are going to succeed. That is why, for example, the research on "Al Caribe" has had about seven or eight different endings, we haven't finished it because we don't find the right ending. It is not cynicism, on the contrary, it is a permanent obsession for not having found a true answer and not just an easy one.

Mariana Leguía Actually, the round table's topic was the role of the architect, so in that sense it seemed important to me to mention how in the last international exhibits this new role of the architect as a social agent appears and there is a lot of debate over it. There is a group of people that considers that an architect should only be a designer, an artist. I would like to know your position on this.

Supersudaca Félix said that he liked to build pretty buildings…

Supersudaca Yes, I can say it again, it does not embarrass me. I believe that there shouldn't be an internal frustration over this, I am still interested in designing a beautiful building.

I don't think that for every project and topic we have to question the validity of the world. One must be critical when it is necessary, not just as a pose. Sometimes to build a pedestrian bridge it is just enough to explore a shape that is efficient and not the social dynamics. We have to enjoy life too because that brings joy to everyone.

Mariana Leguía Well, the point of the question was not meant for you to self-flagellate or anything.

Supersudaca It doesn't mean that we don't want to enjoy life but there is an underlying theme such as the *value of the incomplete*. The issue of one single truth or a single defining reason worries me. We have already played with this existentialist attitude in which architecture did not have any meaning, so we had to look for one and the most interesting thing was that permanent search, which can be translated into this constant change of vines, where the vine itself is not important just the ability to change from one vine to another. Many times, the group changes and Supersudaca would not be so attractive for me if it weren't just for the different points of view. Supersudaca would not be present today if it were not like that.

I am uncomfortable with the word *solution* in general. I believe in the experience of confronting ourselves with what we criticize and we are already living. A theme gets complex when it turns into a moral matter and I believe that is where the cynicism lies. This is why we have always played with the glass half full/glass half empty metaphor, or a way to hold on to the innocence that we don't want to lose – even though we have foreseen the problems that could arise from this – because it could be taken for cynicism. It is actually that dose of humor that allows us to solve things and to go further and not to stay behind. This is where architecture loses its condition of art form or its social role, because definitely we cannot solve the world with architecture, but, on the other hand, architecture does good.

There is something that we still believe in. I don't know if it is a sedative or a sort of pause in one's hard daily life, but there is something that makes it more pleasant, that outlines that side of pure art. That pendulum still looks attractive to us.

Supersudaca I agree with Juan Pablo. I think that what unites us as a group is its version of morality. It is so difficult not to bring up any moral issues. I think you can feel it in all of the projects; it is very important. I think it is still important to do

6. See chapter "Direct
Architecture Genealogy"
pages 26-37.

beautiful things, but for me that is not necessarily an end in architecture, but a means. I see it that way, it is not the goal to make nice things or be funny or cynical.

Supersudaca That is apparent in "To the Caribe" project. As a student or as a young architect one is better trained to see how ugly a capital turned out and that they painted it gold. But, actually, the problem was on the other side! To be able to change your point of view one has to deviate from the training one had.

Supersudaca One time, an Art Institute in Curacao invited us to do a project with high school students studying art. We had started in the morning to explain what "Direct Architecture"[6] is and how to intervene in the city. But then there was a conflict with the teenagers because they said they had to make something nice, "a statue!" And we said: "No, that's not what we want. You have to understand the city and add something worthwhile." I think I understand the difference, the position of the architect and the artist can be in conflict.

Supersudaca Something really funny happened recently with Stephane, at the Canadian Center for Architecture with a group of thirteen-eighteen-years-old and we had five days to produce something. This center has the most important collections of architecture, that of Peter Eisenman, that of Gordon Matta-Clark... I saw the adventure with quite skeptical eyes. With ten years of experience as a teacher, I did my calculations and said: "Thirteen to eighteen -year-old children, five days, impossible! So, let's see what happens and we'll do the best we can and I let go!" There was this obsession with wanting to plan, define what they had to do every single hour, to make sure that the right thing was indeed being done! But then we realized that planning didn't make sense either, because in the next hour everything could change! So, there are those curious anecdotes where finally and independently this process happens and we give the possibility of making mistakes and that is felt directly. In this case it worked, I don't know if that will always be possible.

Mariana Leguía I find it interesting that you mention Matta-Clark, because of the similarities to the way you take something and cut it, and peel it, and synthesize it, and then show it again. It is a methodology of synthesis. I actually mentioned the word *cynical*, because it seems to me that there is such a serious problem behind everything you show, yet somehow it sounds like so much fun, or it actually makes listening to it not tedious; like in the Latin American movies where you end up laughing at problems.

Supersudaca The thing about humor is curious, because people always tell us that we use it a lot. However, you have to think about it the other way around, for architecture in general – I don't know if art is in the same situation – it's supposed to be done without humor!

Enrique Bonilla I think there is a reading that probably comes from the other side, the opposite of humor is bad humor. Seriousness is not the opposite of humor; in other words, one can be totally serious and have a great sense of humor, as I believe you do. To me the truth is that even though it is not finished yet, the work of "Al Caribe" seems impeccable in what it wants to express, in the readings of those ideas. There have been many things that probably put in a different way could have been tremendously empty or difficult to assimilate. But for example, the territorial readings that Supersudaca makes are equivalent to the best planning classes, they seem to me to be extremely serious, extremely well developed and put with enough humor so the message can be adequately assimilated. This has to be clear, being serious and having a sense of humor are not contradictory.

There are people who love solemnity and it ends up getting really tedious. In the morning I would talk with Félix and he would tell me a little about the consistency of the group, he would tell me "We are a little bit anarchic" and I would tell him that the anarchists of the 20th century had two rules: the first one is that there are no rules and the second rule is that the first rule is relative. Obviously, this group has a well understood kind of anarchy and that helps a lot. The fact that they start a project because of it being contradictory seems fantastic to me! Or when we suddenly realize that we have to agree, but because we have to agree a priori.

Participant from the Audience I was listening to the presentations of the architectural projects, and then listening about the concerns that they have and about their research, and I could not find the common thread. There are so many people, so many concerns and many times it seems that these investigations never end, they still will continue to change, but the investigations and concerns are contributing in small doses to the projects. Those little things reflect this kind of knowledge that is the kind you acquire through research.

Supersudaca In any given location when we are researching something, we are not against reality, rather we try to understand it and we try to develop projects taking into account the problems that we are understanding. For instance, we are not against tourism, we rather study how it happens and we can then see that it has its own problems. We do not say that the country lives off tourism, something we are critical of; therefore tourism must be eliminated in order to solve the issue. We understand that those who develop tourism have serious reasons to do it in whatever particular way, but we also understand that there are always options so things can be improved, and people can also work in this other way. When one operates on the other side, everything you've learned will always end up being used later.

Participant from the Audience 2 I wanted to comment on how you use humor as a conversation strategy, you should be on television (laughs). This way of communicating makes everything much more accessible for people who are not architects. I think it is important for society to understand and assimilate, as we have done, this light and fresh ability to face challenges and to be able to see *vines*. How do you see communication with an audience of non-architects?

Supersudaca I always wanted to have a show on TV (laughs). By the way, one of the Supersudaca actually has a show on the radio in Bueno Aires (laughs).

Participant from the Audience 3 This irreverent spirit, this way of understanding the world, where you share certain geographical locations that will remain; but will you at some point retire?

Supersudaca I take this question seriously, that is why I was asking Enrique about the moment your vines started breaking apart and some of you were left alone? Because we are a network, and every generation has its own network, but when the network starts breaking apart then one is left alone. And yes, I think it is a problem of age, so the thing is to be connected.

Supersudaca I think the good thing about these ten years is that we have already been through many things and many

7. Walter Benjamin. "A Short History of Photography," *Screen* 13, no. 1, Spring 1972, 5-26.

situations, beyond babies and separations – Max and I were husband and wife – and moving! (laughs) We have already matured, I think that the interest of being together makes it possible for one to be there in a given moment and not in another moment and then to go on, because we have so much in common, friendships in common, and this is flexible and there are still many things.

Jorge Villacorta I would only like to emphasize one thing, that I think we should not lose sight of, and that is that research is not just where data is accumulated. It is not only a question of volume, of information, but of making information intelligible, that is, being able to communicate and cross check ideas. When I saw the images, Supersudaca was, especially the photographs and precisely the way they organize the photographic material reminds me of Walter Benjamin and "A Short History of Photography."[7] An image of the façade of the factory suffices for the argument. It does not tell us anything about the factory working conditions. I think that many times we think and take for granted that everything we see is absolutely what it is and there is nothing else behind it. In other words, there is no meaning, there is no inquisitive will, and we content ourselves with the photo on the front page of a newspaper, the vision of the building and, above all, with the photos that are published in architecture magazines. It is as if somehow, in the way in which architecture is packaged and sold to us, it is a photograph that says nothing about the world. It is not something that is a certain kind of knowledge. It is something that is rather hermetic and closed in itself. I think that, precisely, one of the strongest things about Supersudaca is that they force us to get rid of that type of attitude; and because of the way in which they organize information, visual, graphic, and images is a way that definitely has all the characteristics of a work of art for me. If art is a form of knowledge and a form of communication, then Supersudaca's work is a confirmation that what the architect does is an art form as well. We must not lose sight of the fact that this is not just about accumulation of data or volume of information, there is an organization and a meaning, and that the meaning mutates through time – and, above all, it can be revised and renewed. This seems to me to be its most valuable thing. An open experience, because one is free to retrace one's own steps, decide that one has made a mistake and look again and try again to realize the real, in the most honest and sincere way possible.

Enrique Bonilla I think that this group has gotten stronger and it is good that there is a feeling of permanent disagreement. That thing about *never finishing* seems important because the day you finish there will be no more vines, so that is a bit of an issue. I think that this should not happen to them, I believe that this enthusiasm to find other things, other paths, other alternatives should not be lost. On the other hand, it is true that this is a group that has concrete things, things done etc. A group which is also dedicated to producing results etc. However, I believe that they should not lose that other spirit. Rather, I think provocation is its most obvious strength. The vines will not be lost and as long as the spirit of the *unfinished* remains, the vines will continue to turn up.

Second Day
September 16, 2011

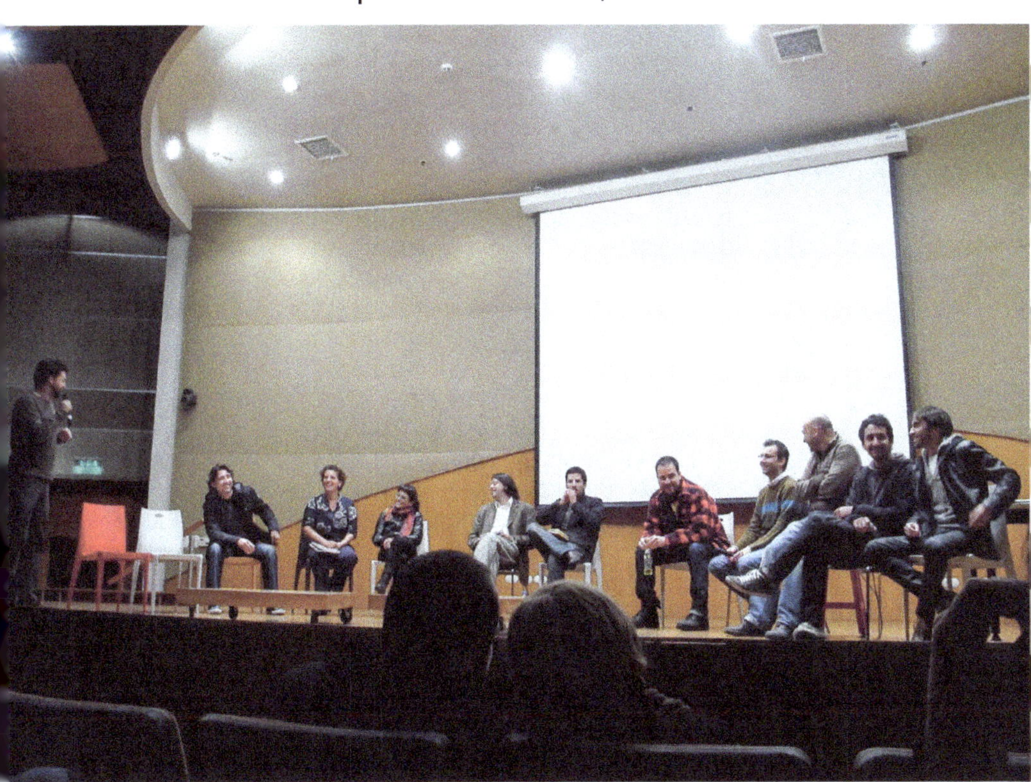

Supersudaca So that we have a discussion – stemming from what we have demonstrated – about what could be expected in the future, today I would like to invite Elio Maruccelli, architect and architectural historian. He was our professor and we are always interested in what he has to say, because of this he couldn't have not been here. Let's see if he helps us now.

Our other guest is Jorge Sánchez, he is also an architect, and he represents the under 35 years old generation. He has been writing about architecture in an intelligent manner for *El Comercio* newspaper. Therefore, we are very interested to hear how Jorge sees all this that we are talking about.

Elio Martuccelli It has been a couple of intense and beautiful days with Supersudaca, talking about what they think and what they do together as well as individually, and you have seen that they have ventured into many areas. Supersudaca can be an office, they can be a school, they can be a research workshop, and, above all, a travel agency. In your work I think there is an explosive mixture of art, sociology, economics, and other things.

So, I'll start from the beginning…

To begin with, I'm going to say that I like the name Supersudaca. It's very good, it's provocative, it's naughty, it's combative. Supersudaca helped you to find your place in the world from a cultural and geographical condition: The condition of having been born on this side of the planet. It implies the double condition of recognizing and recognizing yourself, and exile in fact helps in many ways while identity is present in this collective, but not only to look at the things of this continent, but of the world. And that is another enormous difference with the regionalism of a few years ago.

Secondly, if they are together and if they are here, it is because at some point in their lives they were in Holland. And Holland has a long tradition of builders who have invented a country on the sea and a long tradition of architects. And in the last two decades of the 20th century, a new generation of Dutch architects became famous, who designed, who published, who promoted themselves. And the new wave comes in part and since then from Holland, and the name Rem Koolhaas bring along others such as his professors at the Berlage. And they have carried out formal experiments, objects in unusual and diverse containers, not all of them with the will to be built, but with the will to reflect. There, Rotterdam presents itself like a laboratory of changes, and the Supersudaca have drunk from those sources. Some more than others, and they try to apply those ideas; and surely others – and many more – in their own realities. Now, in the second decade of the 21st century, it is worthwhile to make these considerations, which in fact have served to understand this world of overflowing metropolises, of fragmented areas, of rough areas, of confrontation. Specifically, the Dutch influence is noticeable in the form of communication that you use, with statistics, with short phrases, with collage, with photomontage, with video clips.

I say all this because I did not hear in these two days many comments about what influences you feel you have had in your training, and I think it deserves a comment. On the other hand, I like that the theme of these talks has been "The City," and in other cases, more than that, the territory. It is a gaze that has to do with geopolitics, fed by all your travels, and that opens up an interesting field for speculative architecture. This has constantly led them to the problem and the issue of public space and citizenship. And when you have shown specific architectural projects, you have done it so from the perspective of the city; from a broader strategy. They have faced problems at all scales: To the scales of our countries we could always use the *extra small* strategies, low cost and really small, but precise and powerful interventions. And that they have also done. They have shown us at "Mueblenstein" and "Direct Architecture:" The minimum effort with the maximum impact.

In this era of frenetic construction, it is always necessary to vindicate this scale of the *extra small*, and in everything they have shown there is this interesting will to unite theory and practice, in times when an architectural office is conditioned by haste and profit. So, within the concerns of the team, there are the investigations. Some of the research is very serious, very deep, like the one on tourism in "Al Caribe" or the one on "Y Previ,"[8] full of data.

There is happy thoughtfulness in this group. What should be the norm, but is not. It is not, specially nowadays with greater concern about built square footage. So, these investigations are either ongoing or open investigations. Last night people in the audience demanded concrete results... Anyway, we have to see how these investigations land, how they become real or not. That's another issue.

In fact, these are readings of the reality that continue to be refined and researched and can eventually feed in the most unusual way, your projects and buildings. Of course, "sin querer queriendo" (unintentionally but intentionally), quoting the "Chavo del 8" another cultural reference with which you all identify (if we talk about influences). So, what I rescue from this multinational group is all the reflections on the city that you make departing from each one of your projects.

I have looked up your work on the internet, and what you have done is impressive: In quantity, some of you more than others; and in quality it is quite even. I found a wide range of projects, but there are common denominators when proposing some strategies. Each one of you in your offices, beyond experimental projects as Supersudaca, you have produced concrete projects as well. You have said it already; you do not deny the possibility of working, of designing houses and other buildings. You have produced them, and it's good to do them, and they have to be done well. That's what it's all about.

I like how you use humor and irony as ingredients in some of your proposals. They are well thought out provocations and others are like visions of the future. And humor is an ingredient that does not detract from the depth of the proposals: It is in your work a powerful communication tool. Do not lose it. And I kept thinking about the value of unbuilt projects. You are architects, and anywhere in the world you would be considered young architects. There are architects who were born at the age of fifty, so patience. It doesn't matter that there is more enthusiasm than clients; it's good that way.

This is an experimentation moment. Some projects are done and others are there waiting for their opportunity and you have to give yourself a margin of freedom, which is fundamental, trying out things that can later be applied and brought to reality; and hopefully this moment of experimentation that you have collectively... This moment of experimentation will never really end. And again, I say all this in times of real estate success like the ones Lima is going through; and we have more construction and less city, and you have poignantly raised, again, today, the issue of how to make a city and not just housing.

I am finishing now. We professors are almost condemned to optimism and obviously the problems are enormous, in Lima, in Peru, in Latin America, and in the world. But you have, above all, two things: Good spirits and an enormous capacity to get in trouble. And I praise you for that.

This round was to wrap up some ideas and so you could finish telling us how we are going to save the world then. Last night I kept thinking about a couple of your phrases. If you haven't noticed, Supersudaca is also a factory for making good phrases and you have said in different ways yesterday and today that architecture cannot save the world. It is clear; but it can do it good. And architecture – you said it too – is more a means than an end. Yes, and I agree with that. We architects can still do something good for the world and I want to believe that architecture is a means, yes, to well-being and happiness.

That's it for now.

Jorge Sánchez I will stay with two concepts. I start with the concept of the *designer*, which can suddenly answer this question. I am interested in the architect as a non-specialist, as this idea of de-specializing. Which is actually the opposite of what is happening now in the world, which calls you to specialize, to be more efficient as a way to succeed.

A few months ago, I interviewed a Spanish industrial designer; a graphic designer, actually, called Manolo Jimenez, who talked to me about the *designer 3.0*. For him, the *designer 1.0* was the designer who stood behind his drawing board and waited for the work to come in and was the great genius. The *designer 2.0* was the one who begins to incorporate people from other disciplines. The *designer 3.0* – which is the current situation for him – was the designer who begins to work in networks, which is what this group does. That he can build a project in Santiago from Lima but coordinating with an office in Shanghai. He has a phrase: "New designers must be aware that everything that surrounds them is of interest or should be of interest to them." I found it very interesting, like this idea about not being a specialist, but being interested in everything a little bit.

And I also find it curious, with respect to the topic of "To the Caribe" – and I think this has been the most interesting presentation – that, when Supersudaca was presenting it, we did not know whether we were listening to an economist, a sociologist, an urban planner, a journalist, a hotelier or even a comedian. It could be any of the possibilities and I find that super interesting. The curious thing is to talk about design when, apparently, it is the last thing, or what is considered least important. Except for what Félix said yesterday about this obsession for still wanting to make the building beautiful, what we have heard the most are phrases such as: "Well, there is the project but I will not go into details;" or "Well, the project, there you have sections, photos, but that is not the important thing;" or "Well, there are also double heights, and there is light, and all that what is expected." That is always heard from the 51-1 or "it is irrelevant" with respect to the project itself. Manuel today said (the word *design* came out): "No. It is a system." There is this idea of relegating the design issue.

9. Nomena Arquitectura Files. "Positions". Peru, 2010.
10. "Latin America at the Crossroads."

And the other issue, which Jorge Villacorta mentioned yesterday, was how the architect takes on the role of editor, as a selector of information, as a communicator. We, as Nómena Group, presented exactly a year ago a book that we edited.[9] The book consisted of selecting information instead of producing it, transforming it, and inventing and reinventing a way of communicating it.

Yesterday, the panel also mentioned *AD Magazine* latest issue on Latin America[10] and they also talked about the importance of the editor. One reads that magazine; there are all the articles – on Aravena, Supersudaca, Echeverri, among others – and one wonders: "What is the editor's job, if it has not written anything?" But there is really a great job done in the selection process, in having a clear framework, in selecting the information and devising a way of communicating it. And it seems to me – as Villacorta said yesterday – that this is where your value lies right now. At a time when information is just a click away, it is no longer a virtue just to find the information, but how to transmit it.

Well, in both cases I will leave with a phrase that I liked and I think that summarizes or is something that unites the two days: As Ana said, "a lot of baggage and a lot of culture." I believe that this is something that is present in each of your interventions.

And as a final anecdote, suddenly it has something to do with communication – but in another sense –, I am impressed by how you have managed to maintain such a solid mental structure, in spite of not sharing physical space, that even allows them to be able to explain a project that is not their own. It belongs to the group, but in which they have not had major participation, like Félix explaining Parque Francia, or talking about "Y Previ," and talking about Fernando Belaúnde to the Peruvians. But it seems that he is the expert – or suddenly he is – it is surprising that there is this connection. Each one of them could explain any of the 100 projects they could have or will have done together as a group.

Supersudaca I wanted to answer Elio's statement about the references. Jorge, I think you also said something about it. How is it that we have a Supersudaca brain that thinks one way, that has a particular way of looking at what we all share? It started because we were together, very much together, for a long period of time in Holland. Very close because we were basically a family, and we shared a lot of moments, situations, and we already came with a lot of ideas, our own views, and this grew over time. Even though we were in different places, we always kept talking about the same topics and we worked on the same subjects. But, on the other hand, I like to think that our references are more like music groups – like "The Clash," "Sex Pistols" etc. – because it is a bit of that rock attitude that I have left from Supersudaca. But it can also be David Byrne from "Talking Heads," because he has a similar look much like Supersudaca, about things a bit more alternative of what happens in the world and also that Byrne not only plays, but he is a producer of other people's albums. I also like to say that we are influenced by Tim Burton, because he creates a world; and Supersudaca somehow creates a world. And all of us, when we are apart, we send each other pictures or make comments – "this belongs to the Supersudaca world" –, something we see, something we read and all of this is always feeding us.

Supersudaca When Supersudaca started, we realized that everyone knew Jean Nouvel, everyone knew Rem Koolhaas, everyone knew MVRDV, everyone had their *El Croquis* magazines, they knew who Steven Holl was, everyone knew all that. But nobody had any idea of who Fernando Belaúnde was; nobody had any idea what "Y Previ" was; nobody had any idea of what had happened with STAFF in Buenos Aires. And those were the most interesting influences for us. What makes us different in the beginning is explaining our cities to ourselves and saying: "Wow, I've been studying the Europeans and I have no idea what happens next to my house."

It's one thing to get your influences from magazines, and a totally different thing the influence you get when you go to Cambodia through this *travel agency* that is Supersudaca, and spend all that time talking about your projects; among us, as friends, one absorbs influences in a much more powerful way than from a magazine that one can buy or see in *ArchDaily*. A friend once said: "You know what you want." And since we love each other so much – well, more or less – we know each other so well, that we influence each other a lot. I think that's the biggest influence. Without being like a Mennonite or an autarkic club. We're completely open to the world, but we're very much influenced by ourselves.

And finally, the offices that we are talking about, the Dutch ones, like MVRDV or Rem Koolhaas, we know them from the inside very well, we worked there, and we know very well how they work, and often we do not love them so much. We know that what's said there arises in a very forced way, that the air that we breathe is completely rotten, there is a lot of elbowing

and a lot of *dirty details* that we don't even want to know. I
would have preferred not to have worked with Rem Koolhaas,
because I loved what they did, but once I worked there, I
noticed all this dirt. I don't want to hear about it anymore. I
like listening to the Supersudaca much better. And finally you
realize that Rem Koolhaas in the end is full of us. Who does all
those projects for them? Some Latinos and some Asians and
some from India. It's not the Dutch alone...it's all of us.

Supersudaca Jorge wondered if Félix was an expert or not?
And, on the other hand, he mentioned the issue of de-specialization. I would be interested in establishing this difference,
this issue of specialization versus becoming an expert. We are
not interested in specialization in the sense of focusing only
on one thing, but each of the things we do is very important
to us and there is a rigor (beyond the humor we can put into
explaining it) in being experts and knowing everything about
that particular subject. That entails working mornings like
you have no idea, going on these trips where architects don't
normally go, and when there is money for a ticket, five of us
go, and that means taking the most absolutely absurd flight
connections one can imagine. Fortunately, we have friends all
over the world and they welcome us – once in Tokyo five of us
slept in three tatamis. The goal of becoming experts is central.
For example, when you see our presentation of "Al Caribe,"
you realize that the amount of information and experiences we
have been accumulating is pouring out of our pores. So, it is
not that anything goes. It's that in what you do and what you
get into, you have to know everything. And knowing everything
is extremely demanding. We have won some awards, but I
know that we have only won them when we have pulled out
our souls. To "pull out our souls" means having broken records,
without sleep, one after the other, and that is important to
know.

And about not giving much importance to the design,
each and every one of those projects that have been shown,
comply with the usual rules that have to be expected of any
architect. That's why we say it's normal, it's almost like an ethical duty; if you are making a building, that building has to con-
form to standards of quality that we take for granted. Maybe we
should start doing conferences in which we go back to: "Here
is the entrance, and you turn around, there is the window, and
that is the detail." That's what we wanted to bring up in this
marathon of an afternoon, all these scales. Where that image
of the Kiltro house was so important, with the little corners and

every bolt thought of; as could be some exploration of going to the Australian Parliament to present an absolutely utopian proposal but which proposes to face an issue.

Supersudaca I am fascinated by floor plans, and I see all the floor plans and I see the rest of the Supersudaca and I begin to have a series of doubts. For example, the floor plans in Lima are totally different from the floor plans I am used to. Because of having studied in Switzerland, in Holland and developed in Chile, the subject of orientation is fundamental. The subject of every space, of the square meters etc. – especially in Switzerland – was a whole issue. And quickly one realizes that this issue is not present in the floor plans in Lima. Because the sun does not determine the orientation of the floor plans etc. There aren't the usual eaves for protection from the sun here and there.

For me that is an issue that remains pending. I don't know if this is just dirty laundry. Manuel mentioned this article once, it was by Héctor Velarde,[11] who said that if there was a disaster and then someone from the future came to explore Lima archaeologically, this person would find that in these ruins there were houses with gabled roofs etc., a very strange climate, and would begin to describe the civilization but, in reality, this would have nothing to do with what was happening in Lima.

I think there is a pending issue, almost at the level of pure design, which obviously (once again), we cannot fulfill, (there is a need for) a serious debate at that level; we get distracted and there are many fireworks.

Supersudaca I think looking at all the exhibitions, for example, if we look at everyone's work, I think what we are doing is to "let's let the world change architecture."

Looking at Ana's work, in a context in Uruguay, with all the *posh* houses and her there trying to reach the scale of the small town, putting it in context and bringing that context to her architecture. Another example of that: The MAMM; it's like bringing the "Paisa" world or the favela to the museum, very literal. And I think that's actually what we're doing.

Supersudaca I want to talk about what Jorge was saying, about de-specialization. I loved the concept. I think it should be called that. We have tried to promote it, but there has been great resistance. For example, we were contacted by a very important magazine, from a very important university that I do not want to mention now – the most important and the most expensive in the world – and after months of negotiation and after we sent them the material, they did not publish anything, nor did they respond to our emails ever again. The material was basically a *manifesto* against specialization, which is exactly what they teach.

So that is not going to be so easy, and it's not going to be so easy to convince the dean and say to him: "Try not to let everybody specialize in having a mind this tiny." It's complicated. I don't know if we're doing the right thing. Maybe this is even criminal in a way. Maybe we are recommending something dangerous. Maybe you should specialize to make sure your job is safe. Maybe… I don't know. Maybe you shouldn't listen to us so much.

Supersudaca Isn't this directly linked to the Latin context, where you have to do everything? In Holland I was a large-scale urban planner, and only that. And now that I live on a fucking island (Curacao), I have to do everything!

Participant from the Audience 1 I'm not so clear about the topic of specialization… Finally, you are the product of having gone abroad to specialize.

Supersudaca In Spain there were many graduate courses specialized in theory, history, restoration, interior design whereas at that time in Holland – I don't know how it is now – the objective of the graduate course was to understand the world around us, a world that was changing, to be able to take a stance. We are the last generation of architecture students to learn to draw by hand with stylographs and the first to start using AutoCAD. We grew up in a polarized world between communism and capitalism. We started studying architecture right at the time of the fall of the Berlin wall; nothing was clear at all and then in Holland what they wanted from us was for us to find an agenda. I tell the story of how in my first year at Berlage I was surprised that every Tuesday an architect came to give a lecture, and if one week one architect came and clearly stated that 2+2=3, the next week another one came and consistently said 2+2=8, and after a year of having heard all the possibilities of 2+2. In the second year, they told us: "Now it's your turn. Set your own agenda." The word agenda – which perhaps we use quite a lot – is fundamental.

It wasn't a specialization. At Berlage, the thing we didn't use was AutoCAD. The only thing we didn't do was design. At

that time in Holland, architecture was more interested in poli
tics, in sociology, basically in relation to the topics that Elio was
explaining.

Participant from the Audience 2 I am a student at Villareal
University, what is your outlook on how architecture is taught
in your countries?

Supersudaca Many of us teach in our respective countries
and the truth is that teaching is very heterogeneous in the
places where we work. There are models ranging from private, highly fragmented teaching, as in Chile or here in Peru
where there are many universities, to models where there is
basically one large university, as in Uruguay or at the Technical
University of Delft where Félix works, which is very important
at the European level.

Supersudaca Nowadays it is all about making careers shorter
and shorter, especially in countries where we have public universities. The idea is to reduce architecture's base program,
so that later on you can pay for all the extra courses you want
to take. Well, there are issues of market, business and profit
with education that are happening everywhere, and added to
that there are styles of education particular to each country.
In Argentina the method it's still based on the École de Beaux-
Arts model, where the head of studio is a renowned architect
and teaches what he knows and the students learn to do
exactly what the teacher says. In Buenos Aires there are a lot
of schools: There is the public school, and also you have all
the private schools. Some function as universities and some as
small schools.

Supersudaca Maybe it doesn't matter so much where they
study, but they should come back. In Curacao we have a *brain
drain* problem. Students all go to study in Holland and stay
there. And we are left with the fools. (laughs)

Supersudaca Sofía you have to leave that island soon.

Supersudaca Going back to the topic of education, it's super
complex. I think I've been teaching architecture longer than I
have been practicing it. But the strange thing about the situation we experienced at Berlage was that they advanced the
doctorate. At the beginning, a master's degree deepens knowledge and later in a doctorate you can question that knowledge.

At Berlage, it was like a compact thing. At that time, we were simultaneously transmitted certain knowledge, certain queries, and we reviewed all the texts.

And I remember that on the first day of class they would ask: "What do you stand for? And you repeated (almost like a parrot): "Well, I just want to make a design that is efficient in this, and minimal and blah, blah, blah." And they would answer: "But that's Rem Koolhaas, that's what's next door. We want to hear something else." Uff... It was very difficult to have to answer and answer. And that generated the obligation to ask the other students what they thought about it. And unlike what Manuel says, I think there was a lot of AutoCAD. I had never drawn so much in AutoCAD as at Berlage because we had to make these renderings for Winy Maas in three days (crazy).

What was interesting about that situation, with everything Manuel has said, is that there was also a possibility to react. And there were several people who reacted to that. In fact, in our own class, there was a group that said: "We are bored of reading about sociology and all that. We want pure architecture." Almost as a kind of cathartic situation. "Why are we working as journalists if we are architects?" Because they had an excess of distance with that (architecture). And (with that) they had made a point as well. The strange thing is that people who come from that context, suddenly see themselves reflected in identical Latin America. They have the same diagrams, the same discourses.

Returning to the subject of education, today, there is no formula to guarantee education in almost anything, or at least in architecture. Architecture still has a component that educators both fascinate and dislike. Architecture is one of the few careers in which the dialogue that is established pedagogically has to do with what the student brings. But on the other hand, evaluation in architecture is really difficult. No educator understands what are the patterns of evaluation in architecture. But, once again, changing from one point to another enhances this personal project that sometimes becomes collective. I believe that this questioning prevails over training.

Supersudaca Manuel told us that in Holland they were studying the world, and quite a few things have happened in the last few years. A few days ago, it was the tenth anniversary of the fall of the twin towers and the following year – when we arrived in Holland – the Euro was born; in other words, the European Community was economically consolidated.

12. Roberto Bolaño,
Los Detectives Salvajes
(Barcelona, Anagrama,
1998).

Big things happened, the world we know was broken; and this was a subject of study that was there for the taking. At that moment Supersudaca became interested in studying everything that happens in the world, what happens in the cities, and in the territories. And Supersudaca does all this while enjoying it, with a non-fatalistic vision, although sometimes denouncing things. With an attitude of: "Well, we are not necessarily that bad."

I think that it is very important the *how*, more than the *what*. Supersudaca has a *how*, which is very clear and strengthens us. Internally or externally, there may be different opinions, but I think there is an important strength in how things are done.

Supersudaca In the past ten years, many times we have felt like "Forrest Gump." Not because of the run, but because I don't know how, we always end up in interesting places under interesting circumstances: Supersudaca was in Cuba, by coincidence, the day of the 50th anniversary of the revolution in the middle of the street celebrations; we went to Bangladesh and we were there right on day of the 30th anniversary of the biggest massacre in history, something we haven't even heard about before.

Supersudaca I think that the strongest things that has happened to us is being in the most extremely poor places in the world – like Cambodia or Dharavi in India – or talking to people in the poorest neighborhoods of Caracas. I remember the most intense and most amazing moments, because it has been really getting to know the world from all sides, in all the corners of the world.

Participant from the Audience 3 I perceive that there are important questions that have not been answered up front (I don't know why) and I see that there are some coincidences with a book written by Chilean Roberto Bolaño called *Los Detectives Salvajes*[12] (or the savage detectives, in free translation). The author references a group, the "real viceralistas," where this group turns "magical realism" on its head. It was a new generation of Latin Americans who met in Mexico, then in Barcelona, and they were very *Olympian*: They made quotations without quoting, they sent well-known and badly translated poems by Andre Breton to contests. But referring to magical realism, they always gave credit to William Faulkner,

13. Rem Koolhaas et al,
Mutation (Barcelona,
Actar, 2001).
14. Bart Lootsma, *Super-
dutch: New Architecture
in the Netherlands* (New
York, Princeton Architec-
tural Press, 2000).

aware that what they were doing was not discovering (let's say) "the recipe for ice."

In your case, let's say it seems to me that there is a lack of that part of giving credit to someone. Doesn't the book *Mutation* by Rem Koolhaas[13] and the Harvard project sound familiar to you when they show what Villacorta did not hesitate to call art? I do not hesitate to call art, because of the fascination that those trips caused, with that layout, that way of placing more images. Does that book sound familiar to you? It sounds very familiar to me. That is, the language itself. In that sense, I wouldn't give it that marvelous disbelief produced by images put in a novel way, when they are not so novel. They have been being done that way for a long time.

The other thing is that – without ignoring the projects, which I think are wonderful, I'm talking more about the theoretical part, the staging, the show and so on – it seems to me that as if we are missing some credits and address the sincerely question of the influences. That of Tim Burton? Yes, but no, yes but no... It seems to me that it could be answered in another way, but – because of the irreverence that you propose – I think that it has been answered perfectly well.

Supersudaca When you refer to communicating architecture or thinking about the world: The way we basically think... That aesthetic, that methodology is not coined. It is not copyrighted. It is part of a general culture, of a way of thinking about architectural culture, which is identified and localized (but not exclusively) in the Netherlands. Rem was a guest lecturer every semester at Berlage. Winy Maas worked at OMA and in fact teaches with the man who is walking around (Félix).

It's the stuff we're made of. It's like if "The Clash" had to say: "Look our influences are punk etc. etc." You quote when you literally use someone else's material. When you share the same culture, there is no need to quote.

Supersudaca And also that's what we all came with when we entered Berlage. That's why we went to Holland: Rem Koolhaas, Winy Maas, Willem Jan Neutelings... They were all part of why we went to Holland. *Mutations* was made there, *SuperDutch*[14] was done at that time. I don't even remember anymore, it was a lot of books and things that were going on. Colors magazine, which I always use as an architectural reference, is part of all this. Surely all of those are our references, but at the same time, I like to move away from what is strictly architecture. Because if not, we always keep talking about

architecture when the world is much wider and what we do
is much wider as well. In the end, we are architects and you
are architects, and we come to see each other. But I love it
when we cross the border and talk about art. But for all that to
happen, you also have to look at other things. That's why we
talk about how the references are music, and cinema, and any
other things that are happening.

Supersudaca Thank you (Participant 3) because I like problems. (laughs)

You are mistaken in one part; I am not sure about
Mutation". Mutation is the "Arc en Rêve," from Bordeaux and
Rem did his part with what he had just started in Harvard.
But it is not from Harvard at all "Shopping" and "The Great
Leap Forward" are part of the "Project on the City" at Harvard.
Careful with references.

But it's exactly the same with that topic, in this sense. What
you are saying in the background maybe is: "Why don't they
announce things clearly, why don't they say that they effectively worship the Dutch and that, in reality, there is some kind
of screen. That we are putting the Latin American name but, in
reality, they are repeating exactly what the Dutch were doing?"

Yes and no. I think that – perhaps Félix was explicit for us,
but it turned out to be very subtle or not very clear, and Manuel
also announced it – the instance that took place in Holland, of
confluents; in the sense that many people arrived, attracted by
the opportunity, to debate about architecture, it was special. It
was very special. And that obviously generated a lot of by-prod-
ucts and things. And the debate about that generated different
ways of expressing oneself. And maybe the criticism is: Have
we advanced in that or not? And why do we also have to repu-
diate everything?

The same generation that came later on has repudiated
everything. That is to say, the generation that came later on in
Europe no longer makes diagrams, they are no longer interested in this or that. But for us this is a way of communicating.
In Chile many times they say the same about me. Well, it is
part of being an emigrant, isn't it? I mean, when I arrived in
Switzerland I was Chilean, when I was in Chile I was Swiss,
and when I was in Holland I was also Swiss, and so on. It is
part of your *mestizo* condition. Part of your condition is to value
certain things, to reuse them, to look for what hybrid vigor is
generated, to avoid inbreeding. If we don't like it, or if we consider it a repetition, we are ultra-critical; and if there are still

things that still serve us to communicate, then: Why not just keep using them?

I have a lot of problems with that in Chile. They tell me: "Ah, you are a publicist!" I wish I earned money like publicists do, but no. Those are the tools with which I can communicate better. That lesson from the 1990s, of making the effort to communicate better – not only among architects, which is kind of insular – in a Latin American context that is reflected in many contexts, still seems valuable to me. I don't see why we should hide it. And it is not the exclusive right of this or that. I see it a little bit that way. I don't see why we should hide it. And it is not the exclusive right of so and so. I see it a little bit that way.

Supersudaca And repeating what Félix said a while ago, all those offices and all that production are suddenly made by foreigners. Perhaps many foreigners, from the peripheral countries, who contributed wilder visions than those they could have had there about what was happening. And maybe not only wilder visions, but points of view of a certain naivety, which made things be seen from a different perspective.

Participant from the Audience 4 First of all, congratulations; because all the projects are very interesting and I personally feel that an architect has a lot to do, even if he doesn't have a project to carry out. Maybe research or something like that.

Here in Lima there are quite a few schools of architecture. But in Lima you don't use an architect that much. For example, my house was built by a master builder (and he is already cracking up) two years ago. (laughs) But the question I wanted to ask is: What do you think about that? Why are there so many schools of architecture, if you don't use an architect so much? For example, I think they mentioned that in Paris there were two schools of architecture and here in Lima – where an architect is less used – there are more than twenty or eighteen, something like that. Thank you very much!

Supersudaca Well, people made houses and shelters long before architects existed. So, that the house is made by a master builder is not unusual, and, above all, there are a lot of needs that anyone understands because they are the same needs you need yourself. And he can participate in it. In taking decisions, what happens is that an architect is dedicated intensively to think about that. The person who makes his own house or if the master does, meets the basic needs and perhaps reaches places where architects did not dare to go.

15. Bernard Rudofsky, *Architecture without Architects. An Introduction to Non_Pedigreed Architecture* (New York, Museum of Modern Art, 1964), https://mo.ma/3OcW8Zb.

Suddenly they are not present even though they should be. In the "Y Previ" project you can see that people know how to build, they know how to follow their needs – maybe with some mistakes (covering the patio where light should enter)– and they manage to build their places of refuge and housing.

Supersudaca And how do we learn from that? I think the intent of the Medellin Museum process is that. How can we learn in an unprejudiced way that most of the construction in Latin America – about 70%, if I am not mistaken – is without architects? But that does not mean that it is bad.

Supersudaca Bernard Rudofsky's *Architecture without Architects*[15] is a well-known book, where through techniques and improvements people build their own cities, and sometimes it works better than what an architect from the outside would have designed.

Supersudaca I think that self-construction it's very good. We have no problem; the important thing is perhaps that they are aware. Here in Lima, that it is also a right. That does not happen, for example in Holland – where everything is controlled, and you could no longer build your own house. There was a whole debate (my husband was very involved in that) that we had to reopen the *wild living*, the *wild housing*, and that the State had to give back the right to the people to build their own house.

Supersudaca But at the same time, what Manuel was saying is that at one point, when everything was already *non plan*, anything goes and the architect for what... I don't know either.

It was a discussion that started with Alejandro Aravena. He appeared with the study of public housing, the "23 de Febrero:" There was an initial basic structure and the users finished it. At the time, there were two different visions. Those who wanted to self-build (or those who have only that left) and those who wanted to solve everything with mega-blocks. But there is a third experience, which is the fission of those two things: The typical struggle of liberty versus equality; and, finally, fraternity is the one that allows to solve those issues. And that in-between is more interesting than the two extremes.

155

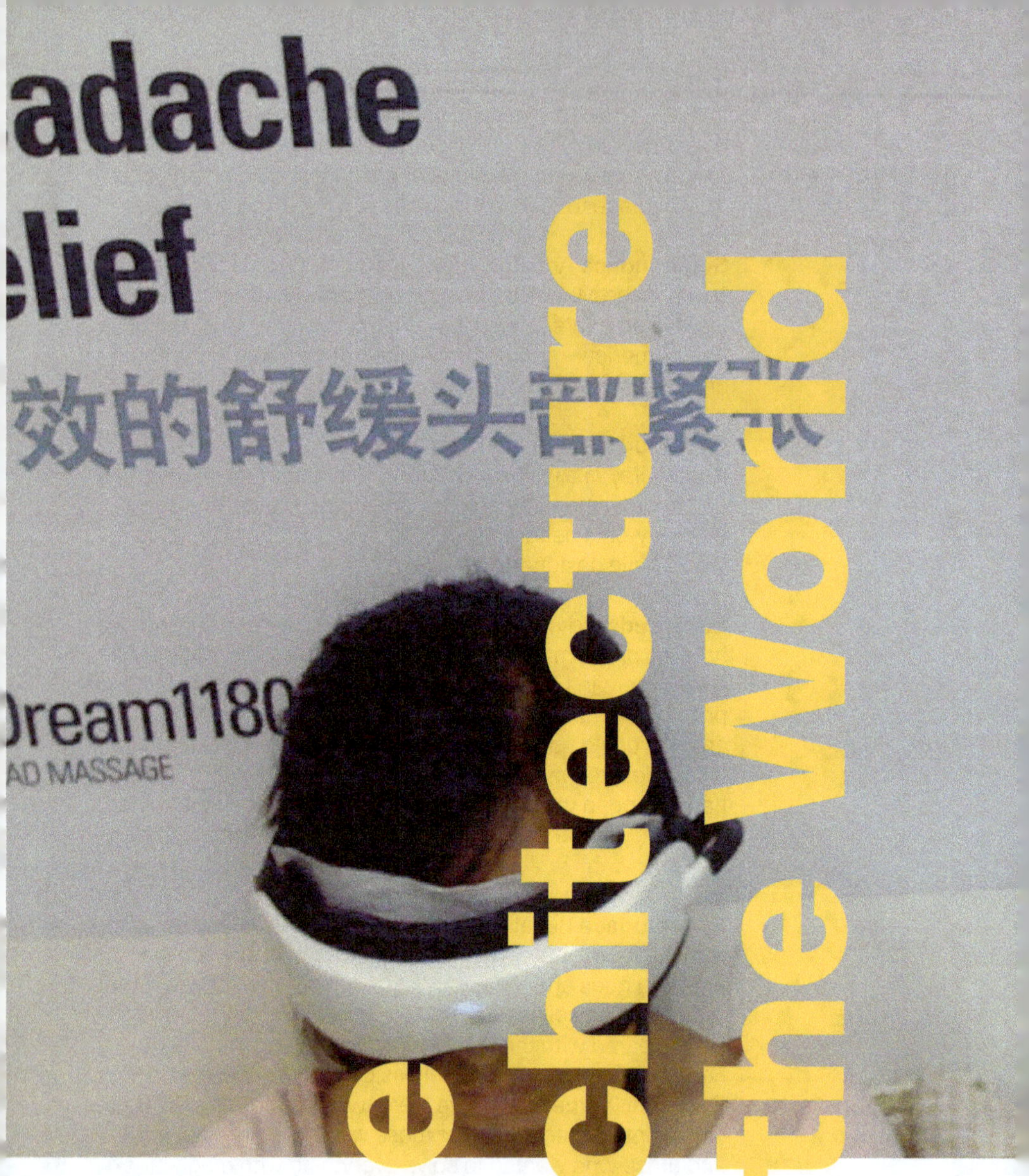

Headache
Relief
高效的舒缓头部紧张
Dream1180
HEAD MASSAGE
The Architecture of the World

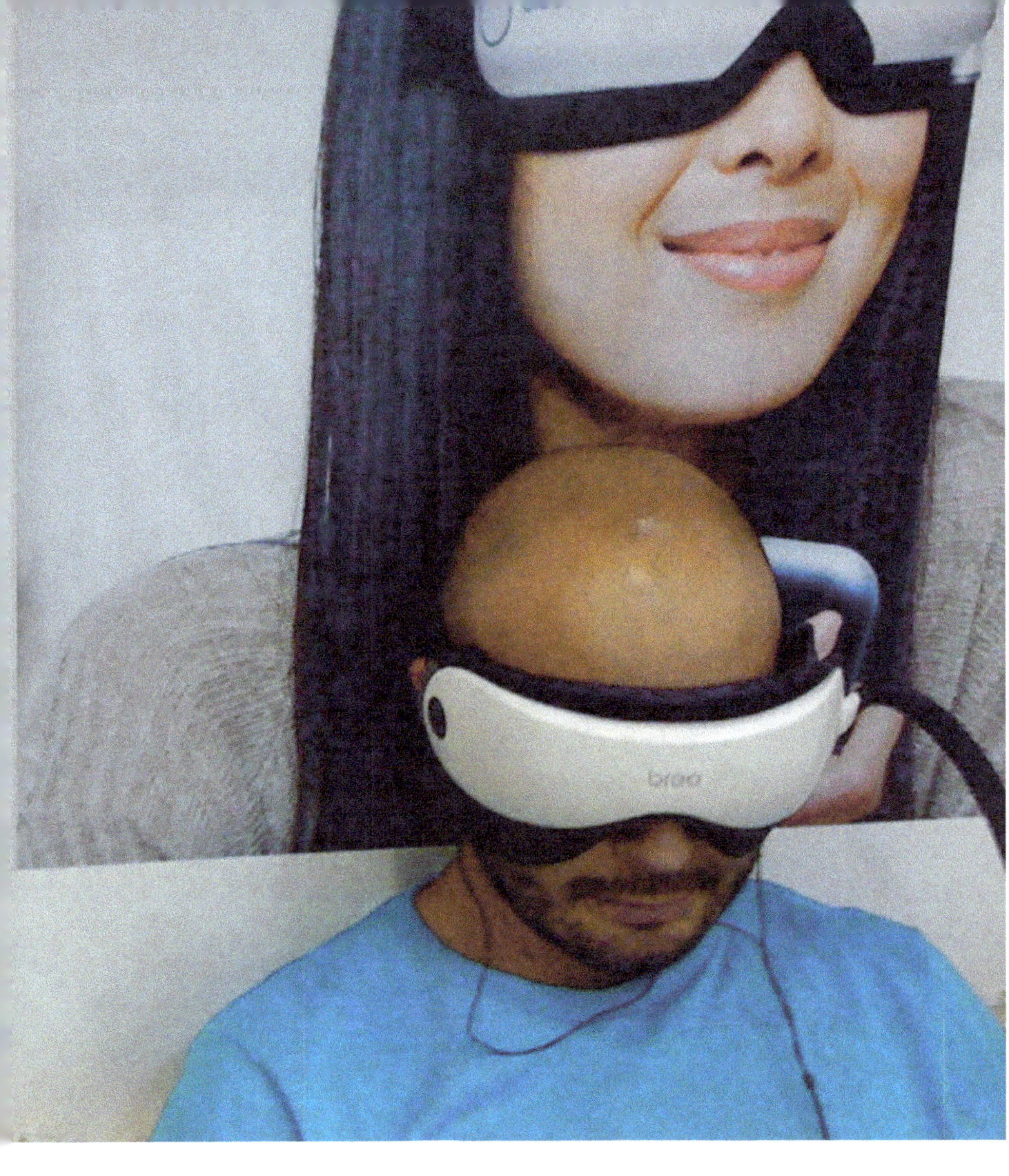

breo

Europe,
We Need
to Talk

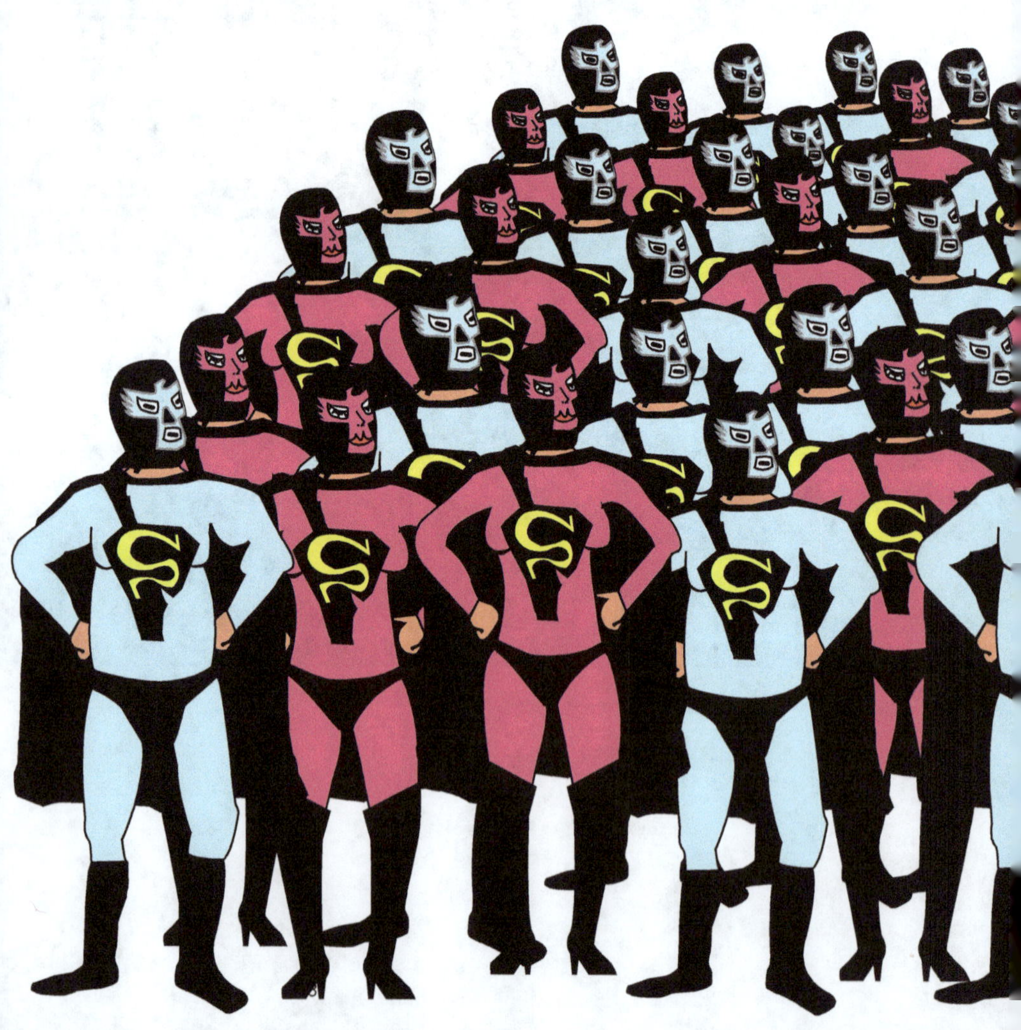

We are part of a generation that saw the emergence of the plotters, floppy disks and yet we were taught on to how to use ink pens, Leroy scriber or erase ink mistakes with razor blades. We belong to the group that changed the drawing table for computers, that saw in the master degree abroad the only way to know the sources we admired. Most of the Supersudaca's traveled to Europe or the United States to study or work. We never thought that something of value could have occurred down the street.

It could not have been a coincidence; in Latin America we were indoctrinated to take as starting point the fact that we belong to what is called "the West." Therefore, in our courses, the architectural history goes from Egypt to modernism through Greece, Rome, Romanesque, Baroque, Gothic, Renaissance, Industrial Revolution, Art Nouveau, Art Deco, Bauhaus, Modernism. (Nobody taught us what Postmodernism was.)

When we arrived in Europe (a.k.a. the true West), in the year 2000, we discovered that our part of the West – Latin America – was not represented in any discussion of contemporary architecture, urban planning or spatial policy. It was a time – and still is – where the East (near and far) occupied much space in the concerns of "the West." But it was not only the West that ignored us, we experienced mixed feelings of relief and shame when we realized how ignorant we all were

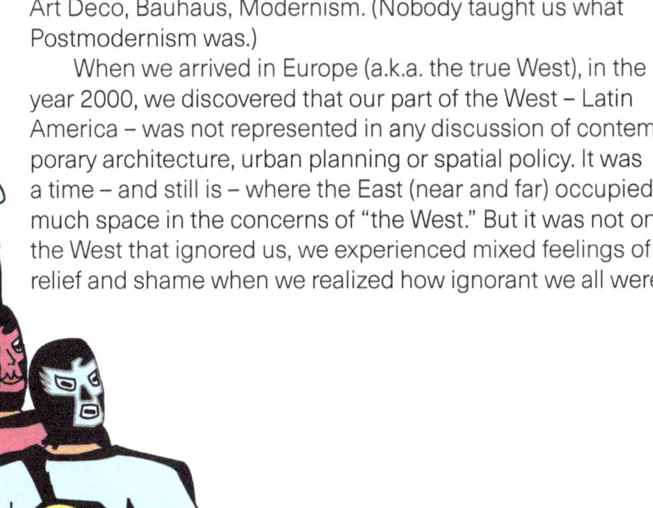

1. The fifteen years refers to 2015, year of this text original publication.

on the countries that we had next door in Latin America, especially embarrassing were the matters related to the production of culture. Luckily, we agreed to have a similar reading (albeit sometimes from opposite points of view) of the social and political situations, analogies diagonally sprouted everywhere.

It is perhaps due to this sense of wounded pride that we found refuge in the part ignored by the West and previously by us also: Latin America. From the distance we began to rebuild it with discussions and PowerPoints. If we had nothing to say, if there was nothing new to contribute, if there was no self-made knowledge, then there was no option but to surrender to the dominion of "the West." Fortunately, we realized that the bank of knowledge was huge and mostly unexplored, that the similarities between the different Latin American urbanisms were not merely accidental. Finally, we realized that our generation that broke with the drawing tables should also break the inertia of blindly following what was recognized in the West.

With a strong colonial past, the region developed recursive forms of survival strategies within complex and often unfair situations that showed a great capacity for social cohesion during drastic changing situations. Without having thought about this before, we noticed that this equipped the region with a special way of dealing with life in the era of global capitalism, and somehow, instead of being behind the times (developing countries) we passed to the forefront of knowledge on how to operate in the present. The current neoliberal world that promotes privatization of spaces and services, which is careless about balancing between wealth and precariousness, is now arriving at the discussion tables of the West, that very same world Latin America already experienced decades ago. We even dared to advice the Dutch that if they wanted to get prepared for the future they should study what happens now in Latin America. Hence, we proposed to them to value of human solidarity that exist in times of insecurity. That was almost fifteen years ago.[1] This year, when the Dutch government launched a proposal that makes responsible by law all those direct relatives of the old, it sounded like *deja vu* for us. The European welfare state shows signs of warnings everywhere, perhaps the Latinos can help them rethink it.

On the other hand, it was funny to realize that in the minds of "the West," people in Latin America mostly live in an unspoiled and exotic landscape, ignoring the fact that the ratio of urbanization in Latin America has been above 80% for a long time. The region has witnessed the growth of huge metropolis that concentrate large percentage of the urban population, megacities not so much in disarray but instead readily willing to perpetual adaptation to upcoming crises. Informal urban developments mixed with American style suburbs proliferate, but above all it is the awareness of the mix (sometimes brilliant, sometimes lethal) between speed of urbanization, lack of planning, improvisation and freedom. Nevertheless, we believe that Latin America today represents an interesting middle point between the vertical planning policies of China and the blurring undefinition of some African cities. We sincerely believe that these regions have more to learn from Latin America (from their mistakes and achievements) than from the West.

Finally, in a time where relations don't need any more to be North-South or *center-periphery* Latin America can now understand that its separation from the West, understood retroactively (we never belonged), should lead us to achieve a strong cultural independence in order to become an urban world actor.

That's why we want to work with global agenda issues of territory and space policy which the Latin American experience brings knowledge and experience beyond the vernacular architecture, global modernity updates and cute beach houses that will be anyway published until the end of times and do not need people from our generation for that.

Al Caribe!

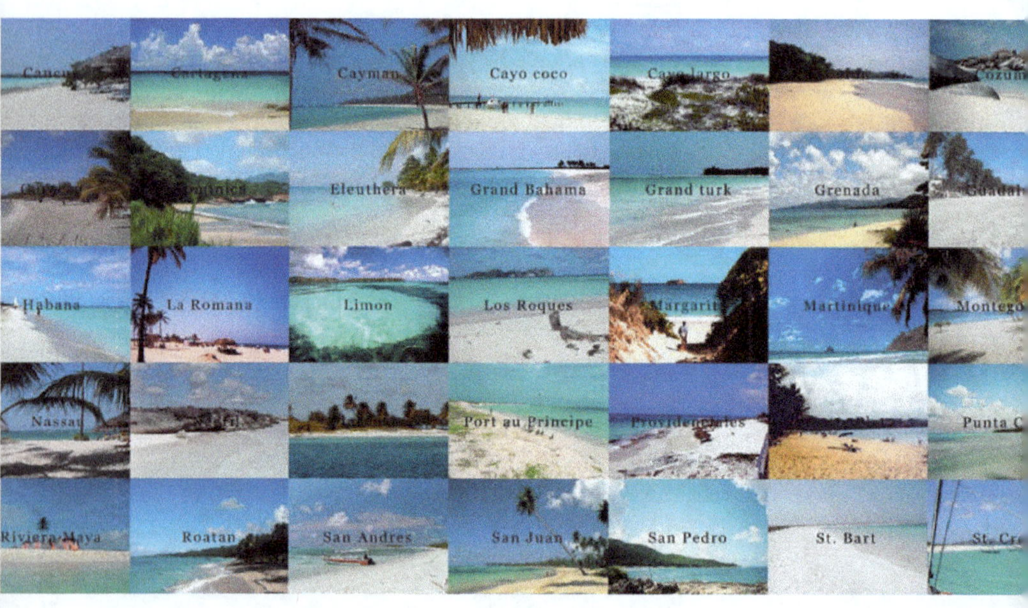

Cancun
Cartagena
Cayman
Cayo coco
Cayo largo
Cozumel
Eleuthera
Grand Bahama
Grand turk
Grenada
Guadal
Habana
La Romana
Limon
Los Roques
Margarita
Martinique
Montego
Nassau
Port au Principe
Providenciales
Punta C
Riviera Maya
Roatan
San Andres
San Juan
San Pedro
St. Bart
St. Cr

The world is experimenting at an unprecedented speed an amazing accumulation of matter along the coasts, led by the tourist *avant-garde*. Buildings, money, food, vegetation, bacteria, waste and plenty of people concentrate more and more in narrow bands parallel to the shores. Tourism, as the largest industry in the world that benefits directly with the increase of free time, is becoming the key of global urbanization.

To investigate such a phenomenon, it is greatly needed for architects, not as an alibi to avoid design, but as a way to inform it, question it, put it in context. This was the main goal of the Second International Architecture Biennale of Rotterdam that took place in 2005 in Las Palmas. It was a space for discussion and debate that took seriously the long run down idea of understanding the urban process. Together with seventeen teams from different points of the world, the Biennale aimed at starting a discussion on the impacts of tourism in the environment. Supersudaca was invited to contribute with the Caribbean region. Here are some of our findings.

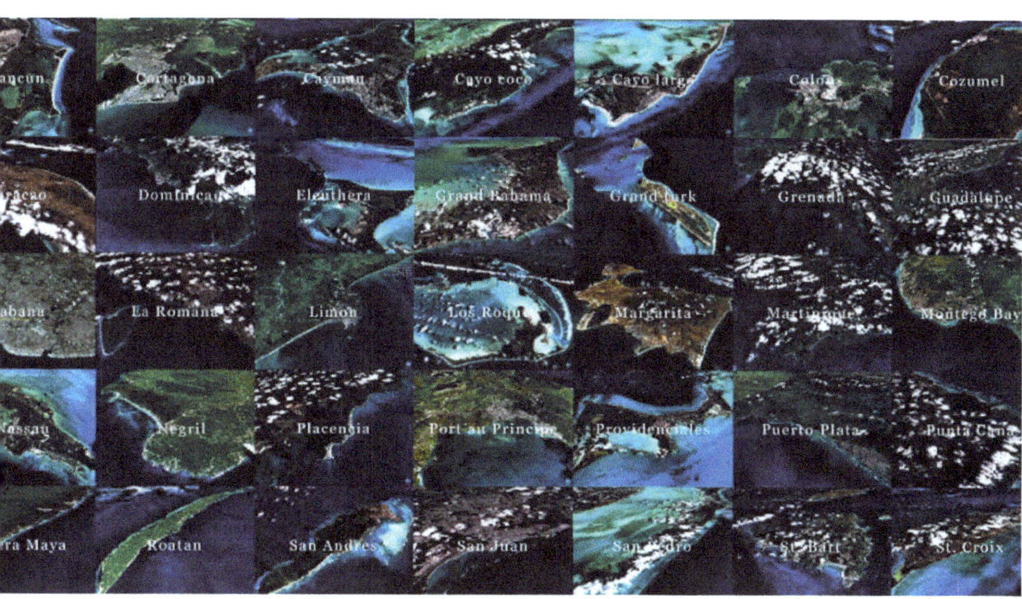

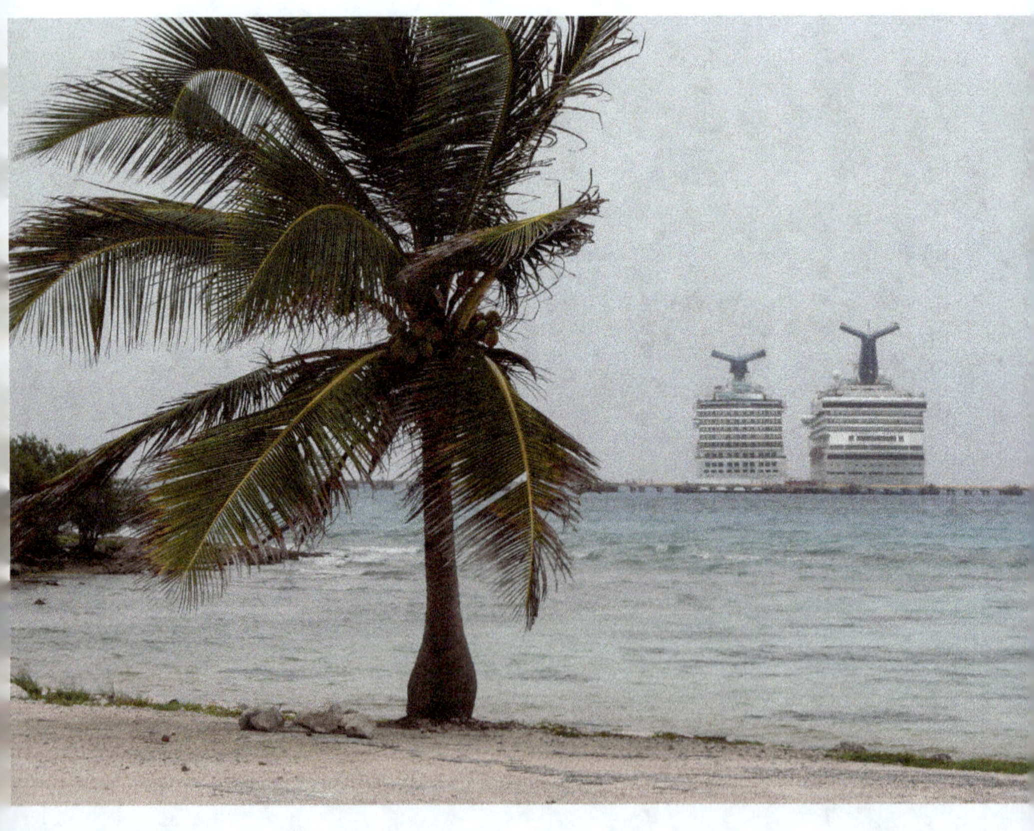

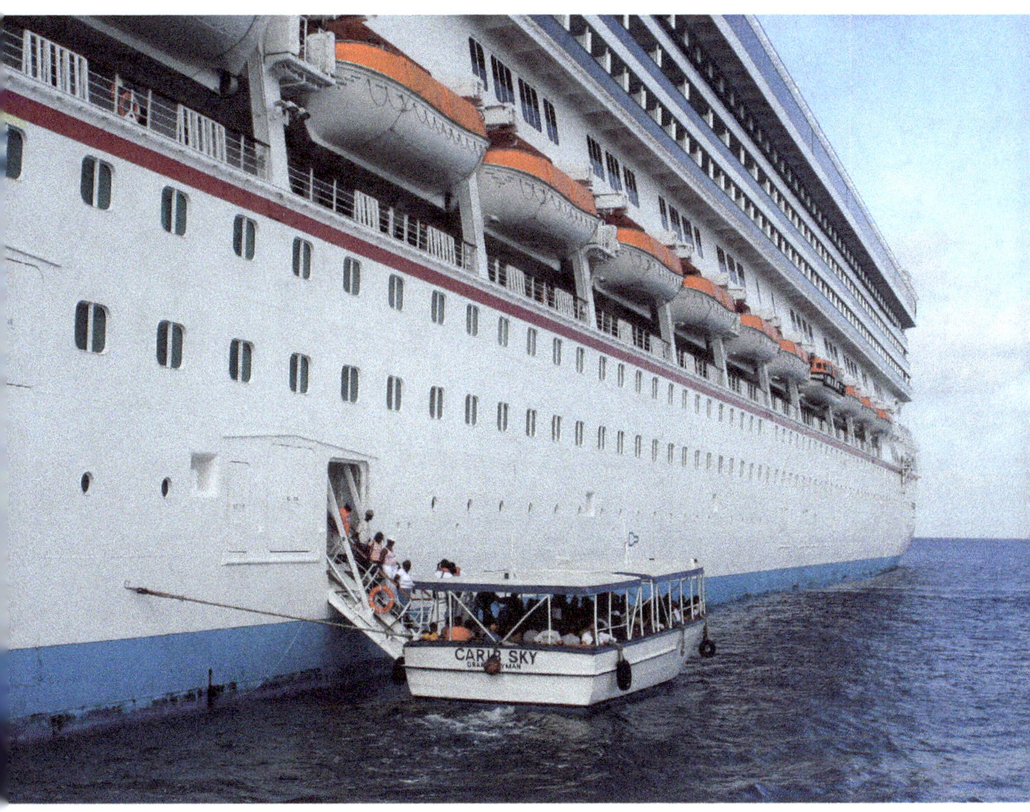
CARIB SKY

In terms of tourism, the Caribbean represents a modest
2.3% of the world market share, with twenty million visitors per
year. There are less hotel rooms in the whole region (266,000)
than in small countries like Greece (317,000) or Austria
(310,000). Yet as farming exports are in great danger of competition from bigger economies of scale and manufacturing
is going east, tourism remains as the last great "resort" that
could take the region out of poverty. The increasing dependency on tourism in the Caribbean is striking, representing
above 50% of their economies. But this can be as high as
95%, as in the cases of the British Virgin Islands, Antigua and
Barbuda.

Dependency on tourism is also a dependency on foreign
investments, a path that reflects the pattern of recent (or current) colonial history, a "coincidence" that affects the local population perception that are beginning to suspiciously see tourism as the latest form of colonial domination by the strongest
powers. Spanish control of the all-inclusive resorts is matched

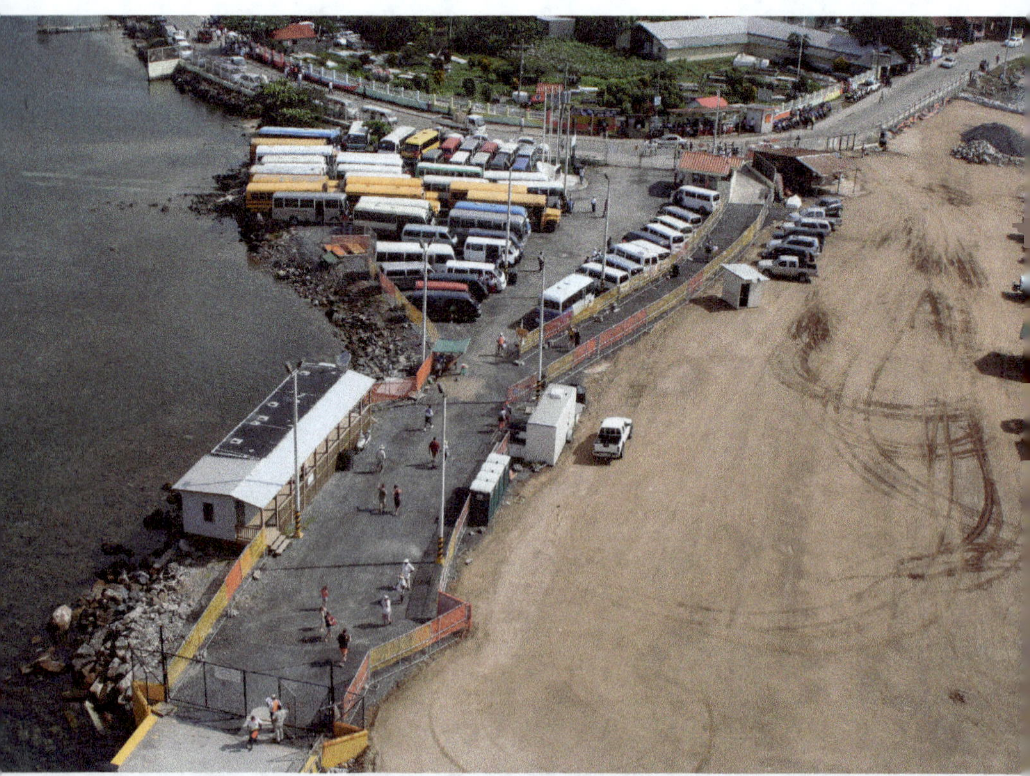

by the amount of American owned tour operators, airline providers and on-line reservation agencies.

When considering the different types of tourism, two stand out clearly as key in the region and in both the Caribbean is the global leader: cruises and all-inclusive resorts. The Caribbean has a 50% market share of the global cruise ship industry that relies greatly on two big companies, Royal Caribbean and Carnival, both of them based in Florida.

The biggest territorial impact of tourism consists of resort strips. The recent history changed since 1995 with places like the Dominican Republic or Mexican Caribbean that have grown at an average rate of 3,000 rooms per year!

The Caribbean's dependency on tourism has made the industry's main players gain enormous power in the region. But what we found surprising is that in the last five years, a process of verticalization of the industry has occurred without much notice. That means that corporations have been buying all the components in the tourism supply chain. Giant groups like Touristik Union International (TUI), First Choice, Accor, My Travel, Carlson, Thomas Cook or Cendant own tour operators, travel agencies, airlines, car rentals, accommodations, cruise lines, excursion operators, hotel schools, even voucher systems and software to track potential customers via credit card behavior. This means the power in the region has concentrated in a few powerful hands that are either in Europe or the USA.

The powerful combination of all-inclusive and verticalization versus rendered local economies at the periphery and local individual enterprises leaves only very little of the tourist's expenditures in the destination. For every dollar spent by a tourist in an all-inclusive package, only three cents remain in the destination. 89 cents stay in the origin country for paying the airline, tour operator, travel agency, hotel owner etc. Of those eleven cents that do arrive in the destination, eight cents go out of the country again to pay foreign managers salaries, advertising, credit interests and above all, imports for tourist demanded products. From the three cents that finally remain, are spent to pay the workers' salaries etc.

Spatially speaking, touristic strips developed in the last decade have increased dramatically in length and detachment from the existing city. The innocent four kilometers long strip of Barbados in the 80's that merged with the city, looks innocent in comparison to recent strips, like the one in Punta Cana that is now reaching 35 kilometers without any connection with the city whatsoever, a parallel world.

With that excuse of disconnection precisely they have generated a – fantasy island – landscape detached entirely from the local reality. Every link of the supply chain is rationalized for profit. Disconnection today with the local population could not be greater. Servants, chefs and taxi drivers arrive "from God knows where" to the resort. They sing, they clean, they smile and then they disappear after the perimetral wall. Where do they go?

Where do they live? Is there such a concept as a city of tourism workers? Just like there was a city of Indians? Or worst, there is not even a place for them, as they dispersed in niches around the hinterland territories close to infrastructure nodes. The all-inclusive strip has surpassed the now dull and even social American suburb, the metropolis, the edge city. The tourist strip is the ultimate non-city of tomorrow, it is here in the Caribbean, an almost lawless place, that the future of urbanization is being tested at its present tense, its laboratory being most likely the poorest countries of the region that desperately need jobs at any price.

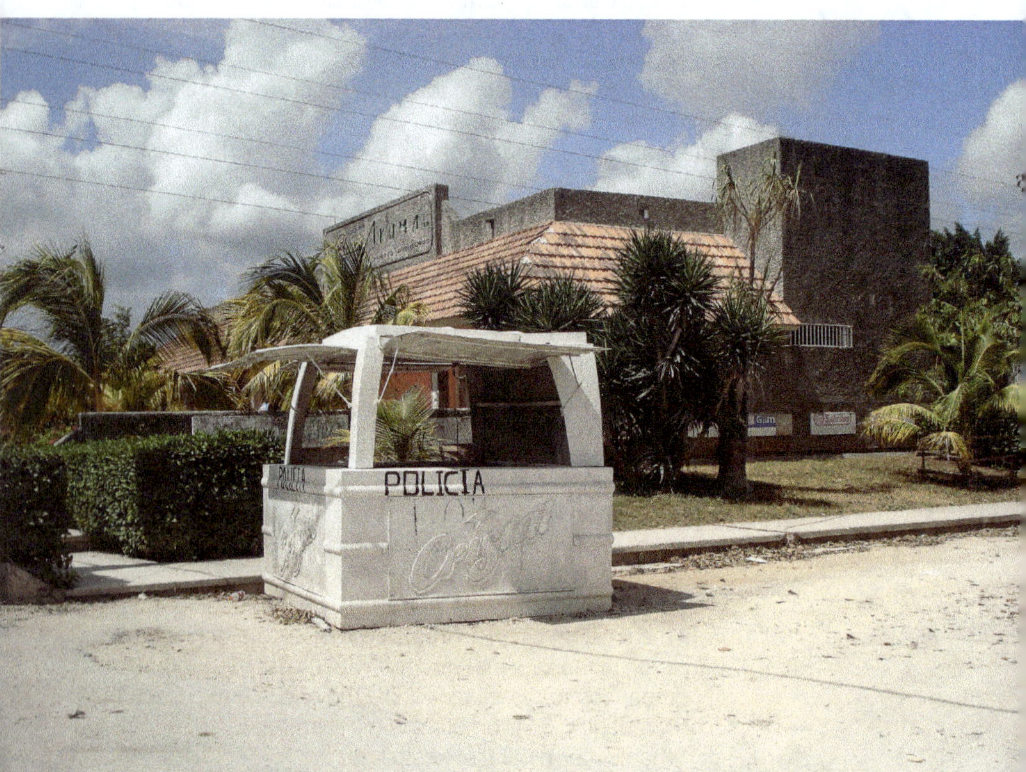

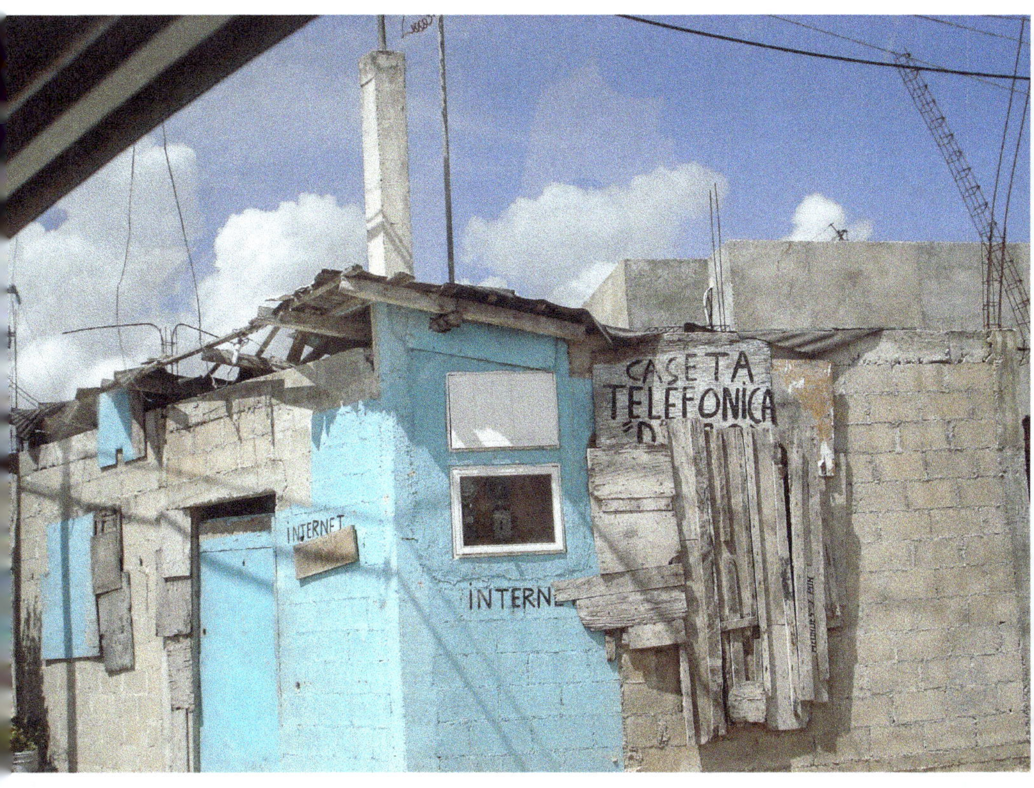

INTERNET
INTERNE
CASETA
TELEFONICA

3,608,332km2
EUROPEAN UNION
2,561,228km2
ARGENTINA
2,621,201km2
MEDITERRENEAN SEA
2,715,892km2
CARIBBEAN SEA

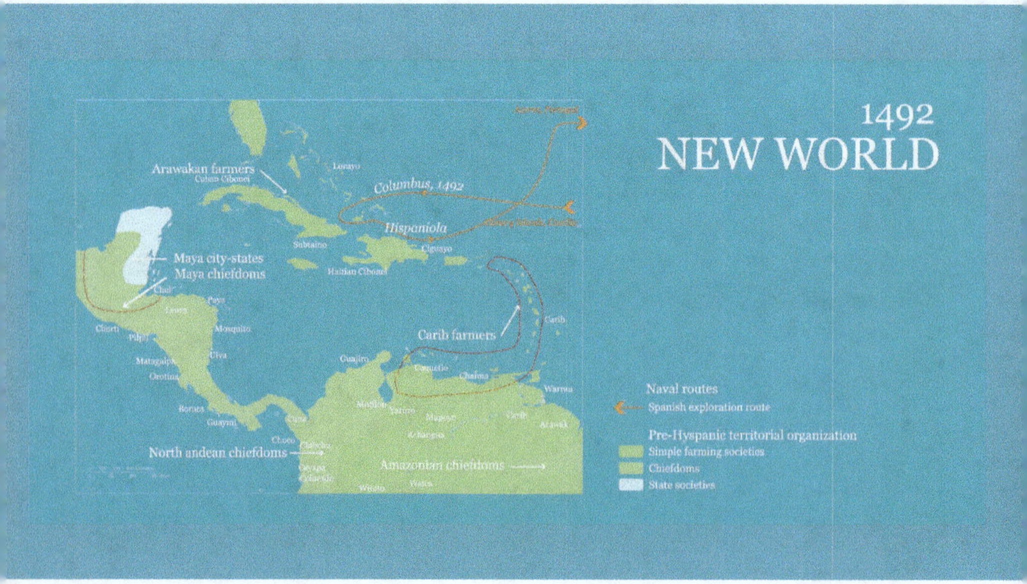

1492
NEW WORLD
Arawakan farmers
Cuban Ciboney
Lucayo
Columbus, 1492
Hispaniola
Subtaino
Ciguayo
Haitian Ciboney
Maya city-states
Maya chiefdoms
Chol
Paya
Tzutuj
Chorti
Pilpil
Mosquito
Uva
Matagalpa
Orotina
Boruca
Guaymi
Cuna
Choco
Coiquer
Cayapa
Colorado
Guajiro
Caquetio
Chaima
Carib farmers
Carib
Warrau
Naval routes
Spanish exploration route
Pre-Hyspanic territorial organization
Simple farming societies
Chiefdoms
State societies
North andean chiefdoms
Amazonian chiefdoms

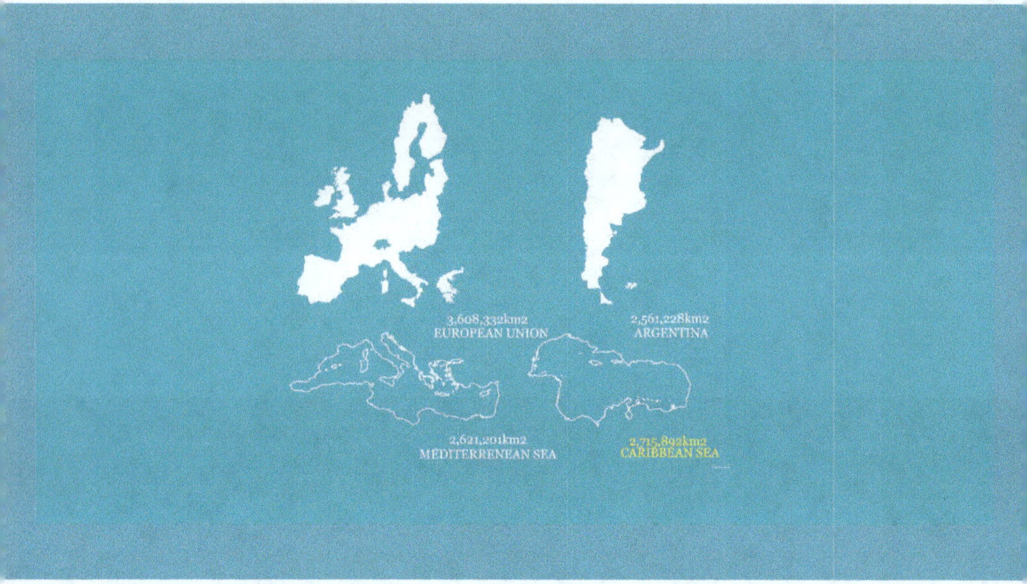

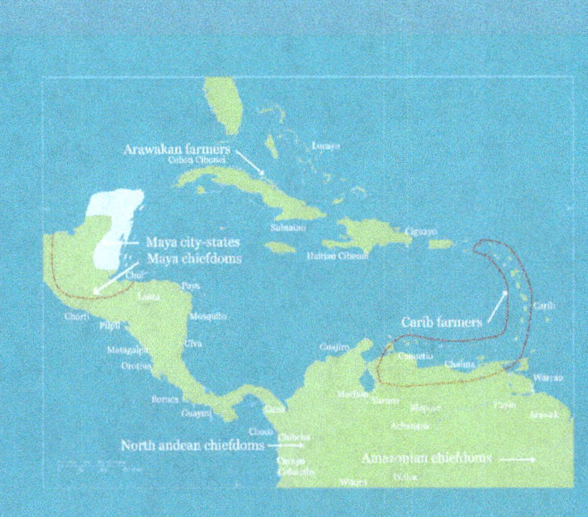

1492
OLD WORLD
Arawakan farmers
Ciboni Ciboney
Lucayo
Sabaino
Ciguayo
Maya city-states
Maya chiefdoms
Haitian Ciboni
Chol
Poya
Lenca
Chorti
Pilgui
Mosquito
Carib
Metagalpa
Ulva
Orotina
Guajiro
Carib farmers
Cometio
Chaima
Borica
Medano
Warao
Guaymi
Gira
Maracu
Mapoye
Toriu
Aruwak
Achaguus
North andean chiefdoms
Chibcha
Choco
Cuevas
Colorado
Amazonian chiefdoms
Wikira
Uaba
Pre-Hyspanic territorial organization
Simple farming societies
Chiefdoms
State societies

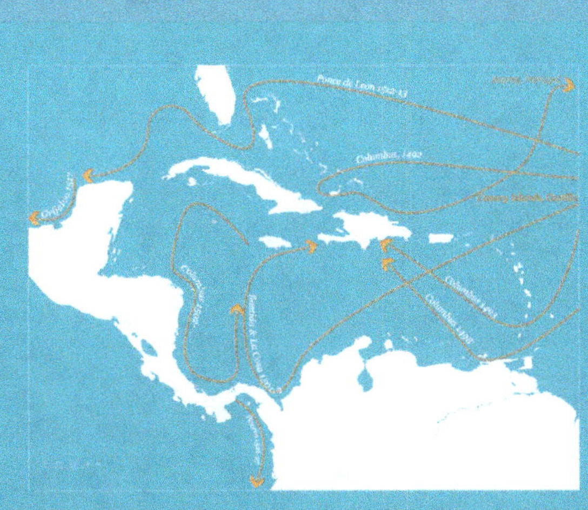

1492-1798
EXPLORATION
Ponce de Leon 1512-13
Columbus, 1492
Orellana
Naval routes
Spanish exploration route

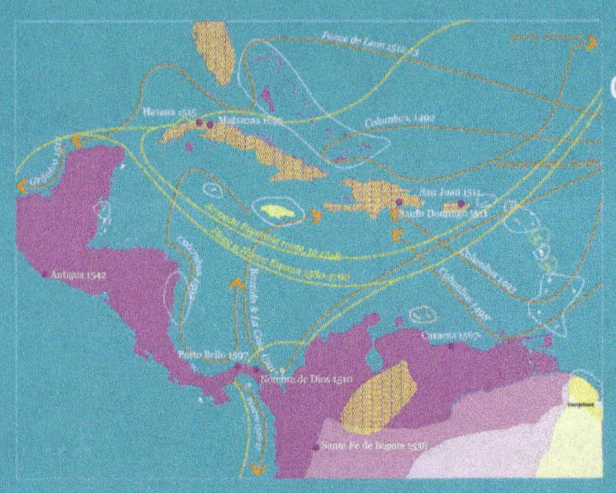
1492-1798
COMMERCIALIZATION
Ponce de León 1512-13
Columbus, 1492
San Juan 1511
Santo Domingo 1511
Havana 1515
Matanzas 1696
Antigua 1542
Caracas 1567
Porto Bello 1597
Nombre de Dios 1510
Santa Fé de Bogota 1538
Naval routes
Spanish exploration route
Spanish trading route
Early settlements or trading post
Spanish
Territories
Spanish territory, 1650
Spanish territory, 1750
Spanish frontier land, 1750
Portuguese frontier land, 1750
British territory, 1750
French territory, 1750
Dutch territory, 1750
Slavery
Concentration of african slaves XVIII Century

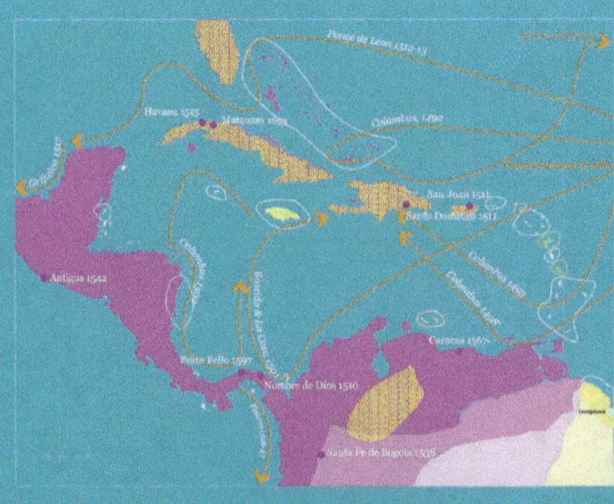
1492-1798
EXPLOITATION
Ponce de León 1512-13
Columbus, 1492
San Juan 1511
Santo Domingo 1511
Havana 1515
Matanzas 1696
Antigua 1542
Caracas 1567
Porto Bello 1597
Nombre de Dios 1510
Santa Fé de Bogota 1538
Naval routes
Spanish exploration route
Early settlements or trading post
Spanish
Territories
Spanish territory, 1650
Spanish territory, 1750
Spanish frontier land, 1750
Portuguese frontier land, 1750
British territory, 1750
French territory, 1750
Dutch territory, 1750
Slavery
Concentration of african slaves XVIII Century

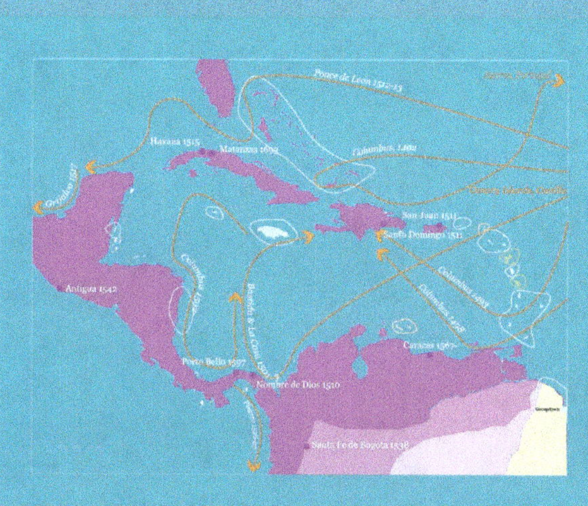

1492-1798
COLONIZATION

Naval routes
Spanish exploration route

Early settlements or trading post
Spanish

Territories
Spanish territory, 1650
Spanish territory, 1750
Spanish frontier land, 1750
Portuguese frontier land, 1750
British territory, 1750
French territory, 1750
Dutch territory, 1750

1783-1914
UNITED & INDEPENDENT

Territories held by European Powers, 1783
Spanish territory
French territory
British territory
Netherlands territory
Independent republics & federations
Gran Colombia
United Provinces of Central America
Republic of Haiti, 1804-08, 1822-44
Leeward Islands Federation, 1871
Winward Islands Federation, 1876 (abortive)

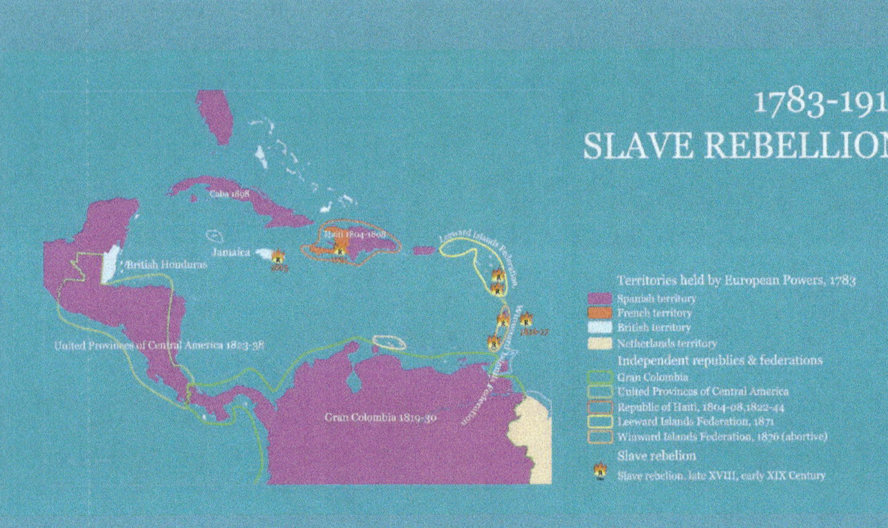

1783-1914
SLAVE REBELLION
Cuba 1898
Haiti 1804-1808
Jamaica
British Honduras
Leeward Islands Federation
United Provinces of Central America 1823-38
1826-27
Gran Colombia 1819-30
Territories held by European Powers, 1783
Spanish territory
French territory
British territory
Netherlands territory
Independent republics & federations
Gran Colombia
United Provinces of Central America
Republic of Haiti, 1804-08,1822-44
Leeward Islands Federation, 1871
Winward Islands Federation, 1876 (abortive)
Slave rebelion
Slave rebelion, late XVIII, early XIX Century

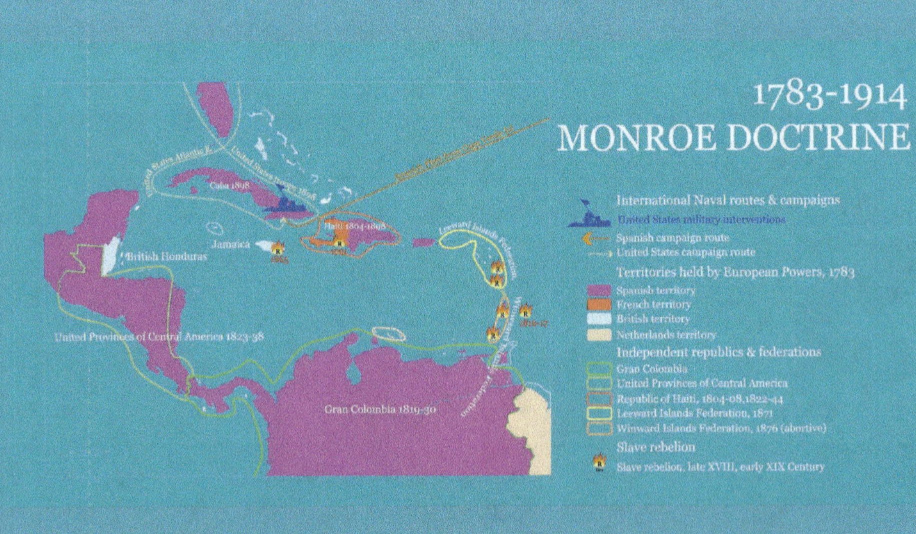

1783-1914
MONROE DOCTRINE
United States Atlantic &
United States Pacific Fleet
Spanish Caribbean Fleet
Cuba 1898
Haiti 1804-1808
Jamaica
British Honduras
Leeward Islands Federation
United Provinces of Central America 1823-38
1816-17
Gran Colombia 1819-30
International Naval routes & campaigns
United States military interventions
Spanish campaign route
United States campaign route
Territories held by European Powers, 1783
Spanish territory
French territory
British territory
Netherlands territory
Independent republics & federations
Gran Colombia
United Provinces of Central America
Republic of Haiti, 1804-08,1822-44
Leeward Islands Federation, 1871
Winward Islands Federation, 1876 (abortive)
Slave rebelion
Slave rebelion, late XVIII, early XIX Century

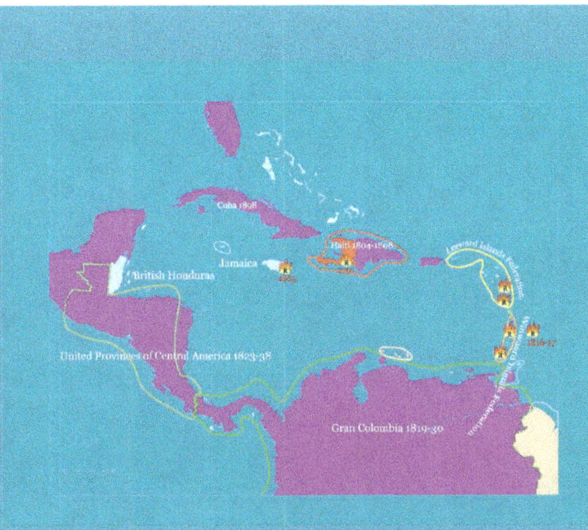

1783-1914
SLAVE REBELLION
Cuba 1868
Haiti 1804-1808
Jamaica
British Honduras
Leeward Islands Federation
United Provinces of Central America 1823-38
Gran Colombia 1819-30
1816-17
Territories held by European Powers, 1783
Spanish territory
French territory
British territory
Netherlands territory
Independent republics & federations
Gran Colombia
United Provinces of Central America
Republic of Haiti, 1804-08,1822-44
Leeward Islands Federation, 1871
Winward Islands Federation, 1876 (abortive)
Slave rebelion
Slave rebelion, late XVIII, early XIX Century

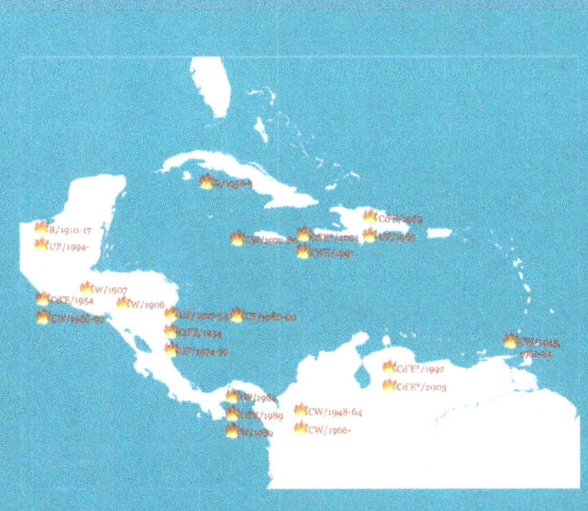

1914-2005
INTERNAL REVOLUTIONS
R/1958-9
CdE/1963
R/1910-17
CW/1972-79
CdE/2001
UP/1965
UP/1994-
CW/1991
CW/1907
CdE/1954
CW/1906
UP/1950-53
UP/1980-60
CW/1960-96
CdE/1954
CW/1948-
UP/1974-79
CdE/1992
CW/1948-
1979-84
CdE/2005
UP/1906
UP/1989
CW/1948-64
W/1969
CW/1966-
International and domestic conflicts
W (International War)/Date
CW (Civil War)/Date
CdE (Coup d' Etat)/Date
UP (Uprising)/Date
R (Revolution)/Date

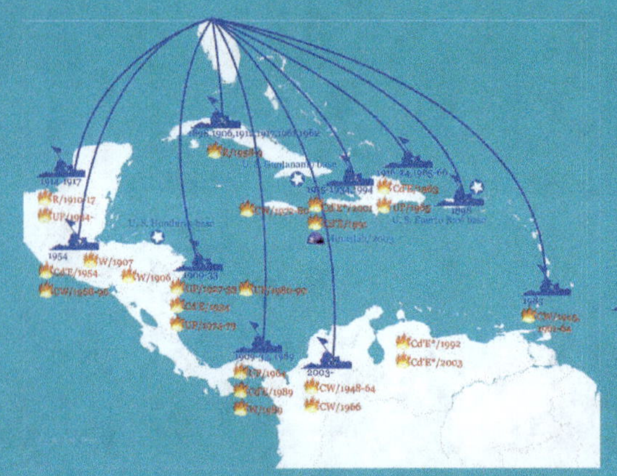
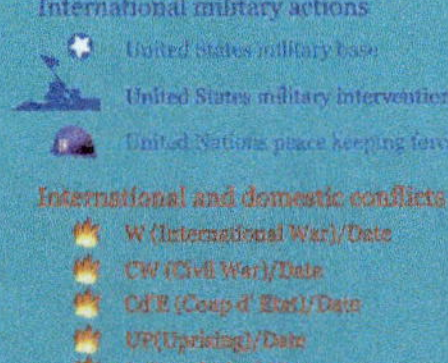

1914-2005
EXTERNAL INTERVENTIONS

International military actions
United States military base
United States military interventions
United Nations peace keeping forces

International and domestic conflicts
W (International War)/Date
CW (Civil War)/Date
Cd'E (Coup d' État)/Date
UP (Uprising)/Date
R (Revolution)/Date

Tourism Impact
Flows, dependency and verticalization

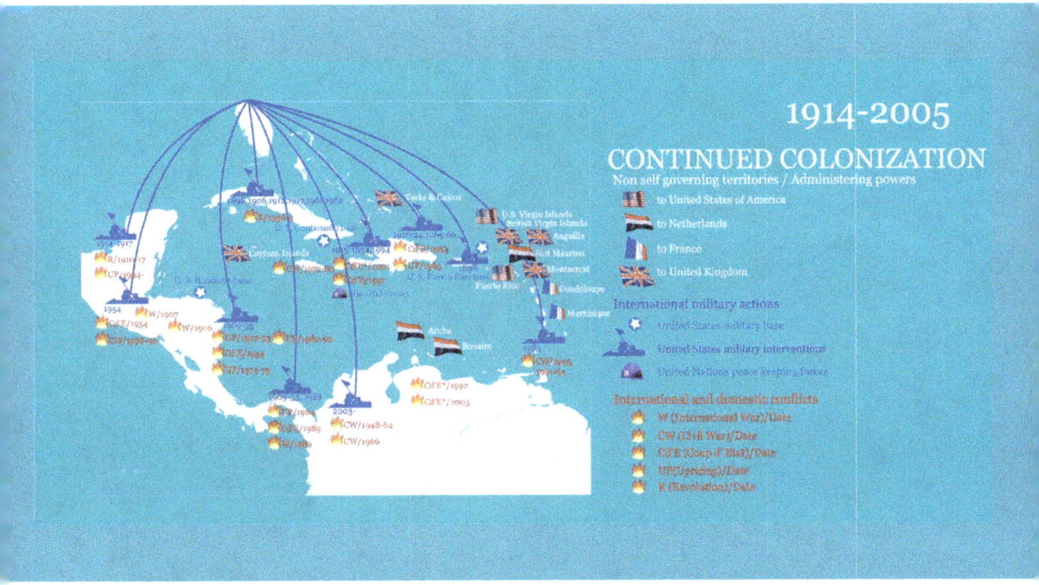

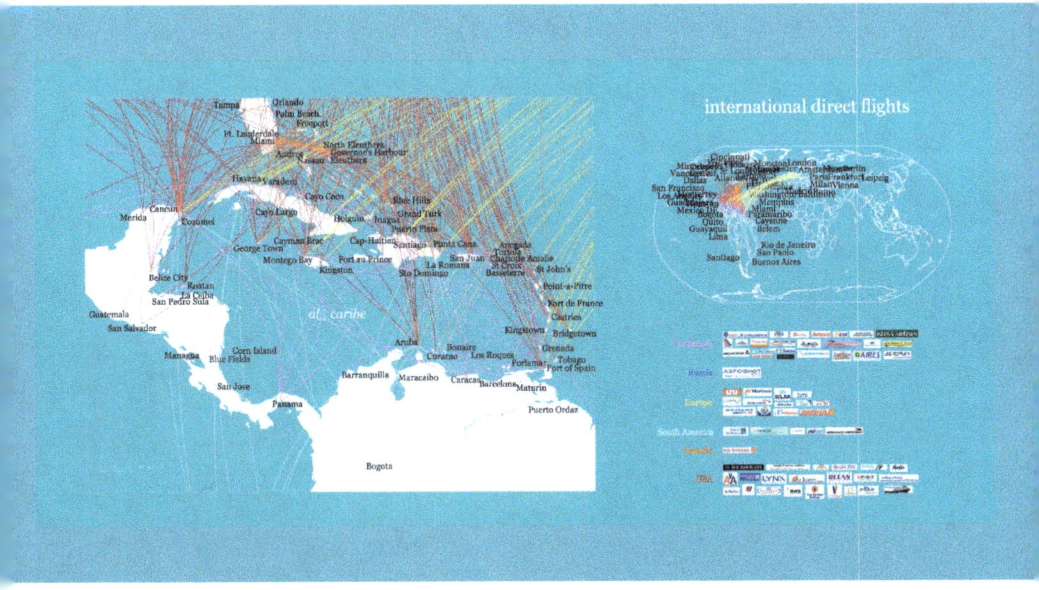

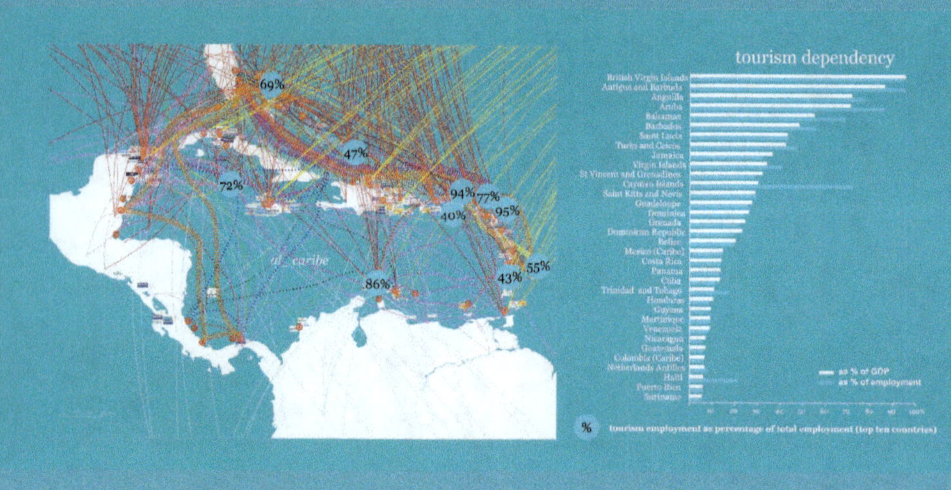

tourism dependency
British Virgin Islands
Antigua and Barbuda
Anguilla
Aruba
Bahamas
Barbados
Saint Lucia
Turks and Caicos
Jamaica
Virgin Islands
St Vincent and Grenadines
Cayman Islands
Saint Kitts and Nevis
Guadeloupe
Dominica
Grenada
Dominican Republic
Belize
Mexico (Caribe)
Costa Rica
Panama
Cuba
Trinidad and Tobago
Honduras
Guyana
Martinique
Venezuela
Nicaragua
Guatemala
Colombia (Caribe)
Netherlands Antilles
Haiti
Puerto Rico
Suriname
as % of GDP
as % of employment
%
tourism employment as percentage of total employment (top ten countries)
69%
47%
72%
94%
77%
40%
95%
86%
43%
55%
el caribe

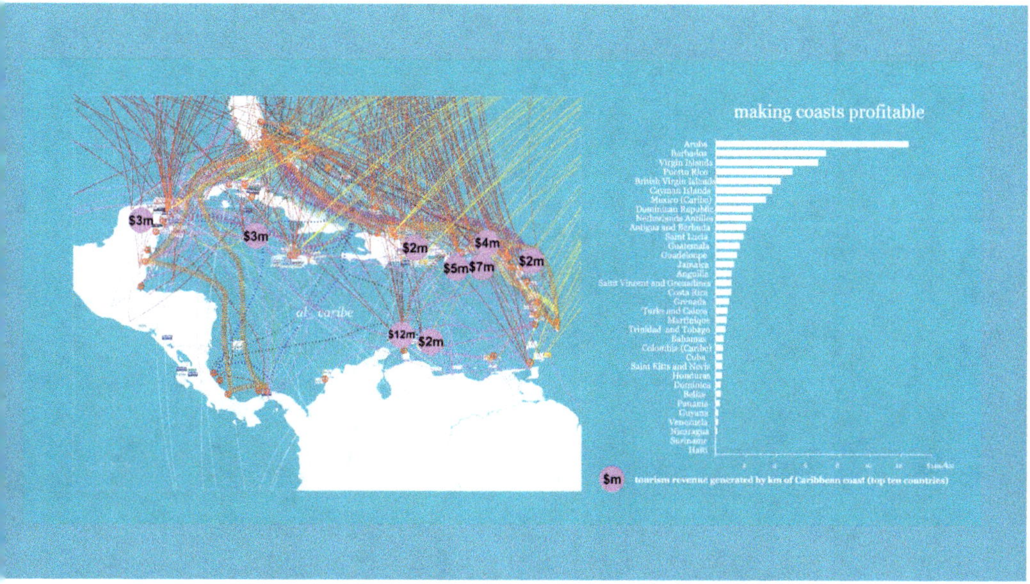

making coasts profitable

verticalization of Caribbean tourism
main corporations

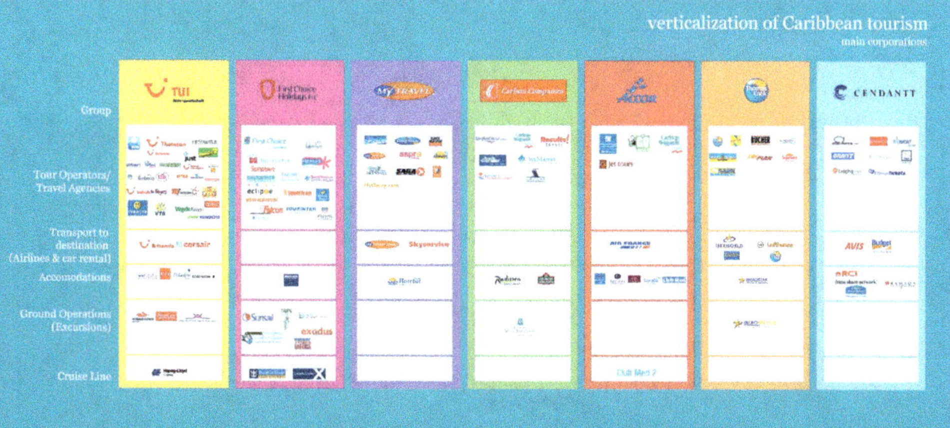

Main Players
All inclusive & cruise

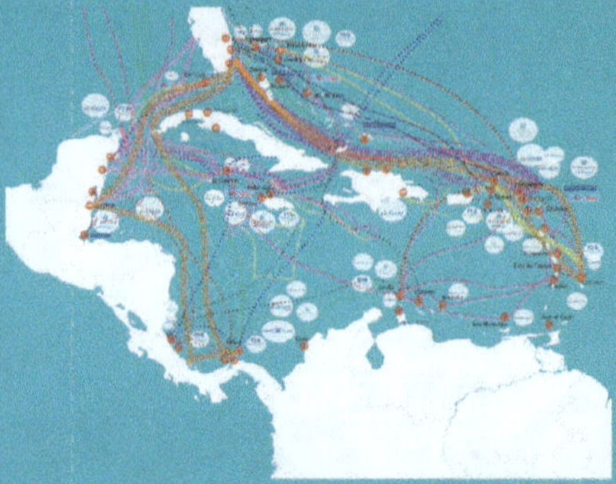

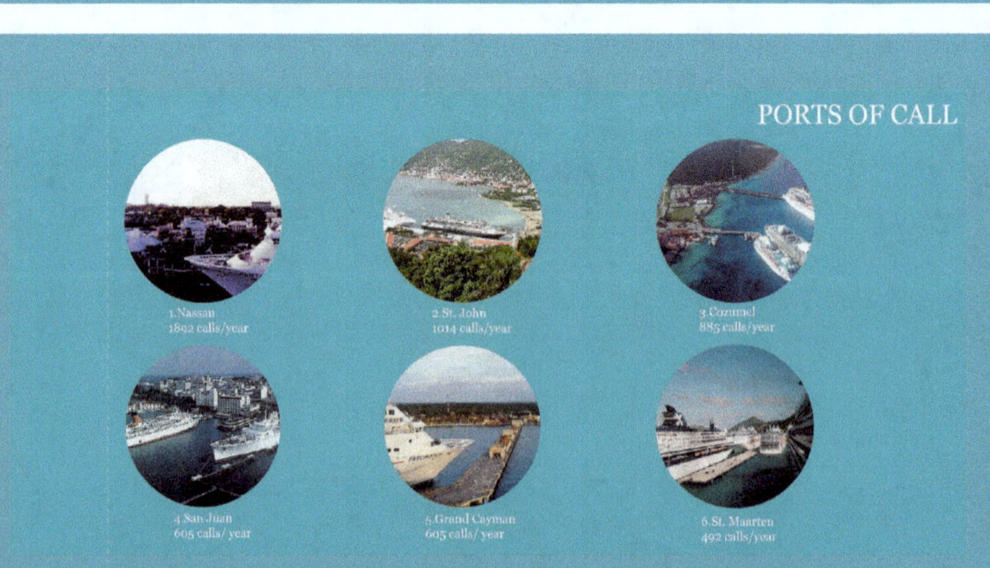

GROWTH

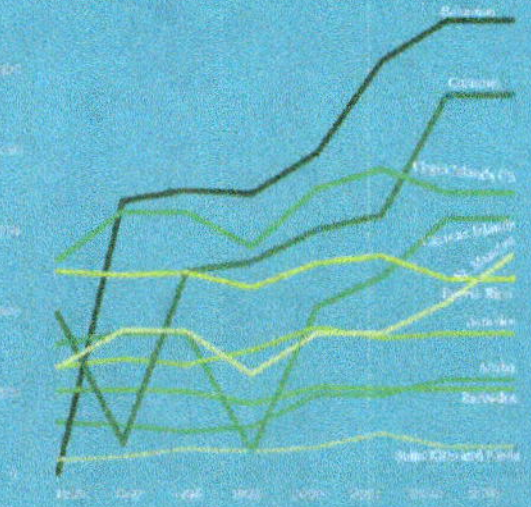

CRUISE PASSENGER ARRIVALS

OCCUPANCY RATE 90 %
Caribbean cruise passenger capacity grew
by 21,8 % in the year 2000

LEAKAGE

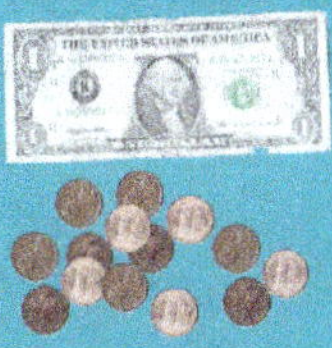

CRUISE TOURISM

For every dollar spent by a
tourist on a cruise
package,only 14 cents
only stays in the caribbean

ALL INCLUSIVE

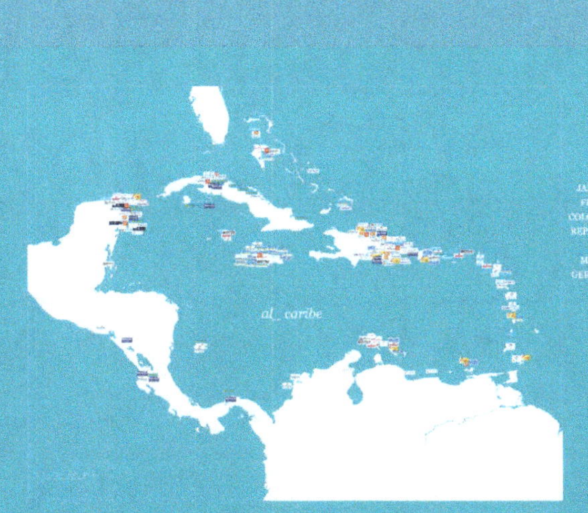

The Caribbean is the World's leader
by a very wide margin in quantity and
quality of all inclusive resorts.
source: WTO, Caribbean report

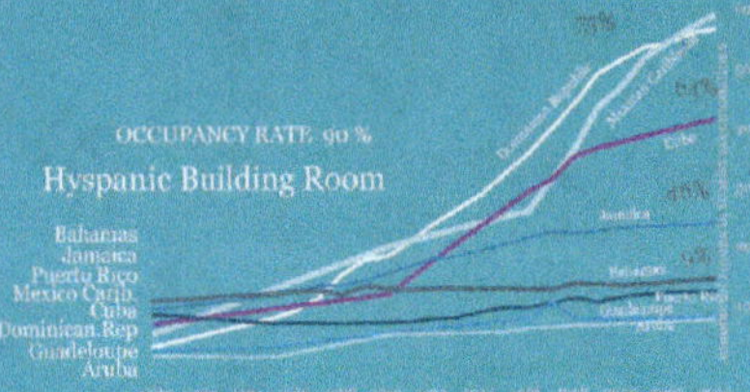

THE ALL INCLUSIVE EFFECT

OCCUPANCY RATE 90 %

*Accomodation capacity of Caribbean increased from 88,000 rooms in 1980
to 266,000 last year. In that period 140,000 of the new rooms were built mainly through all-inclusive resorts in the Mexican Caribbean, Dominican Republic, and Cuba.

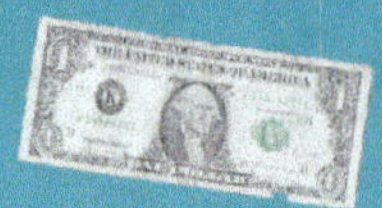

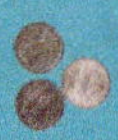

HOTEL TOURISM

For every dollar spent by a tourist in an all inclusive package,only 3 cents stays in the caribbean

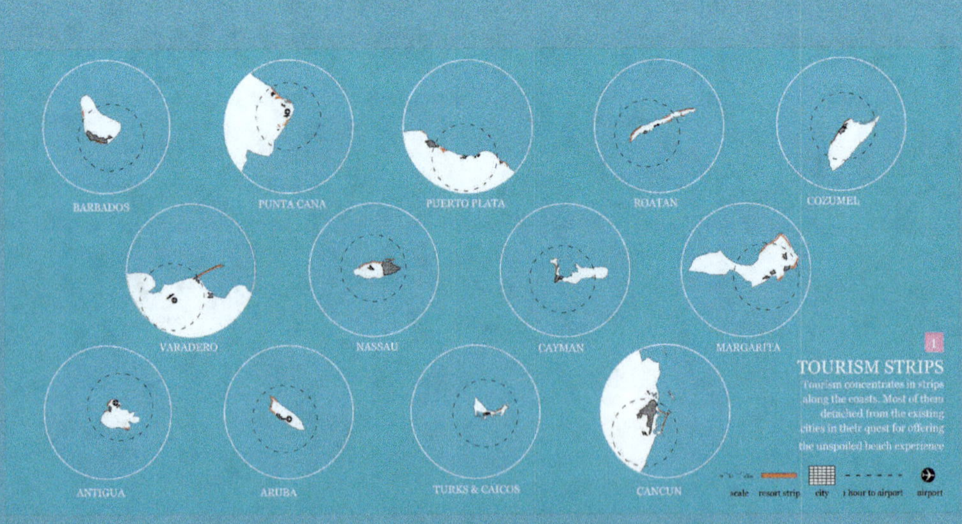

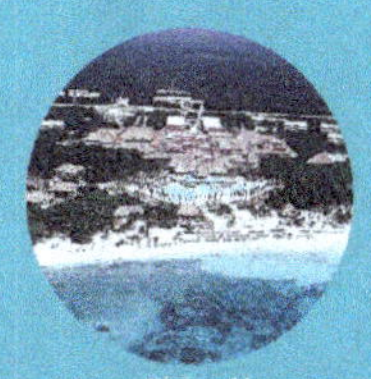

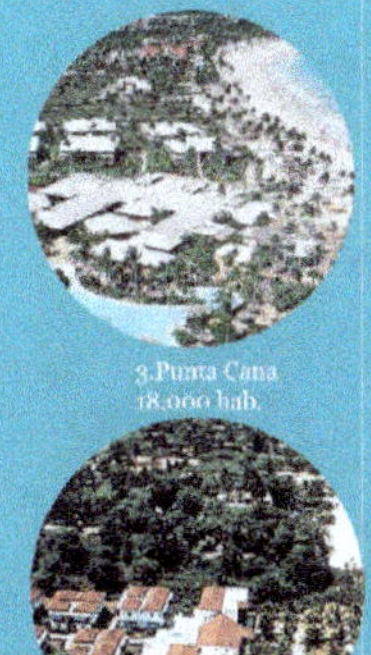

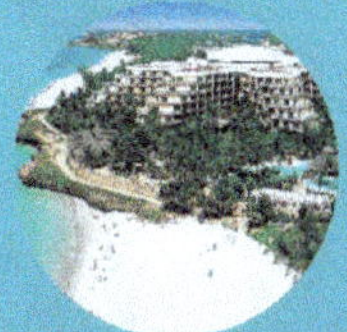

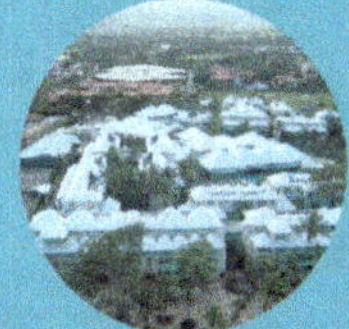

1.Cancun
27,522 hab.

2.Riviera Maya
23,512 hab.

3.Punta Cana
18,000 hab.

4.Varadero
15,723 hab.

5.Puerto Plata
15,000 hab.

6.Negril
5,647 hab.

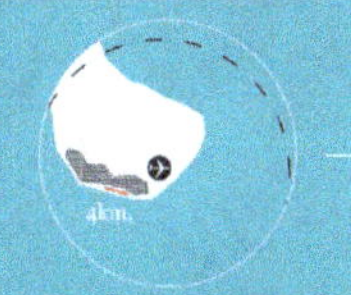

2 LONGER AND MORE ISOLATED STRIPS
Strips developed in the last decade have increased dramatically in length and detachment from the city.

3 HOLIDAY SUBURBS
Latest strips are monofunctional programmatically (100% resorts) and stylistically echoing an unrolled American suburbia

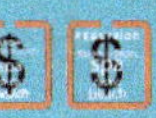

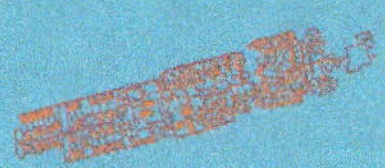

4 PARALLEL WORLDS
Strips isolation nursed the All-Inclusive concept into an unavoidable option, generating a parallel world, where this fantasy islands detached from the local reality and rationalized every link of the supply chain for profit.

5 ROOMS FULL
All-inclusive strips are extremely successful among consumers. Promise of high security at 'strange land' and controlled expenditure becomes unbeatable.

84% occupancy

⚠ UNSUSTAINABLE GROWTH
6 All-Inclusive formula -paradoxically- excludes local economies by marginalizing local enterprises and beyond damages when removal of essential mangroves, coral reefs and sand dunes in their construction, the unprecedented scale reached by some resort strips has proven socially, economically and ecologically unsustainable.

7 NO FACILITIES
Resort growth hasn't been accompanied by facilities further than roads and airports.

-How to turn sustainable those extensive resort strips and avoid their decay?
How to unlock the all-inclusive regime so other operations could coexist?
-How to introduce the missing programs in such elongated territories?

8 RETROACTIVE URBANIZATION

1. Concentration
urban mass is required for many programs to become usable (schools, community centers, hospitals, etc.)

2. Integration
system's efficiency depends largely on integration level of its components

3. Coast Access
beyond leisure opportunity, coasts are important income source for local residents involved in marine activities

4. Beach Front
image for resorts is much as possible increases its economical value.

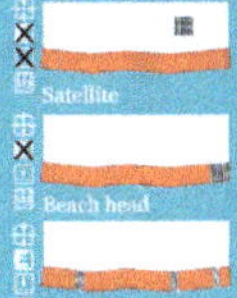

-with a retroactive urbanization, actual tourism strips would be the caribbean cities of tomorrow >>>>>

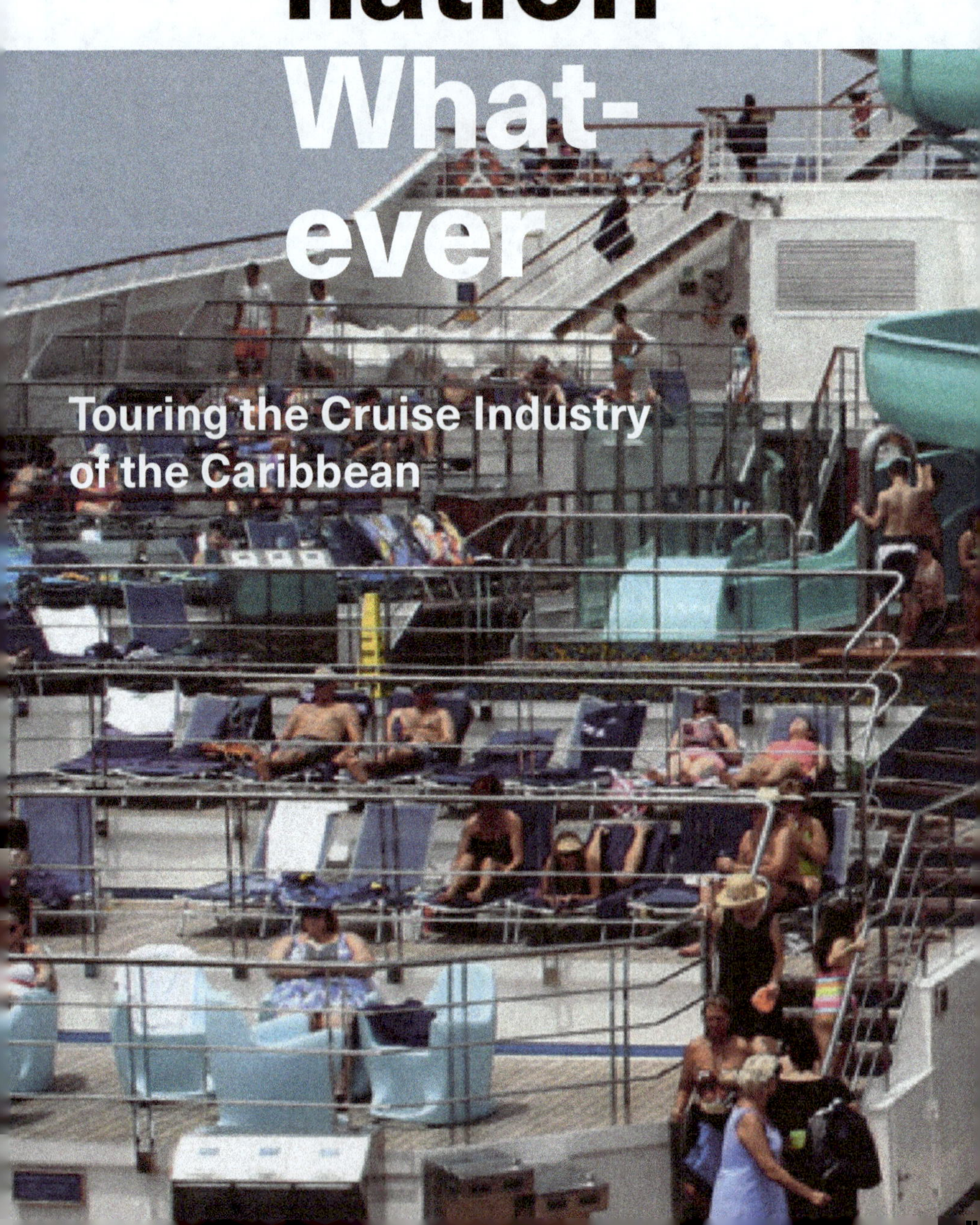

Desti-
nation
What-
ever
Touring the Cruise Industry
of the Caribbean

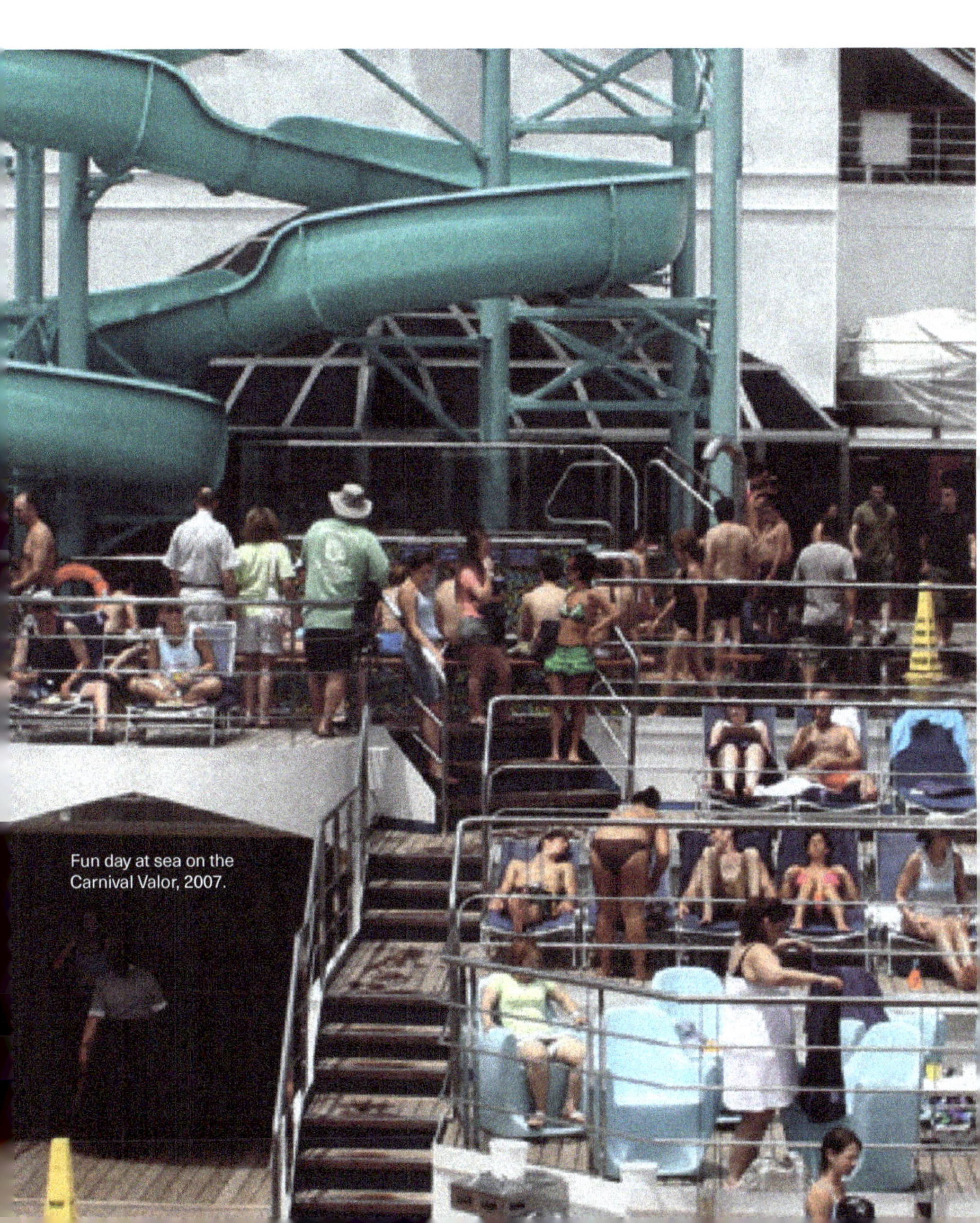

Fun day at sea on the
Carnival Valor, 2007.

1. Labadee, Haiti. Port
explorer and shopping
guide. RCCL© 2010.
2. Ibid.
3. Ibid.

With open, smiling mouths and wide, fixated eyes, a group of ethnically diverse *wholesome* families is featured against the new slogan of Royal Caribbean Cruise Lines – RCCL®: "Our ships are designed to WOW." Notable here is the emphasis on the ships' design, not any particular destination. As ships grow in size, scale, and amenities, the travel experience is designed to make the floating experience a highly familiar and comfortable one. The process of interiorizing hundreds of atmospheres into one floating mega container has much to do with design, engineering, and management – but mostly economics. And the effects of the current generation of cruise tourism in the Caribbean are only beginning to unfold.

Adrenaline Beach, Barefoot Beach Club, Dragon's Plaza. Entering Columbus' Cove, *Freedom of the Seas* sails into Royal Caribbean's Buccaneer's Bay. The bay is flanked by recreational attractions including the world's longest zip line, Dragon's Breath, and the Dragon's Tail Coaster atop Santa Maria Mountain. The only landmark and reminder of where you might be is the 19th-century citadel sitting above the horizon – 9,840 feet above sea level, the fortress is named for Henri Christophe Laferrière, a key leader of the first black slave rebellion that lead Haiti to independence from the French in 1804.

The boat, Royal Caribbean's flagship, docks on the Northwestern coast of Hispaniola Island, a territory called Labadee® – a registered trademark – and Royal Caribbean Cruise Lines leased the peninsula from the Haitian government on a 99-year contract. According to Royal Caribbean's *Port Explorer & Shopping Guide*, the leased land is "strengthening the cooperative effort between the government of Haiti and RCCL® [...] and has been solidified by extensive on-site development through the company's investment of tens of millions of dollars."[1] Testifying to the economic humanitarianism of the deal, the guide mentions that "it is a clear vote of confidence in the people, nation, and future of the country as our guests continue to have the exclusive opportunity to enjoy a relaxing fun filled day in the clear blue waters of Haiti's northern coast. The sailors who joined Christopher Columbus and first came ashore here centuries ago obviously knew a good thing when they saw it."[2]

Since the 1980s, Royal Caribbean Cruise Lines has held exclusive rights to docking at the once small fishing village and coastal town of Labadie, named for the first French settler in the late 17th century. Anglicized, Labadee® "was specifically designed and built to provide guests with a variety of opportunities to have fun in the sun."[3] As the guide claims, Royal Caribbean "is honored and proud to be a pioneering partner with a people and country which has such a rich heritage and the tremendous potential to become one of the Caribbean's premier tour destinations."[4]

These private destinations – compounds really – have become the new ports of call for big cruise ships. Today, nearly ten private islands are owned by eight major cruise operators in the Caribbean. By buying or leasing islands, or anchoring at an unregulated, deserted stretches of beach, cruise operators can reduce the number of days in official ports and divert the expenditures of travelers to locations under control of the industry. Piers, once perceived as extensions of land that connected ship to destination, have today become extensions of ships. Usually fenced or cordoned off, these extensions are fictional territory: They guide travelers away from local neighborhoods and people, toward areas owned and scripted by the cruise companies. These extensions of the ship are programmed to deliver isolated, worry-free experiences supplementing those offered by the ship itself – pristine water, white sand, Caribbean beaches. Off-site excursions are limited to day-trips to tourist-friendly destinations – a colonial city, or pre-Hispanic archaeological ruin.

Bigger Boats, Bigger Piers

As ships grow, they become destinations in themselves, ultimately devaluing the role or necessity of destinations. From the already impressive 961-foot, 2,200-passenger *Queen Elizabeth* in the late 1960s, the size and scale of cruising vessels has nearly tripled to a whopping 6,300 passengers (Royal Caribbean's *Allure of the Seas*). The increase in size of cruise ships, in width as much as in height, enables considerable spatial and programmatic complexity – streets, entertainment spaces, dining rooms, bars, pools, stores, water parks – with nonstop events that keep passengers entertained, day and night. Ships are designed as small, floating cities. Like an urban theme park, the ships include a multiplicity of landscape decks, terraces, surfing pools, and running paths that consumes all available space on the ship's roof deck. Although the layout of vessels is organized around a double-loaded corridor down the middle – the *main street*, which provides each room with exterior views and direct access to amenities – it is the central kitchen that forms ships' cores and ensures their functionality. Precisely engineered and impeccably designed,

5. See: Wendy Little-field, "How a Cruise Ship Feeds 4,000," *The Atlantic,* July 15, 2009, https://bit.ly/3mS8ES8.
6. "Financial Break-down of Typical Cruiser," *Cruise Market Watch,* https://bit.ly/3tFsi7D.
7. Steve Inskeep, "Royal Caribbean Pro-vides Tourists, Relief to Haiti," *National Public Radio,* January 19, 2010, https://n.pr/3mOqeGA.

ship kitchens provide food tailored to a wide range of dining experiences, from luxurious, romantic dinners to basic midday snacks. Upwards of fifteen thousand meals can be served in one day, delivered through tirty different menus. Onboard infrastructure is vital: Desalination plants for drinking water, crushing and compacting systems for recyclables, dehydrators and incinerators for food waste, with leftover ash disposed of offshore.[5]

The bigger the boat, the plusher the interiors; the more exotic the entertainment, the less relevant the destination. These floating worlds, with their new interiorized experiences, pay off. Onboard sales of goods now outpace ticket sales as the primary producer of profits, especially on Disney Cruise Lines, where the average passenger spends over $1,000 on an eight-day trip, making five-star resorts comparatively less expensive.[6]

While Caribbean destinations compete for the business of these floating hotels, the investment expected of ports to build and maintain big piers is ballooning, and is oftentimes out of reach. If Caribbean ports of call are unable to expand and modernize pier infrastructure to accommodate the increasing size of ships, tour operators look elsewhere for destinations that comply with burgeoning demand. In some cases, cruise companies share responsibility and investment for upgraded infrastructure with local partners. In other – more profitable – cases, they develop, manage, and operate ports themselves. Meanwhile, at *outdated* facilities, cruise companies negotiate anchoring fees down to meager sums. Faced with growing congestion in the Caribbean and stiff competition from emerg-ing economies worldwide, a port's inability to upgrade leads to the danger of obsolescence and abandonment. The threat of abandonment leaves ports paralyzed – investing large sums of money to upgrade facilities only leads to subsequent obso-lesce, but not upgrading means no business at all.

As cruise line operate more and more independently, distance between travelers and islanders grows at an alarm-ing rate, with dramatic levels of dispossession and inequity. For example, Royal Caribbean was noticeably absent in the immediate aftermath of the 2010 earthquake in Haiti, and pro-vided continuous service to Labadee®. Indifferent to the crisis, President and CEO of RCCL® Adam Goldstein admitted on National Public Radio that the decision to keep business going as usual, on the edge of a disaster zone, was a "pretty easy decision [...] a no-brainer."[7] Although the Haitian government requested that they maintain their voyages for both economic

8.   Jim Walker, "Haiti to Charge Royal Caribbean Passengers $2 More to Visit Labadee," *Cruise Law News*, August 19, 2014, https://bit.ly/3zVTFyr.

9.   Elizabeth Becker, "Destination Nowhere: The Dark Side of the Cruise Industry," *The Saturday Evening Post,* April 17, 2014, https://bit.ly/3NXXJCa.

10. "Cruise Industry Overview 2014: State of the Cruise Industry," *Florida-Caribbean Cruise Association*, https://bit.ly/3NXQuKr.

benefits and some relief efforts (they provided the transport of goods), maritime lawyer Jim Walker questioned motivations by asking: "Is it appropriate to sail into the idyllic port of Labadee, Haiti on a pleasure cruise when the dead remain unburied and the impoverished country writhes in chaos?"[8]

Cruise line operators now sometimes work like infrastructure banks, offering loans to governments at local destinations to fund cruise-based infrastructure projects. In 2007, Carnival Corporation PLC and St. Maarten signed a $34.5 million agreement for the enlargement of their pier, anticipating bigger ships to revive the tourist economy in the British Virgin Islands. Destinations have no choice: Upgrade their piers or die.

Caribbean Incorporation

The majority of cruises sail to the Caribbean and serve a primarily North American market, but not a single ship that cruises the Caribbean is Caribbean-owned – or US-owned, for that matter. Company headquarters are often on US soil, but most companies sidestep US incorporation and go offshore to avoid high taxation. Carnival (number one in terms of market share), which owns Holland America Line (number four), is incorporated in Panama; Royal Caribbean (number two) is *based* in Liberia; and Norwegian Cruise Line (number three) is registered with the Genting Group in Malaysia. It's a matter of economics. As journalist Elizabeth Becker noted, "during its two-decades-long civil war, Liberia earned at least $20 million every year by acting as the off-shore registry for foreign ships."[9]

For the past decade, cruise tourists have made up about 40% of all tourists in the Caribbean, yet they have accounted for less than 10% of overall tourist expenditures. Despite periodic efforts to raise port passenger fees, they remain extremely low in the Caribbean. Bermuda charges $60 per visitor, far more than the majority of islands, which often charge less than $10 per visitor. Efforts by Caribbean islands to form a united front as a way to collectively negotiate with cruise lines have been less than successful. If anything, governments feel compelled to give generous tax exemptions to lure ships into their ports and to contribute to local economies, regardless of how paltry the amounts.[10]

Black Clouds, Murky Waters

Until 25 years ago, cruising was reserved for the wealthy of Europe and America. But growth in ship capacity has made

11. Mike Melia, "Caribbean Cruise Ships Dump Garbage at Sea," *Associated Press*, March 1, 2009, https://bit.ly/39puol5.
12. See: Annex IV and Annex V from the International Convention for the Prevention of Pollution from Ships, https://bit.ly/3xun9jY.
13. Monica Hesse, "Carnival Triumph Disaster: A Drama of Discomfort," *The Washington Post*, February 15, 2013, https://wapo.st/3xv0PH1.
14. Jay Herring, *The Truth About Cruise Ships. A Cruise Ship Officer Survives the Work, Adventure, Alcohol, and Sex* (The Colony, SaltLog, 2011).

luxury leisure available at much lower price points, closer to half the cost given inflation. The increase in numbers means a decrease in operational expenditures, making cruising an affordable vacation for a larger population. But greater economies of scale bring greater risks, with hazards on the rise: Technical failures, navigational blunders, sanitation lapses, and health epidemics. For example, any given boat loads 24,000 bottles of water every week, which eventually turn into waste. Destinations are often unable to treat the massive amount of waste, leading cruise ships to dump tons of waste in international waters.[11] It was not until 2011 that the Caribbean was designated as a "Special Area" (with regard to garbage only) by MARPOL, the UN-based International Convention for the Prevention of Pollution from Ships that regulates the dumping of waste overboard, including sewage, sludge, garbage, oil, and exhaust. Although MARPOL was adopted in 1973, the dumping of waste in the ocean is still widely practiced, albeit regulated beyond a certain distance from "the nearest land."[12]

Problems at sea don't end with waste, they start there. The larger the vessel, the bigger the engine, the bigger the risk of repairs, breakdowns, or fires. Shorter periods in port mean lower cycle times for repairs and inspections, much like planes.

On February 14, 2013, Carnival's *Triumph,* a post-Panamax, 102,000-ton cruise ship was towed into Mobile, Alabama, after being stranded at sea for nearly five days. The ordeal began with an engine fire, which despite being quickly and safely extinguished, resulted in a loss of power and propulsion. The ship floated in the Gulf of Mexico with no running water, no air conditioning, and limited food and fresh water. Carnival's inability to provide solutions for proper waste disposal for passengers and crew led news media to dub it the "poop cruise." Carnival offered passengers a full refund in cash, $500.000, and credit toward another Carnival cruise. One passenger interviewed on the *Today Show* said of the crisis: "It was like post-natural disaster, but stuck on a boat."[13] A cruise operator like Carnival, with 25 Fun Ships in seven different classes (Fantasy, Triumph, Spirit, Conquest, Splendor, Dream, Sunshine, Vista) sailing to over sixty destinations, is no stranger to disaster on board. In fact, its 1972 inaugural voyage ran aground on a sandbar. And just one year prior to the *Triumph* disaster, the *Costa Concordia* (operated by Costa Crociere, a subsidiary of Carnival Corporation) capsized and sank off the coast of Italy, killing 32 passengers.

15. Scott Neuman, "As Cruise Industry Grows So Have Its Problems," *National Public Radio*, February 15, 2013, https://n.pr/3HsZ81h.
16. See: Jean-Paul Rodrigue and Theo Notteboom, "Transportation, Economy and Society," in *The Geography of Transport Systems*, ed. Jean-Paul Rodrigue, Claude Comtois and Brian Slack (3rd ed.; New York, Routledge, 2013); Jean-Paul Rodrigue and Theo Notteboom, "The Geography of Cruises: Itineraries, not Destinations," *Applied Geography* 38 (March 2013): 31-42.

lay Herring, former senior officer at Carnival and author of the book *The Truth about Cruise Ships*[14] says that safety during these catastrophes is of growing concern as ships become bigger and the number aboard increases. He says that with more than three thousand passengers, evacuation becomes a major problem: "Imagine you have this little bitty boat, bobbing up and down, and you're trying to transfer passengers from a ship that's essentially stationary, walking across a gangway. It's just so dangerous."[15] The *Costa Concordia* wreck caused the cost of protection and indemnity insurance to skyrocket despite the fact that the captain was singlehandedly at fault for neglect.

The bigger the ship, the higher the risks. In January 2014, Royal Caribbean, the second largest cruise ship operator after Carnival, had to return its *Explorer of the Seas* to its port of origin in Cape Liberty, New Jersey, after an outbreak of norovirus symptoms – nearly 20% of it's three thousand passengers and 5% of its 1,100-person crew suffered from extreme diarrhea and vomiting, setting the record for the highest number of passengers and crew sick on board a vessel in recent history. Seasickness is no longer just from the seas; it comes from the ship.

The Terrorism of Tourism

As massive cruise ships sail away from their old ports of call and lay course toward small, nearly uninhabited territories, the ratio between visiting and stable populations on shore shifts. In some isolated islands of the Caribbean, high season produces extreme spikes in population – Cockburn Town, Turks and Caicos, for example, quintuples during peak cruise season, with neither conflict nor negotiation. When boats undock, destination ports and leisure infrastructure are essentially abandoned. Cruising in the Caribbean sometimes result in massive land vacancy, creating idle lands and unoccupied territories that remain unused by locals, melancholically waiting for the arrival of the next floating city to bring meaning and money with it.

Tourism is a global, economic force, and the annual global growth rate of the cruise industry – around 7% – shows remarkable stability.[16] This statistic is a testament to the industry's resiliency, despite recent global recessions. According to the Cruise Line Association, in 1970, cruise ships worldwide were carrying about five hundred thousand passengers annually; forty years later, that number had reached over 20

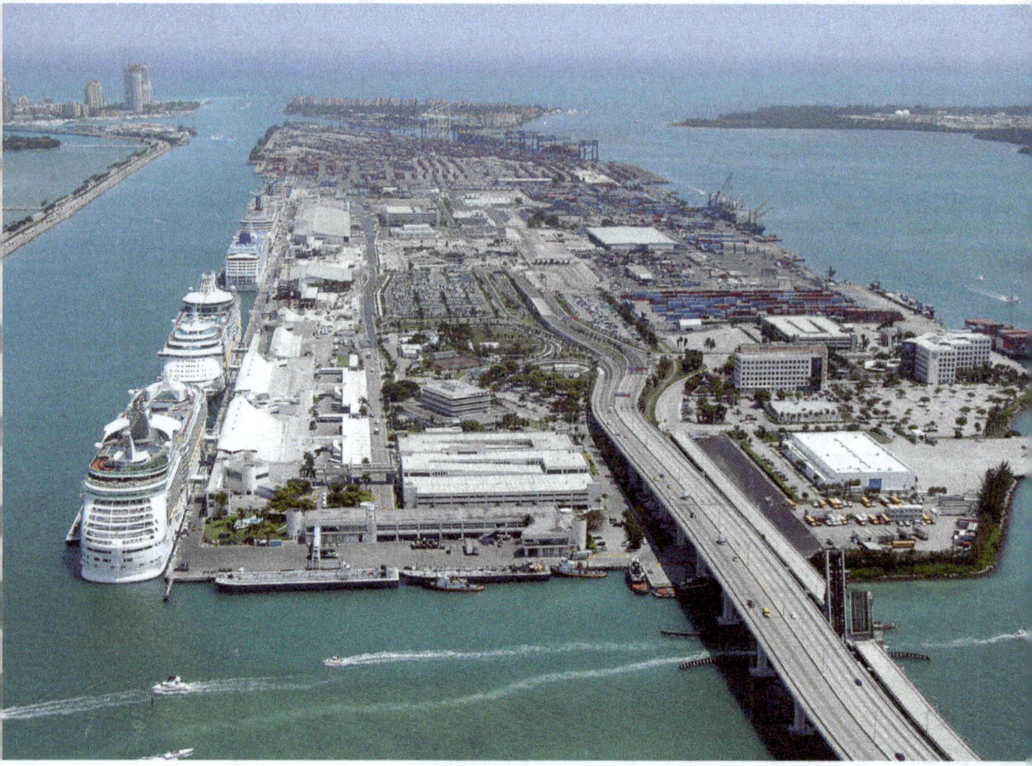

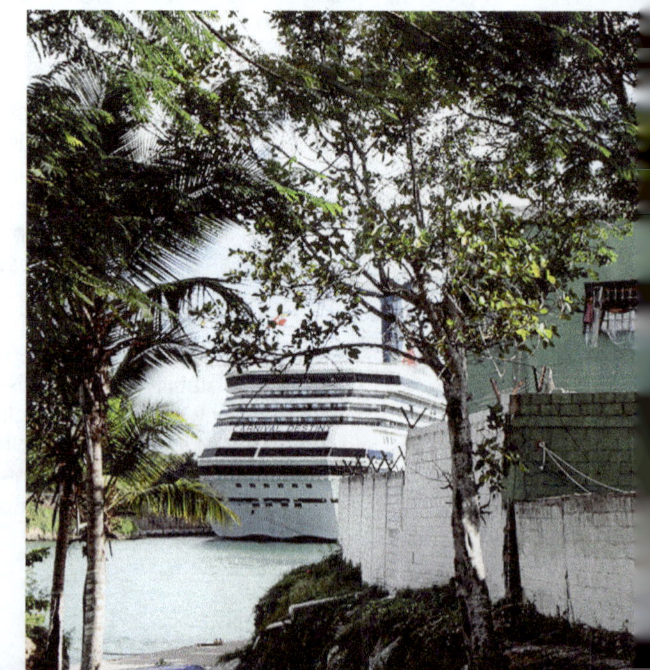

million, a growth of nearly 1,000 percent. In spite of its modest beginnings, the three companies that grew the industry have become the largest operators in the world. Norwegian began sailing in 1966, Royal Caribbean in 1968, and Carnival in 1972. These three companies not only survived the advancement of the airline industry as prime examples of transnationalism; the maritime experience of programmed leisure, guaranteed happiness, and catered fun that they provide, it seems, is the perfect antidote for the point-to-point logistics of the aerial age.

But, in an industry nearly monopolized by three companies, competition for exotic destinations grows ever fiercer. The Caribbean and the Mediterranean comprise more than 60% of all cruise destinations, with the rest divided between Asia, South America, Alaska, and Australia. During the winter months, two-thirds of cruises travel to the Caribbean. Although the cruise industry, and tourism more broadly, has been relatively successful, its success – calculated in passenger miles and smiles – comes with hidden costs unknown injustices, where profits often come at the expense of destinations that continue to risk economic atrophy.

If tourism accounts for one of the biggest sectors of the world economy, and cruise tourism is its flagship industry, at what costs must tourism sustain itself in the future? And what role do North Americans – as the dominant cruisers – have? The growing inequalities between cruise tourists and largely dispossessed local populations must be addressed, and cruise companies need to be held accountable.

Perhaps for the foreseeable future, the rise of itineraries to Private Destinations™, and FUN© packages designed for the 20 million happy passengers may become hotly contested political territories, where the design and docking of increasingly big, precise, efficient floating fantasies cruising the warm waters of the Caribbean will potentially become economic albatrosses, en route to somewhere other than paradise.

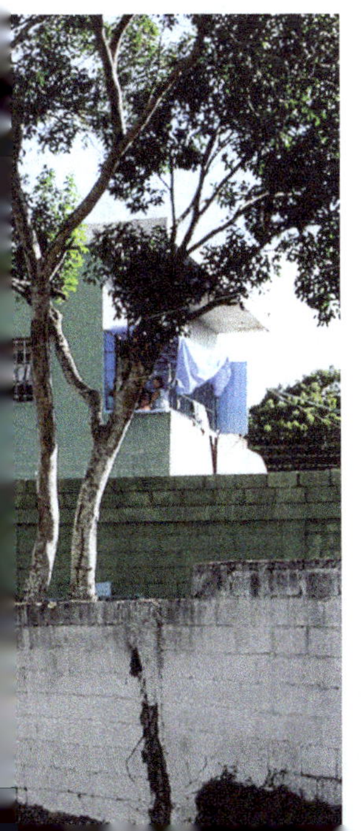

From Heritage to Feritage

How Economic Path Dependencies in the Caribbean Cruise Destinations Are Distorting the Uses of Heritage Architecture and Urban Form

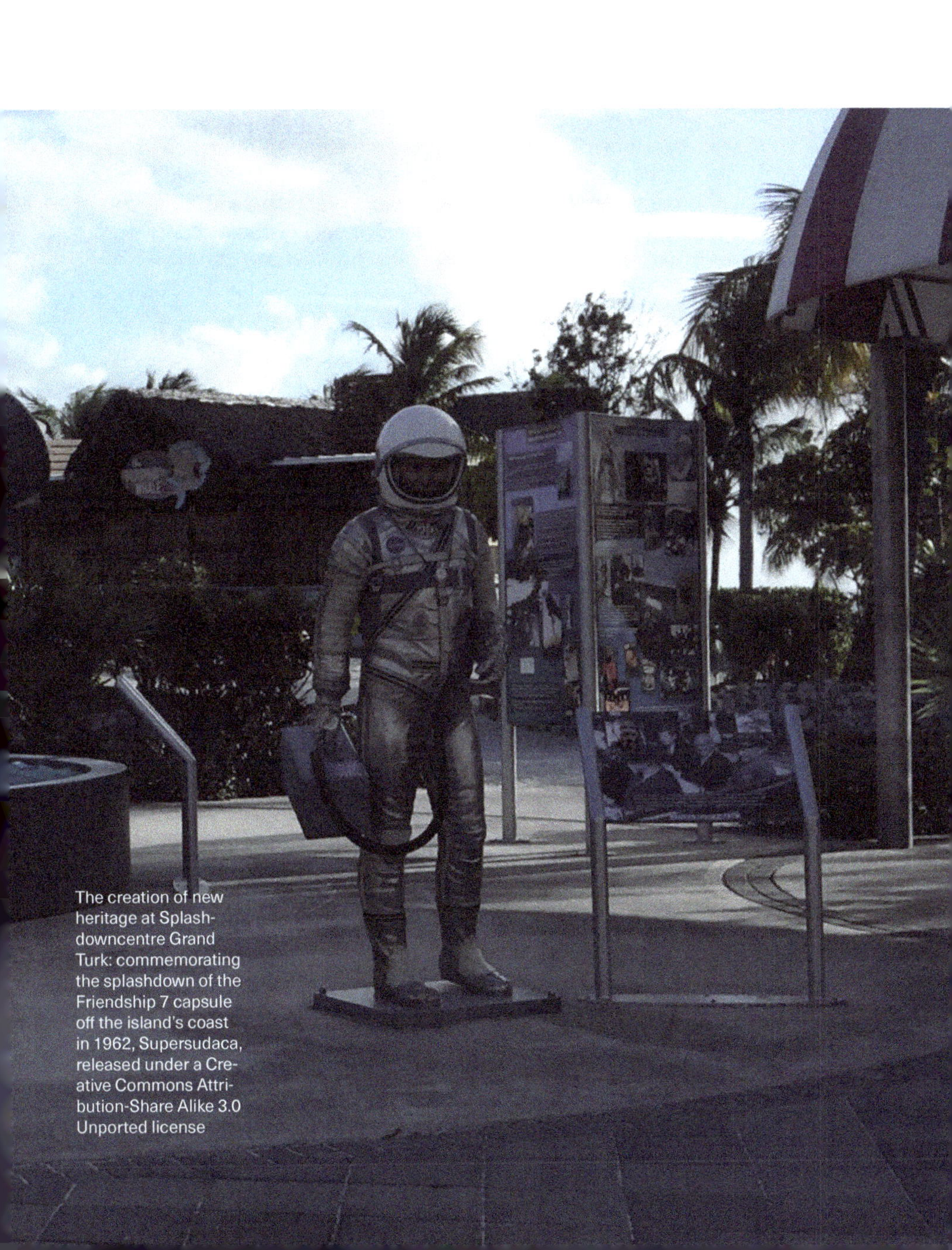

The creation of new heritage at Splashdowncentre Grand Turk: commemorating the splashdown of the Friendship 7 capsule off the island's coast in 1962, Supersudaca, released under a Creative Commons Attribution-Share Alike 3.0 Unported license

Since the early 16th century, economic considerations have influenced the built heritage of Caribbean port cities. The similarity of the colonial exploitation model and the current operating modes of cruise tourism unveils how historical patterns are repeated in new forms and the essence of power relations – in which the main economic decisions are still in the hands of foreign investors – remains identical. We coined the pun *feritage* to show simultaneously how contemporary Caribbean cruise destinations are distorting the uses of heritage architecture while resembling spatial and economic practices of colonial times. The title of the paper *feritage* is a reference to the ongoing deformation of the use of heritage for the purposes of the cruise industry. For example, the constant improvements of replicas are challenging what local tourist boards considered essential and irreplaceable for the tourist purpose of visit: to experience authentic places.

1. Jean-Paul Rodrigue and Theo Notteboom, "Transportation, Economy and Society," in *The Geography of Transport Systems*, ed. Jean-Paul Rodrigue, Claude Comtois and Brian Slack (3rd ed.; London, Routledge, 2013); Jean-Paul Rodrigue and Theo Notteboom, "The Geography of Cruises: Itineraries, not Destinations," *Applied Geography* 38 (March 2013): 31-42.

2. Carola Hein, "Port cityscapes: conference and research contributions on port cities," *Planning Perspectives* 31, no. 2 (March 2016): 313-326, https://bit.ly/3tSbdHP.

3. Robert J. McCalla, "An Investigation into Site and Situation: Cruise Ship Ports," *Journal of Economic and Human Geography* 89, no. 1 (February 1998): 44-55; George K. Vaggelas and Athanasios A. Pallis, "Passenger ports: Services Provision and their Benefits," *Maritime Policy & Management* 37, no. 1 (January 2010): 73-89, https://bit.ly/3tN863W; Lorenzo Gui and Antonio Paolo Russo, "Cruise Ports: A Strategic Nexus between Regions and Global Lines, Evidence from the Mediterranean," *Maritime Policy & Management* 38, no. 2 (April 2011): 129-150.

4. Erica Avrami, ed., *Harboring Tourism: An International Symposium on Cruise Ships in Historic Port Communities* (New York, World Monuments Fund, 2013), https://bit.ly/3tZrvPg.

5. Hein, "Port cityscapes."

6. Megan Epler Wood, "The Cruise Industry – Empire of the Seas," *Sustainable Tourism on a Finite Planet Environmental, Business and Policy Solutions* (London, Routledge, 2017), 225-260.

7. Ibid.

8. Kieran Corcoran, "Cruise Ships Are Being Banned from Sailing through Venice after Locals Got Sick of them Dwarfing their City," *Business Insider Nederland*, November 9, 2017, https://bit.ly/3OI8IFI; Will Coldwell, "First Venice and Barcelona: Now Anti-Tourism Marches Spread Across Europe," *The Guardian*, August 10, 2017, https://bit.ly/3zUcHFc.

9. Ross K. Dowling, "Looking Ahead: The Future of Cruising," in: *Cruise Ship Tourism*, ed. Ross K. Dowling (Wallingford, CABI, 2006), 414-434.

10. Jarkko Saarinen, "'Destinations in Change': The Transformation Process of Tourist Destinations," *Tourist Studies* 4, no. 2 (August 2005): 161-179, https://bit.ly/3bghoPc; Reiner Jaakson, "Beyond the Tourist Bubble? Cruiseship Passengers in Port," *Annals of Tourism Research* 31, no. 1 (January 2004): 44-60.

11. Jaakson, "Beyond the Tourist Bubble?"

12. Carola Hein and Felicitas Hillmann, "The Missing Link: Redevelopment of the Urban Waterfront as a Function of Cruise Ship Tourism," in: *Waterfronts Revisited. European Ports in a Historic and Global Perspective*, ed. Heleni Porfyriou and Marichela Sepe (London, Routledge, 2017), 222-238.

13. David B. Weaver, "Model of Urban Tourism for Small Caribbean Islands," *Geographical Review* 83, no. 2 (April 1993): 134-140, https://bit.ly/3zTzrFa.

14. Sofía Saavedra Bruno, "Cruceros en el Caribe/Caribbean Cruisers," *Arquine*, no. 42 (Winter 2007): 96-107, https://bit.ly/39Nf3eh. Also see chapter "Destination Whatever. Touring the Cruise Industry of the Caribbean," pages 184-193.

15. Sofía Saavedra Bruno, Felix Madrazo, Martín Delgado and Pablo Roquero, "Fair Play: Turks & Caicos Feasibility Study on the Cruise Industry," https://bit.ly/3tS79XR.

Cruise ship tourism is one of the fastest growing and most stable industries,[1] and the landside tourism it generates has transformed urban form, urban function, and heritage architecture around the world.[2] Scholarly research on cruise tourism has nevertheless focused on isolated aspects of the cruise industry, notably economics, or on the need for tourist-geared adaptation of the historic built environment and the port facilities; it has not engaged with heritage debates.[3] In turn, most literature that does explore cruise tourism and heritage is focused on preserving these values in the face of increasing economic pressures.[4] The relationship between (cruise) tourism and cultural heritage values of local communities is only starting to be looked at by academics, including Carola Hein[5] and more briefly Megan Epler Wood.[6] The sociocultural challenges that cruise lines bring to the shores of their destinations and attempts to formulate planning solutions have only recently been explored.[7] But locals comment strongly and express concern on the impact of cruise shipping on heritage values of local communities, notably in the media. Venice and Barcelona have been at the forefront of recent protests against cruise tourism.[8] Social media has also covered and commented on these protests, but those conversations have yet to be studied.

Ross K. Dowling probably offers the most comprehensive overview of academic work on cruise shipping,[9] but the stress in such studies on the industry rather than its destinations is remarkable. A range of significant studies on destination evolution under the influence of tourism[10] identifies the area in the port visited by tourists as a "tourist bubble"[11] consisting of a core and a periphery. Nonetheless, a need remains for a more comprehensive investigation of the effects of cruise shipping on historical urban areas,[12] and of the transformative effect of the cruise industry on the spatial relations between city, port, and hinterland.[13] Through various research formats, our research group of architects and planners, Supersudaca – *Sudaca* is a pejorative term among Spanish people for a Latin American – has investigated the impact of the latest business model of cruise tourism and the spatial relation between city, port, and hinterland in the Caribbean;[14] more recently, Supersudaca was asked to advise the government of Turks and Caicos.[15] In our report, we aimed to unveil the mechanisms behind the changing spatial relationship of the cruise pier with the urban territory as a dynamic relation of interdependence between local and foreign actors; we concluded that new policies are needed to improve and integrate cruise shipping with the local population and their economy. Meanwhile, heritage remains sidelined by strategic positioning of the pier far from the historic center. Yet, the role of tourism and heritage within the larger relationships between actors has not yet been investigated. In this article, we explore how heritage debates today play out in discussions on cruise ships on the Caribbean Waterfronts.

Over the last twenty years, some of these debates have created a distinctive power balance in which policymakers and planners focus on the economic side of the cruise ship industry and consider urban form and heritage architecture only as supporting elements of the tourist offer instead of seeing heritage as an integral part of the cultural values of the local population. The dominant discourse often adopts a short-term perspective that supports this approach, mainly looking at tourist arrivals and expenditures, leaving aside local actors, their agendas, their interest in urban form and heritage, and their specific identity concerns. But the complex interaction of (cruise) shipping with port, city, and hinterland requires a multifaceted approach that acknowledges long-term development.[16]

With scholars of historical institutionalism, we argue that the current model of cruise tourism contains a pattern of historical development with trajectories that are inherently difficult to reverse, so-called path dependencies.[17] The decision points during which new institutional configurations are established and new developmental trajectories are launched – usually referred to as "critical junctures" – are crucial to the future direction of each destination.[18] In line with Marco Bontje, Sako Musterd and Peter Pelzer,[19] we propose that city

16. Hein, "Port cityscapes."
17. Jacob S. Hacker, *The Divided Welfare State. The Battle over Public and Private Social Benefits in the United States* (New York, Cambridge University Press, 2002); Paul Pierson, *Politics in Time: History, Institutions, and Social Analysis* (Princeton, Princeton University Press, 2004); James Mahoney and Kathleen Thelen, "A Theory of Gradual Institutional Change," in: *Explaining Institutional Change: Ambiguity, Agency, and Power*, ed. James Mahoney and Kathleen Thelen (New York, Cambridge University Press, 2009), 1-37; Andre Sorensen, "Taking Path Dependence Seriously: A Historical Institutionalist Research Agenda in Planning History," *Planning Perspectives* 30, no. 1 (December 2014): 1-22, https://bit.ly/3tQAfqH.
18. Ruth Berins Collier and David Collier, "Critical Junctures and Historical Legacies," *Shaping the Political Arena: Critical Junctures, the Labor Movement, and Regime Dynamics in Latin America* (Princeton, Princeton University Press, 1991), 27-39, https://bit.ly/3xGbSgE; Giovanni Capoccia and R. Daniel Kelemen, "The Study of Critical Junctures: Theory, Narrative and Counterfactuals in Historical Institutionalism," World Politics 59, no. 3 (April 2007): 341-369, https://bit.ly/3OactOE.
19. Marco Bontje, Sako Musterd and Peter Pelzer, *Inventive City-Regions. Path Dependence and Creative Knowledge Strategies* (London, Routledge, 2011).

region's attraction to the creative sectors and their potential
economic development is influenced by the path of historical
developments. Using the concept of path dependence theory and including the built environment as another actor, we
analyze the influence of cruise shipping on the development
and architectural heritage preservation of port cities in the
Caribbean islands.

How Historical Political and Socioeconomic Dependencies Shaped Both Caribbean Port City Heritage and Current Operating Modes of Cruise Tourism

Historical political and socioeconomic dependencies shaped
Caribbean port city heritage – both urban form and architectural production – in ways that are still visible in the current
operating modes of cruise tourism. This is in part due to the
continuation or resurgence of geopolitical structures of the
past, but perhaps more interesting is the current relevance of
spatial strategies for the cruise industry from that distant past
that had as its primary objective the control of flows of capital
in the Caribbean. Cruise tourism in Caribbean port cities relies
on principles of mercantilism and monopoly control that were
normal practice in the region in the 16th and 17th centuries.

What we perceive as the oldest heritage now represents,
sometimes in diagrammatic clarity, the economic and cultural
policies intended to create an urban system that facilitated
trade, security, and stability. Furthermore, the spatial configu-
ration of Caribbean port cities – their grid systems and fortifications – expresses how the market did not allow competition
from other places. Culturally, port cities appeared to be neutral
spaces but a closer look reveals that they were highly hierarchical, pushing local indigenous populations to the fringes of
the system. Emerging models of tourism today echo several of
these dynamics.

The mostly European built heritage of the Caribbean
islands dates to the beginning of the 16th century. This legacy
is closely interrelated with the history and interests of the colonial exploitation of the region. The colonization model follows a
pattern of discovery and conquest, after which colonizers identified resources to exploit, and, depending on their importance,
protect them militarily with city fortifications and (later) force
on the high sea. More specifically, once colonizers had discovered a new place, they founded a city: Distributing land among
conquistadores, building up the infrastructure of extraction,
organizing and distributing forced labor, and setting up the

logistics of trade to bring the products of exploitation back
to the metropole. The model involved the private sector, with
strong support and guidance from the state, paralleling today's
private-public partnerships to some extent. The newly founded
cities might then grow or collapse, depending on the presence
and quantity of metal and available labor.

In general, the first phase of Spanish colonization lasted
from 1492 until the conquest of Mexico in 1520 and Peru
in 1532.[20] The discovery of vast reserves of silver and gold
in Mexico and Peru meant drastic change for Caribbean
islands and ports, which had to refocus their economies on
other activities, such as sugar and tobacco production. As
Caribbean port cities became key nodes of logistic trade,
bringing precious metals to Europe and importing European
products to the colonizers,[21] they accumulated treasures themselves and became more attractive to pirates. This all pushed
port cities into a new phase of vulnerability at the end of the
16th century. The most drastic change of this phase came in
the 17th century, after the conformation of the Triple Alliance
of 1596 between France, England and the Republic of the
Seven United Netherlands. The Treaty of The Hague recognized the Republic of the Seven United Netherlands for the
first time, and it implied a common enemy in the Caribbean:
Spain. Not long after the French, Dutch, and English too began
to claim territory and establish plantations in the region.

From a spatial point of view, the built heritage of several
Caribbean port cities corresponds to that of a fortress, most
filled with gridded streets. Yet most of these locations did
not have fortifications in the first decades of conquest. San
Juan de Puerto Rico is a clear example of this, being an open,
unwalled city for 130 years and based on an old reference
to Plato's disdain for walled cities.[22] Historically, before the
Spanish conquest of America, the port cities of Canary Islands
were open structures, that is, unwalled ports promoting a
message of free trade in a harbor city. Leonardo Torriani, a

20. Edwin Williamson, *The Penguin History of Latin America (The Penguin Press, 1992).*
21. James Lockhart and Stuart B. Schwartz, *Early Latin America: A History of Colonial Spanish America and Brazil* (New York, Cambridge University Press, 1983).
22. Arleen Pabón-Charneco, *The Architecture of San Juan de Puerto Rico. Five Centuries of Urban and Architectural Experimentation* (London, Routledge, 2017).
23. Leonardo Torriani, quoted in: Pabón-Charneco, *The Architecture of San Juan de Puerto Rico*, xx.
24. Jorge Enrique Hardoy, *Urbanization in Latin America: Approaches and Issues* (Garden City, Anchor Press, 1975); Anthony Edwin James Morris, *History of Urban Form Before the Industrial Revolution* (3rd ed., London, Routledge, 1994); Jean-Francois Lejeune, *Cruelty and Utopia: Cities and Landscapes of Latin America* (Princeton, Princeton University Press, 2005).
25. Edwin Williamson, *The Penguin History of Latin America (The Penguin Press, 1992).*
26. Ibid.
27. Ibid.

16th-century Italian naval engineer, described San Cristobal de
La Laguna in Gran Canaria, San Juan's most prominent prec-
edent, as "a city made from peace for peace. No fortresses
and no walls".[23] The now so-called Ciudad de La Paz (or city of
peace), also known as Ciudad Marítima (or maritime city) was
characterized by the presence of a main square facing the sea
(Plaza del Mar), which a grid linked to the main square (Plaza
Mayor) containing the main civic buildings and the church.
Later, the Spanish used this grid to lay out their new open city,
probably for reasons of speed, order, and the availability of
rudimentary tools such as cord and ruler.[24]

The system of colonization moved from a standard strategy of founding cities to one of specializing ports. This had to
do more with central planning of the region from Spain rather
than with local demands. Ports that dealt with export-import
duties to Spain had their duties drastically reduced to single
tasks: Veracruz became the ancillary port of Mexico City that
controlled the flows of silver from Mexico; Nombre de Dios
(also known as Portobelo) in the Panama isthmus controlled
the resources (mainly metals) coming from Peru by way of
the Pacific Ocean; Cartagena de Indias (nowadays Colombia)
served as a stopping point for refueling ships and eventually
a hub for trading slaves from Africa. Havana meanwhile was
the port where ships coming from Peru and Mexico joined the
Spanish naval escort to return to Spain.[25] Some ports suffered
from this re-configuration: San Juan and Santo Domingo for
instance lost some or most of their early importance.

The *Ciudades de La Paz* model was eventually tested by
Spain's enemies. British, French, and later Dutch pirates damaged key ports. In 1572, Sir Francis Drake attacked Portobelo;
in a turning point in the politics of city defense,[26] the Spanish
king Philip II responded by commissioning an engineer specialized in fortifications, Battista Antonelli, to improve the
security of Portobelo and other key cities, especially of those
ports on the main route of import-export monopoly known as
the *Carrera de Indias*: Cartagena, San Juan de Ulua, Havana,
and San Juan in Puerto Rico.[27] Thus, the built heritage in the
Caribbean port cities has historically been a product of the
Spaniards, who designed cities first to maximize speed of construction and the efficiency of water trade and later for defense
and customs.

Today that same heritage is being recycled to maximize cruise tourism, another product of foreign exploitation.
Although the theory of path dependency normally refers
to a continuous sequence of events, it is worth noting the

similarities between these two phases – colonial exploitation and cruise tourism –, despite the time that separates them. In colonial times, most of the economies of the Caribbean relied mainly on a single form of exploitation at the regional scale, protected by the monopoly of the market regulated by the Spanish crown through its Casa de Contratación, fortress architecture, and naval escort. The relatively recent emergence of tourism in the Caribbean as the main source of the economy also offers one type of product for the region. Recent cruise centers in a few Caribbean destinations strikingly recall the fortress strategies of colonial times, and like them are aimed at maximizing control of the economic benefits of the enterprise.

At the same time, it is important to observe the differences between these histories. Tourism differs from mining and sugar industries, with many more economic sectors affecting the business. Cruise tourism is what scholars call a vertical industry, in which giant companies control several sectors of the economy.[28] That means that we are not talking of monopolistic control of one product but of intensive concentration and deformation of the market by few companies. Flows and success or failures of port cities related to cruise tourism are linked to the decisions of foreign-controlled industries, mainly located in Florida. "The majority of cruises sail to the Caribbean and serve a primarily North American market, but not a single ship that cruises the Caribbean is Caribbean-owned – or US-owned, for that matter. Company headquarters are often on US soil, but most companies sidestep US incorporation and go offshore to avoid high taxation. Carnival (number one in terms of market share), which owns Holland America Line (number four), is incorporated in Panama; Royal Caribbean (number two) is based in Liberia; and Norwegian Cruise Line (number three) is registered with the Genting Group in Malaysia. It's a matter of economics"[29] for the host countries as much as for the cruise companies. As journalist

28. Supersudaca, "Gran Caribe: Al_Caribe: Supersudaca," *Archivos de Arquitectura Antillana*, no. 23 (2006): 47-57; Sweenay N (2002) A regional tour operator for the Caribbean? Caribbean Development Bank 29. Chapter "Destination Whatever. Touring the Cruise Industry of the Caribbean," page 184.
30. Elizabeth Becker, "Destination Nowhere: The Dark Side of the Cruise Industry," *The Saturday Evening Post*, April 17, 2014, https://bit. ly/3NXXJCa.
31. Jeb Sprague-Silgado, "The Caribbean Cruise Ship Business and the Emergence of a Transnational Capitalist Class," *Journal of World-Systems Research* 23, no. 1 (Winter/Spring 2017): 93-125, https://bit. ly/39NSqqd.
32. "The Caribbean the Impact of Travel &Tourism on Jobs and the Economy," *World Travel & Tourism Council*, https://bit.ly/3niDrHL. See page 23.
33. Ibid. See page 65.
34. Ibid. See page 65.
35. Ross A. Klein, "The Cruise Industry's Business Model: Implications for Ports," in: Avrami, *Harboring Tourism*, 48.

Elizabeth Becker noted, "during its two decades long civil war, Liberia earned at least $20 million every year by acting as the off-shore registry for foreign ships."[30] Thus historical patterns returned in new forms while the essence of actor power relation remains identical: The main economic decisions are still in hands of foreign investors, whose interest might prevail above local agendas of preservation.

Two foreign-owned cruise lines, each formed by multiple associated brands, monopolize the Caribbean cruise market. Together they hold 70% of the world market share,[31] and their turnover sometimes triples the Gross Domestic Product – GDP of local Caribbean countries. Their power to stabilize economic dynamics in the long run can be termed economic lock-in. As in colonial times, the benefits for the region are clearly not the foreign investors' priority. Although the Caribbean islands are the most active cruise tourist region of the world, the revenues do not correspond to the size of the business. A 2004 report from World Travel and Tourism Council stated that "Given that the Caribbean attracts around 50% of the world cruise market, its contribution to overall tourism earnings is nonetheless relatively insignificant accounting for between 8 and 10% of international tourism receipts only."[32] Cruise tourists constituted about 42% of all tourists to the Caribbean in 2000, yet the same report stated that they accounted for only 12% of overall tourist expenditures. Nor is the news always good for all destinations. As competition increases so do the problems of growth. Continuous growth of the industry does not automatically guarantee success for all players.

Against the criticism of scarce economic benefits for the region, the report makes the argument that cruise tourism "presents destinations with the opportunity to convert cruise visitors (many of whom admit to being on a familiarization tour of the Caribbean) into future stayover tourists."[33] It calls for "further research as to market perceptions of the two products [cruise and land base tourism], the degree of direct competition and demand substitution between them, or the extent of conversion to stayover visit."[34] But the theory of conversion goes against the current trend of tourists spending less time on shore, which diminishes the chances of the destination to promote itself. Besides cruise lines are controlling shore excursions more and more, as "another source of income" for the cruise industry that "provide solid revenue for the cruise line in form of sales commission."[35] The waterfronts and ports catering to mass tourism from the cruise industry are becoming a product controlled by the cruise tourist industry that with its "status as a single sector economy raises the spectre of future regional ruination."[36] Cruise ships are always becoming bigger "floating theme parks,"[37] requiring ports of call to invest more and more money to build, maintain, and modernize big piers. When some Caribbean ports are unable to afford these ballooning expenses, tour operators look elsewhere for destinations that can meet burgeoning demand or they negotiate anchoring fees down to meager sums. In some cases, cruise companies share responsibility and investment for upgrading infrastructure with local partners. In other – more profitable – cases, they develop, manage, and operate ports themselves. "Cruise line operators now sometimes work like infrastructure banks, offering loans to governments at local destinations to fund cruise-based infrastructure projects. In 2007, Carnival Corporation PLC and St Maarten signed a $34.5 million agreement for the enlargement of their pier, anticipating that bigger ships will revive the tourist economy in the British Virgin Islands."[38] The loans are calculated based on the head taxes that the governments receive from the flow of cruise tourists. With growing congestion in the Caribbean and stiff competition from emerging economies worldwide, a port unable to upgrade can face abandonment. "The threat of abandonment leaves ports paralyzed – investing large sums of money to upgrade facilities only leads to subsequent obsolesce, but not upgrading means no business at all."[39] Once again, as in colonial times, the control of the demand and supply is in foreign hands, but the destinations have no choice: "Upgrade their piers or die."[40]

36. Patrick Brouder, Salvador Anton Clavé, Alison Gill and Dimitri Ioannides, *Tourism Destination Evolution* (London, Routledge, 2017), 3.

37. Robert E. Wood, "Caribbean Cruise Tourism: Globalization at Sea," *Annals of Tourism Research* 27, no. 2 (April 2000): 358.
38. Chapter "Destination Whatever. Touring the Cruise Industry of the Caribbean," page 184.

39. Ibid., page 184.
40. Ibid., page 184.
41. Saavedra Bruno, "Cruceros en el Caribe/ Caribbean Cruisers," 106. Also see chapter "Destination Whatever. Touring the Cruise Industry of the Caribbean," page 184.

42. Ibid., 104.
43. Ibid.

Heritage Architecture of Caribbean Cities and Cruise Lines' Economic Interests

Since cruise ship tourism depends on heritage, the first actors that were interested in heritage conservation were the cruise industries. Therefore, the preservation strategies for heritage buildings and urban spaces play a major role in marketing the Caribbean islands and are closely related to the attractiveness of the cruise ship industry. In Curacao, for example, the world-famous Dutch canal house-style facades of the waterfront street, the Handelskade, have always attracted cruise tourists, but on the other hand, the Curacao Government learned from a marketing study that their city should appeal to what the tourists have in mind for a *Caribbean* location. They planted palm trees along the public areas near the terminal – but those palm trees are not actually indigenous species of the island, so the government is importing them from Cuba, as payment on an earlier debt. The supposedly Caribbean landscaping of the passage that guides the cruise tourists into the shopping district has led to the "situation that on the same square (Brionplein) two sorts of lamps are used: those paid for by the tourist industry along the path of the cruise tourists and the old and the less kitschy public lamps that remain standing on the square"[41] – all this reflects the absence coordination among the local tourism and planning authorities.

Some of the shops on St Maarten's Front Street literally turned their orientation 180° to face a new walking boulevard for cruise tourists, reorienting urban form; at the same time, when four cruise ships in St Maarten simultaneously unload, their 10 thousand passengers instantly cause a traffic jam.[42] In Curacao, the design of public space guides the cruise tourists carefully from the Megapier through a shopping center onto the "swinging old lady" bridge to Punda, the old city center that is now full of luxury duty-free shops. This route literally turns its face away from the main shopping street for locals in Otrabanda, whose "shopkeepers have always expressed that they want to keep orienting themselves to the local client, considering it a more stable factor."[43]

At first, the interest of the cruise industry in heritage was not only ethical but economically driven, therefore more stable. Yet recent cases point in a different direction, indicating that the cruise industry is comparing the costs and benefits of this model to those of a new model of total control in which they fabricate *heritage* assets elsewhere, preferably far from the city and authentic heritage.

The cruise lines have constructed cruise line-owned shopping destinations in no man's-lands and leased (or sometimes bought) beaches, creating tourist bubbles[44] disconnected from actual heritage sites, real cities, and local lives. According to researcher Caroline Cheong, "port communities may be predisposed more so than other tourist areas to commodify their heritage for tourists" given the concentration of tourist activity and the revenues generated in the "tourist bubble".[45] She quotes Robert E. Wood, saying "that increased interaction between visitors and local communities furthers processes of globalization and homogenization."[46] According to her, "this process is sped up within the host community when the ratio of visitors exceeds that of the local community, a phenomenon that [Juan Gabriel] Brida and the United Nations World Tourism Organization note is especially prevalent in the Caribbean."[47]

In some isolated islands of the Caribbean, the population spikes in the high season. "Cockburn Town, Turks and Caicos, for example, quintuples during peak cruise season, with neither conflict nor negotiation."[48] If the main attraction was first heritage sites, it then became itineraries and ports and later the ship itself in combination with beach and water-related activities, often on leased islands in the middle of nowhere. Yet, according to Cheong, despite cruise lines' separate shopping and beach areas for their passengers, "heritage sites remain a main attraction."[49] Nonetheless, she notes: "Though many studies found that cruise itineraries and ports of call remained primary motivators for cruise travelers – acknowledging the need to provide satisfactory offshore experiences – the literature indicates that there is a consumer-driven shift toward the ship itself acting as a the primary attraction."[50] Our recent analysis of Caribbean excursions on shore reveals that this tendency goes hand in hand with the tendency that most current excursions ashore in the Caribbean region focus on water and the beach rather than heritage.

44. Jaakson, "Beyond the Tourist Bubble?"
45. Caroline Cheong, "Impacts and Trends: A Literature Review," in: Avrami, *Harboring Tourism*, 29 and 30.
46. Ibid., 29.
47. Ibid. Caroline Cheong quotes: Juan Gabriel Brida and Sandra Zapata-Aguirre, "Cruise Tourism: Economic, Socio-Cultural and Environmental Impacts," *International Journal of Leisure and Tourism Marketing* 1, no. 3 (January 2009): 205-226, https://bit.ly/3yj4JUU; World Tourism Organization, *Cruise Tourism: Current Situation and Trends* (Madrid, UNWTO, 2010).
48. Chapter "Destination Whatever. Touring the Cruise Industry of the Caribbean," page 184.
49. Cheong, "Impacts and Trends," 27.
50. Caroline Cheong, "Appendix A: Annotated Bibliography," in: Avrami, *Harboring Tourism*, 126. The author quotes: "2012 Industry Update," *Cruise Lines International Association*, 2012, https://bit.ly/3QMEhtR; Konstantinos Andriotis and George Myron Agiomirgianakis, "Cruise Visitors' Experience in a Mediterranean Port of Call," *International Journal of Tourism Research* 12, no. 4 (July 2010): 390-404, https://bit.ly/3ykDKZg.

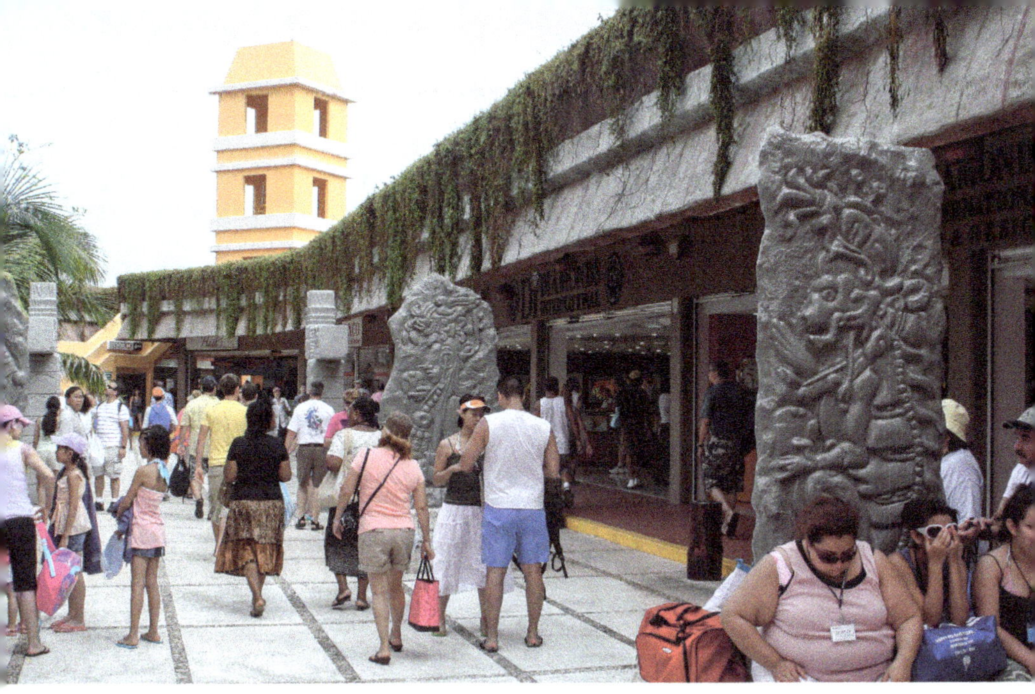

Contemporary Modes of Cruise Tourism in the Caribbean and their Impact on the Heritage of Caribbean Port Cities and their Hinterland

It is hard to shake the impression that cruise ships have become entirely self-sufficient. The exponential increase in ship sizes has turned into a metaphor for the cockiness of the cruise industry: The bigger the boats, the less the companies seem to care about the quality, variety, or authenticity of destinations. If cruising in the Caribbean not long ago meant wandering old colonial cities like San Juan, walking beach promenades in Cozumel, buying goods near the pier, or having a taste of local cuisine of Santo Domingo, the latest cruise development has tended to diminish the importance of destination-specific values.

As cruise companies have succeeded in engineering a diversity of life on board, they call into question the relevance of destinations. The plurality, potential insecurity, and lack of guarantees in real places surely overshadowed any advantage they might offer. In places such as Cozumel, where tourists still are able to reach the local shops, cruise directors warn passengers to avoid the uncertified and unsafe shops of the locals. It even seems that ships could just stop anchoring at local nodes.

One apparently insignificant shift is actually a crucial move changing the role of destinations in the power game of tourist spatial economics. Originally, the pier was the extension of the local economy of a touristic destination. As the extension of the touristic destination, the cruise pier had to lead tourists carefully to the destination charms, seducing then to spend as much time and money as possible in locally owned shops during their short stay. As the cruise industry is now financing, building, and deciding the position of new piers, they "have today become extensions of ships."[51]

The dominant new model for handling cruise tourism ashore is to provide a fenced bus terminal and a shopping area attached to the cruise pier, sometimes far from the city or on an unexploited island. This cruise village immediately attached to the cruise pier is providing leisure and (often cruise line owned) shopping wrapped up in duplicates of historical villages, divorced from existing cities and their economies.

With the new piers increasingly far from historic destinations, the tourist has fewer options to venture into town (and they run the risk of not catching the cruise when it departs). It is easier and easier to stay on the secure grounds of the new ports of call that are under industry control. It is estimated that "at each arrival of the boat to the port, 15% of the passengers never leave the cruise ship."[52] But this move could not be completed without a revolution on the ship itself. The transformation of the boat has been so massive that many tourists now decide that destinations are less crucial to their experience than in the past.

As ships grew, they "decreased dependence of the ports of call as the ship itself has become the destination."[53] This has enabled cruise lines to maximize their benefits for the cruise industry. The only remaining role of real places is fulfilling the few tourists wishes unattainable on the boat: Authentic experiences of a tropical colonial city, pre-Hispanic archaeological ruins, and an unspoiled beach. Even this remaining niche is

51. Chapter "Destination Whatever. Touring the Cruise Industry of the Caribbean," page 184.
52. Lems K (2010) Economic valuation of USVI coral reefs. Is the USVI's tourism industry the seed of its own destruction? IVM Institute for Environmental Studies, p 51

53. Wood, "Caribbean Cruise Tourism," 358.
54. Ibid., 361.
55. Ibid., 363.

56. Saavedra Bruno, "Cruceros en el Caribe/ Caribbean Cruisers," 106. Also see chapter "Destination Whatever. Touring the Cruise Industry of the Caribbean," page 184.

57. Wood, "Caribbean Cruise Tourism," 363.

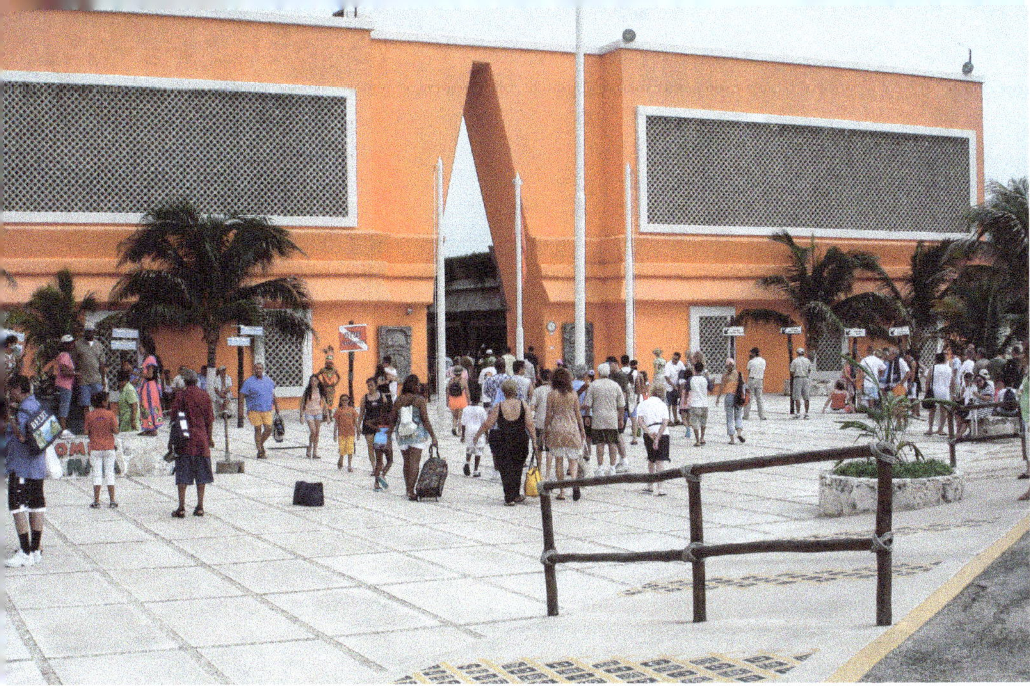

Photo 19.1 Cruise center Costa Maya. Source Supersudaca, Al Caribe research with auspices of Prince Claus Fund; released under a Creative Commons Attribution-NonCommercial- NoDerivatives 4.0 International License

now also being contested by the cruise industries that are creating "fantasy escapes on board and on land."[54] Colonial port destinations where the cruise industry is a big lobby, such as Curacao, control the routing of tourists in a nearly perfectly orchestrated choreography; and to "some extent Caribbean destinations are imitating the cruise ships, introducing theming in port city landscapes (such as in Aruba, whose main street feels very much as a theme park) and creating man-made, artificial attractions, divorced from the geographical environment as in St Maarten."[55] To meet tourists' demand for exotic architecture, the cruise industry has built a place in Mexico called Costa Maya from scratch and in the middle of nowhere. It includes a shopping area and restaurants in neo-Mayan style, owned and operated by the industry, while a plaster church tower recalls Spanish colonial times. Fake "stone sculptures and Indian dancers on the shopping plaza recall Mayan culture."[56] Not only did Grand Turk promote a replica of the Nasa Friendship 7 capsule, which splashed into the Atlantic in 1962 a few short miles from the island, as one of the island's main excursion attractions on land, but it copied it again when it built the Grand Turk cruise terminal and center. To a significant degree, Wood points out, by extending "the fantasy environment of the ship" the ports also "reproduce in new form the enclave development long characteristic of the region."[57] Furthering this tendency, the Caribbean region has been a laboratory since the 1970s for the development of all-inclusive resorts, a world parallel to the cities where the locals live.

Ports of call like Curacao and Aruba, where the tourists can walk directly from the terminal into the old city center, became quite exceptional in the Caribbean. When mapping the cruise terminals and their direct surroundings, we found that "most emerging cruise terminals are situated several kilometers away from the closest inner city."[58] But in order to get the local beach environment that tourists demand, one of the last remaining niche for destinations, "cruise lines are also reducing the days in port by buying, or leasing islands or by anchoring at a deserted stretch of beach."[59] Of the eight major lines that now operate in the Caribbean, ten own private islands.[60] Royal Caribbean owns Coco Cay in Bahamas, for example, and leases Labadee in Haiti – which they tell tourists is Fantasy Island, in order to not spoil their holidays.[61]

As cruise companies have developed and refined their business models, they have affected the spatial relation between the city, port, and hinterland by strategically positioning docks in new places outside the old city. Their new constructions and new uses affect the historic spatial development of both urban form and heritage (local identity). But neither public actors – local politicians, tourist agencies, planners, heritage actors – nor citizens themselves have been involved in the ongoing transformation.

58. Saavedra Bruno, "Cruceros en el Caribe/Caribbean Cruisers," 106. Also see chapter "Destination Whatever. Touring the Cruise Industry of the Caribbean," page 184.
59. Wood, "Caribbean Cruise Tourism," 361.

60. Chapter "Destination Whatever. Touring the Cruise Industry of the Caribbean," page 184.
61. Polly Pattullo, Last Resorts: The Cost of Tourism in the Caribbean (2nd ed., London/New York, Latin America Bureau/Monthly Review Press, 2005), 164.

62. Hacker, *The Divided Welfare State*; Pierson, *Politics in Time*; Mahoney and Thelen, "A Theory of Gradual Institutional Change;" Sorensen, "Taking Path Dependence Seriously."
63. Capoccia and Kelemen, "The Study of Critical Junctures," 341.

64. "Work in Progress 2011-2013," *International New Town Institute*, 2015, https://bit.ly/3Oljc2b.
65. Robertico Croes, "Measuring and Explaining Competitiveness in the Context of Small Island Destinations," Journal of Travel Research 50, no. 4. (2011): 431-442, https://bit.ly/3bl3RWJ.

Conolusion

Cruise tourism has rewritten the urban form and architectural heritage of the Caribbean region and their functions in the last twenty years with urban form thematization (often *disneyfication* of the historic inner cities, including waterfronts) and simulations of historic ports. We have analyzed how the most recent cruise business model has affected both urban form and heritage architecture by (1) strategically positioning docking at new places outside of the old city or in the middle of nowhere, (2) reproducing heritage architecture, objects, and landscapes in replicas and simulations, and (3) recodifying heritage to suit the demands of the tourists and to exclude local economies.

The rapid growth of the cruise industry and its concentration in a few companies has established distinctive power relationships between the cruise industry and Caribbean governments. We understand that this emerging dynamics follow path dependencies,[62] so what now seems like a dynamic process could actually be heading toward a static relationship among the key actors over time, making change increasingly difficult. As Capoccia and Kelemen have argued, "long periods of path dependent institutional stability and reproduction are punctuated occasionally by brief phases of institutional flux – referred to as critical junctures - during which more dramatic change is possible."[63]

We are currently at such a *critical juncture*, in which local actors and heritage institutions can both prevent the cruise lines from seizing complete control of heritage areas while simultaneously luring them to stay in heritage sites (and not abandon them altogether). Caribbean governments are increasingly recognizing the role that heritage plays in attracting cruise tourists and the role that cruise tourism could play in preserving heritage and making it valuable in the future. In Havana, for example, the government has increasingly tied the renewal of the waterfronts to cruise tourism. A new port has taken over large-scale transport activities, leaving behind the historic port, which is being redeveloped primarily for cruise tourism. That process had already started, but the recent political opening of Cuba has accelerated it.[64] Similarly, according to the Winning the Future report Aruba has recently recognized the power of cruise tourism and has decided to invest part of the revenues from it directly into preserving heritage.[65] The cruise lines are often behind the scenes, still deciding where that money is being invested. The government of Grand

Turk, for example, planned to use revenues from cruise tourism to turn an old building in the historic center into Carnival's welcoming cruise center, but the cruise line would not use it without the guarantee that cruise revenues on the other side of the island would be high enough.[66]

Cruise tourism triggers new institutional configurations in Caribbean cruise destinations, including collaboration between heritage and water-related planning institutions to ensure the future of historic port cities and to keep inherited patterns from further distorting uses of heritage architecture and urban form.

66. Bruno, Madrazo, Delgado and Roquero, "Fair Play," 45.

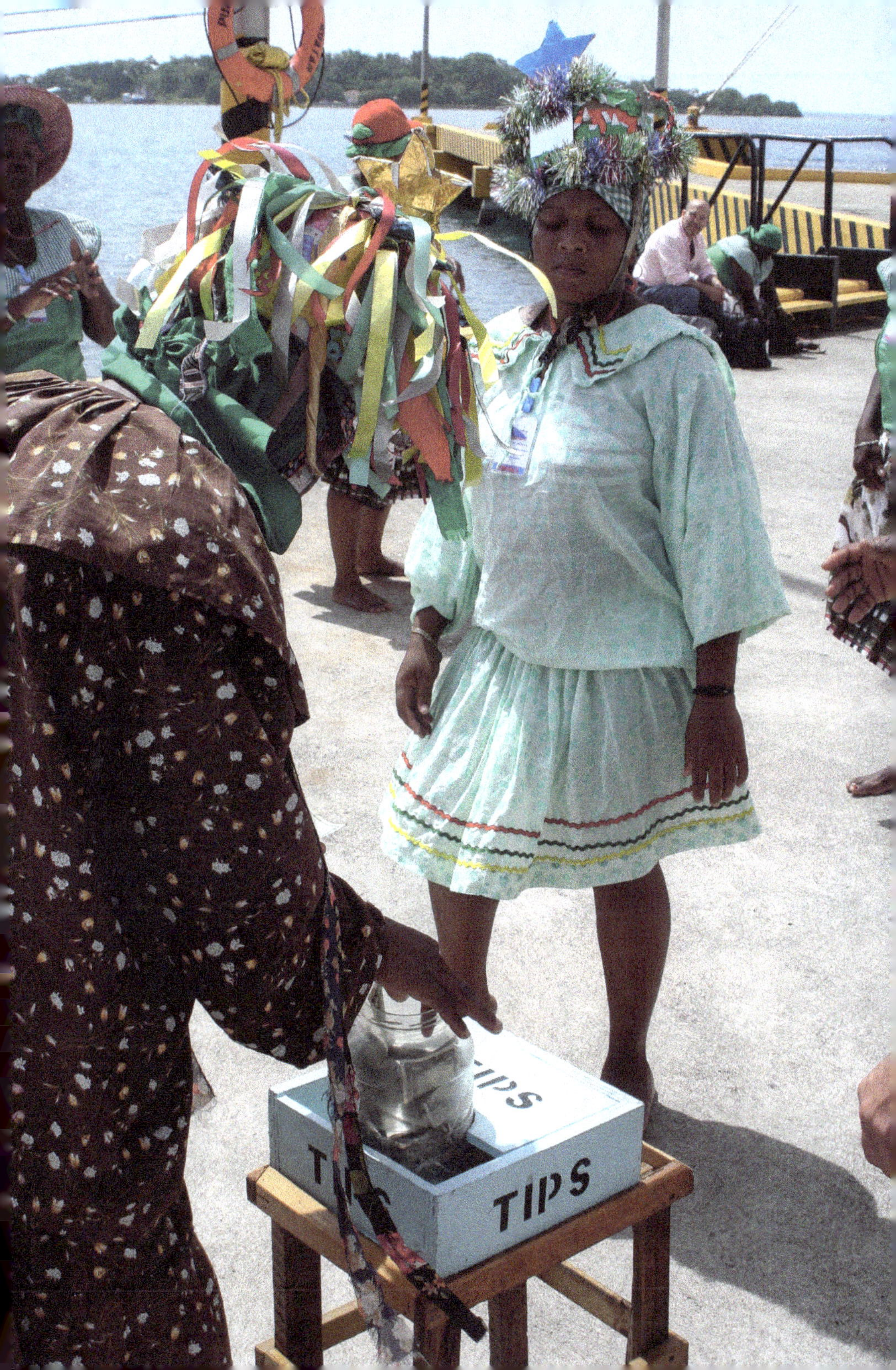

TIPS
TIPS

At Any Rate

ONCE UPON A TIME, not long ago the world was dominated by 2 ideological blocks: some people call them the bright & THE DARK SIDE

After the fall of THE DARK side the planet became entirely bright (well, almost!)

The new world privileged DEMOCRACY over IDEOLOGY, people were in charge at last, enthusiasm spread all over

As discussions were no longer focused on politics, innocent questions were increasingly answered by one famous sentence: 'it's the economy, stupid'

Enthusiasm started to fade away and optimism slowly became replaced by a more obscure term: ECONOMIC REALITY

But people from all countries were happy at the beginning, the new bright world was free after all

It all started to get complicated later when economic crisis became more and more frequent

At the same time, more and more countri[es] started to become evaluated, classified a[nd] rated not anymore by Secret Agents but by Rating Agencies. EXPLAIN…

STANDARD & POOR'S DOWNGRADES US CREDIT RATING
STEELERS LB WOODLEY LANDS 6-YEAR, $61.5M D

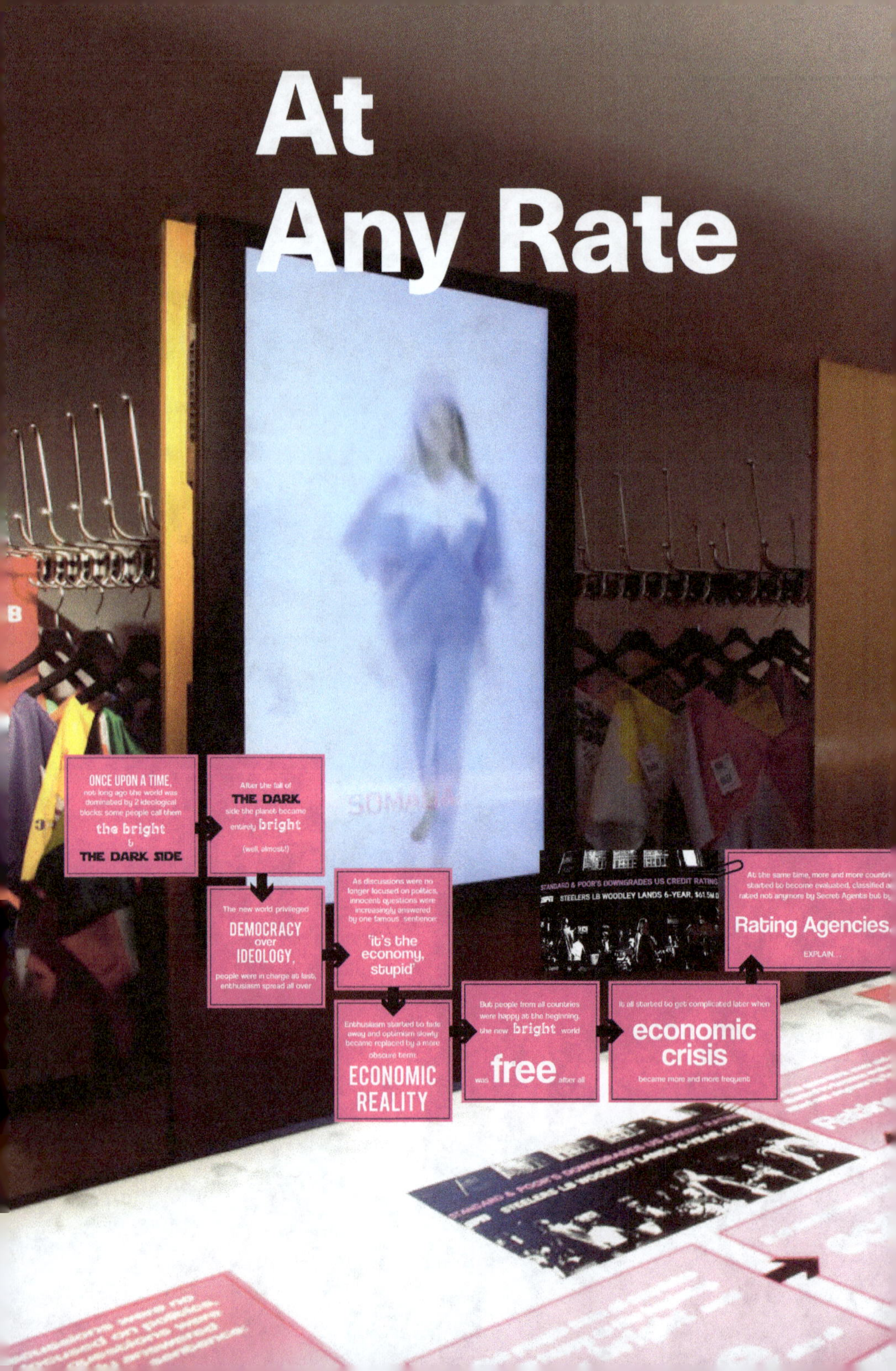

While the Cold War was dominated by geo-political tensions, our current world seems to be tenuously tied together by finance. In making the judgment of who gets good loans and who gets bad ones, credit rating agencies have stumbled into a curiously powerful position. In one single rating, they can cast a country to the economic periphery, or ensure its position as a central global player. Supersudaca explore this new global superpower and ask the question: Where's the accountability?

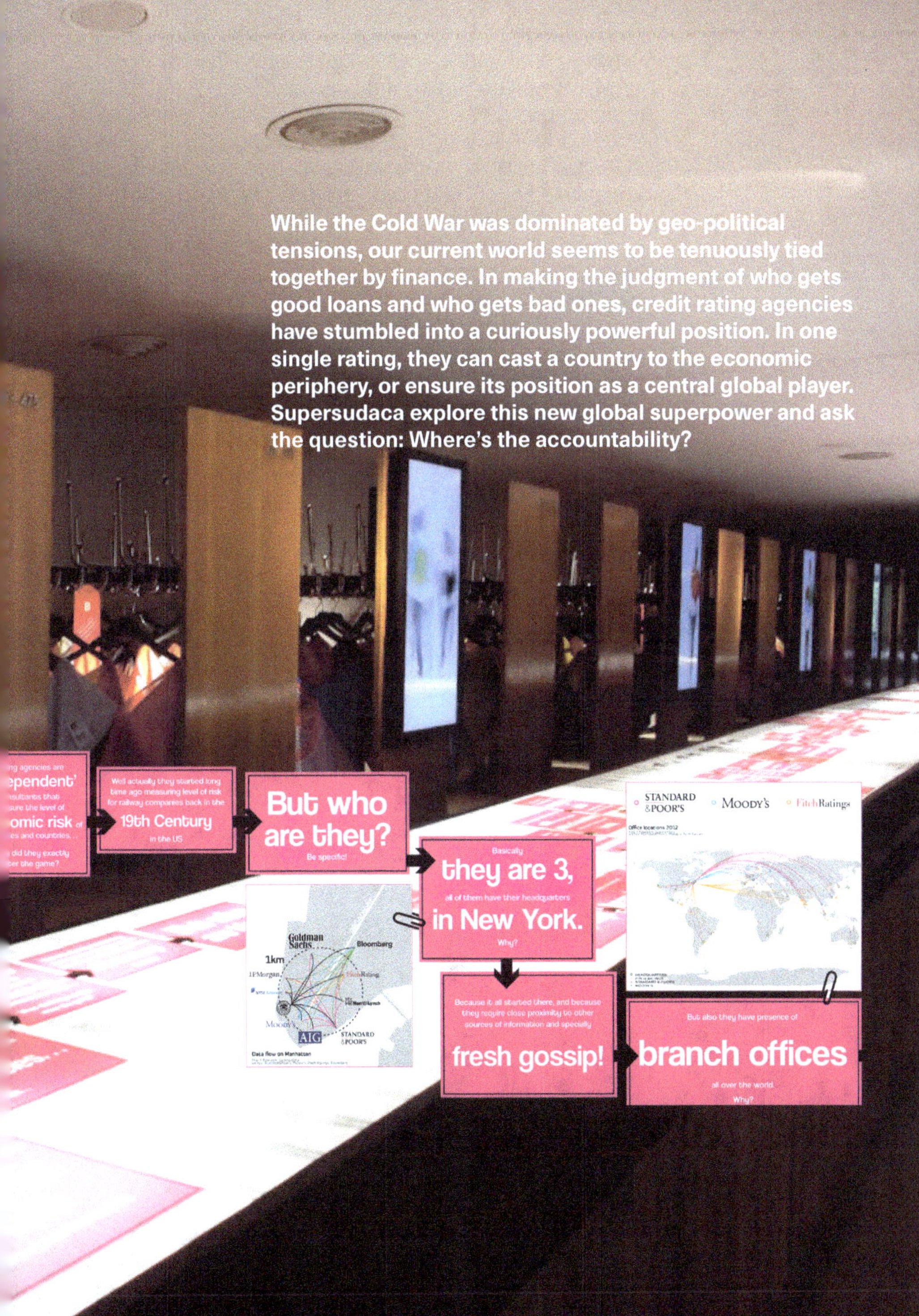

NA. This text is part of a research shown at the exhibition *Between Walls and Windows. Architecture and Ideology*, held by Haus der Kulturen der Welt, in Berlin, from September 1st to September 30, 2012. See: Valerie Smith, ed., Between Walls and Windows. Architecture and Ideology (Berlin, Hatje Cantz Verlag, 2012).

After the fall of the Berlin Wall, politics became no longer the forefront of a country's destiny; market dynamics and tensions have replaced the confrontations and impulses of the old superpowers. No more East versus West; not even South versus North. The world is more homogenous; countries are not divided between *good* and *bad*. We understand the world through the lens of numbers overlaid with geography no longer affected by political signs.

Market sensitivities have become the main theme of the discussion in the city. Not long ago these discussions were merely based on the performance of the stock exchanges or the value of foreign currencies. But lately the most influential gossip in town is the upgrading and downgrading of countries on the world financial rating system.

Returning quickly to the start: Are credit rating agencies the new superpowers? Can we blame them for our current tensions? While they aren't countries, they do resemble what

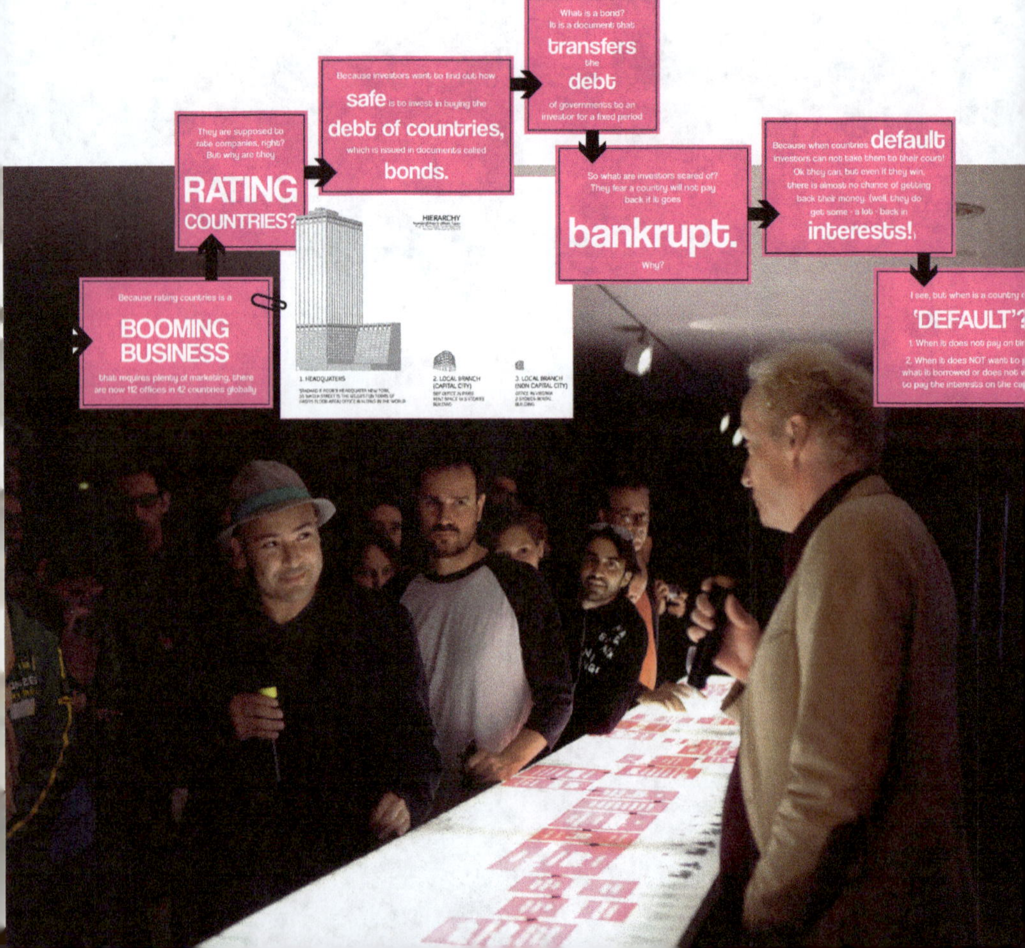

political lobbies were for the politics of the recent past; in both cases their campaigns are a means to promote or degrade a certain worldview, according to their own ideology, differentiating between what is good from what is evil in economic terms. The main difference between political lobbyists and rating agencies is that political lobbyists campaign openly and negotiate privately to achieve such goals while rating agencies research privately and their final judgments are public but not meant to be negotiable, thus are meant to be without politics. Is that believable? OK, the question is not only about finding out how trustworthy and unbiased the rating agencies' judgments are, but about realizing who gave them so much power and why. Who actually pays them when they rate countries without being requested to obtain their services? And if you did request to be rated, can you claim neutrality of judgment when a payment is pending to be transferred?

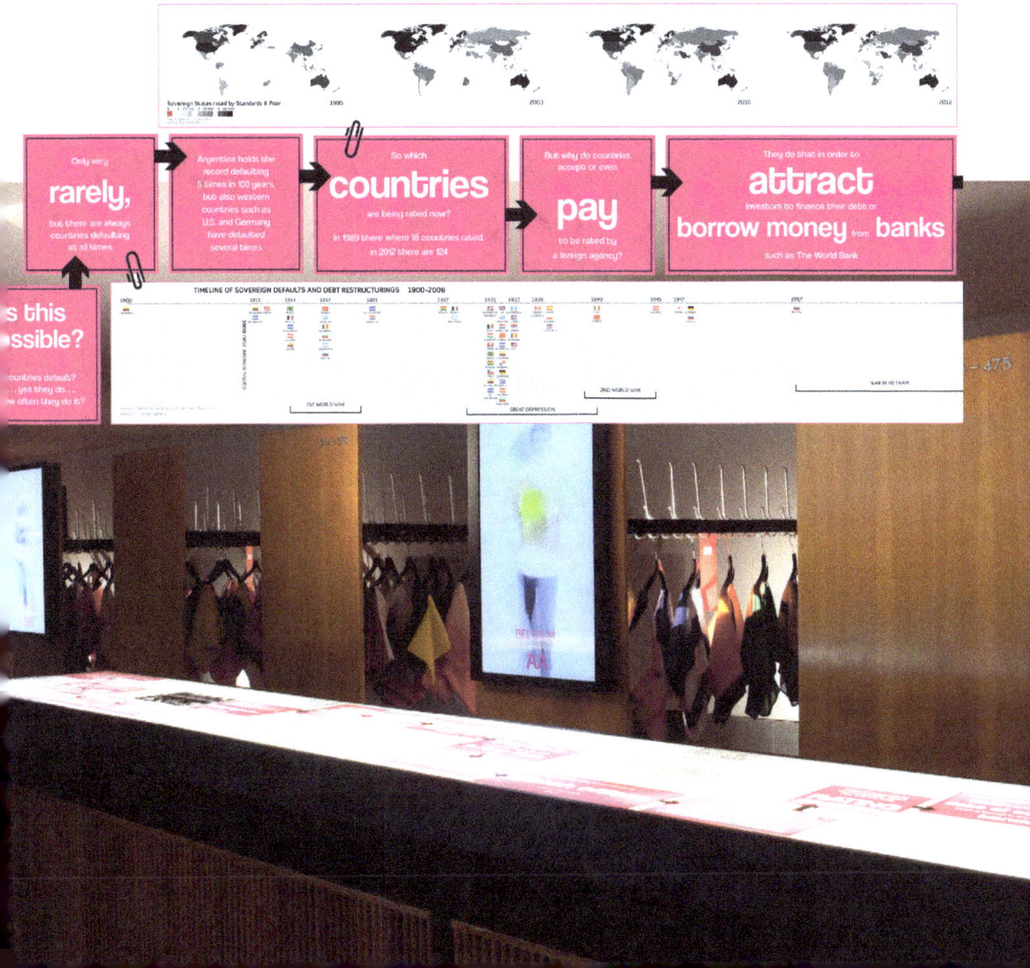

1. Cf. Andrew Fight, *The Ratings Game* (New Jersey, Wiley, 2001).

Back to School

Credit rating agencies first emerged in the United States, and have actually been there for a while – since the American railway expansion to the West in the 19th century. The two most important agencies, Standard and Poor's and Moody's, have a long-established history; but it's only since the 1990s that their expansion to the rest of the world accelerated at a growth rate of 25% per year,[1] coinciding nicely with the fall of the Berlin Wall. Their epicenter located in Manhattan expanded their branch offices to Japan and Europe in the 1980s while the current network now spreads over many countries. Yet their spatial presence in Costa Rica, Guatemala, or other non-*global cities* such as Calcutta point to their increasing need for outsourcing of data processing. In any case the presence of offices worldwide indicates how increasingly it's not just companies being rated, but countries as well.

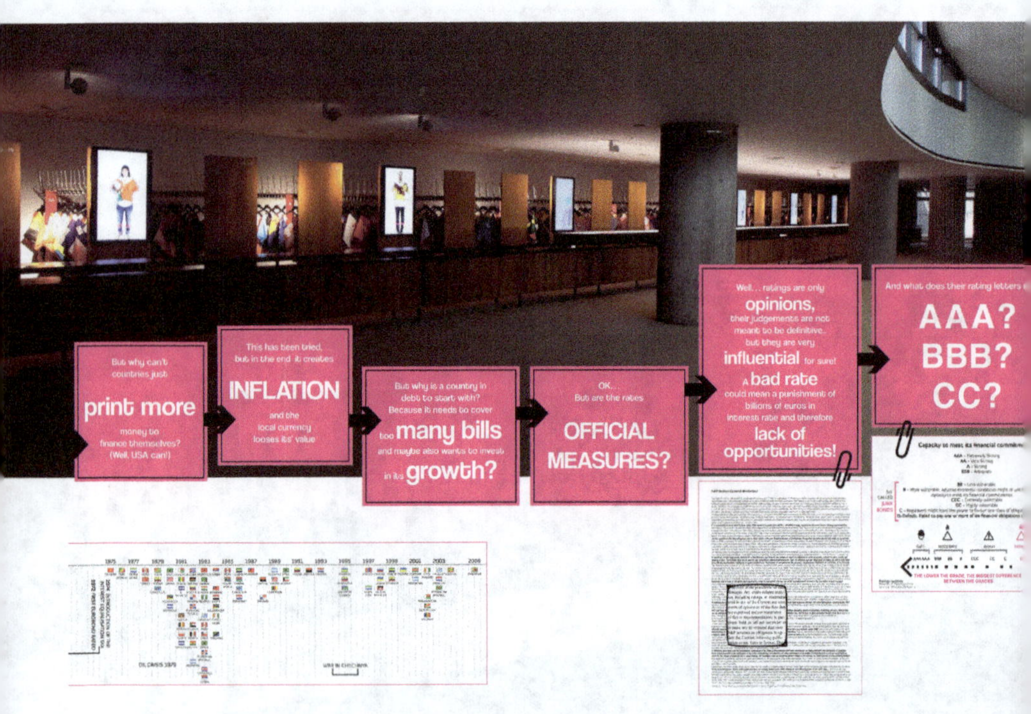

218

Towards an Obedient World

It is worth noting that on average, despite all the stressful news we are confronted with on a daily basis (or perhaps because of it), the average inhabitant of the world is actually rated within the A-range and actually that average has improved since the crisis of 2008. However, you could also conclude that countries are now more than ever obedient to the orthodoxies of what is considered to be responsible financial management dictated from the epicenters of panic: Wall Street and the rating agencies. While most countries' ratings reflect that they are strongly capable of respecting their financial obligations, to take a policy step in what rating agencies consider the wrong direction could instantly cost a country exponentially more fiscal punishment, reflected in higher costs of borrowing, higher amounts of debt, tougher payment conditions, and ultimately might lead to the loss of sovereignty over political decisions to control their internal budgets. Spain and Greece are the latest exemplary cases that are presented to the world with a clear message: No one will be safe from agencies' judgmental power and their lethal influence on the markets.

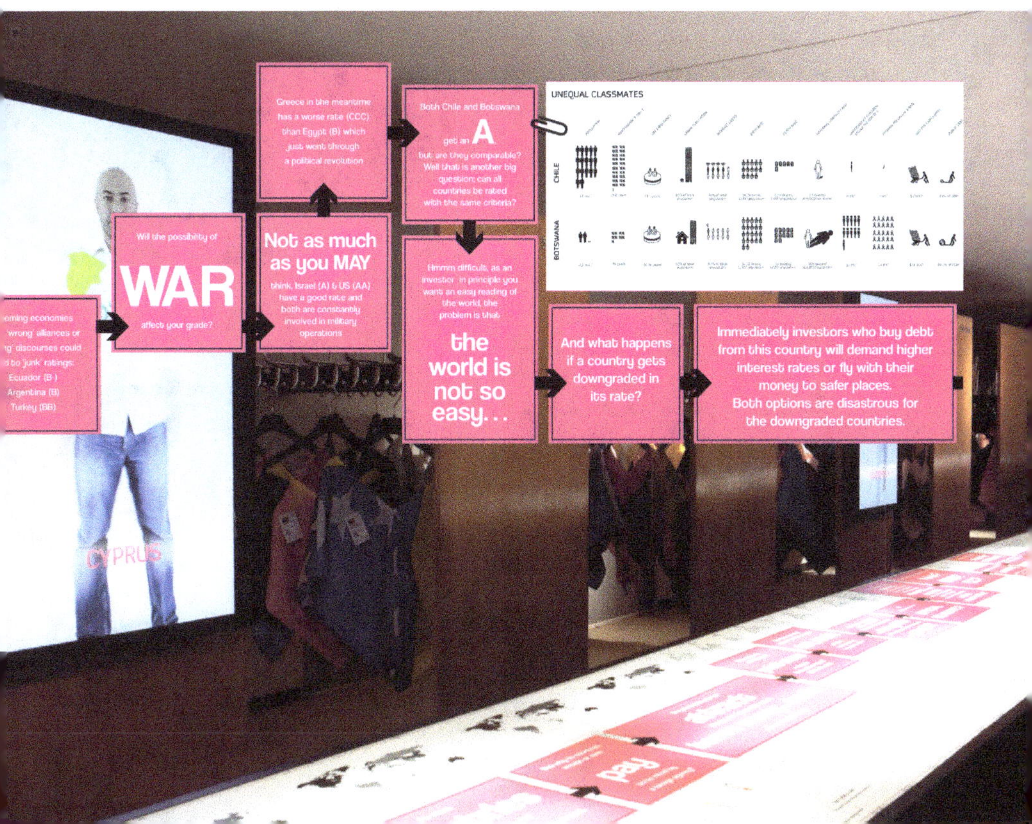

At Any Rate

So why play the game, why is it so critical to be in the club of the rated? For one, without a rating record, countries and companies cannot obtain credit in many financial institutions, especially in the United States. A good rating for a country meanwhile could improve its negotiation capacities for acquiring credit at fairer rates. The absence of such a record or a negative outlook on the other hand could mean that borrowing costs escalate in accordance with the rating reports. That is why countries are proud to show the triple assessment of the experts to calm any source of alarm for potential investors, turning rating agencies into a great business without real competitors.

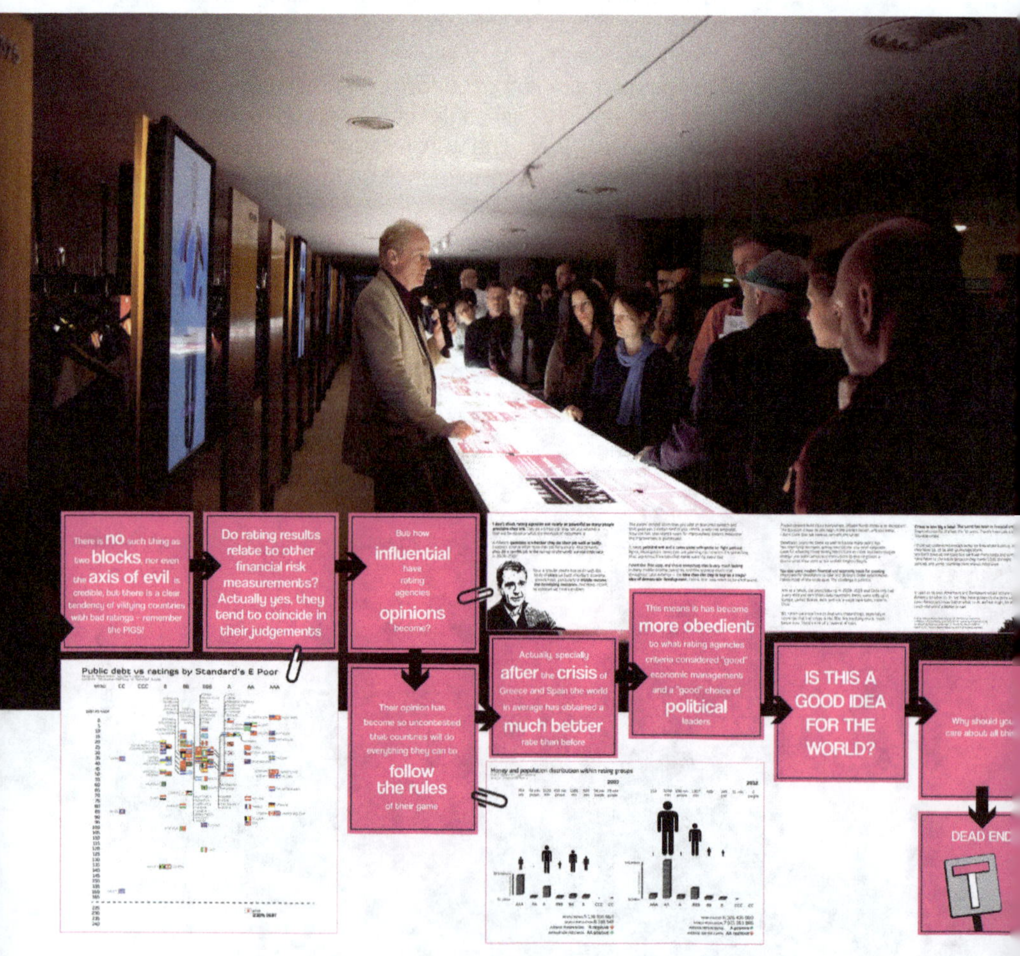

Disclaimer

The rating agencies have a protected status within the United States and therefore have no responsibilities concerning the damages they could cause to companies or countries for inaccurate ratings. To achieve this status has meant that only three rating agencies dominate the rating world: Standard and Poor's, Moody's, and Fitch Ratings. The ratings themselves are only opinions of the mentioned companies intended to inform investors on the willingness and capacity of a country or companies to honor their debts and interest payments on time.

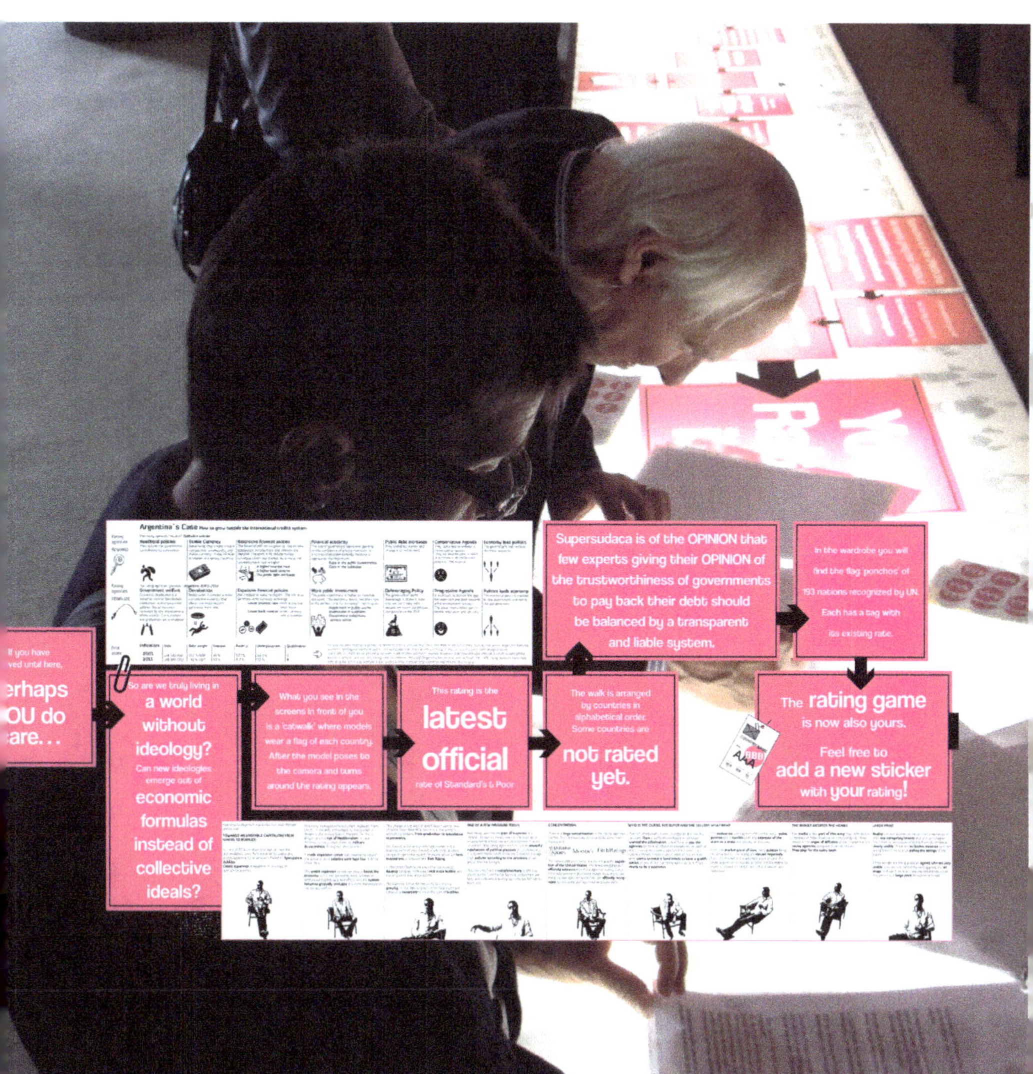

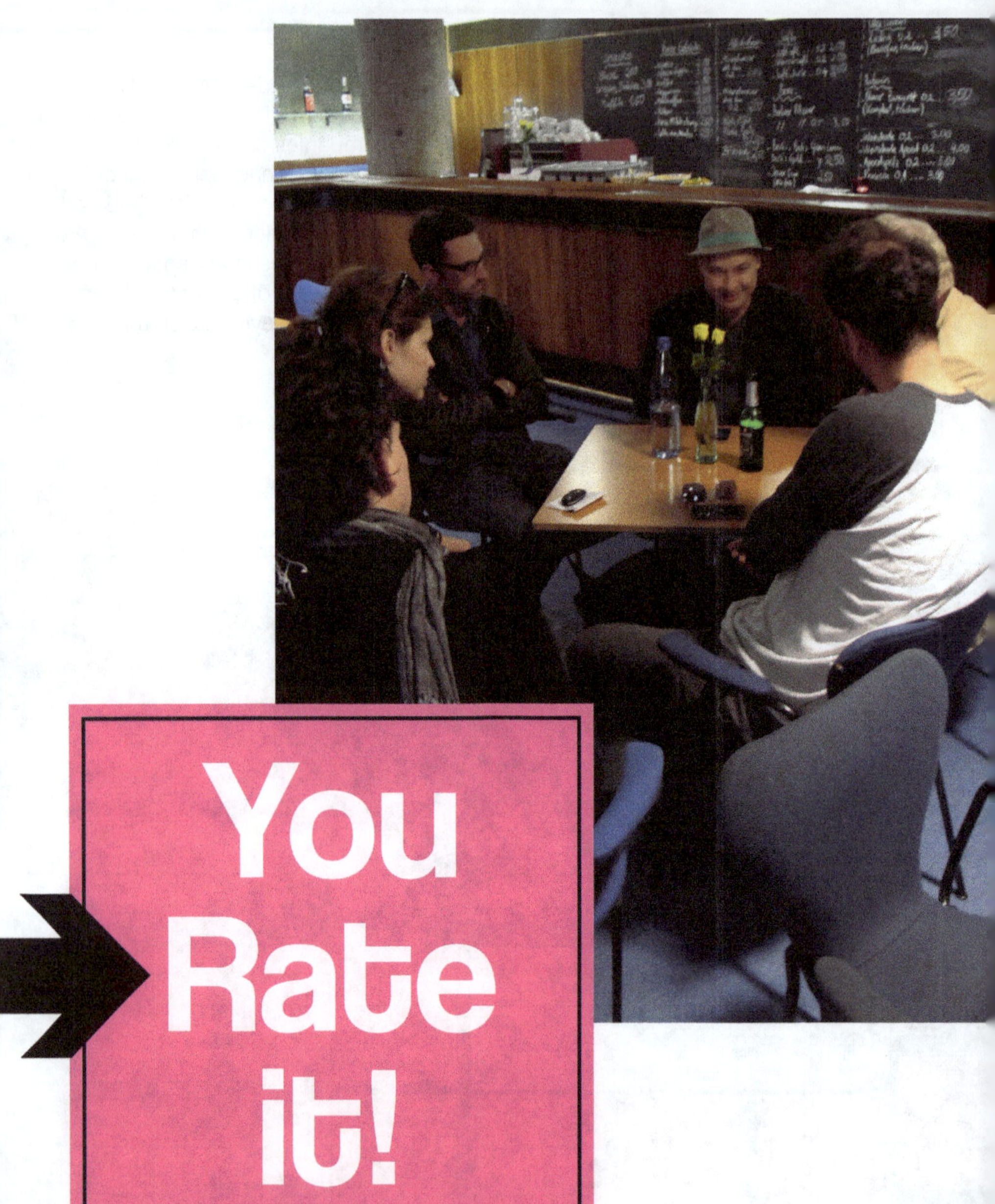
You
Rate
it!

Myth and Power of the Rating Agencies

It is not that we expect credit rating agencies to be perfect, or neutral, nor even censored. But why don't we at least expect our governments to monitor them more strictly? It is no secret that rating assessments do include a high degree of political judgment over which type of government is more likely to honor its debts. Their rating methods are hardly transparent in this regard. They also rely largely upon gossip heard at world summits, with rating agencies relying on their agents much as secret agents of the past. So crucial are their *opinions* that billions of euros and more absurdly millions of people depend on their fair judgment – all the more reason not to let them get away with it so easily.

China tu Madre

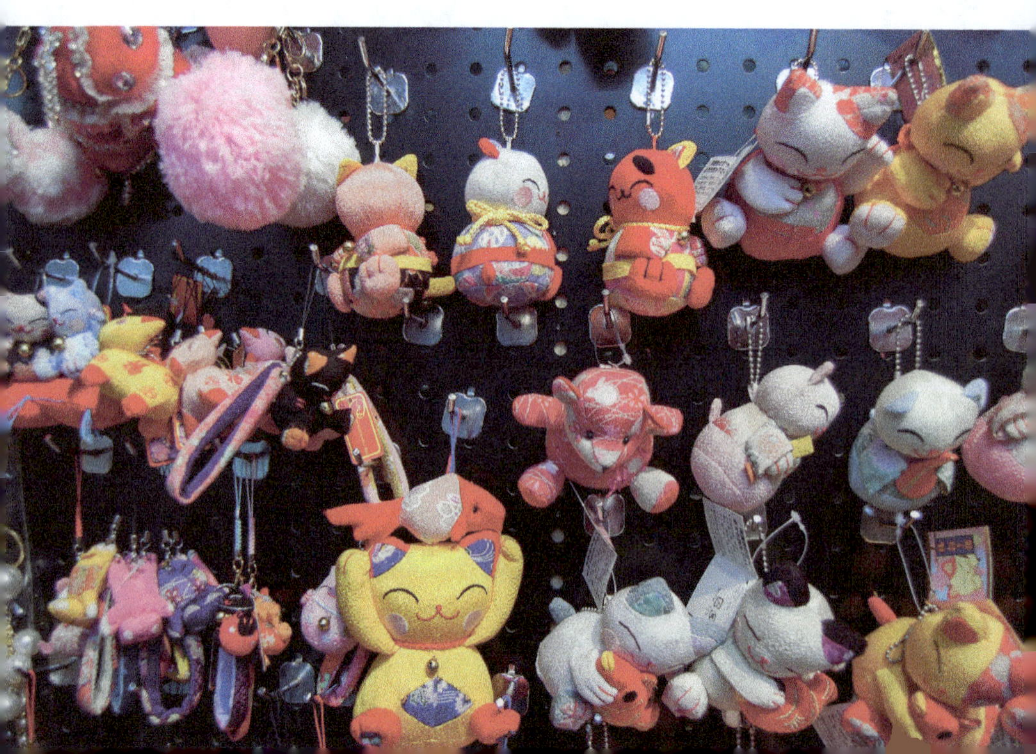

When the theme of culture comes to the fore, the first thing
that comes to mind for Latin Americans is that their culture is
a product of Western civilization. At school, one is educated to
understand how each of the countries that form Latin America
belongs to the so-called Western civilization. High school
teachers place so much emphasis in making sure no student
leaves without knowing the names of Charlemagne, Catherine
the Great, or Carlos V. It is only when you inhabit the core of
the West that you are able to understand and digest that the
so-called epicenter of Western civilization does not give much
thought to Latin America, nor does it think of Latin America
as part of the West. San Martin, Andres Bello, or Benito Juarez
are unknown names for most European high school students.
Living in the core makes you also realize that the so-called
West is much smaller than the European continent; more
specifically, the West is both the completion – and future
projection – of a few European (and American) cities that have
been the epicenters of power and influence over centuries
and across vast amounts of land abroad, including European
territories.

So, if the West has a core, what is the need and purpose
of the periphery? The core defined colonial policies, but also
the concentration of profit from investments abroad. The core
needed the resources from the periphery to generate industry
and profit. Core and periphery, despite needing each other

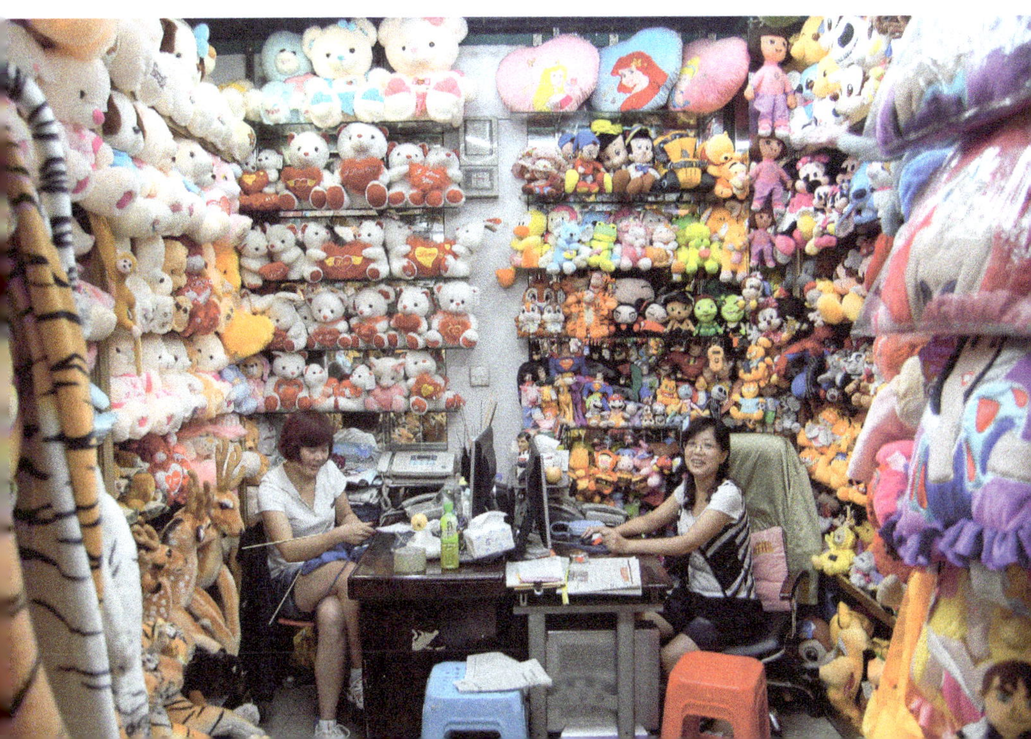

1. See: Manuel Lucena Giraldo, *Naciones de Rebeldes: Las Revoluciones de Independencia Latinoamericanas* (Madrid, Taurus, 2010).
2. Fernand Braudel, *A History of Civilizations* (1963; repr. New York, Penguin, 1994), 171.
3. "Videographic: Which Country has the Biggest Economy?" *The Economist,* October 15, 2014.

to survive, did not mean that each were the same. In fact, the clearer the difference, the better. Claims from noble groups at one periphery – in Latin America – to a legitimate voice within the core were mostly ignored. Ignorance, in turn, backfired with the surge of independence movements in Latin America against Western foreign rulers.[1] These were the first episodes that eventually will affect the new relations between the West, Latin America, and the new world power: China.

Independence, despite invoking massive introspection, never dared to wipe out a Western cultural inheritance. Most Latin-American countries were, and still are, proud to be associated with the cultural canons of the West, *la madre patria*. One key factor that encouraged adherence to the Western canon was its world economic domination. Although Western dominion was only rather recent in history, the overall feeling was that the West had always been at the top of everything. It is only now that China (and also India) are coming back, that the rise of the West is being studied within the trajectories of a much longer historical context. French historian Fernand Braudel reminds us that China's latent power, "however slowly… was never immobile."[2]

A recent video podcast from *The Economist*[3] also reminds us that it was actually China and India that have dominated world economic power since 1 AD until 1870, when these countries were overshadowed by the United States. The 20th

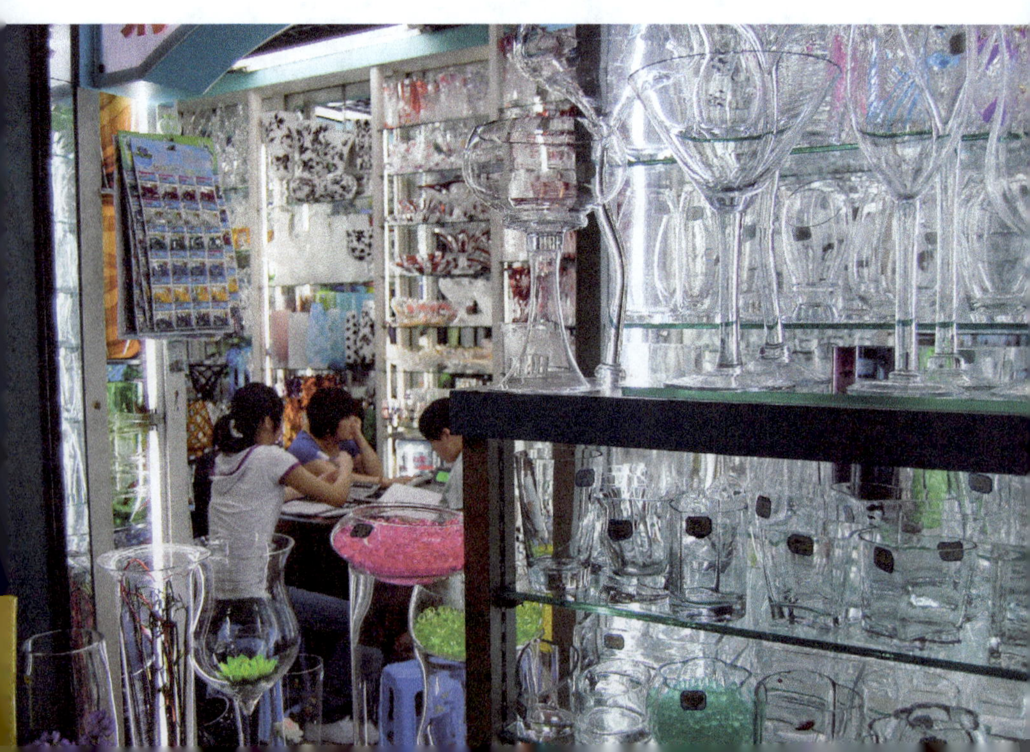

1. Mark Loonard, *What does China think?* (New York, Public Affairs, 2008), 117.

5. Braudel, *A History of Civilizations*, 194.

6. Ibid., 195. See also: Fernand Braudel, *Capitalism and Material Life, 1400-1800* (New York, Harper and Row, 1973), 1973.

7. Braudel, *A History of Civilizations*, 196.

century made a terrible blow that brought China to its lowest point since its long-standing dominance.

As shown in this 2014 podcast, China has since recovered its global economic lead, with around 18% of all economic output, followed by the United States and then India. The dominion of the West that we still refer to is merely a mirage. The effects of the new paradigm are still to be seen. What is sure is that history is far from over. And for people and "governments in Africa, Central Asia, Latin America, and even the Middle East, China's rise means that there is no longer a binary choice between assimilation to the West and isolation."[4]

But, before we dive into China's new global influence and its relation with South America, we want to dig a little further into what brought China to a standstill until its 1945 revolution; what made it so vulnerable to dominance and humiliation by the West? Braudel theorizes that one key problem was China's refusal to embrace the city as a territory of free enterprise.[5] And while the West relied on new instruments to provide money for businesses via credit systems, in China "there was no credit system, at least until the 18th century and (in some places) the 19th century."[6] Without free trade amongst its cities, China further lagged behind in its infrastructure; it "suffered from poor internal communication and still more limited links with the rest of the world."[7]

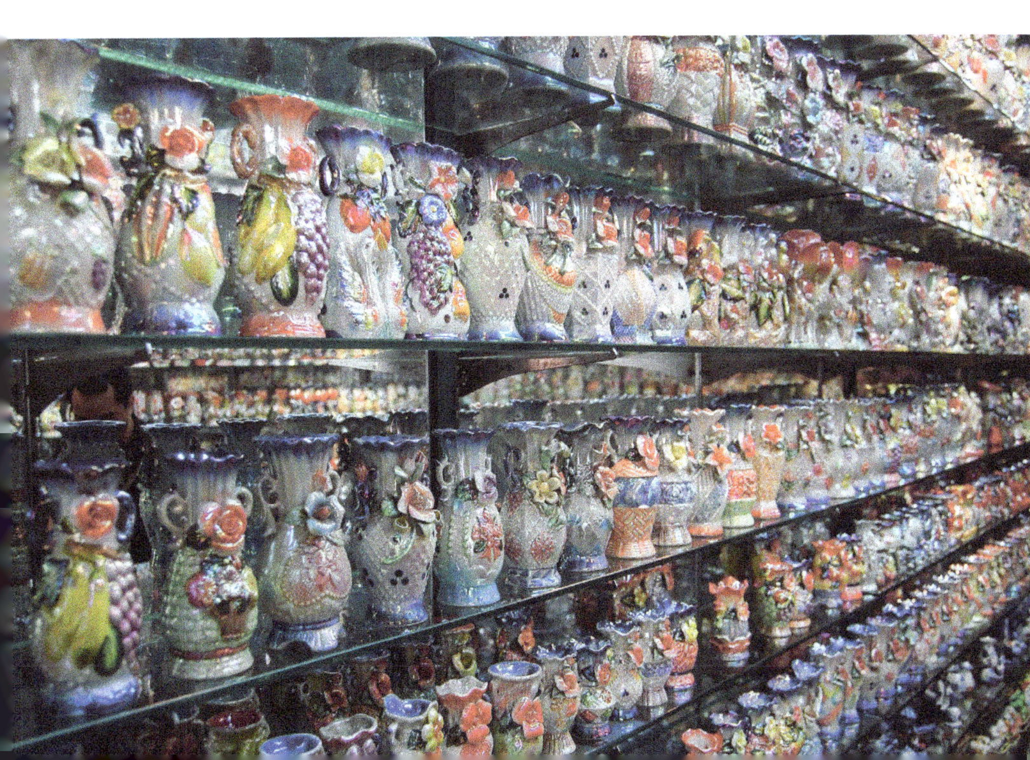

8. Ibid., 201.
9. Ibid, 197.
10. Ibid.

When the West decided to take advantage of China's large market potential, it made sure to control its market logistics. Although it did help modernize China, the West did so with a price tag of dependency. Until the beginning of the 20th century "Western powers controlled part of the railways and customs – guarantees for the payment of interest on foreign loans."[8]

Further, and perhaps as Braudel suggests, China's impasse in technological innovation was due to an excess of labour: "Excessive wealth of manpower necessarily had drawbacks. It probably prevented technological progress. Teeming humanity made machines unnecessary, as slavery had in classical Greece and Rome."[9] This did not significantly change until the revolution in 1945. Whereas at the time, China "was unable to make a motor-scooter; by 1962 she was on the brink of producing an atomic bomb."[10]

If one were to summarize China's recent history from a Western perspective, the anecdote would present itself as follows: Discovery > military dominion > colonial trade > monopoly > struggle for independence > commercial dominion > financial dependence > cultural inheritance. We wonder what sequence (if at all different) China will follow in its own incursion across the globe, including within South America.

The arrival of China in Latin America must be weighed within this longer historical context. We think it is no

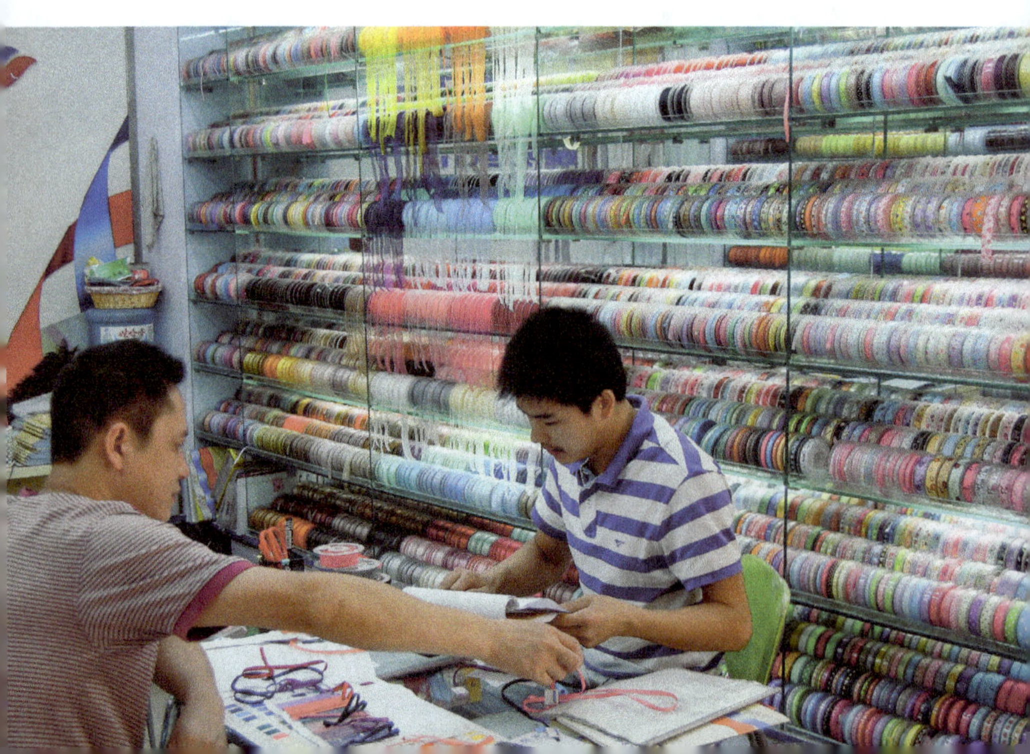

coincidence that China has deliberately followed a policy path distinguished from that of the West. Though objectives might be the same, China's implementation has certainly branded itself as the antipodes of Western dominion.

The reasons behind these distinctive policies are what interest us most. Do they come from centralized governance out of mainland China? Or do they instead come from a decentralized Chinese business diaspora that also includes powerful Taiwanese? Are policies of investment and trade self-organized or vertically determined? Is Chinese foreign policy really different from that of the West? What is the role of Latin America as a source of raw resources? How does this role affect development, and in particular, how does it impact territory, environment, cities, and culture? How is it all linked: Credit, foreign investment, import-export relations etc.? What is the role of building projects in the equation? We briefly explore three themes that, when presented together, might offer a better reading of emerging relations between China and Latin America.

Credit

The dominion of credit rating agencies in Manhattan is renowned. Within a few blocks from each other, these mega consultants define, with a simple grade, the level of risk

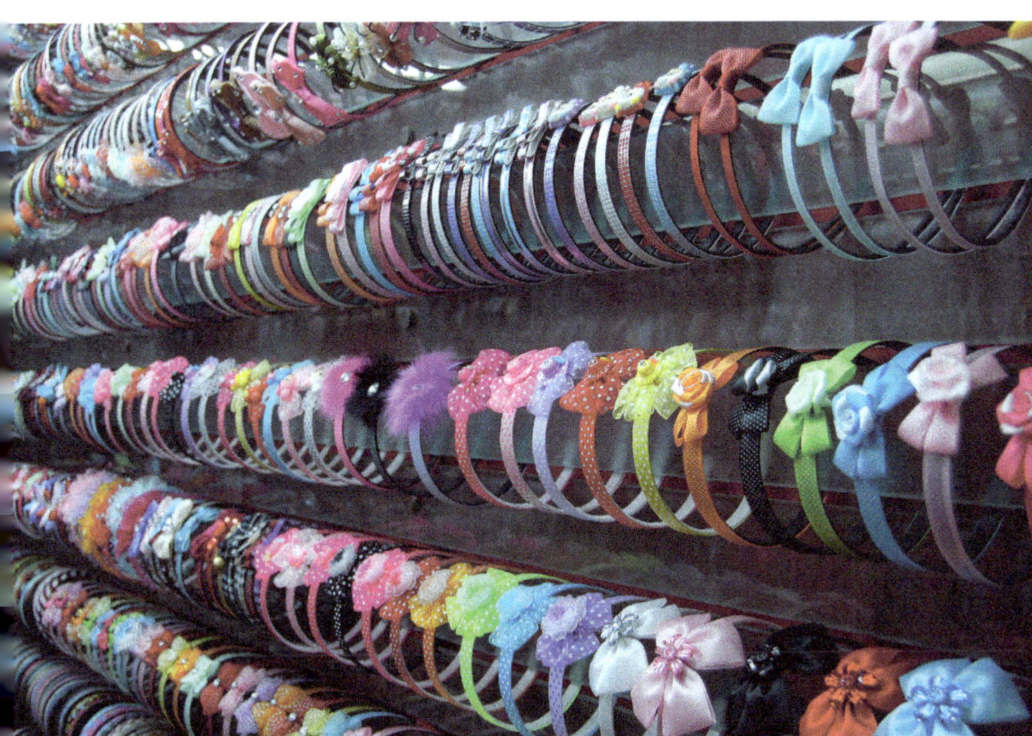

11. "Overview," *Dagon Global*, 2012. Interestingly enough, Dagon Global does not exist anymore, was suspended for corruption charges and later absorbed by the Chinese government.

12. Ambrose Evans Pritchard, "Chinese rating agency strips Western nations of AAA status," *The Telegraph,* July 12, 2010. https://bit.ly/3satPB2.

13. "China Weighs Risks to $50 Billion Investment After Chavez," *Bloomberg News*, March 6, 2013.https://bloom.bg/3HqWLuZ.

involved in lending money to governments of foreign countries. Standards and Poor – S&P, Fitch, and Moody's, all share one thing in common: The power to define the future of global finance. If a country has shown too many signs of distrust or free will in its institutions or political figures, the rating agencies quickly downgrade the credit level of the country. This means that for most credit institutions, the interest rates that are negotiated with governments escalate to a level at which the country is almost left out of credit.

China has made two crucial moves in this regard. First, it has created its own rating agency: Dagong Global Credit Rating Co[11] that, according to China, is not biased in the interests of the West.[12] Second and most importantly for Latin America – affected by un-payable interest rates of Western credit institutions – Dagong Global has offered credit to countries with bad ratings through processes that involve creative negotiations for guarantees or re-payment protocols.

Take, for example, Venezuela. For many years it has had a *junk* rating; as a result, credit and investment from abroad had nearly frozen. "Moody's Investors Service rates Venezuelan long-term foreign-currency debt B2, or five levels below investment grade, the same as Honduras and Cambodia."[13] China has come to Venezuela's rescue by offering credit worth $50 billion dollars. To secure repayment, China has planned an extensive and long-term oil-for-loans program. (Gold is also

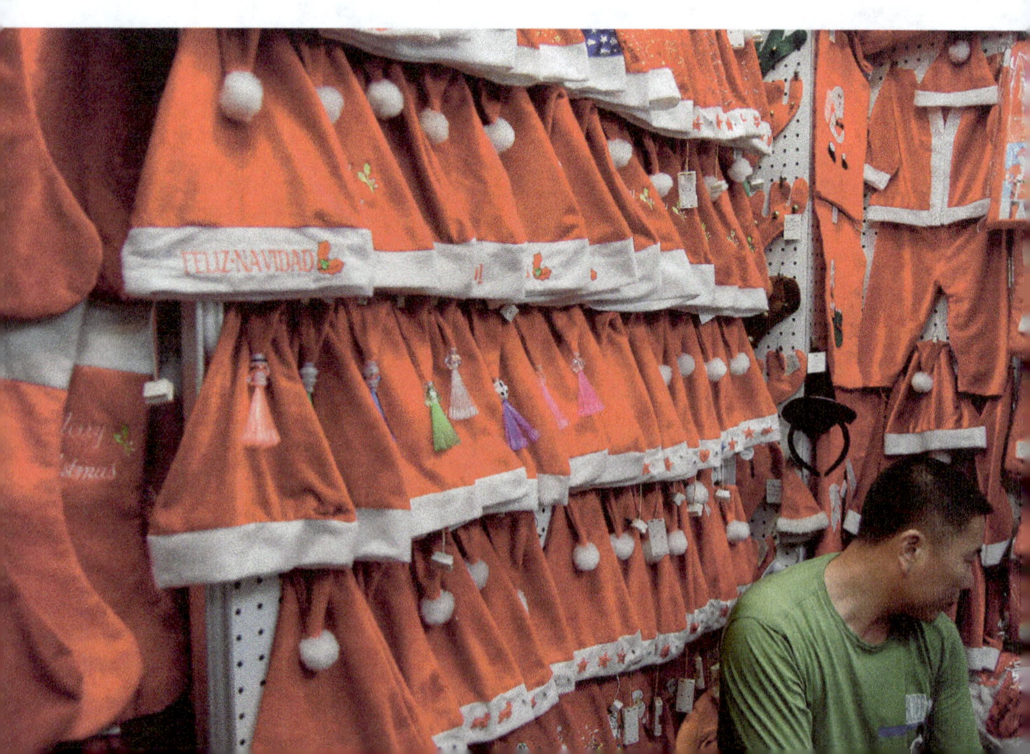

14. Ibid.

15. Maolis Castro, "Obras de Ciudad Tiuna marchan con lentitud," *El Nacional,* February 14, 2012.

16. Kevin P. Gallagher, Amos Irwin and Katherine Koleski, "The New Banks in Town: Chinese Finance in Latin America," *Inter-American Dialogue* (March 2012): 7, quoted in Jon Brandt et al., "Chinese Engagement in Latin America and the Caribbean: Implications for US Foreign Policy" (American University School of International Service, December 2012): 5, https://bit.ly/3J1pzKO.

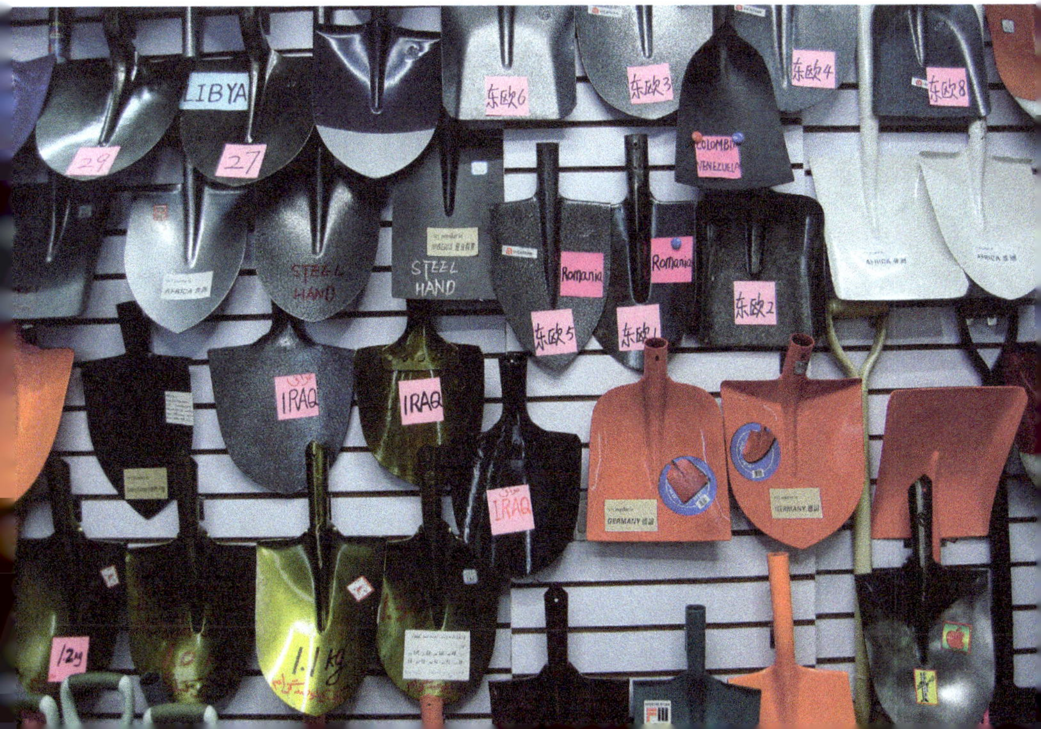

being explored as an alternative repayment method.) In the scheme, Venezuela has granted China several public contracts for infrastructure projects worth $11 billion dollars.[14] Within this complex array of deals, China has also invested massively in building public housing along with Russian and Belarusian contractors.[15]

The scale of loans is by no means irrelevant: "As of 2010, China loaned more to Latin America than the World Bank, the Inter-American Bank and the US Export-Import Bank combined."[16] Clearly, Latin America is a top priority for China. Up to

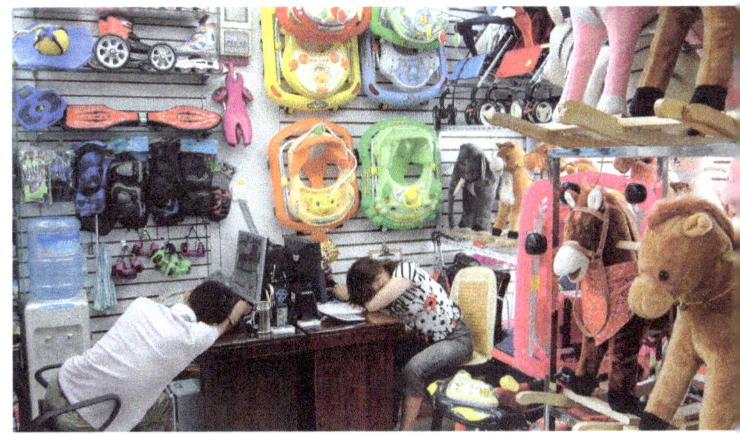

17. OECD, CAF Development Bank of Latin America and Economic Commission for Latin America and the Caribbean, *Latin American Economic Outlook 2016. Towards a New Partnership with China* (Paris, OECD, 2015).
18. Keith Collister, "Why S&P Raised Jamaica's Rating Outlook to Positive," *Jamaica Observer,* September 24, 2014.
19. Sandra Laville, "Beijing Highway: $600m Road Just the Start of China's Investments in Caribbean," *The Guardian*, December 24, 2015, https://bit.ly/3onmUDt.

91% of all its international credit lines from 2005 to 2014 were directed to the continent.[17]

Jamaica, a close neighbor, is yet another case where China has come to the financial rescue. The case of Jamaica was not one disadvantaged by bad credit ratings (actually, Jamaica recently was promoted by S&P to a stable B-[18]), but rather by cuts in nationwide infrastructure projects made in order to better these ratings. China has made its first strategic move in the country by investing in a superhighway nicknamed the Beijing Highway, connecting Kingston with Ocho Rios. This is China's biggest investment in the Caribbean, but not for long, since plans to build a port are already underway. "In a country in the grip of austerity imposed by the International Monetary Fund, and where poverty has doubled since 2007, according to the Centre for Economic Policy Research, the arrival of the Chinese is seen by many as the only hope."[19] Jamaica's case also shows China's reading of strategic partnerships in the region, particularly since traffic through the Panama Canal is likely to become important global trade access for decades to come.

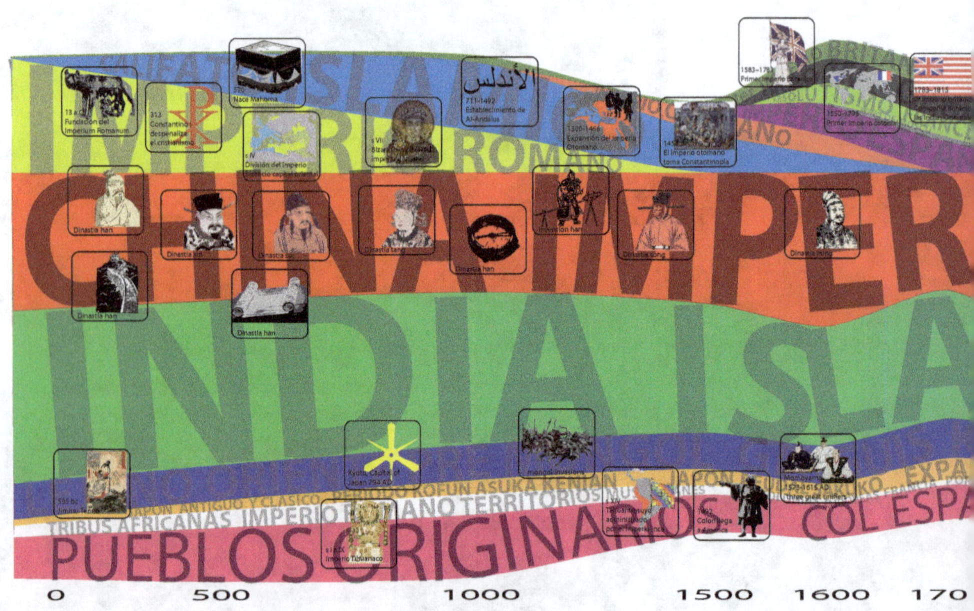

20. Leonard, *What does China think?*, 97.
21. Brandt, "Chinese Engagement in Latin America and the Caribbean," 5.
22. Charlie Devereux, "China Bankrolling Chavez's Re-Election Bid with Oil Loans," *Bloomberg Finance* (September 26, 2012), https://bloom.bg/3s5xhwE, quoted in Brandt, "Chinese Engagement in Latin America and the Caribbean," 6.

Chinese credit does not follow Western protocol of exerting one-sided conditions on political institutions, human rights, or the environment. Instead, lending follows a more straightforward strategy of *no strings attached*. Regardless of the internal politics of each country, China's position is to provide credit without sovereign conditions. "Where Western donors increasingly tie their aid to demands for protection of human rights and political reform, Beijing is avowedly non-judgmental."[20] In any case, it is worth remembering that "most of China's loans, which have grown immensely in the past decade, are aimed at natural resource extraction."[21] This is shown by China's $42,5 billion dollars loan to Venezuela, "collateralized by revenue from its oil reserves."[22]

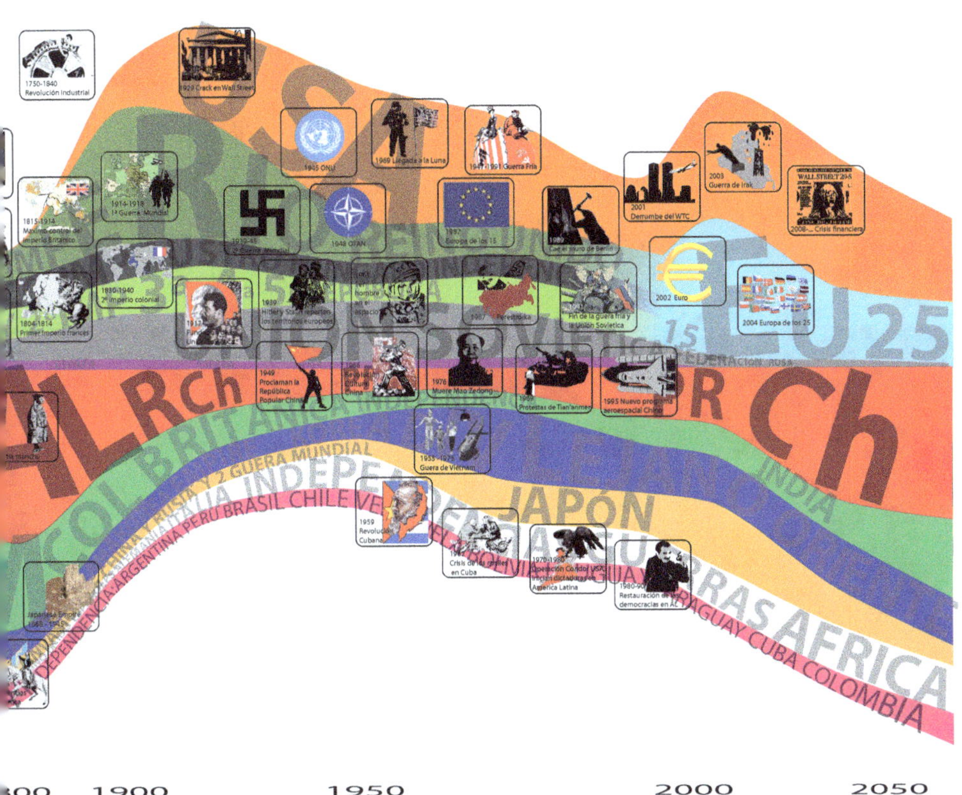

23. Alexander Simoes and César Hidalgo, "The Economic Complexity Observatory: An Analytical Tool for Understanding the Dynamics of Economic Development," *25th AAAI Conference on Artificial Intelligence* (January 2011): 39-42.

Extraction

China's dependency on natural resources is well known; of the many questions surrounding the relation between this dependency and Latin America, few can be answered fully or precisely. We have begun to draw an outline of our main questions: What resources is China specifically after in Latin America? What does China export to Latin America? With whom does China trade more and what are the trade balances with each country? How does China's search for resources impact environmentally sensitive areas? Does the search of depleting resources suspend the development of more advanced technologies? How will the discovery of resources elsewhere or their obsolescence affect local economies? Or, finally, how will the many ongoing political shifts from left to right in Latin American countries affect trade dynamics and economic performance in these countries?

The first question concerning types of resources is crucial for all the rest. There are mainly three types of resources China is after: Energy, metals, and food. All of these are crucial to keep China's current economic growth rate. For data, we have used the collections and beautiful graphics of The Observatory of Economic Complexity.[23]

For energy, China has focused on securing crude petroleum mainly out of Venezuela, Brazil, and Colombia. Whereas

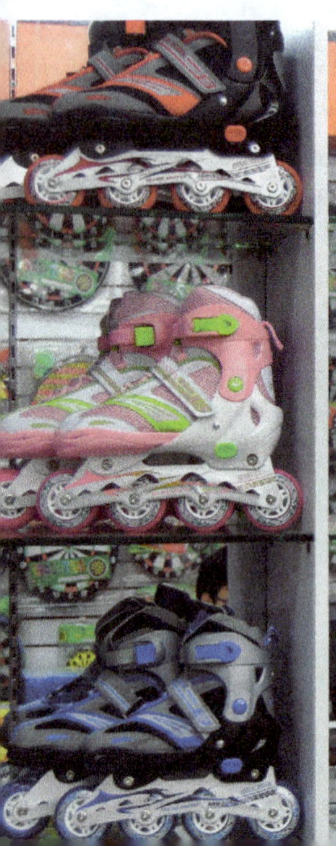
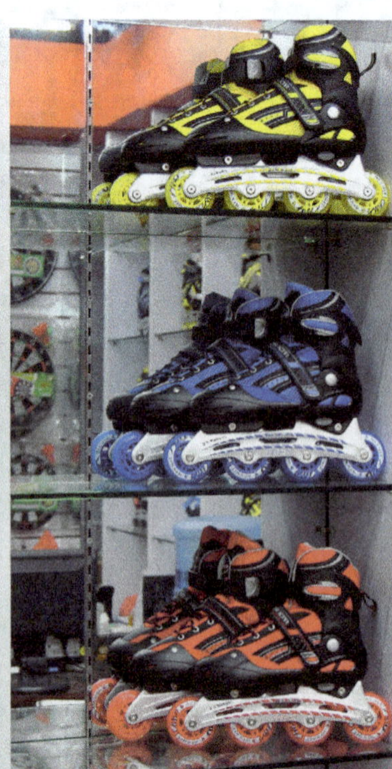
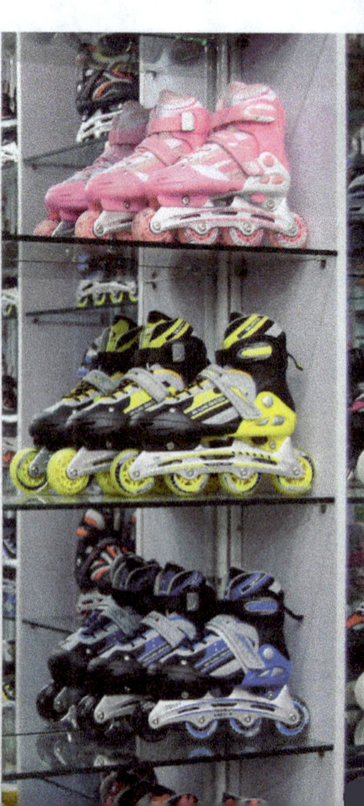

ten years ago, China imported more processed resources such as refined petroleum, now the pattern is to import crude resources only. For example, Venezuela's refined petroleum or asphalt exports to China have practically disappeared in a few years. The latest data shows that 95% of all Venezuela's exports are now crude petroleum. Colombia and Ecuador, although at a much lower volume, are also funneling most of their crude petroleum exports into China.

A very similar pattern has occurred with metals. China is interested in importing primarily raw materials, retaining the economic and employment benefits of processing within. China is in search for several types of ore, with particular interest in those containing iron, zinc, lead, and copper. It is also interested in ferroalloys containing aluminum. With few exceptions, such as Chile's refined copper, most of current exports from Latin America to China are raw resources. Yet China exports a multitude of products back into South America, products beyond those made from the processing of South American resources.

Besides metals and energy, China needs to ensure its own food security. China's national demand for soybeans, for example, goes beyond its production capacity; as a result, China has become the world's largest importer of soybeans. Soybeans make up around 60% of all Argentina's exports to China, having a value of around $33 billion dollars per year. Meanwhile,

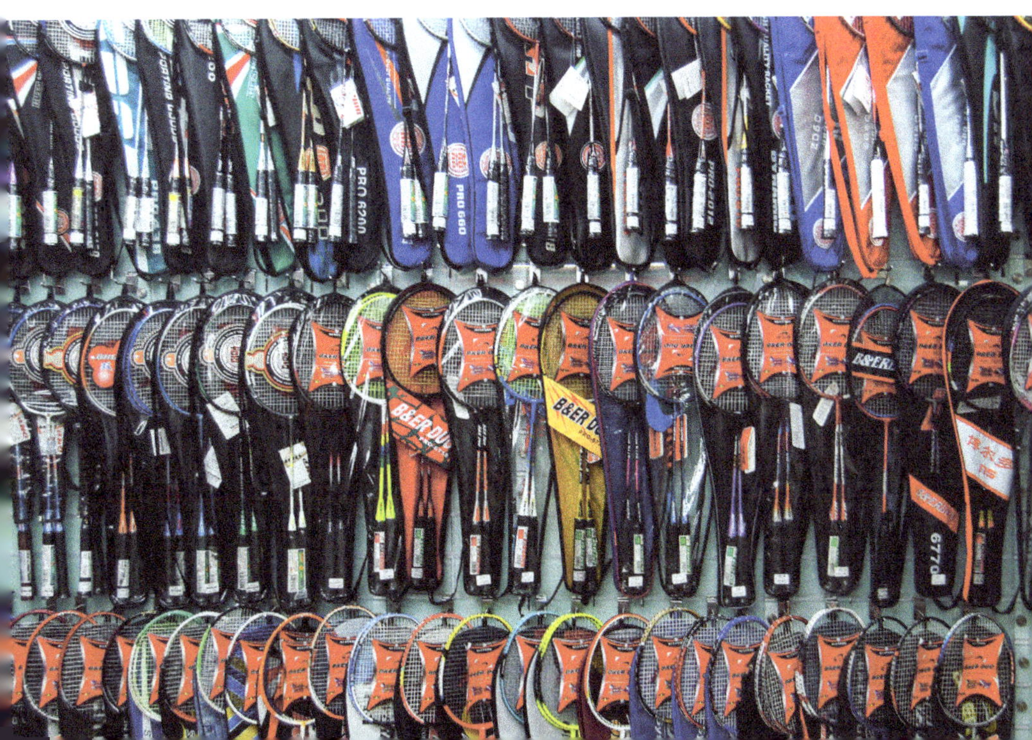

24. Rhett A. Butler, "Suriname (Surinam)," *Mongabay*, February 9, 2006, https://bit.ly/3rw1zKh.
25. Conrado Hornos and Paul Simao, "Chronology – Argentine, Uruguay dispute pulp mill, *Reuters,* April 20, 2010, https://reut.rs/3HndL5u.
26. Butler, "Suriname (Surinam)."

Brazil's 36% amounts to an even higher annual volume worth $90 billion dollars. China also imports soybean oil, but in much lesser quantities than in previous years, now preferring raw imports, similar to the cases described for metals and crude oil.

Finally, two more export providers are worth mentioning. 80% of all Suriname exports to China are raw lumber, not surprising for a country whose land is 95% forest area.[24] Meanwhile, Uruguay's second most prominent export after soybeans is Sulfate Chemical Woodpulp. These last examples represent two of the biggest challenges Latin America faces regarding environmental risk. Disputes recently arose between Uruguay and Argentina due to the activities of Uruguay's pulp mills.[25] Suriname, despite having a low rate of deforestation, is now confronting challenges of environmental protection and updated forestry protection laws.[26]

Anonymous Things

China's interest in extracting raw resources from South America are paralleled by an interest in exporting the products it makes out of these resources. And although we may forget this bilateral relationship, much of our daily contact is with objects of Chinese origin. It is hard to grasp the scale of production until you visit Yiwu, China's export hub for *anonymous products*. In one of its complexes (Yiwu has numerous)

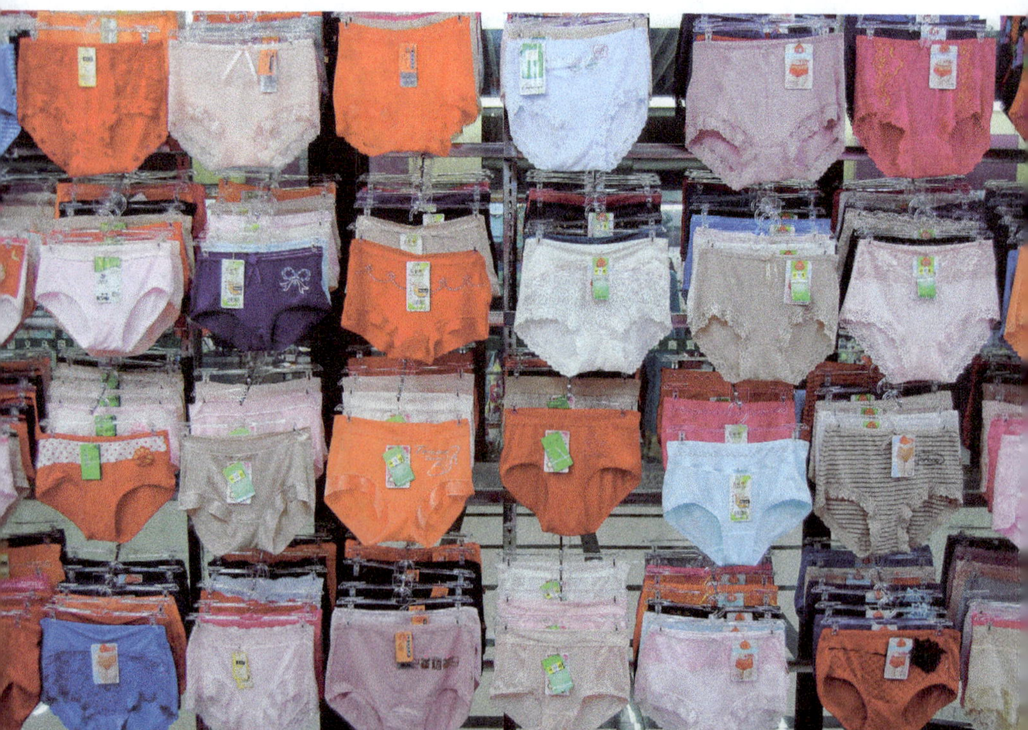

Extraction: Latin American export to China as percentage of total. 1995-2015

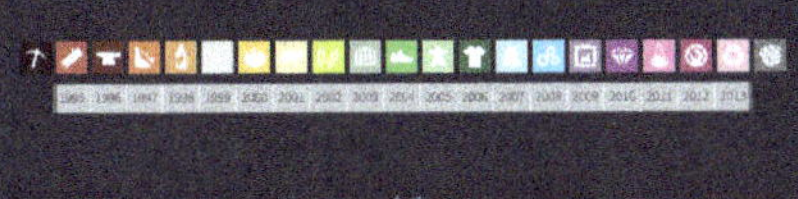

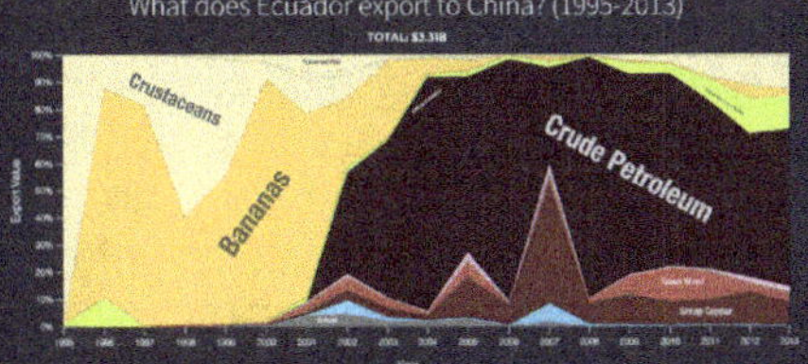

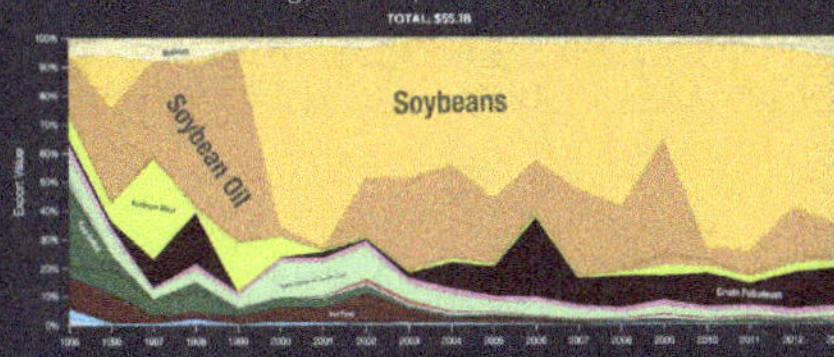

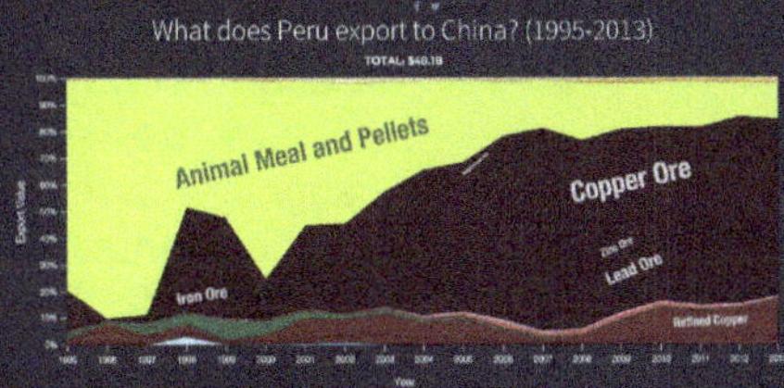

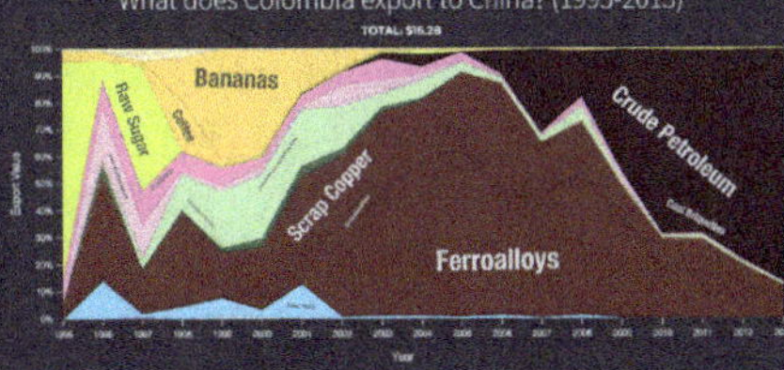

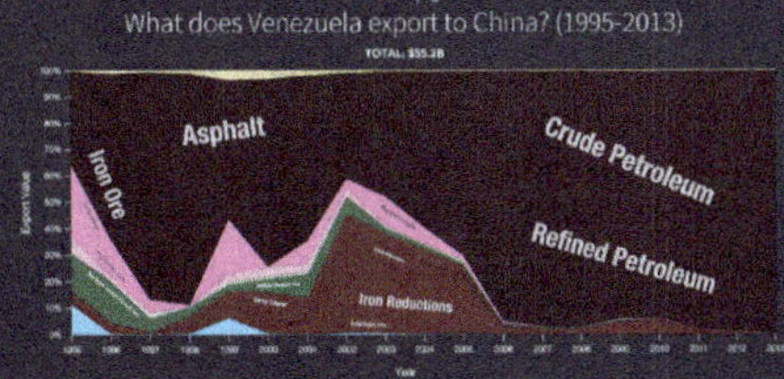

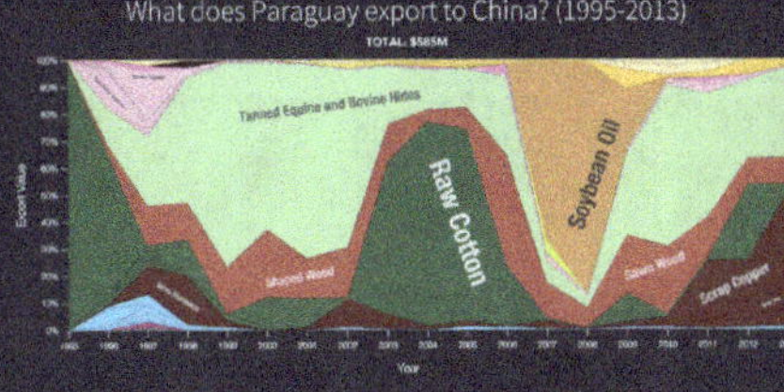

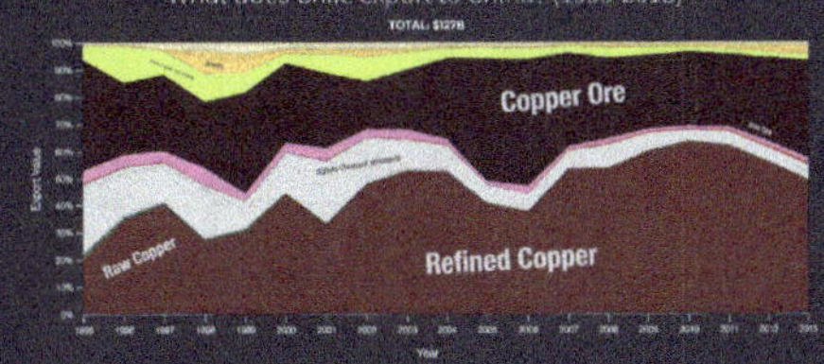

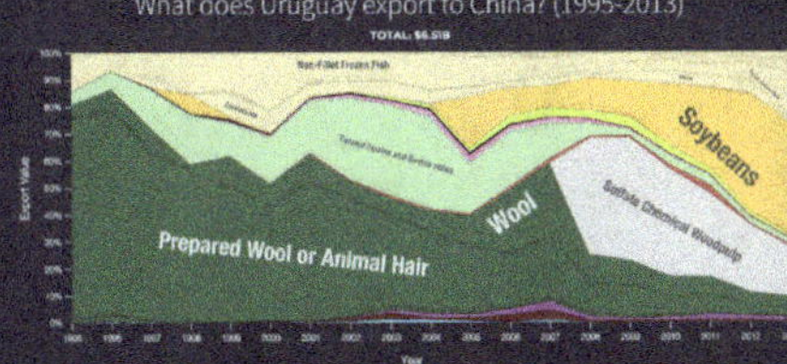

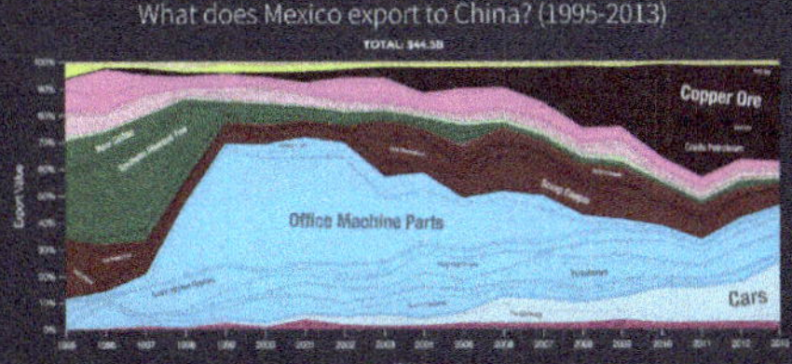

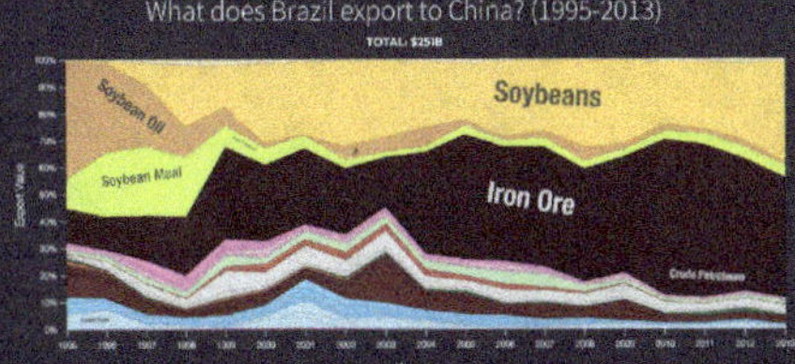

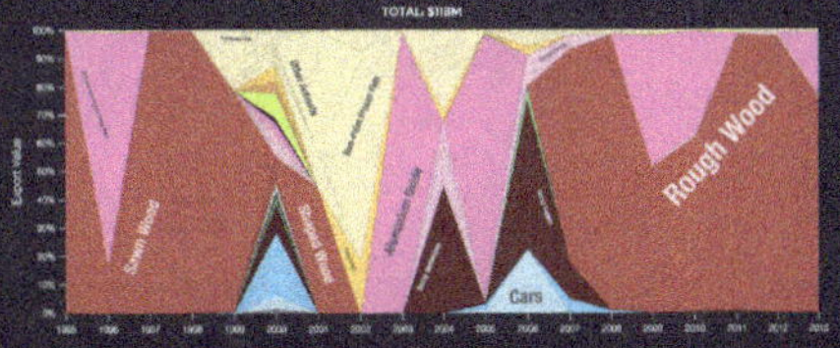

27. Jose Reinoso, "Viaje al hipermercado del mundo," *El País,* April 26, 2010, https://bit.ly/34u1j5c.

– around 4 million square meters of retail area and 100 thousand front shops – deals are made with clients worldwide to export approximately 1,7 million different products.[27] Once inside this complex, you feel you are face to face with The Architect, as if living in *The Matrix*. Everything you have known from your childhood memories comes to the fore immediately. The calendar from your uncle's shop, your school supplies – pencil sharpeners, rulers, pens –, your current cup, your spoon, the lamp hanging above you, the carpet on your floor, the floor beneath it, the video equipment that secures your house, the toys of your children, your sunglasses, your computer mouse, your Barcelona Messi shirt, your flip flops, your daughter's Barbie doll or your sex toys (although these are in another complex). Anything. Everything. An enormous *no-logo* flood of useful junk. And while you might think that all this *junk* is generic or useless, there is an endless array of products that are indeed needed in our everyday life; some products are similar to those produced in different parts of the world, yet China is a lesser advocate of standardization, respecting local customs and winning the hearts of its clients. An example of this regional differentiation is to find, in one of these shops, a wall display with around forty different shovels, all of which have a similar price, but are slightly different. Each shovel has a tag that may read: "Preferred in Slovakia," "preferred in Bolivia," or "preferred in Uruguay." The variations of angle, length, and

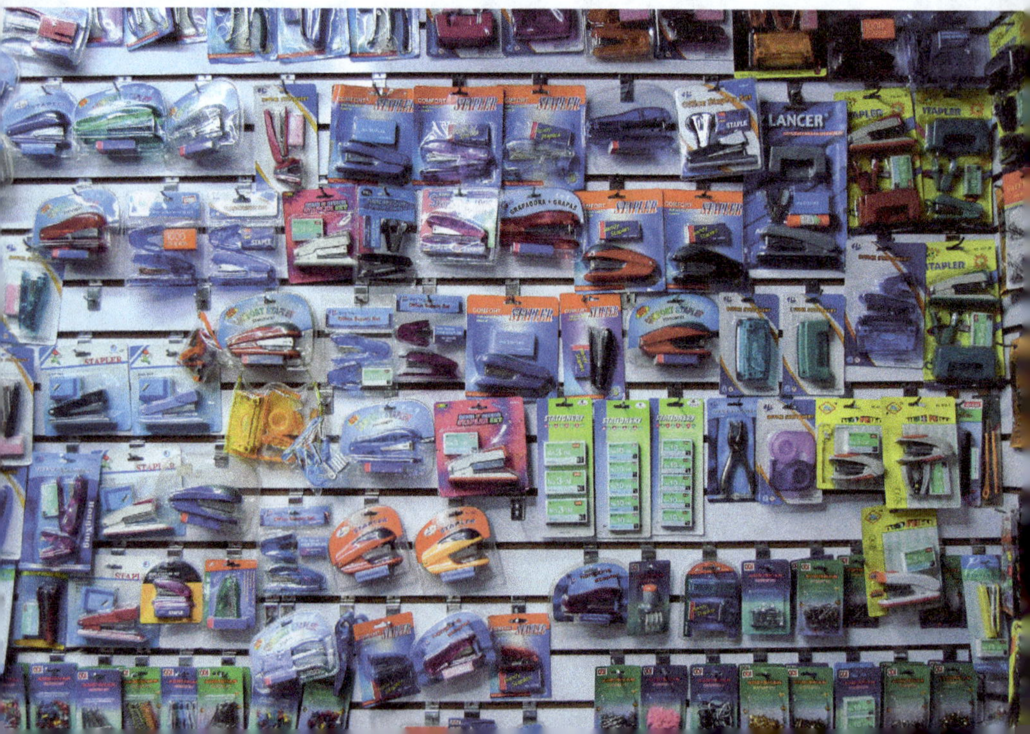

Import and export between China and Latin American countries. 1995-2015

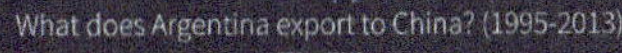

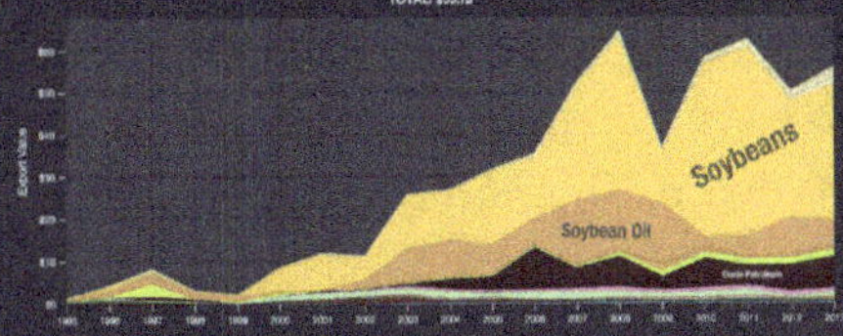

What does Argentina export to China? (1995-2013)
TOTAL: $55.3B

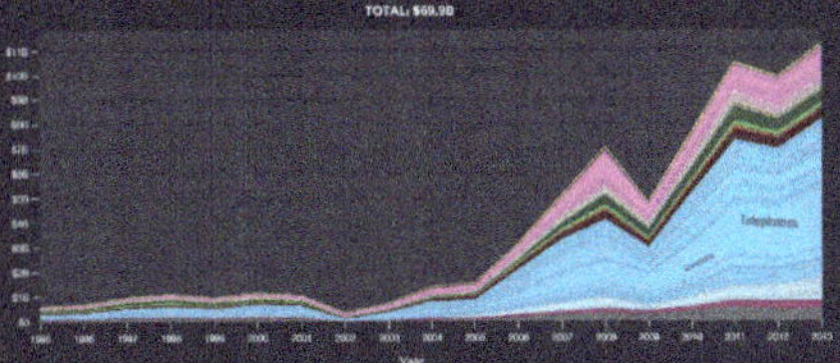

What does Argentina import from China? (1995-2013)
TOTAL: $69.3B

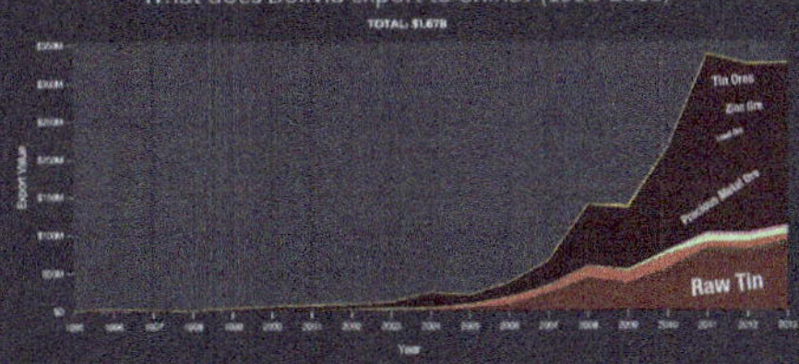

What does Bolivia export to China? (1995-2013)
TOTAL: $1.67B

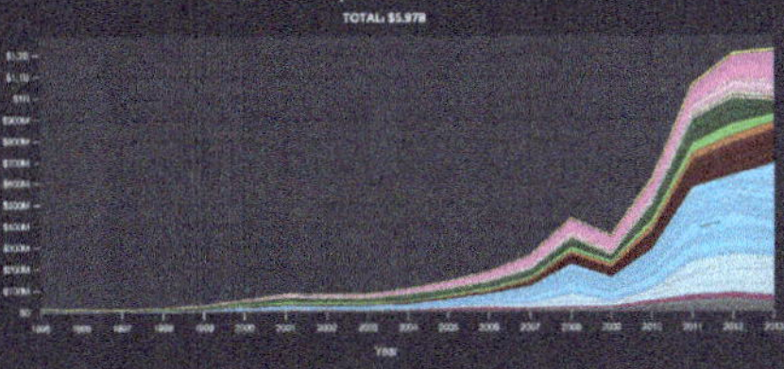

What does Bolivia import from China? (1995-2013)
TOTAL: $5.97B

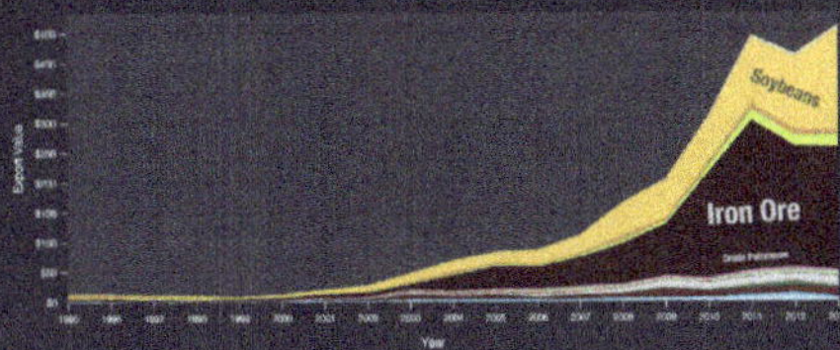

What does Brazil export to China? (1995-2013)
TOTAL: $251B

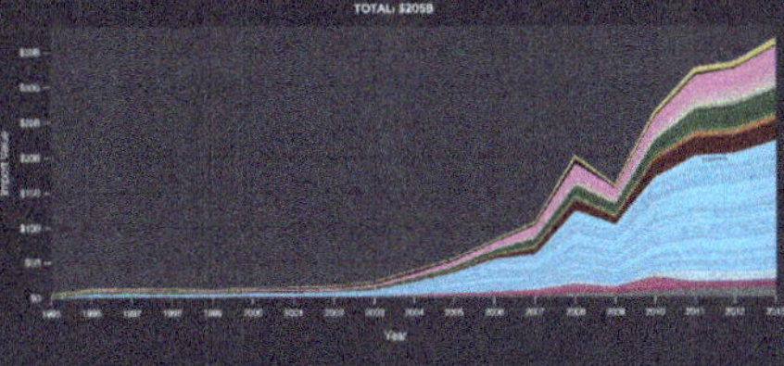

What does Brazil import from China? (1995-2013)
TOTAL: $205B

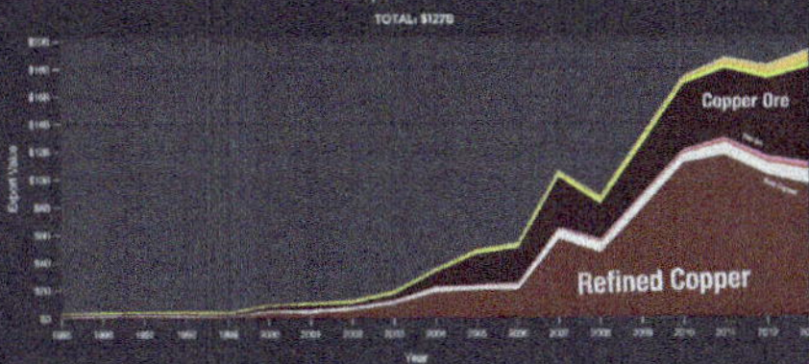

What does Chile export to China? (1995-2013)
TOTAL: $127B

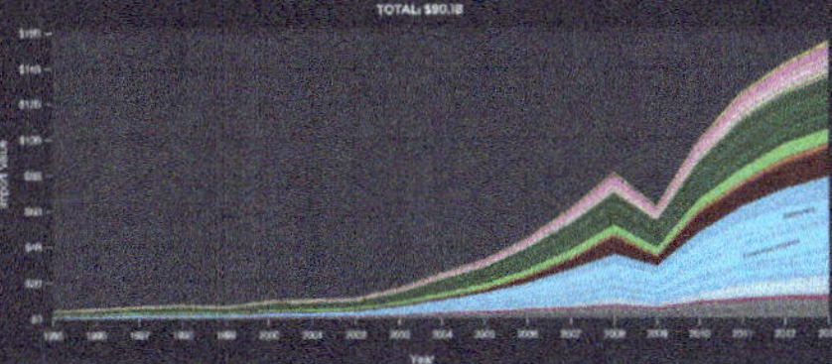

What does Chile import from China? (1995-2013)
TOTAL: $90.1B

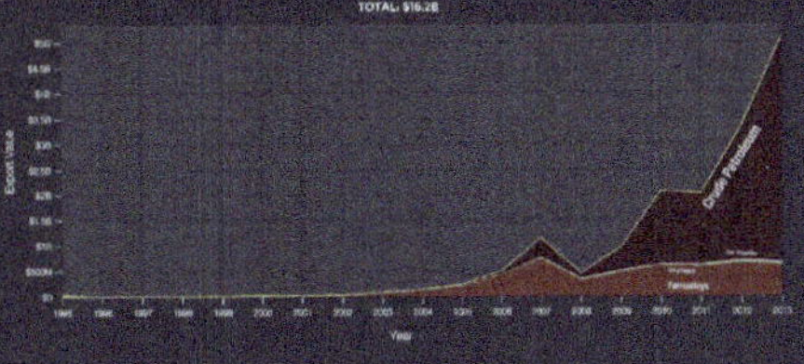

What does Colombia export to China? (1995-2013)
TOTAL: $16.2B

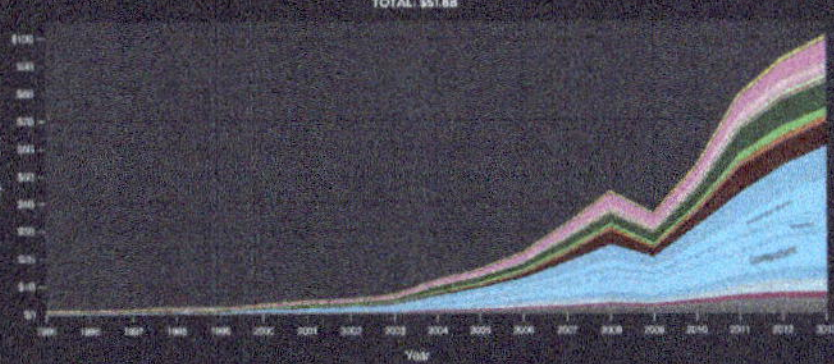

What does Colombia import from China? (1995-2013)
TOTAL: $51.6B

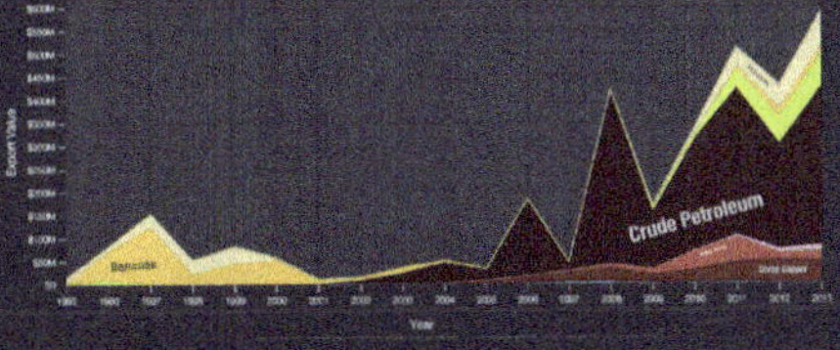

What does Ecuador export to China? (1995-2013)
TOTAL: $5.31B

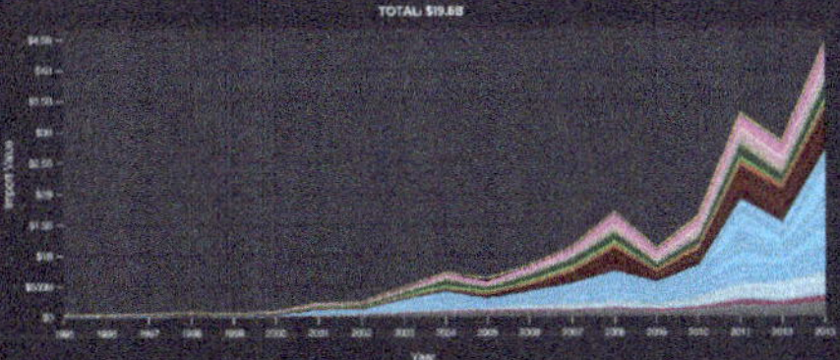

What does Ecuador import from China? (1995-2013)
TOTAL: $19.8B

28. "One could, of course, simply redefine the term *capitalism* to include "power to manipulate markets" as a constitutive part of its meaning." Manuel de Landa, *A Thousand Years of Non Linear History* (New York, Zone Books, 2000), 48. Fernand Braudel suggests to name this behavior of manipulation as "antimarkets."

curvature are minimal, perhaps, but it seems that China's care and skill to accommodate these variations makes it an irresistible foreign trade partner – not to mention prices are pretty much unbeatable.

So where is all this in terms of quantity? Take, for example, Argentina's imports from China. Telephones are the main product incoming from China, yet they make up a mere 2% of China's market share in imports. That is, most imports represent only a fraction of the total, but they all count – stuffed animals, baby carriages, railway passenger seats, video recording equipment, headphones, copper pipes, iron chains, aluminum cans, cutlery, scissors, rubber footwear, pesticides, vitamins, and so on.

With so many little things being imported, one wonders how these products are distributed, which companies take the time to find the right selection of, say, measuring tapes, mouse pads, and so on. Here comes another dimension of China's soft landing on Latin American ground – the Chinese diaspora and the operation of thousands of small shops all over Latin American cities, a logistical feat mirroring the organization of Yiwu. The anti-brand and seemingly bottom-up, self-organized Chinese system reflects more on – what Manuel de Landa would call – market driven dynamics, as opposed to that of capitalist speculation relying on big brands and their manipulation of the market.[28]

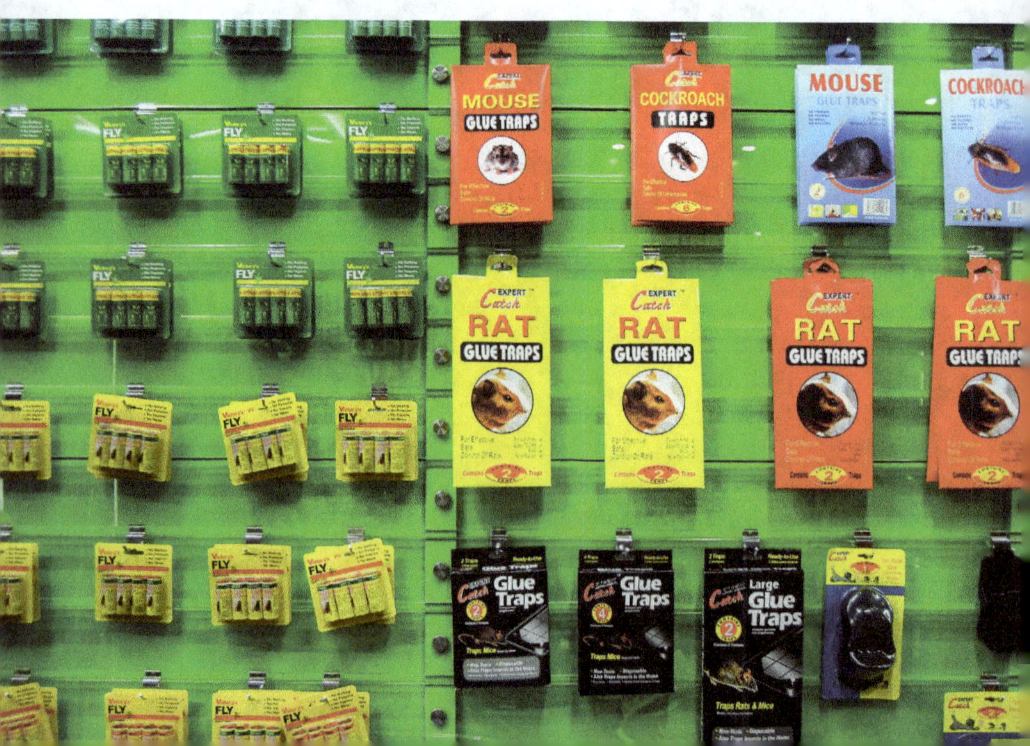

Import and export between China and Latin American countries. 1995-2015

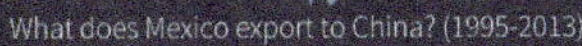

What does Mexico export to China? (1995-2013)
TOTAL: $44.5B

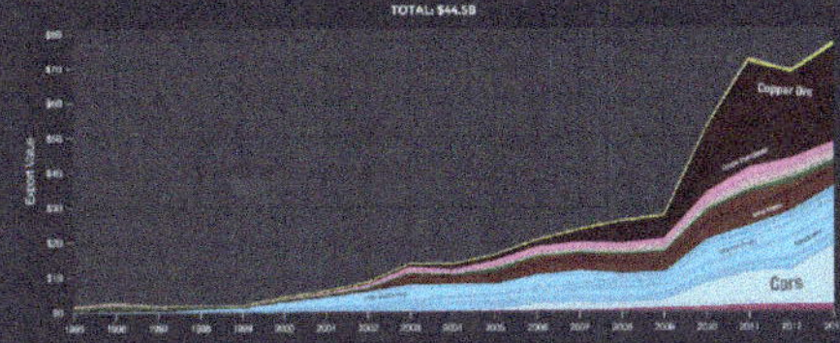

What does Mexico import from China? (1995-2013)
TOTAL: $350B

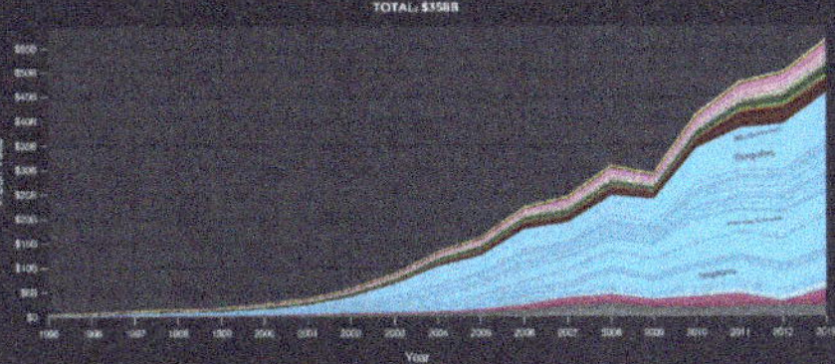

What does Paraguay export to China? (1995-2013)
TOTAL: $185M

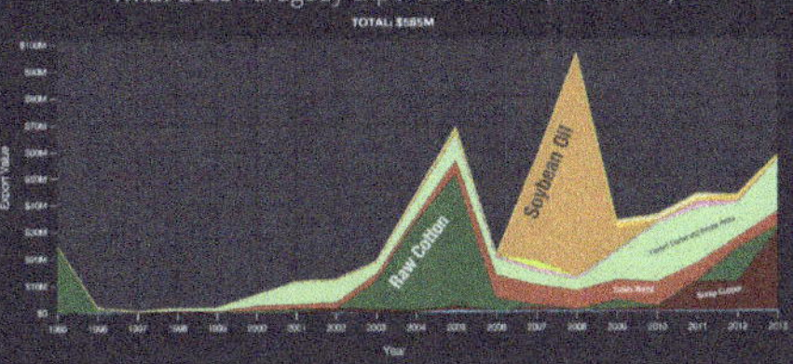

What does Paraguay import from China? (1995-2013)
TOTAL: $25.3B

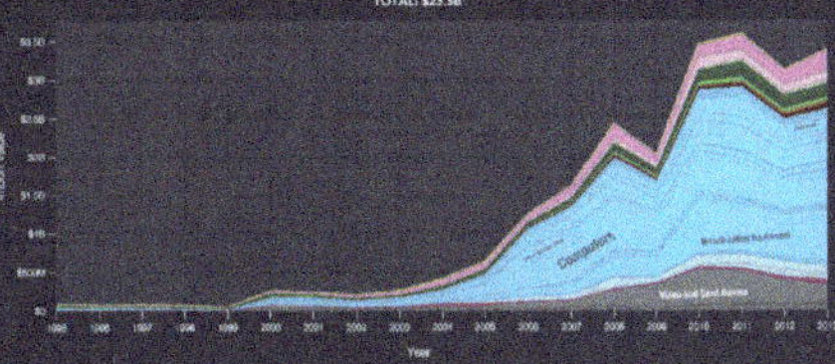

What does Peru export to China? (1995-2013)
TOTAL: $46.1B

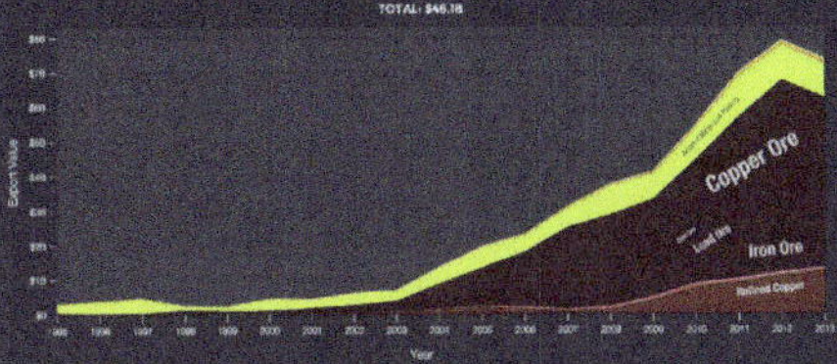

What does Peru import? (1995-2013)
TOTAL: $333B

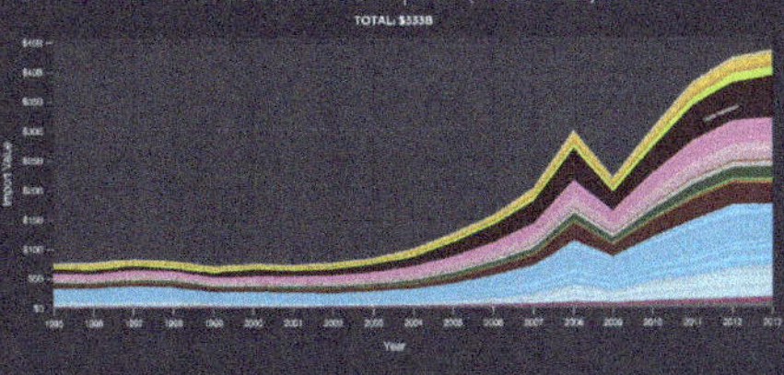

What does Uruguay export to China? (1995-2013)
TOTAL: $6.51B

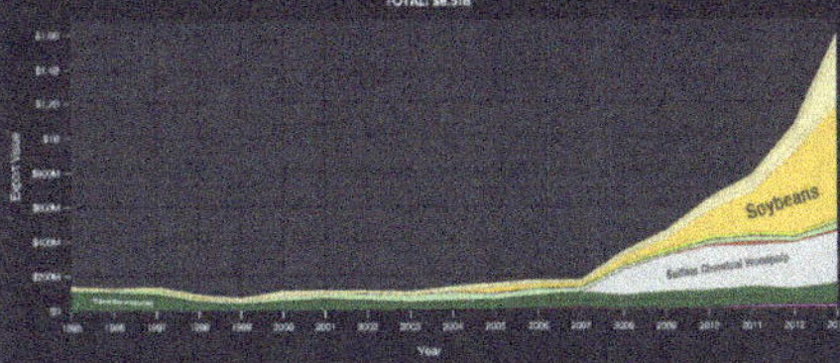

What does Uruguay import from China? (1995-2013)
TOTAL: $10.3B

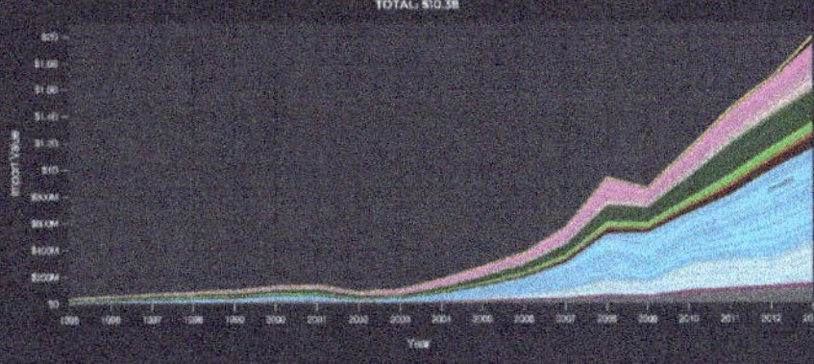

What does Suriname export to China? (1995-2013)
TOTAL: $118M

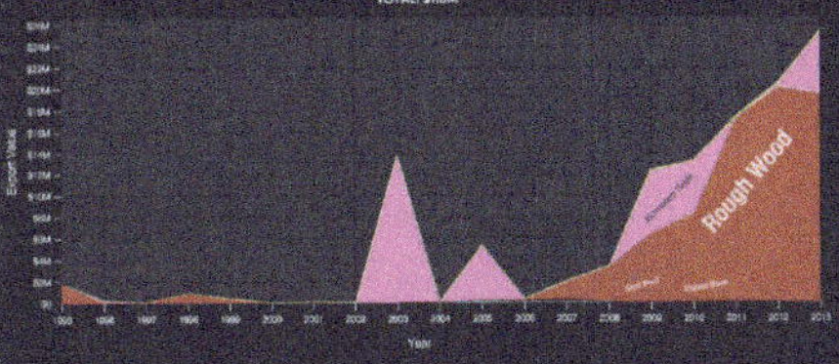

What does Suriname import from China? (1995-2013)
TOTAL: $1.14B

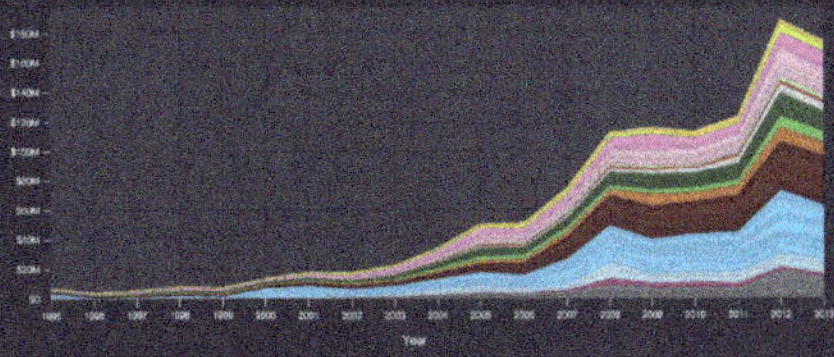

What does Venezuela export to China? (1995-2013)
TOTAL: $55.2B

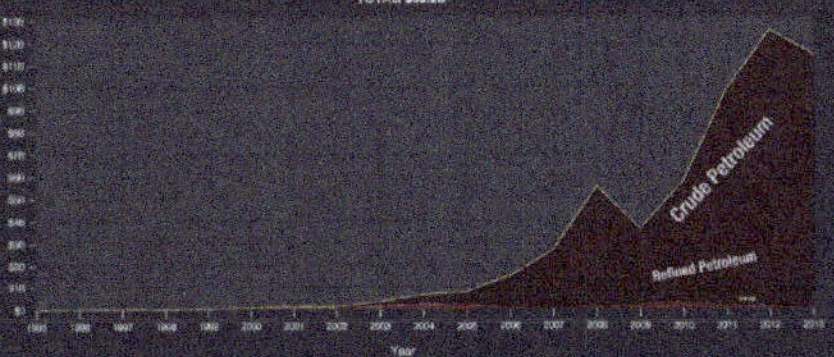

What does Venezuela import from China? (1995-2013)
TOTAL: $40.1B

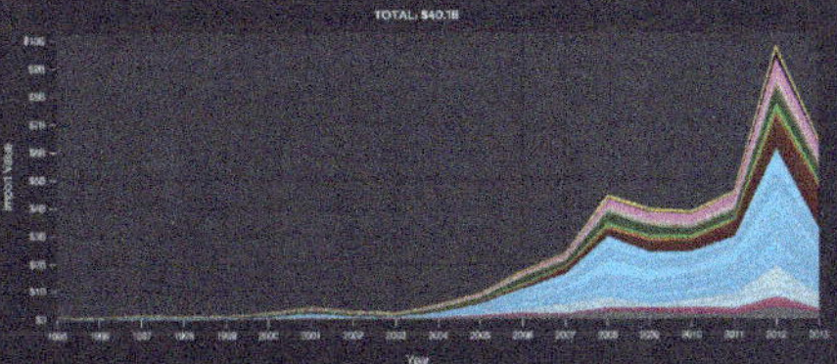

From these initial observations, we made a quick survey of Chinese mini markets in Buenos Aires, not only the established Chinatown, but also the anonymous presence of corner shops in every neighborhood. In just over a decade, the Chinese diaspora has opened thousands of mini markets, which now constitute over 90% of the offer of convenience stores in Buenos Aires; this growth in ownership can be associated with the consolidation of Chinese communities within nearly every country in Latin America.

It would be an oversight to think that we are still living, and pursuing, the Western canon in Latin America – to forget the effects of new trade dependency on China. Although it would seem as if culture is not important to China's foreign policy, this assumption ignores the power of objects in everyday life. While the West focuses its efforts on exporting mega brands, such as Ikea, Ford, or Apple, China has taken the opposite approach, conquering millions of hearts via pure practicality.

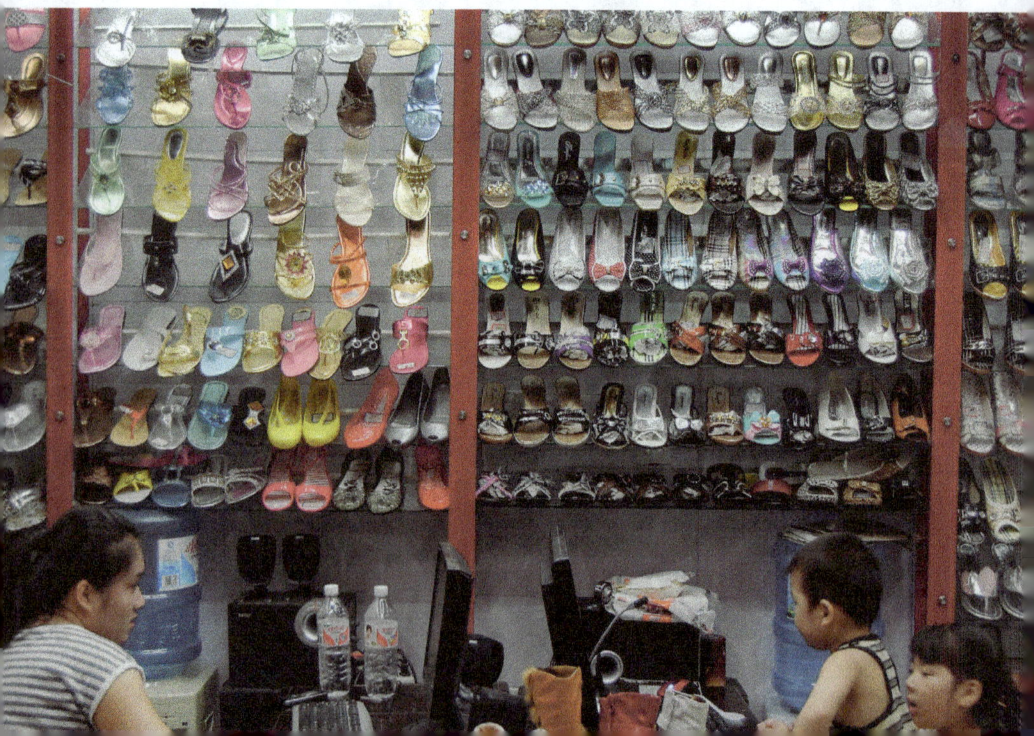

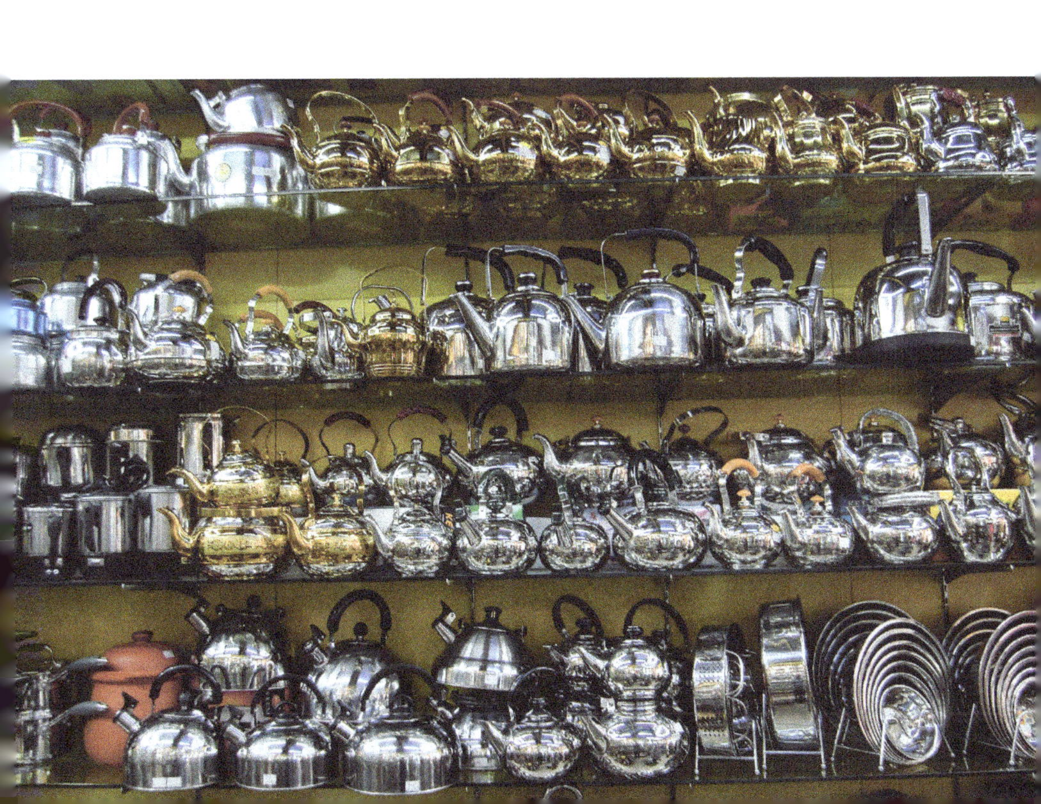

Talking Around the World

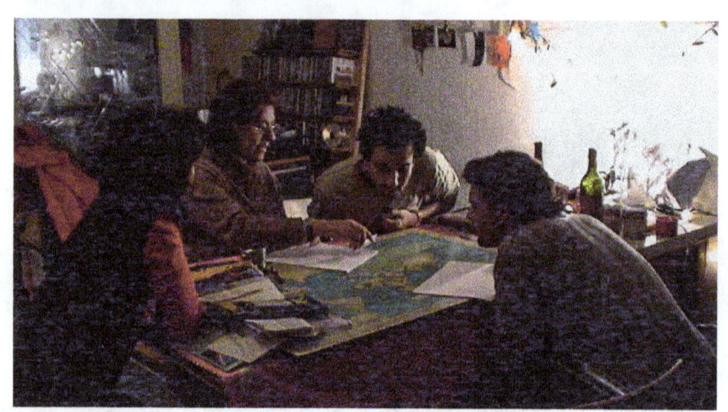

Interviewing Mirta Demare

Rotterdam
November 6
2002

Prologue for Incomplete Works

Mirta Demare became a dear protective and aunt-like figure
to us the instant we met her in our first months of stay in
Rotterdam. Back then Mirta was an Argentine art gallery owner
who spoke with us mixing words from six different languages.
In her gallery we got to know a world of interesting people,
migrants from various places, especially South Americans.

In what became an increasingly close relationship, she
revealed herself a globetrotter, one who was exiled in Europe
since Argentina's dark years of the military dictatorship. Mirta,
the exiled, ended up making refugee camps all over the planet
especially in the most dangerous and inaccessible places.
Supersudaca was just beginning to exist and one of our initiation projects was to interview this extraordinary character who
turned out to be, without us realizing it at the time, one of our
first mentors.

We sat down one night with a map of the world and a few
glasses of wine to go over her adventures. Looking back, we
can see that all the topics we talked about that long night were
fundamental to the research and vision of the world that we
developed in Supersudaca throughout these twenty years.

I am an Architect

1. Lúcio Costa (1902-1998) was the Brazilian architect and planner that created the master plan for Brazil's new capital city, Brasília.

Supersudaca Do you speak Portuguese because you studied in Brazil?

Mirta Demare Yes and, added to that, when I was studying architecture in Brazil just for fun I also started studying Brazilian literature at the Center for Brazilian Studies. It was the time of the Bossa Nova. And I loved it. My first teacher was the daughter of the writer Carlos Drummond de Andrade. He is the most beautiful and important poet of the last fifty years. I always loved reading. I went on a scholarship and I stayed. And because I finished the first part of the literature course very fast I had almost eight months of scholarship left. I was good friends with Vinícius de Moraes. Vinicius took me to see Oscar Niemeyer; and from there to Lúcio Costa.[1]

Supersudaca Were you already an architect?

Mirta Demare Not really, I was almost finished, but I was missing some history courses and Design 5. But when I came back to Argentina I started doing only what interested me. At that time, there were no social projects in studio classes at school, only bizarre projects such as museums, sculptures etc. In Design 4 we had already done something interesting which was a psychiatric hospital.

Then I came back and there was this intensive summer course on social housing in Neuquén. The project included peasants' houses based on modular structures and self-construction, this was in 1973. It was an experimental studio; it was implemented only in that one year and then never again because we ran out of time.

Supersudaca When did you go to Brazil?

Mirta Demare In 1968 I went to Brazil traveling back and forth from Argentina. I wanted to go see Brasília, because it was being built at the time. They were starting to build satellite cities to house the social part of the project. In a few words, Brasília was very big and beautiful, but there were no people there. Where were all those people who were not ministers or presidents going to live? I started there, and then they gave me the opportunity to work for two years as a sort of a master's degree.

Supersudaca Building the satellite cities?

Mirta Demare I was working in the satellite cities and then working in Rio de Janeiro, within the university, with them and also within the studio. So, it was a very practical thing. I had a lot of knowledge of the basics because already in Argentina I had always been more interested in urbanism, more planning than architecture.

Supersudaca What were the references? Which were the books and who were the architects?

Mirta Demare Ivan Illich, Paulo Freire, John Taylor, William Mangin, C. Abrams, G. Huizer, Oscar Lewis, Louis Wirth.

It was the new theory, to break up the old cities, open them up, and start making many more connections. The problem from 1955 to 1965 was the migration from the countryside to the city. So, you couldn't continue in South America or in the third world with closed cities. Because our cities are not zoned, it's all like boom!! On the one hand there is the government house, and a bank, and the universities, and on the other hand the dormitories, all mixed up. That is one of the problems we have in Buenos Aires.

So there was no planning. Nor was there ever a long-term urban planning. When people started coming to the city, slums were a problem, a tangential problem. It still is a problem to this day.

Supersudaca What does it say in your passport? What is your profession?

Mirta Demare Architect

Supersudaca Do you still feel like an architect?

Mirta Demare I am an architect, yes. I have never built a house.

Supersudaca How did you get from Buenos Aires to Khao-I-Dang? Because that was your first job, right?

Mirta Demare I left Buenos Aires as a political refugee in November 1975. The military was not in power yet, but there were already lots of "missing" people. At that time, I lived in Buenos Aires with my husband, the Dutch Jim Dobson, and at that time I worked, not only in the organization of the slums, the one of Retiro, but I also worked in an architecture studio that did everything concerning the

2. The Montoneros is
a Argentinean armed
guerrilla group of
peronista affiliation that
was later massacred by
the military dictatorship
(1976-1983).
3. By *blacklist* Mirta
Demare is referring to
the list of people the military wanted to eliminate.
4. Jan Pronk (1940)
is a left wing Dutch
politician that, in 1975,
was serving his first term
of office as Minister for
Development Coopera-
tion (1973-1977).

food industry such as meat processing plants, dairies, and others. And what interested me the most was the organization of cooperatives.

Back then I spent a lot of time in the provinces because we had thousands of places in Arroyo Seco, in Misiones. But what I am trying to get to is that my husband's cousin was the Dutch ambassador in Buenos Aires, and the Montoneros[2] had kidnapped the president of Philips. And this man, the ambassador, was in constant contact with the Argentinean Intelligence Service – SIDE. And one day he showed up and said: "You two are on the blacklist."[3] There were already people missing. There were people who were in accidents and so on. Then he told us: "You have to leave." We were building our house and since we worked a lot abroad, we left the country for a few weeks, meanwhile my dad would go and take care of the house. One day he went and left the light on but, as I said, we weren't there. And they put a bomb, it blew up the whole house. According to the newspaper it had been a gas leak. But we didn't even have gas. That's when this guy said: "You guys are leaving because I don't want to have three problems here." They gave me a passport, and they took us to Uruguay, and from Uruguay we traveled to Holland.

In Holland, my husband introduced himself to Jan Pronk,[4] because of course, he was a guy who knew a lot, he spoke many languages. We went to live in Bloemendaal, a very posh place. We asked ourselves: "And here what do we do? What are we going to live off?" I said: "I don't want to get into the architecture arena. I don't want to go work in a studio to make houses or buildings, that was not what I wanted." Despite all this, I arrived on November 4 and by January 3 I was working in an architecture studio.

For my husband it was much more difficult because he was very specialized. Then he wrote a letter to Pronk, and considering my husband's knowledge of languages and his background, Pronk told him: "I need people to be inside the embassy." Soon we were moving to Tanzania. But I was not married and Tanzania did not have relations with Argentina and they would not let me in. They did not give me a visa or let me enter the country. That whole process took a year. My husband was then sent to Thailand, and I stayed here. I went to Thailand for a week, sure, but I went to Phuket and Pattaya, at the time when these places

5.   Khmers Rouges
in French or Khmer
Krahom in Cambodian
are the members of the
Cambodian Communist
Party that rise to power
in April 17, 1975 (the
"Fall of Phnom Penh")
and had as its main
leader Pol Pot.
6.   T.N. *Favela* is the
Brazilian term for slums.

were like a paradise. There was not the horrible tourism boom that there is now. Then they sent us to Pakistan.

In Pakistan the representative of United Nations International Children's Emergency Fund – UNICEF was a Filipino, a great friend of mine and who had been the representative in Thailand. At the time, UNICEF was dealing with the problem of the Khmer Rouge in Cambodia and he told me: "I need a planner." Because you have to plan these places for refugees. It was a very big problem. The Cambodian refugees came and went into a place that was sacred for the locals and that created another tremendous problem of hatred and other stuff. The Cambodians were fleeing the Khmer Rouge,[5] and the Thai people did not want them to come there. Cambodians were in the middle of it, like a sandwich.

At the time my husband and I had planned to go diving in Phuket and I mentioned this to my Filipino friend. Then my husband told me: "Travel a week ahead of me, and go talk to him, maybe you can help him with the problem of the refugee camps." I said: "Yes, and maybe I can make a plan or a zoning plan for you." And then off I went to Phuket. I arrived, and well, Phuket, I never saw it. And there I stayed working for about four months.

Supersudaca How useful was what you learned in college?
Mirta Demare Remember that my thesis was on *favela*[6] renovation. In Rio de Janeiro in one of the largest favelas there was. I was able to apply that knowledge to the project.

Supersudaca And how many cities have you designed?
Mirta Demare No, not cities, these were settlements. About fifteen.

For example, I made the Khao-I-Dang plan. It began with tents; I was there in the time of the tents. 1987 was the year of the *destechados*, homeless. Then the Berlin forum invited me to give a workshop and discussion on this issue. At the forum, when I arrived, there were many presentations. I was walking around and there was an architecture exhibition, with photos and so on. I looked at the map and said: "How similar to Khao-I-Dang;" and then I left, because I had to go to the discussion. When the discussion was over, I came back and I saw it: it was Khao-I-Dang. What had happened? Khao-I-Dang had transformed, almost ten years later, into a small town. So the Thai architects with the people of Khao-I-Dang worked adding infrastructure. They formalized the infrastructure, each house with its toilet or a toilet every so often, communal water with one point every four or five houses. So it seemed like a lot of fun to me, because not just anyone gets to see his or her city grow. There are four or five architects who did, among them Niemeyer, Lúcio Costa, the Greek Dioxiadis, and others. There are four or five of them who have been able to see those cities, Brasília, Islamabad.

Well, Khao-I-Dang was formalized and the lines that I drew are the streets, now the same with where I placed water and the hospital.

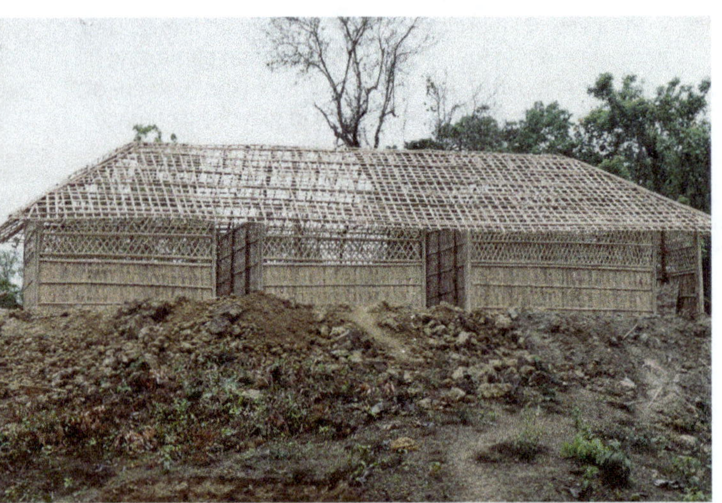

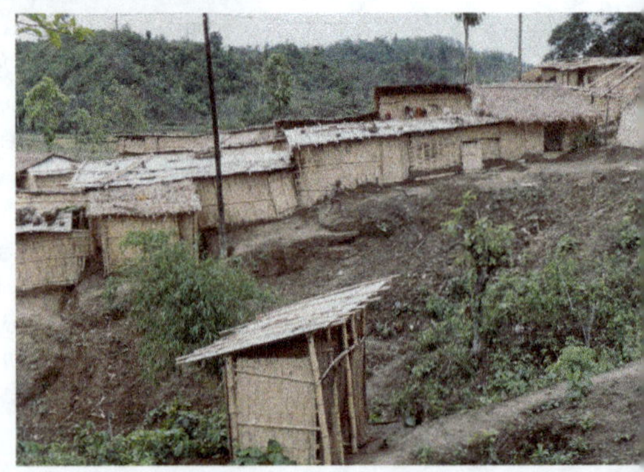

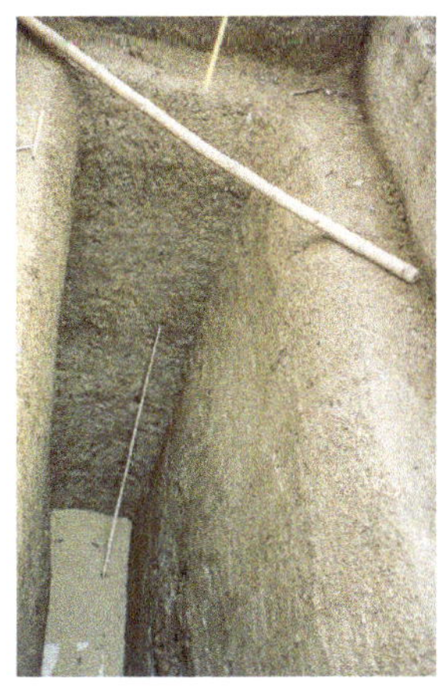

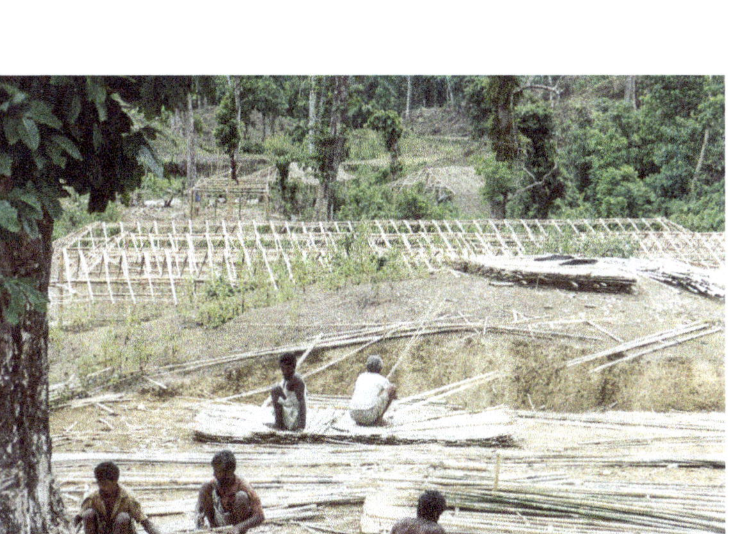

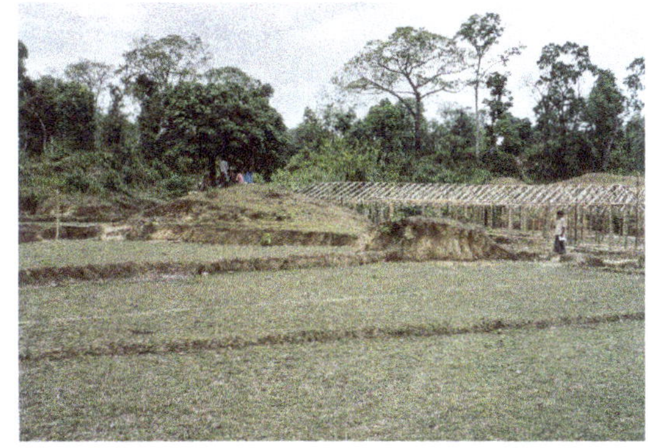

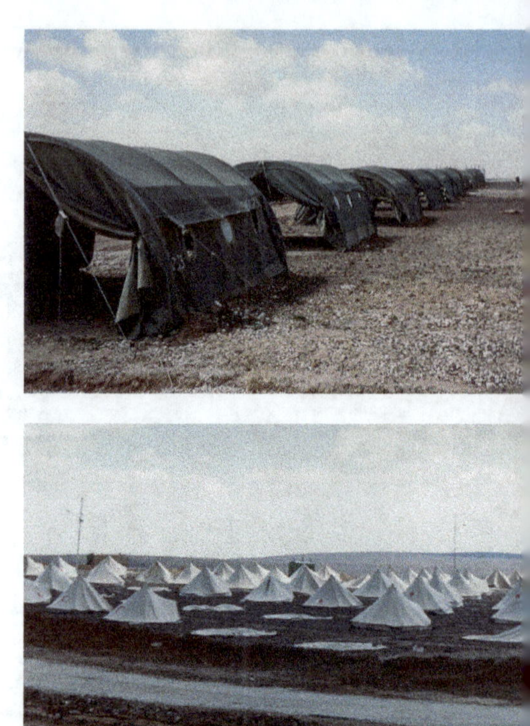

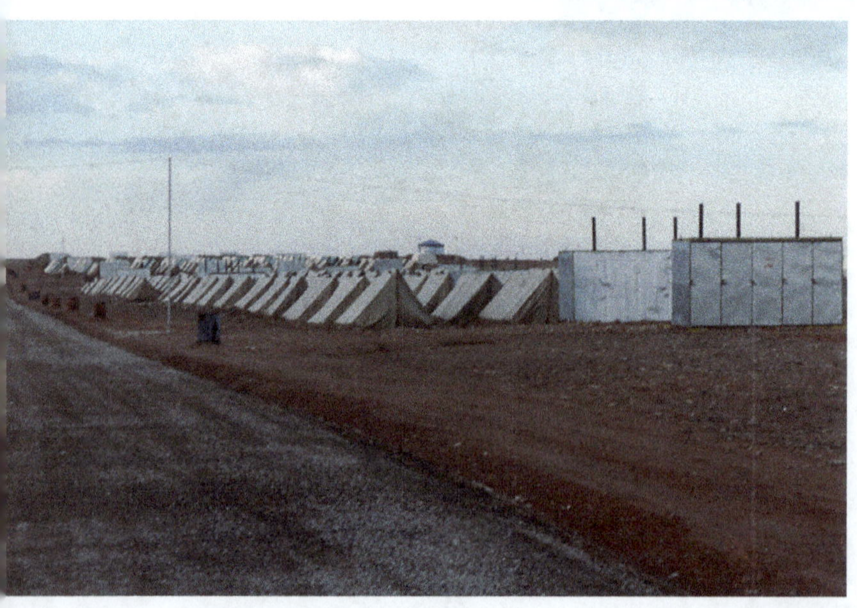

How to Make a Refugee Camp

Supersudaca How does it work with the countries that contact you? How and who reach out to you?

Mirta Demare I plan or redevelop areas or zones that need to be rearranged because of the problems caused by wars or natural disasters. When they call me there is a basic idea of what needs to be done. Institutions such as the International Committee of the Red Cross – ICRC or the International Federation of Red Cross – IFRC reach out to me. The difference between these two institutions is

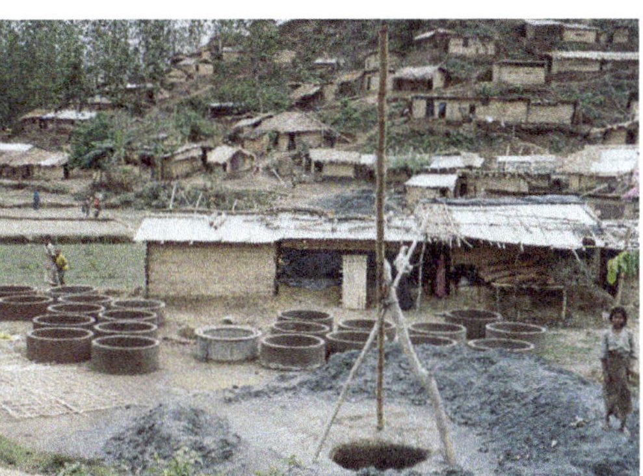 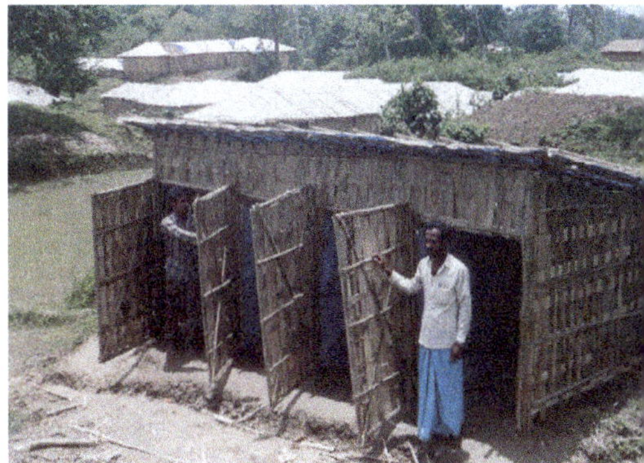

that the ICRC works in all things related to war and the IFRC works in natural disaster areas. For example, they reach out to me and tell me: "We have this problem with the Kurds who are coming because Saddam Hussein is sending them to gas chambers and people are escaping." That's when I go with them. They introduce me to the government and I start by discussing what it is that they want to do. What they know about the situation. For example: We went to this area that, after eight years of war, had huge problems because three quarters of the area were mined. Then you have to start a discussion and try to find a place where to house all these people. The war refugee camps are very different from reconstructions after natural disasters, because in the natural disaster areas there is a structure and we know what needs to be done. In the war refugee camps you don't know how many people are coming, the refugees keep coming and coming, as was the Syrian case. In Syria I visited the whole country, I drew plans of the desert area, visited these areas

7. Mirta Demare is referring to the first Gulf War, that occurred in 1991.
8. T.N. *Zuk* or *zoco* means market.

in order to find a place where to house the refugees and then nobody showed up. There was a war in the gulf,[7] and nobody came because nobody crossed the border. The same happened in Iraq: Everybody thought that after the war in Iraq all the Iraqis were going to leave the country, but nobody left.

Supersudaca What are the criteria to plan a refugee camp?
Mirta Demare The criteria are:
1. The first thing you have to find: Water.
2. That there are natural drains, such as slopes, in order to avoid flooding. You cannot establish a camp in the mountains, because terrace work is very expensive, it is a really difficult infrastructure.
3. That there is shade but it can't be in the forest, because there is already no water. The problem that arises with the forest is that people will cut all the trees down. Also, it could be that the government does not want the refugees either. The biggest challenge is to convince a government of the vulnerability of the refugees.
4. You can't place refuges too close to the border because they will still be in danger.
5. It has to be an easy to control area, because you cannot have people dispersing all over.

Let's see: This is Korea, this is Laos, this is Cambodia, and this is Thailand. The Cambodians started to come from the Northern part of Cambodia and from the mountains. And that poses another problem. If there are mountains it means that there is not much free space. In the valleys there will be an established population, and it is also where the water is and then also valleys usually flood. Snow is also a problem in mountainous areas. You have to know the area issues very well. A place can be perfect in the spring and summer but when the winter comes it fills with water. In the desert it seems like it never rains but, in reality, when it rains in a matter of moments you have a flood and rivers form.

And, because these are cities, you start wondering what are the services that they need? Then you start drafting an area and right after that, the market, which is such a fundamental infrastructure. Refugees are mostly merchants and they need a *zuk*[8] so they build their lines, with pieces of wood and four empty cans and that is when it starts transforming rapidly. Because they start using the dirt around them and when they find good clay they start making hearths for the goats, horses, and camels. And just like that they put together their compound where they live, a set number of families form a compound. And a culturally cohesive neighborhood is born on the spot. To that we also try to add the necessary sanitary accommodations, because here nobody defecates out in the open field. Can you imagine what an open field ends up looking like with 70.000 people going to the bathroom in it?

Supersudaca That's where you get real life educated.

Mirta Demare Yes, it is a forced education. UNICEF is really strict on that. And also other United Nations departments help you and they have their own campaigns. The first thing that I usually place in the project is a school. You have to put the kids in school so they don't bother anymore. Children love water and in particular the systems we create and they are fascinated by these systems, and then it becomes a play area for them. (laughs) Those rascals break everything.

For example, we work with other Non-Governmental Organization – NGOs, which are very specialized, for example the British Oxford Committee for Famine Relief – OXFAM (founded in 1942), it is everywhere, it was the first one to focus on water. To make special tanks for water you have to purify the water, you have to find it, and you have to do the drilling. You have to make sure that the water is away from the toilets. You have to think about the slope so the water is in one place and the toilets are in another. Nor can you take the toilets to a place that is far away, because then they do not use them and they make everything dirty. Toilets are a very big problem at night. They are the only places that have light, because women are continually raped. It doesn't matter if they are Muslim, Christian, whatever, women always end up paying the price.

Supersudaca Is there any security?

Mirta Demare No, the camps are very unsafe places.

Supersudaca But is it different according to the culture?

Mirta Demare In general, rape is a problem consistent across cultures. It does not matter where you are or the level of education. I had an idea that the Kurd camps would be safer because they were more educated, but women are at risk everywhere.

Supersudaca And is this problem determining your plans; do your plans include that this does not happen?

Mirta Demare Yes, we try that it does not happen. We place the women's bathrooms away from the male bathrooms in order to have some control. We ask the governments to add guards, but then that can become the problem, as it was the case with the Blue Helmets who were themselves perpetrating rapes. African women are better organized because they are not under the yoke of men as the Muslim women are. There were lots of rape cases when I was in Zambia. Then, one day, some children showed up there with some whistles. And they blew my head off; they were there, playing around. So I asked the kids where they bought the whistles. There was a man there who sold stuff and toys. So I bought some whistles, and then all the women had one. When they blew their whistles at night, the women knew where it was happening. And all the women ran towards the sound. They repelled those guys with shovels and more than one guy got a blow with a machete.

Temporary Shelters are not Temporary

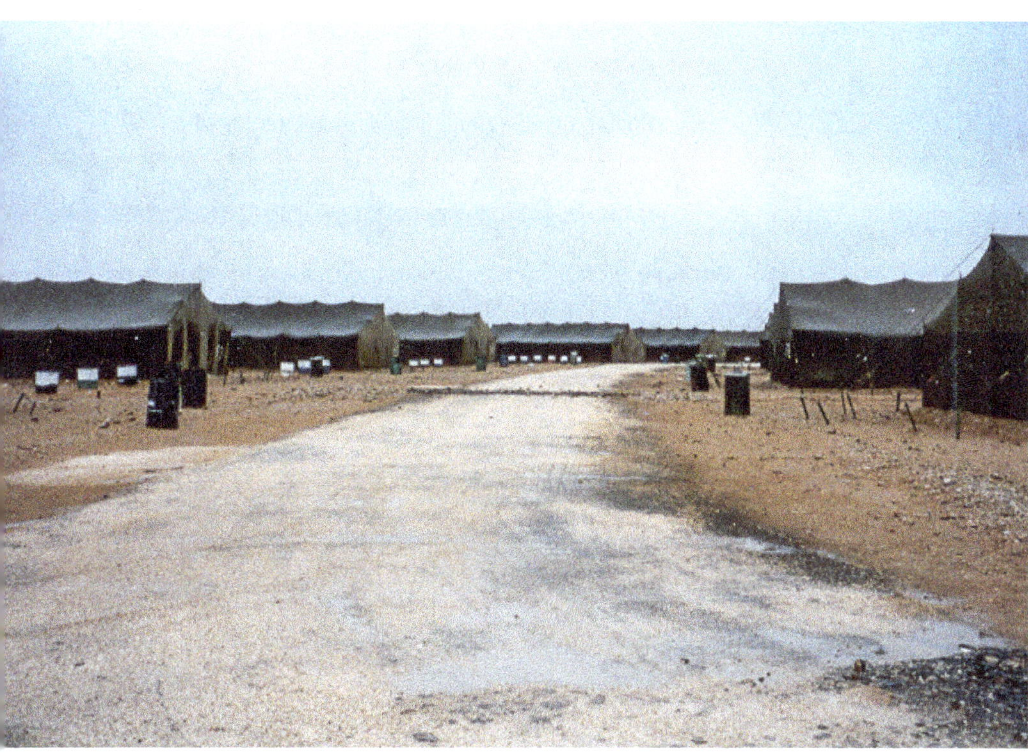

Supersudaca Do you know what percentage returned home? Are there more refugees staying at the relocation camps or do most refugees return back home?

Mirta Demare Yes, I know. The problem is that everyone thinks that a shelter is temporary. And what we have said in recent years is that you do not have to make them temporary because refugees stay there for many years. In general, I think that the cities or fields that I have done, they last a minimum of ten years. When people leave after ten years the shelters are invaded by the local population because sometimes – and that is a very big problem – there is a lot of competition with the local people, as the refugees receive an amount of help while the locals do not receive. We started something in Khao-I-Dang, and we realized that was very problematic because the refugees received a ration of rice and the local people had a much smaller rice ration per day. Then we realized that local people had infiltrated the shelter to get the refugees' ration. At that point we realized that we needed to know the local's ration of rice and then try to balance that; otherwise you can create a rivalry that could end very badly.

Medicine, one thing that I have done in general in the fields in Zambia, was to extend the UNICEF vaccination campaigns to the entire area. It didn't matter who they were, refugees or locals. And then there is also a very funny thing because the mothers enter the refugee camp and start talking to the people…

Supersudaca Of course, if the refugee camp brings a benefit to the area then locals will accept the refugees.

Mirta Demare Then they accept them, but also something else begins there. People from the camps start selling their eggs or a chicken to the locals in exchange for goods they do not have, for example powdered milk. Right there a barter system starts and there is a type of trade. And when you have been around for fifteen years, schools start to open. The school is outside the refugee camp but then the refugee children go to school alongside the village kids. Then a community begins to emerge, because it is not possible for someone who is 5 or 6 or 10 years old to be isolated.

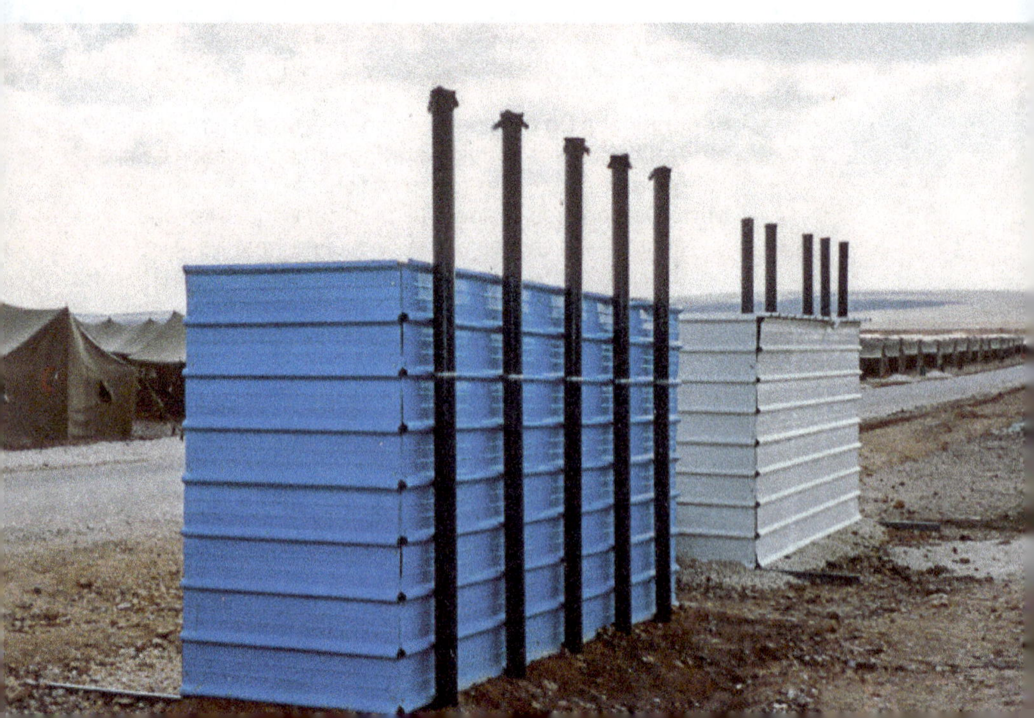

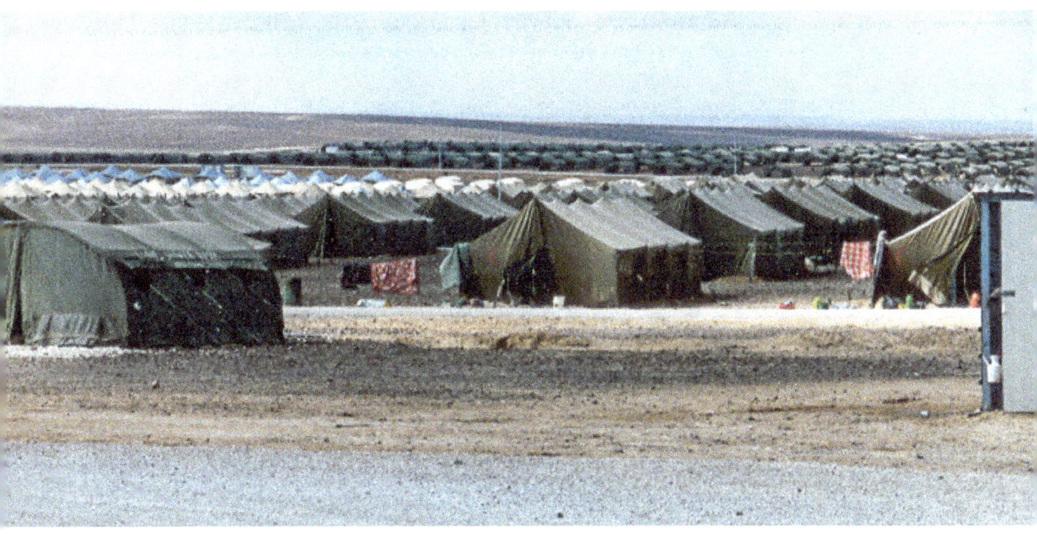

Supersudaca But please go back to the government topic.

Mirta Demare The most difficult thing is to convince governments that those people who come have to be, first, within the Geneva conventions; since there are the Geneva conventions that regulate warfare. Convince governments that these people are going to be around for a long time. Most people initially think that the conflict is going to be transitory, but then it is not. In the early 1950s the average stay in a refugee camp was (it was thought) about two to three years. At the end of the 1970s there were already people who were in refugee camps for eight years. In the 1980s there were people who spent twenty years, like the Mozambicans, who spent more than fifteen years in Zambia.

Supersudaca But that changes a lot because you can't have someone for twenty years in a little tent.

Mirta Demare No. But it is changing, for example: the Angolans were in camps many years because of the problem of the war in Zaire and, in the end, they were given a piece of land. In the case of countries with lots of territory like Zaire, these countries have the capability to accommodate relocations. And don't forget that most of the refugees come from border areas. So, there is always a connection, family, tribe etc. In some places they adapt, or mix, or they relate to the locals. There are other places that are much more difficult.

Supersudaca But your job is to provide shelter at least for the next two years? Are those tents designed for a two-year stay?

Mirta Demare No and yes. Because in the end nobody wants to build a house for the refugees. But they are resourceful and, in general, they are the ones who are building a house. They live in the tent provided and simultaneously they are slowly building with adobe on nearby land and suddenly a city is formed. I saw that happen in Pakistan, when the Afghans were rushed out because of the 1978 Soviet invasion.

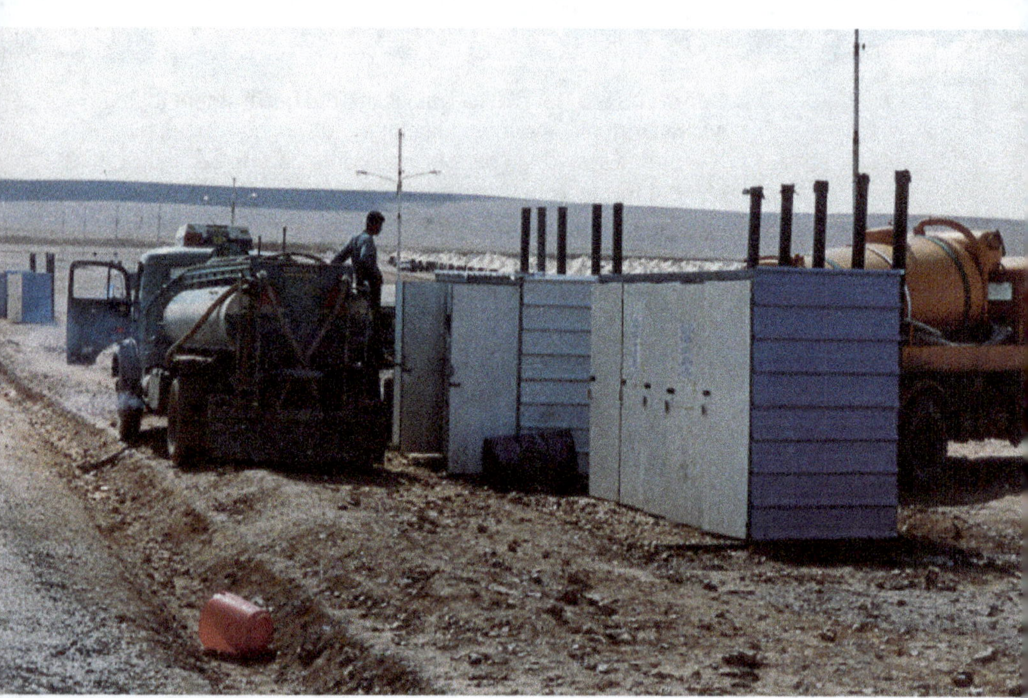

Cultural Resistance

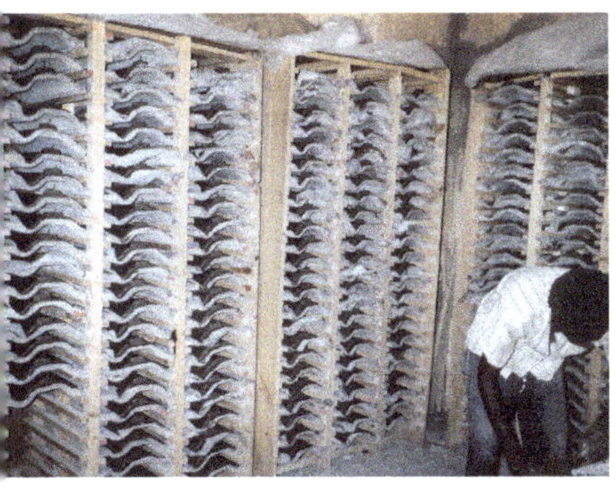

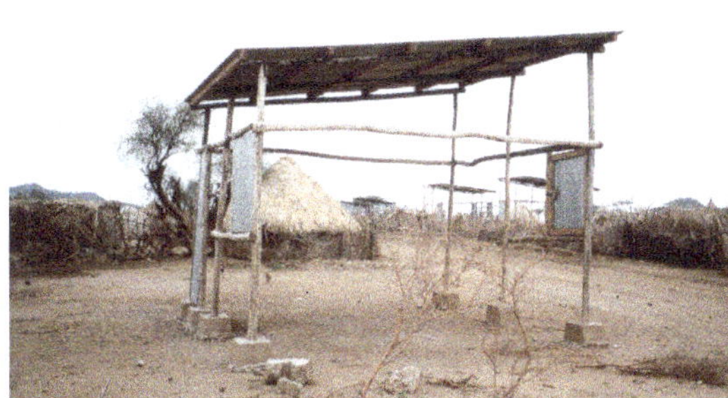

9. T.N. *Construcciones de material* in Latin America means a solid construction made using cement, sand, brick.

Supersudaca Are the desires of the people the same in terms of the *dream home*? Because in Latin America, when a population starts to consolidate, the houses homogenize to the nearest homes aesthetically and materially.

Mirta Demare It is just that the idea of the public in general is that a house is always something that we call in Argentina, made of *material* (a permanent construction).[9] In other words, if someone is talking about an adobe house, that could be big, beautiful, culturally people won't want it. People want concrete, iron, or at least cinder blocks. The problem with brick is that it is hard to find wood to fire them. As an example: In all Central America after earthquakes when you need a lot of houses right away the chosen material is cinder blocks.

Supersudaca Do you know Shigeru Ban, the Japanese architect who does wonderful works of architecture, among them houses and museums but, mainly, he builds refugee houses working with cardboard tubes? Architects think that the solution is brilliant, they think Ban found a solution. Do you think that building with cardboard tubes is a viable solution?

Mirta Demare Yes, I saw the projects, I know him. The problem is that people sometimes resist this type of house. In Eritrea, the Germans built some adobe houses. In Grenoble, France, there is a very good school called Craterre where they teach how to use adobe, and earth, and clay, but at an industrial level. Here – in Europe – there are some beautiful buildings built with that technology. So, these Germans went there and built three different model houses. A square one, very similar to their own houses, with a corrugated metal sheet roof. The other one was a vault, and the third was a cupola. The Germans built a whole compound in Tesseney, Eritrea, which is almost at the border with Sudan and there it is very hot and they had built a hotel as well with domes. And those were fantastic, because in that heat they were delicious. On the other hand, nobody wanted that house. They built the prototypes, and everyone chose the little square one with a corrugated metal sheet roof; very few picked the vault one and nobody wanted the dome model. Nobody wanted to go into that one because they were afraid that the roof would fall down. Because it didn't have any kind of structure. Because they do not have the notion that it resists because of its shape so they did not go in there. So, the ones who picked the dome or the vault models were us all expatriates.

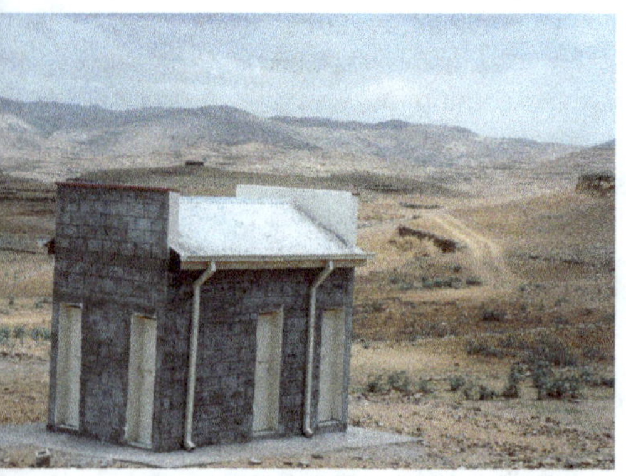

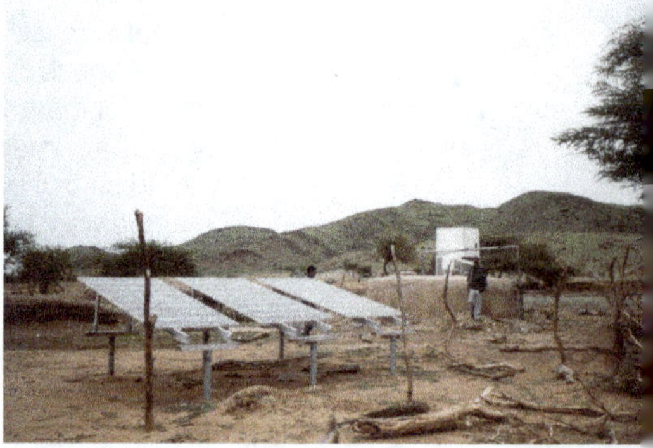

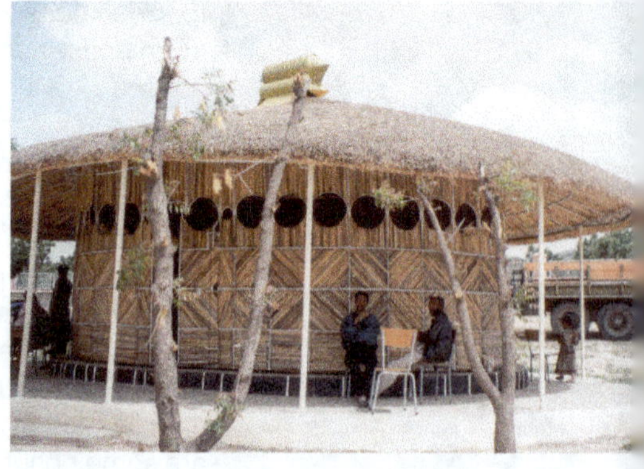

Supersudaca But why if they do accept tents?

Mirta Demare People accept tents, because it is something universal. Not everyone accepts tents, but it is the only thing they have.

Supersudaca Which is the worst weather for tents?

Mirta Demare The cold weather. The first time that we didn't use tents was in Yugoslavia. There, for the summer time, you could but then one just couldn't. Therefore, we had to build wooden shelters. We used some prefabricated elements that came from Turkey. A sort of do-it-yourself house that the refugees themselves built. Scandinavia also sends a lot of wooden paneled houses. And don't forget that if there is money available, the refugees themselves can build their own houses pretty quickly with brick and so on.

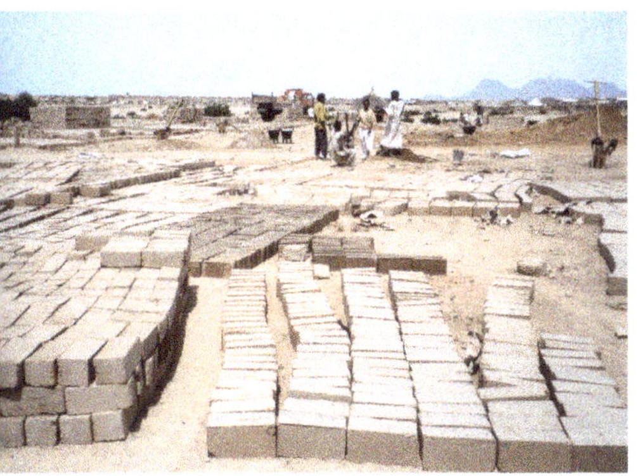

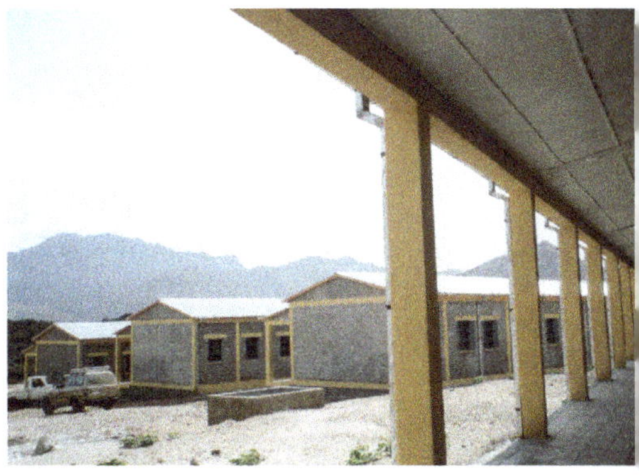

Catastrophe and War

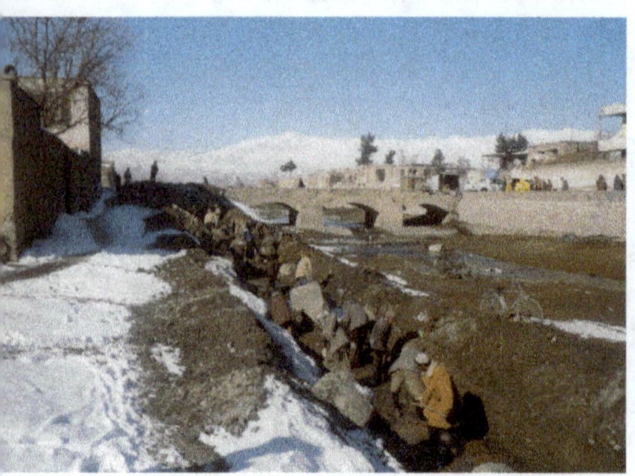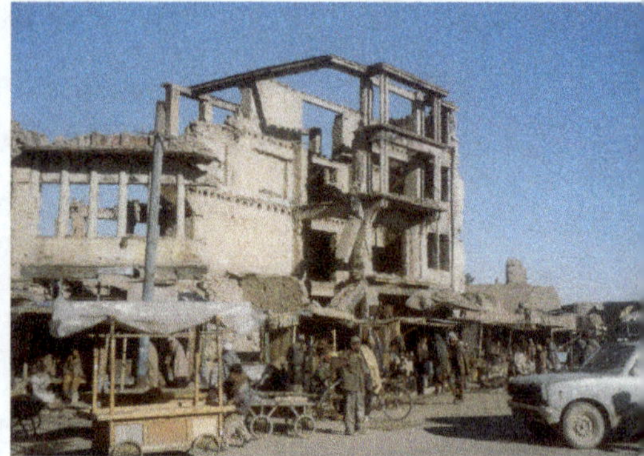

Supersudaca So any plan you build will always end up consolidating as a town or something like that?

Mirta Demare In general, yes. In Asia something very strange happened to me, they took them all and disappeared.

Supersudaca How long had they been there before disappearing?

Mirta Demare A month.

Supersudaca So the only possibility that they leave is that it doesn't last at all, because if they stay there for six months, then they have already settled. In a year...

Mirta Demare Exactly, that the houses don't last at all. In a year it may be that if they leave there will be nothing left. Perhaps. But, in general, there is nothing left.

Supersudaca Does this happen more often with natural disasters?

Mirta Demare In cases of natural disasters people do not want to stay in the place.

Supersudaca Could we say then that in the case of natural disasters refugees will leave the camps, but in the case of wars the camps will most likely become permanent? Is there a huge difference between natural disasters and wars?

Mirta Demare Yes, there are substantial differences between natural disasters and wars in terms of camps. There is a whole line of differences.

Supersudaca So wars are more similar to endemic poverty in that sense because favelas and *villas miserias* (or slums) have more in common with settlements resulting from wars.

Mirta Demare That's right, yes, yes. That is why what I had learned working in the favelas was really helpful in the refugee camps.

Supersudaca Therefore it could be the other way around. We could apply the war case...

Supersudaca No, because they do that all on their own.

Mirta Demare Exactly. No, because in reality the favela has a survival mechanism. In the case of the favela, the inhabitant has no other option than to stay there. While the problem of the refugee is psychological. The refugees do not want to stay, they want to go back, they do not want to stay there. The camp is not their place of origin, while the other ones who are already here in their own land, they are ready to continue living there. And the favela people are in their own place in their own country. There is also a big difference between what we call *displaced people* and refugees. A refugee is someone who crosses a border and goes to another country, a displaced person is the one who moves within its own country. Although displaced people suffer, I have seen it in El Salvador during the war where all the people from the East went to the West and it hurts. And they had to stay there. People who are from the plains and who began to go to the coffee producing region, a very different region because the coffee region is in the highlands, it's cold there and the displaced do not know anything about coffee. But even with this loss of immediate knowledge of the environment, the new area is within their own country and despite the fact that sometimes they feel bad, they speak the same language, they adapt and it is the same.

Supersudaca But going back to the experience that you have gained – not by building favelas, but returning towards the favela–, how far do you think the architect should go? What is the role that the architect can assume today in the circumstances of the favela?

Mirta Demare It is the role of a guide, it is one of accompaniment, it is working as a consultant. Well organized. Last year I had this job in El Salvador, it was a totally destroyed town. Of the 4.000 houses only four remained standing, the rest nothing, not even the church was left. And then I helped them organize. Together we looked at what they wanted to do. This is where the church was and there we stayed under a thing – she refers to the map. That's where it's called, people come to Mass on Sundays and then everyone comes down, the peasants come down, and then we start organizing with them. They come back, then one Sunday you talk to them and tell them what you want and then the other Sunday, the following Sunday then what we are going to do is for everyone to discuss in their own places what they want, what the house would be like. They think about the needs they have in relation to the people; they have to start thinking about the distribution, about materials and other things. And then the next day they show up and it is very interesting because there are people who even come with a small model, made of paper or cardboard, it is beautiful. And they are people who cannot even read but who know very well what they want. Very interesting.

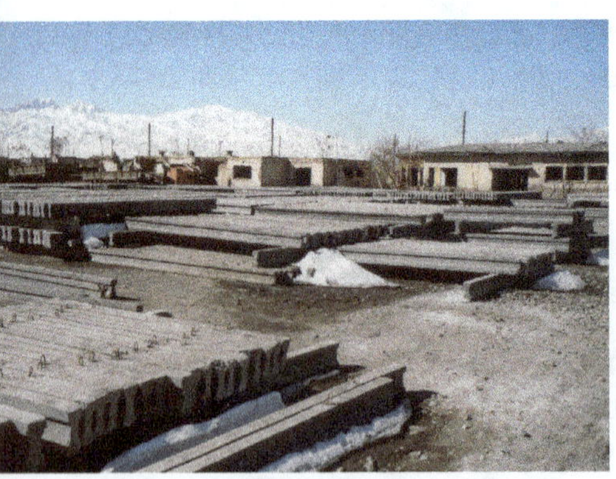

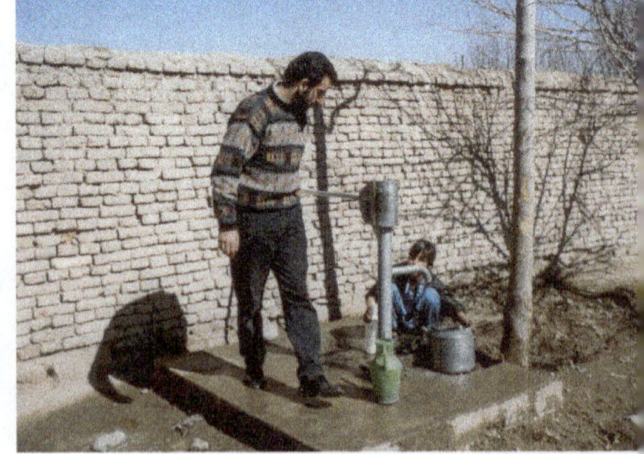

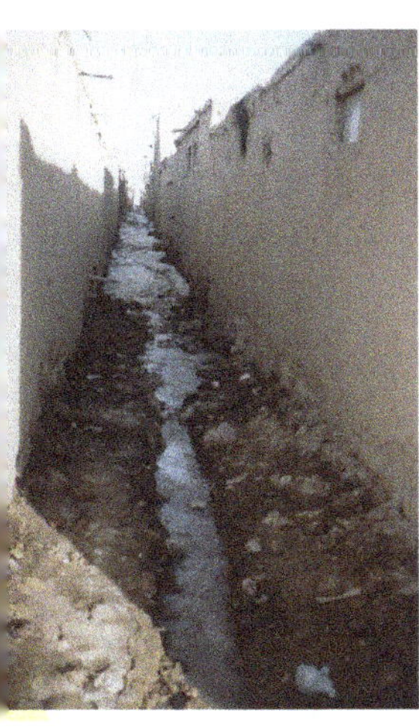

Supersudaca Operationally, what are the differences between natural disasters and wars?

Mirta Demare In a natural disaster everyone feels very united, because it happens to everyone, no matter the position, social class, ideology, there is no enemy. So, the reaction is that people are very supportive, and they react as a community, and they know that, even if it happens again, they will survive, because it happened so many times. Earthquakes are a known threat in South America, and everybody reacts and starts rebuilding. On the other hand, war is a psychological problem. With an earthquake you know that there will be a big shake, and then you might have another seventeen more of them. Last year when I was in El Salvador; you're asleep and you feel the boom, boom, boom every day. That hammock over there swings from side to side. War is a whole traumatic problem. The insecurity created by war is a heavy psychological weight much more traumatic than an earthquake. At any given moment they can take you, kill you, it is so much more. You can run or get out of the building when an earthquake hit. With some knowledge and planning, earthquakes are manageable. In fact, there is a whole preventive system.

Supersudaca Is a flood – the kind where the whole town is flooded and people have to get on their roofs – worse than an earthquake?

Mirta Demare No, no, that is manageable. The war is so much harder.

Supersudaca Besides the usual issues of a war, I assume that sometimes you have operative issues such as political frictions that you might not find in natural disaster situations.

Mirta Demare No, no. A natural disaster happens through a short period of time and the world responds in solidarity. On the other hand, a war lasts years and, in the end, people lose interest. That is the problem with Israel and the Palestinians: They have been fighting for over fifty years. In the last year, when there was an option for peace, then it broke and there was no solution. In 2000 I stayed for three months in Israel.

Moving in between Boundaries

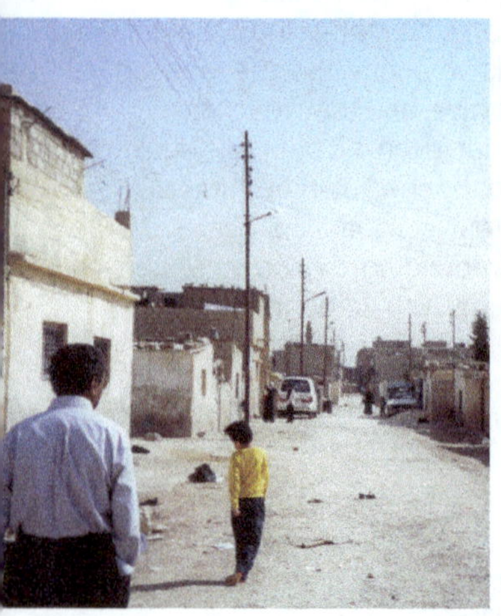
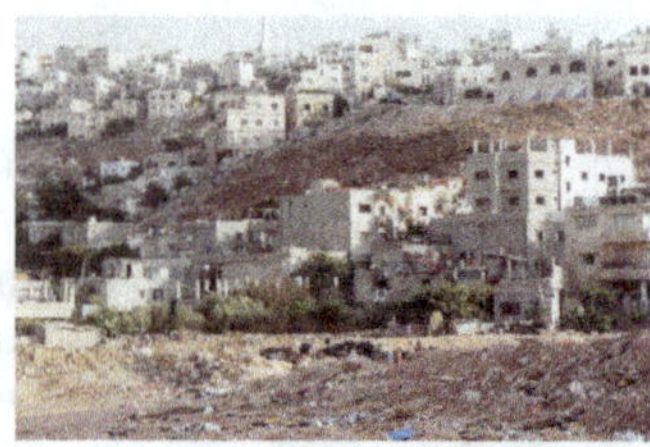
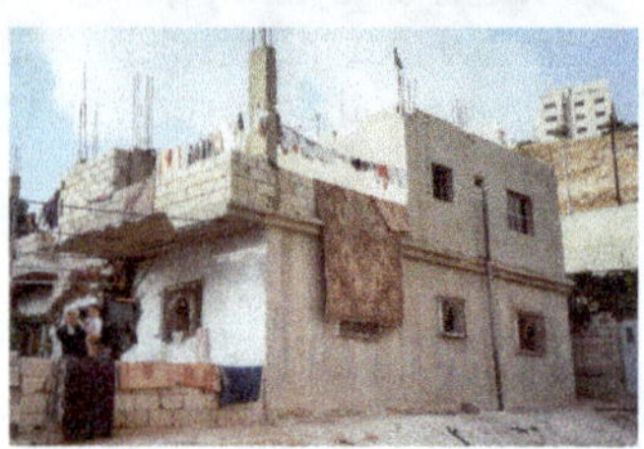
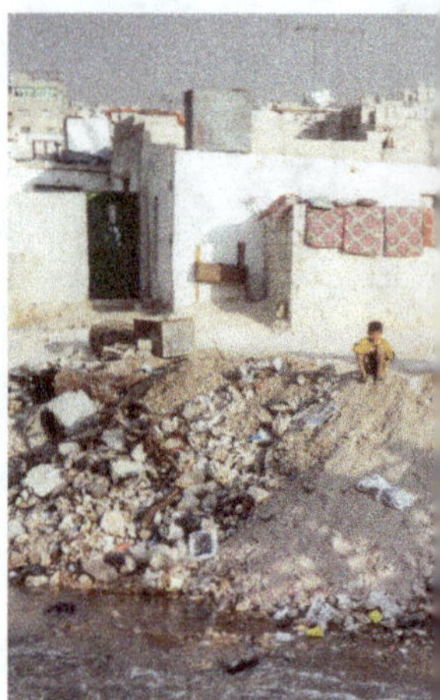

Supersudaca At what point you go from being a technician to a politician?

Mirta Demare When you say something. But they do not let you do such a thing.

Supersudaca Because there is a moment when *saying something* might happen, and somehow, sometimes they can use you.

Mirta Demare No, no. You have to be clever about it. In all the places in which I have been I could not carry a camera. These photos you see exist only because an Iranian man lent me his camera. I cannot have a camera on me, I cannot talk to the press, every time I go to one of these places I have to sign an agreement. Only if they tell me: "You have to go to a press conference;" but I can only talk about the systems, about what we have done, how are people doing, what the problems are.

In other words, it is a very delicate situation to handle politically. In general, the political people, like the ICRC, United Nations High Commissioner for Refugees – UNHCR, have their own mechanisms to deal with the media, they have their own political lobby and all. The only thing that I do is to push for the refugees to get more, for better conditions etc.; for that I fight. But I come really strong with that.

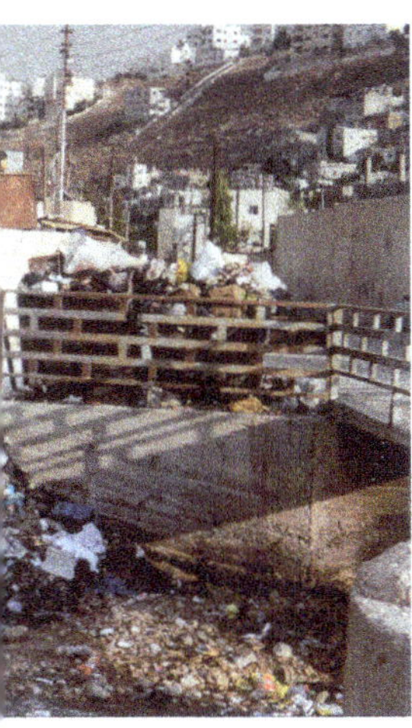

10. By *disappeared* Mirta Demare is referring to those people who were killed by state terrorism and buried in mass graves or thrown to the river a routine practice by the military and para-military groups during the military dictatorship in Argentina (1976-1983).

Supersudaca Are you optimistic regarding the future?

Mirta Demare Yes, I was born an optimist. I believe in looking back at history, there were always wars and people, and there were always refugees and there were always catastrophes.

Perhaps there are more wars and catastrophes with more people in the planet. But in the latest years there is something that also happened. Between 1995 and 1998, there were a lot of people going back to their home countries, that is the one thing one wants. This is the thing: The governments hosting the refugees think that the refugees will be staying for good. And that is a myth, because when you're given the opportunity... Sometimes they don't even let you get out. The repatriation process is a lot harder than the entry process. It takes more preparation, and in general the government or the UNHCR hope that the other side of the border is safer and more peaceful. And then there are people who leave with what little they have, and leave because they just want to go back. Do you think that a Ghanaian guy or any other refugee who has a great local community, where they feel welcome within their family, by their ancestors, by everything; when they get here, to Holland, they die, they die of cold, they don't have any greenery, not even the spaciousness that they have back home, they are discriminated, beaten up, they are foreigners, and on top of that they live in *apartheid*, that and many other things. If that person has the necessary living conditions in his own country, that person would not leave. If they come here it is because they are desperate. Imagine what you have to feel to risk your life, for example, in the case of the group of Chinese people hidden in a container. That is unfathomable. I am really tough for lots of things, but when I arrived here in a few weeks I knew I wasn't going to be able to go back. And then I realized why. After three months of leaving, Buenos Aires became a real disaster. We lost five members of our family, they *disappeared*.[10] When you cannot go back, that changes you and you say to yourself: "I will endure this." The first two months were very tough because I got here and it was the coldest winter in I don't know how many years. I didn't know any refugees; I was the first refugee. I found this group when I came back from Pakistan. I found Ana Falú and a great group of architects too.

Previously Published Works

Foreword
Incomplete Works, 10th Sao Paulo Biennale, 2013.

Supersudaca's Turn
"El Giro Supersudaca." Los Límites de lo Urbano. Circo 222, 2016.

LA Collective: Latin America's Parallel History as Occident's Laboratory Backlash
The Block 21, 2009.
Summa 120, 2012.

From Slum to Slim
Grigoran, Yuri, curator. Archeology of thePeriphery. Moscow Urban Forum, 2013. Madrazo, Félix. "De Slum a Slim: Nezayork, el Perfecto Rascasuelos." *Arquine* 71, 2015 <https://arquine.com/de-slum-a-slim-nezayork-el-perfecto-rascasuelos/>

Susucumbre
Revista Internacional de Arquitectura y Opinión – *A35*, 2012.

Europe, We Need to Talk

Supersudaca Collective. "Supersudaca: China and Africa Have More to Learn from Latin America than from the West." *Architectural Review*, May 27, 2015 <https://www.architectural-review.com/essays/profiles-and-interviews/supersudaca-china-and-africa-have-more-to-learn-from-latin-america-than-from-the-west>

Al Caribe!

"Best Entry Award." II International Architecture Biennale Rotterdam, 2005.
Revista Internacional de Arquitectura y Opinión – *A35*, 2012.
Cantis, Ariadna, ed. "Iberoamérica: Emerging Architecture." *2G Dossier*, 2008.

Destination Whatever

Sigler, Jennifer. "Destination Whatever: Touring the Cruise Industry of the Caribbean." *Harvard Design Magazine* 39, Wet Matter, FW 2014.

Heritage to Feritage

Hein, Carola, ed. "Adaptive Strategies for Water Heritages." *Chapter* 19, Springer 2019, 362-382 <https://link.springer.com/chapter /10.1007/ 978-3-030-00268-8_19>

At Any Rate

Smith, Valerie, curator. "Exhibition Between Walls and Windows Architecture and Ideology." *Haus der Kulturen der Welt*, Berlin, 2012.
Smith, Valerie, ed. "Between Walls and Windows Architecture and Ideology." Hatje Cantz, 2012.
Centers Adrift 32, 2012.
Plot 12, 2013.

China tu Madre

Ibelings, Hans and Powerhouse Company. "China's Turn." *The Architecture Observer*, 2016.

Talking around the World

Materia 04, Ediciones Universidad San Sebastián, December 2011.

Acknowledgements

We would like to thank the following people and organizations that have believed in this collective. Many of them were essential for the creation of the content of this book: Els van der Plas, Joumana El Zein Khoury, Fariba Derakhshani & Caro Méndez from the Prince Claus Fund. Vedran Mimica, Wiel Arets and Winy Maas from The Berlage Institute. Arjen Oosterman and Lilet Breddels from Volume. Catherine David & Tanja Elstgeest from Witte de With. Martín di Peco & Fernando Diez from Summa+. Luis Rojo and Emilio Tuñon from CIRCO Marcelo Arauz from APAC. Roberto Segre, Jorge Peña, Ada Portero y Gisela Diaz from CUJAE. Jasper Goldman from Friends of Havana. Gustavo More from AAA. Jorge Rigau from UPR. Orval Sifontes from PRO ARQ. Francisco Javier Rodríguez from Universidad de Puerto Rico. Ronny Lobo from FCAA. Mark Raymond from CCAU University of West Indies. Deane Simpson from Bergen School of Architecture. David Bade & Tirzo Martha from IBB Curacao. Ergün Erkoçu & Arrelis Vis from University of Curacao. Carlos Pinto from Tridimenciudad Medellín, Ana María González Forero from FEM Cartagena. Danielle Van Zuylen art curator 'When guests become hosts', Haarlem and Porto. Ana Luandina. Bart Pluym from gebermte, Pieter Van den Broeck from KU Leuven. Lucila Urda from ETSAM, SOA from Syracuse University. Michelle Provoost and Wouter Vanstiphout from Crimson historians and urbanists. Yuri Grigoran from Moscow Urban Forum. Anastassia Smirnova-Berlin, Anya Koens & Arseniy Khitrov from Strelka Design Institute. Daravuth Ly from Reyum Institute Phnom Penh. Tom Rivard. Francisco Díaz from PUC. Marcelo Danza, from Taller Danza FA UdelaR. Felipe Assadi from UNAB. Miquel Adrià and Alejandro Hernández from Arquine. Javier Fernández Castro from FADU UBA. Pablo Roquero from Harvard University. Federico Rodríguez from UCR. José Roberto Paredes from 5 Patas al Gato. Matías Echanove from URBZ. Francis Espino from a35. David Basulto from Arch Daily. Fábrica de Paisaje from Uruguay. Christine de Baan as Head of Programme 3rd International Architecture Biennale Rotterdam. Ariadna Cantis from 2G & Fresh Latino. Jennifer Sigler from Harvard Design Review. Martín Huberman from Monoambiente. Prof. Carola Hein from TU Delft. Valerie Smith from Haus der Kulturen der Welt. Florencia Rodríguez & Igo Wender from PLOT Magazine. Hans Ibelings from the Architecture Observer and Nanne de Rue from Powerhouse Company. Ken Young from Asian Design Forum. Pablo Brugnoli from Materia & Mario Marchant for his writing for L.A. Colective as well as Francisco Quintana y Stephanie Fel. Davide Quadrio and Defne Ayas from Arthub Asia. Albert Ferrer from Actar. Arquitaxi from Universidad de Granada. Melisa Vargas from Unibe. Roberto Converti & Miguel Jurado from the Bienal internacional de Arquitectura BA. Lluis Alexandre Casanovas Blanco, Ignacio González Galán, Carlos Minguez Carrasco, Alejandra Navarrete Llopis, and Marina Otero Verzier from The Oslo Architecture Triennale curatorial Team. Ligia Nobre & Guilherme Wisnik from the curatorial team of the São Paulo architectural Biennial 2013. Gabriel Vergara, Renata Sinkevic and José "Pepe" Mardones for their help during Susucumbre. Nicole L'Huillier for her participation in Supersudaca show at Sao Paulo Biennial 2013 and Incomplete Works video creation along with Gabriel & Rodrigo Vergara. Ingrid Sepúlveda for her creation of the video "Gold". Carila Matzelbacher, Marilia Gallmeister & Rodrigo Andreoli from Terreyro Coreografico. Teatro Oficina Uzyna Uzona. Celso Sim. Olly Wainwright from ICON. Mariana Leguía from Architecture Design. Prof. Zhao Pei for the invitation to Papel Latino project & special thanks to Mirta Demare, Teresa Papachristou & Carel Weeber.

Camilo García Barona & Diego Barajas (Husos), Juan Alfonso Zapata & Pablo Guerrero started this journey with us in Rotterdam in 2001, and even if they continued with other paths, they were part of this adventure and are part of this friendship.There are many other people that we crossed in our way that were important in the development of Supersudaca: students, professors, interns, clients, people we met in our trips and investigations that taught us with their stories, points of view, knowledge, expertise and compromise. We thank all of them as well.

Supersudaca 2023

Credits

Supersudaca
Ana Rascovsky
Cesar Becerra
Esteban Varela
Félix Madrazo
Fernando Puente Arnao
Juan Pablo Corvalán
Martín Delgado
Manuel de Rivero
Max Zolkwer
Sofía Saavedra Bruno
Stephane Damsin

Foreword
Text
Juan Pablo Corvalán

**Supersudaca
A Practice of Friendship**
Text
Fernando Luiz Lara

**The World of
Architecture**

Supersudaca's Turn
Text
Juan Pablo Corvalán
Translation
Irina Rivero

**Direct Architecture
Genealogy**
Text
Manuel de Rivero
Juan Pablo Corvalán
Sofía Saavedra Bruno
Max Zolkwer
Félix Madrazo

**LA Collective: Latin
America's Parallel
History as Occident's
Laboratory Backlash**
Editors
Juan Pablo Corvalán
Félix Madrazo
Manuel de Rivero

**Mario Pani Avant
l'Heure**
Text
Miquel Adrià

Supersudaca Collective Cases Timeline
Text
Manuel de Rivero
Sofía Saavedra Bruno
Félix Madrazo
Juan Pablo Corvalán
Ingrid Sepúlveda

**Argentina Megablocks
Lasts**
Text
Ana Rascovsky
Max Zolkwer
Research Team
Leticia Balacek
Francisco Apa

**Barriada Experience:
John F. C. Turner
Interview**
Text
Roberto Chávez
Julie Viloria
Melanie Zipperer
Editors
Manuel de Rivero
Félix Madrazo

Y PREVI?
Text
Manuel de Rivero
Félix Madrazo
Juan Pablo Corvalán

**Montevideo Cooperativo: Gustavo González
Interview**
Text
Martín Delgado
Esteban Varela
Juliana Espósito

**Latin American Know-How: Alejandro Aravena and Fernando
Pérez Interview**
Text
Juan Pablo Corvalán
Manuel de Rivero
Francisco J. Quintana

**From Big Boxes to
Little Boxes**
Text
Mario Marchant

From Slum to Slim
Text
Félix Madrazo

Papel Latino
Text
Félix Madrazo
Max Zolkwer
Research team
Max Zolkwer
Félix Madrazo
Ana Rascovsky
Martin Delgado
Manuel de Rivero
Juan Pablo Corvalán
Franca Ferraris
*Audio transcripts and
public survey*
Franca Ferraris
Barbara Oestereicher
Euge Zoe Massa
Joaquim Gonzalez
Milburn

Susucumbre
Interview Participants
Manuel de Rivero
Ana Rascovsk
Félix Madrazo
Sofía Saavedra Bruno
Martín Delgado
Max Zolkwer
Juan Pablo Corvalán
Esteban Varela
Elio Martuccelli
Jorge Sanchez
Editor
Manuel de Rivero
Translation
Irina Rivero

The Architecture of the World

Europe, We Need to Talk
Text
Félix Madrazo
Max Zolkwer

Al Caribe!
Text
Félix Madrazo
Sofía Saavedra Bruno
Manuel de Rivero
Ana Rascovsky
Max Zolkwer
Martín Delgado
Juan Alfonso Zapata
Elena Chevtchenko
Pablo Guerrero
Victoria Goldstein
Ico Abreu
Translation
Irina Rivero

Destination Whatever
Text
Martín Delgado
Félix Madrazo
Sofia Saavedra Bruno
Zuzanna Koltowska

From Heritage to Feritage
Text
Sofía Saavedra Bruno
Félix Madrazo
Martin Delgado

At Any Rate
Text
Félix Madrazo
Stephane Damsin
Max Zolkwer
Juan Pablo Corvalán
Research team
Sebastian Marsiglia
Marcela Martin
Kathia Sanchez
Andrés Sandoval
Pablo Zolkwer
Zuzanna Koltowska
Teresa Papachristou
Renata Sinkevic
Gabriel Vergara
Elaine Hoffman
Joaquín González Milburn
Martín Delgado
Graphic Design
Guilherme Werle
Teresa Papachristou

With Infinite Slowness Arises the Great China
Text
Félix Madrazo
Max Zolkwer
Manuel de Rivero

Talking around the World. Interviewing Mirta Demare
Interviewers
Max Zolkwer
Manuel de Rivero
Ana Rascovsky
Editors
Max Zolkwer
Stephane Damsin
Translation
Irina Rivero

Image Credits
Andrés Lübbert - p. 26 (top)
Atelier 5 - p. 65
Carel Weeber - p. 182, 183
Carla Hernandez - p. 96, 97, 98, 99
Ciska Rusch, Omar Kuwas - p. 29 (bottom right)
Ergün Erkoçu - p. 29 (bottom left)
Federación Uruguaya de Cooperativas de Vivienda por Ayuda Mutua (FUCVAM) - p. 74, 76
Felipe Fontecilla - p. 85
Google maps - p. 101
Guillermo Zamora - p. 40, 41, 43
Hector García - p. 92
Hugo Ignacio Sanchez - p. 90, 91
Max Zolkwer - p. 6, 7 (watercolor portraits of Supersudacas done while in Zoom meetings during the pandemic)
Miami Port - p. 190
Mirta Demare - p. 250, 251, 252, 253, 257, 258, 259, 260, 261, 262, 263, 264, 266, 267, 268
Reinout Mulder - p. 26 (left), 28 (bottom right)
Rosa Aguirre, Militza Carrillo, Pablo Pedreros - p. 27 (bottom right), 29 (top)
Servicio Aerofotográfico del Perú - p. 62
Supersudaca - p. 16, 26 (bottom right, drawing's photo), 27 (top right, top left, bottom left), 28 (top), 46, 47, 57, 69, 95, 156, 157, 158, 159, 168, 169, 170, 171, 172, 173, 174, 175, 176, 177, 178, 179, 180, 181, 182, 183, 192, 207, 209, 213, 224, 225, 226, 227, 228, 229, 230, 231, 232, 233, 234, 236, 238, 240, 242, 243
Supersudaca, Andrea van Walleghem - p. 244
Supersudaca, Enzo Zolkwer, Bárbara Oestereicher, Tati Vainstein, Félix Madrazo - p. 104, 105, 106, 107
Supersudaca, Juan Zapata - p. 164, 165, 190
Supersudaca, Renata Sinkevic, Pepe Mardones - p. 14, 15, 124, 125, 128, 139
Supersudaca, Rubén Salvador Torres - p. 230, 231
Supersudaca, Teresa Papachristou (costume design), Gillerme Werle (graphic design explanation strip) - p. 214, 215, 216, 217, 218, 219, 220, 221
The Observatory of Economic Complexity - p. 237, 239, 241
Time Magazine, Mar. 12, 1965, cover - p. 65
Tomás García Puente - p. 38, 48, 51

Latin America: Thoughts
Romano Guerra Editora
Nhamerica Platform

Management Coordination
Abilio Guerra
Fernando Luiz Lara
Silvana Romano Santos

**Incomplete Works
Supersudaca**
Ana Rascovsky
Cesar Becerra
Esteban Varela
Félix Madrazo
Fernando Puente Arnao
Juan Pablo Corvalán
Martín Delgado
Manuel de Rivero
Max Zolkwer
Sofía Saavedra Bruno
Stephane Damsin

BR + USA 10

Editorial Staff
Abilio Guerra
Fernando Luiz Lara
Fernanda Critelli
Irene Nagashima
Silvana Romano Santos

Graphic Design
Dárkon V Roque

Translation
Supersudaca
Irina Rivero

Translation Review
Fernanda Critelli
Irene Nagashima
Noemi Zein Telles

Cover image
Supersudaca

Romano Guerra Editora

Editors
Abilio Guerra and Silvana Romano Santos

Editorial Board
Abilio Guerra, Adrián Gorelik, Aldo Paviani, Ana Luiza Nobre, Ana Paula Garcia Spolon, Ana Paula Koury, Ana Vaz Milheiros, Ângelo Bucci, Ângelo Marcos Vieira de Arruda, Anna Beatriz Ayroza Galvão, Carlos Alberto Ferreira Martins, Carlos Eduardo Dias Comas, Cecília Rodrigues dos Santos, Edesio Fernandes, Edson da Cunha Mahfuz, Ethel Leon, Fernanda Critelli, Fernando Luiz Lara, Gabriela Celani, Horacio Enrique Torrent Schneider, João Masao Kamita, Jorge Figueira, Jorge Francisco Liernur, José de Souza Brandão Neto, José Geraldo Simões Junior, Juan Ignacio del Cueto Ruiz-Funes, Luís Antônio Jorge, Luis Espallargas Gimenez, Luiz Manuel do Eirado Amorim, Marcio Cotrim Cunha, Marcos José Carrilho, Margareth da Silva Pereira, Maria Beatriz Camargo Aranha, Maria Stella Martins Bresciani, Marta Vieira Bogéa, Mônica Junqueira de Camargo, Nadia Somekh, Otavio Leonidio, Paola Berenstein Jacques, Paul Meurs, Ramón Gutiérrez, Regina Maria Prosperi Meyer, Renato Anelli, Roberto Conduru, Ruth Verde Zein, Sergio Moacir Marques, Vera Santana Luz, Vicente del Rio, Vladimir Bartalini

Nhamerica Platform

Editor
Fernando Luiz Lara

About the authors

Ana Rascovsky, (Buenos Aires, Argentina 1972) is an architect based in Buenos Aires. She is a co-founding member of Supersudaca. She completed a master of excellence in architecture and urbanism from the Berlage Institute Rotterdam, a master (D.E.A.) in History of urbanism from the Ecole d 'Architecture de Versailles and graduated as architect from University of Buenos Aires -Faculty of Architecture, Design and Urbanism (FADU-UBA, 1996). She is a design professor at University of Buenos Aires (UBA), she co-directs Estudio PLANTA, and develops Acrilia – her art practice.

Cesar Becerra (Lima, Peru1974) is an architect living in Peru. Member of the international collective Supersudaca and its project base practice in Lima: 51-1 arquitectos. Graduated in Architecture and Urbanism from the Ricardo Palma University of Peru.

Esteban Varela is an architect living in Uruguay. Member of Supersudaca and its project base in Montevideo. He has been teaching in UDELAR and UTU, Director of Architecture in Social Development Department of Uruguay and Parliamentary Consultant.

Félix Madrazo (Saltillo, México 1972) is an architect based in Rotterdam, co-founding member of Supersudaca. He also runs the architecture and urbanism practice IND [Inter.National.Design] in partnership with Arman Akdogan. He is a lecturer and researcher at the Why Factory, TU Delft. He graduated as architect from La Salle University in México City and has a Master of excellence in architecture and urbanism from the Berlage Institute, Rotterdam.

Fernando Puente Arnao (Lima, Peru1973) is an architect based in Lima. Member of the international collective Supersudaca and its project base practice in Lima: 51-1 arquitectos. Master in Management of Construction and Real Estate Companies from the Polytechnic University of Madrid (Spain) and Pontifical Catholic University of Peru. Graduated in Architecture and Urbanism from the Ricardo Palma University of Peru.

Juan Pablo Corvalán (Geneva, Switzerland 1973) is a multimedia architect based in Santiago, he is co-founding member of Supersudaca and its project base in Chile: Susuka, realizing projects, researching and teaching in the areas of urbanism, architecture, design, and music. Graduated from EIG, Geneva, Universidad de Chile, Santiago and Master of excellence in architecture and urbanism at the Berlage Institute, Rotterdam, PhD candidate in Geography by the Pontificia Universidad Católica de Chile, Santiago. He is the Dean of the Facultad de Arquitectura, Animación, Diseño y Construcción of Universidad de las Americas.

Manuel de Rivero (Lima, Peru 1973) is an architect based in Lima, co-founding member of Supersudaca and its project base practice in Lima: 51-1 arquitectos. He graduated from Universidad Ricardo Palma (Lima) and the made a master of excellence in architecture and urbanism at the Berlage Institute, Rotterdam and since then, has been teaching in different schools around the word.

Martin Delgado Filippini (Montevideo, Uruguay 1975) architect based in Montevideo, co-founding member of Supersudaca. Currently he is director of the Department of Urban Development at the Intendencia of Montevideo, previously in charge of the Division of Public Spaces. He is a professor of architectural and urban design at Taller Danza and researcher in urban-territorial issues at the Institute of Territorial and Urban Studies at FADU-UdelaR. Director of RE Estudio de Arquitectura. Architect graduated from FADU-UdelaR, Uruguay.

Max Zolkwer (Buenos Aires, Argentina 1972) is an architect based in Buenos Aires. He is a co-founding member of Supersudaca and constituted his base in Buenos Aires with his office: Habitante del Espacio in partnership with Ramiro Gallardo. He studied and taught at the Universidad de Buenos Aires. He is also founder of the playgrounds company LUDUM.

Sofia Saavedra Bruno (Leuven, Belgium 1972). She is based in Brussels and is a co- founding member of Supersudaca. Over the past 25 years she combined urban design practice and cocreative (research) processes with entrepreneurship and societal service in Europe, Northern Africa and the Caribbean. In parallel, she teaches as a volunteering Post Doc Researcher at KU Leuven. She graduated as a civil engineer from Ghent University and has a Master of excellence in architecture and urbanism from the Berlage Institute, Rotterdam and a PhD from KU Leuven.

Stephane Damsin (Brussels, Belgium 1981). Architect graduated in 2005. Worked with different architectural offices in Marseille, Antwerp and Buenos Aires before starting his own practice, Ouest (www.ouest.be). Joined Supersudaca in 2008. Architectural curator in Brussels art center Recyclart between 2011 and 2021. Is now teaching architecture in different universities.

Te fuiste un poco temprano, todos tenemos una sensación de que algo quedó incompleto, que nos perdimos mucho Félix. ¿Aunque a la vez a quién no le gustaría tener una vida tan llena y tan completa como la tuya? Tu espíritu inquieto, estudioso, irónico, generoso, amante de la vida, nos acompañará a todos los que compartimos parte de tu trayecto.

Félix, este libro, que llegaste a terminar antes de irte, es también un homenaje a nuestra amistad y la mirada del mundo que compartimos. Somos testigos que pusiste mucho de lo que te quedaba en este libro, en este legado tuyo y de Supersudaca, del pensamiento y amistad que creció durante estos más de 20 años.

¡Abrazo, Madrazo!

Supersudaca, diciembre de 2023.

Romano Guerra Editora
Rua General Jardim 645 cj 31
01223-011 São Paulo SP Brasil
rg@romanoguerra.com.br
romanoguerra.com.br

Nhamerica Platform
807 E 44th st,
Austin, TX, 78751 USA
editors@nhamericaplatform.com
nhamericaplatform.com

ISBN 978-65-87205-28-1
Romano Guerra
ISBN 978-1-946070-56-2
Nhamerica

Supersudaca: Incomplete Works
Félix Madrazo et al. – São Paulo, SP:

Romano Guerra Editora:
Austin,TX: Nhamerica Plataform, 2024.

280 p. il.
(Latin America: Thoughts BR + USA 10)

ISBN 978-65-87205-28-1
Romano Guerra
ISBN 978-1-946070-56-2
Nhamerica

1. Architecture –
   Latin America - 21th century
2. Architects – Latin America
3. Architects - Interviews

CDD 720.98

Catalogue record prepared by the
librarian Dina Elisabete Uliana – CRB-
8/3760

This book was composed in
Neue Hass Unica.
1st edition, 2023

www.ingramcontent.com/pod-product-compliance
Lightning Source LLC
Chambersburg PA
CBHW051552030726
47592CB00001B/251